FORGET M

CW01023528

THE THRAPSTON DIARIES
1914 – 1921

A MISCELLANY OF
NEWSPAPER REPORTS
FROM THRAPSTON

A COMPANION VOLUME TO
IN THE SPRINGTIME
OF THEIR LIVES

COMPILED BY

ERIC FRANKLIN

INDEXED BY EDDIE SEWELL

A THRAPSTON DISTRICT HISTORICAL SOCIETY PUBLICATION

First published in 2013 by

Thrapston District Historical Society
3 Fisher Close
Thrapston
Northamptonshire
NN14 4UB
UK
01832 732950

www.thrapstonhistorysoc.co.uk

Copyright © Eric Franklin, 2013

ISBN: 978-0-9563642-3-4

Prepared for publication by Eric Franklin

Printed by Inkwell Printing
Units 7 – 7a, The Workshops, Barnwell,
Near Oundle, Peterborough, PE8 5PL
01832 273745
inkwellprinting@btconnect.com
www.inkwellprinting.co.uk

Contents

On each odd-numbered page, the year has been included at the top of the page to assist with readability.

Cover pictures:

    Front - Silk postcard produced in France during WW1 – unused.

    Back   - Crested china bust commemorating the death of Lord Kitchener
             with the Thrapston crest, and made by Carlton China.

    Both from the *EDF Collection*.

Introduction

"Forget me not" is a miscellany of local news stories from between 1914 and 1921. This book covers the months before the Great War started, the war years and up to the end of 1921 when the Peace Park formally became the town's memorial to the men who had made the ultimate sacrifice. Research has taken over seven years. News from home and abroad regularly appeared in the local press, some trivial, some scandalous and many items just reporting the day-to-day lives of local folk. On a number of occasions, usually involving misdeeds, names have been omitted to protect the guilty! I was fortunate to have such an excellent archive available at Kettering Library and am grateful to library staff for their help, tolerance and encouragement.

The forget me not flower was the symbol of remembrance during the Great War, only being replaced by the poppy in 1918. A number of "forget me not" days were held in town during the period covered by this book where funds were raised to provide comforts for serving men. These gifts were received with great cheer, their letters to the organising committee showing just how much they meant. "Forget me not" seemed to me to be the very embodiment of the support Thrapston gave to their boys, and an appropriate title for this volume.

When "In the Springtime of their Lives" was produced in 2009, it was always the intention to produce further volumes to enhance both understanding of the times the casualties lived through and to research earlier conflicts Thrapston men took part in. It quickly became apparent that, although there is some information on earlier conflicts, it would not provide the level of detail hoped for. I hope to produce a booklet giving basic details at some future point. Men currently identified are:

Boer War (1899 – 1902):
Sidney Bone, Obadiah Booth (died of illness), William Chapman, Herbert William Clarke, Thomas R Dodd (died of illness), H. Davidson, St. Vincent Kingsford, Wilfred Lenton, Timothy Parrish, J. Perrin, William Rowell, James Shadbolt (died of illness), Archibald Charles Siddon (died accidentally), M. Sullivan, Thomas Rawson Tusting, W. Wakefield and Cuthbert Wright.

Second Afghanistan War (1878):
David Nicholls.

Indian Mutiny (1857 – 1859):
Frederick John Salmon Bagshaw (died of wounds).

If you have any information about any of these men and conflicts, or others not mentioned, please contact Eric Franklin who is researching people and events up to 1921.

I am grateful to Thrapston District Historical Society for their support in the production of this second book. The town is fortunate to have such an active group of people interested in local history. Funding for this book has come from sales of "In the Springtime of their Lives".

Eric Franklin
July 2013

Acknowledgements

As with production of "In the Springtime of their Lives", this volume would not have been possible without much help from many people and organisations. Specific mention must be made of:

Thrapston District Historical Society for allowing this publication to be produced under their auspices.

Staff at Thrapston and Kettering Libraries, with a special mention for Sarah (Thrapston) and Sheila (Kettering).

Hazel Evans (Isle of Wight) for items donated which appear in this book and form the Hazel Evans Archive.

Celia Hope, page 190, and Aubrey Bygrave, pages 93 and 139, for the loan of original photographs and Ray Barratt for use of the memorial card on page 153.

My team of proofreaders – Sarah Wright (Wright Words), John Dawkins, Philip Pike and Stephne Tewson.

Caroline Wallace for all her work formatting the original into the finished product.

Eddie Sewell for work on the index.

Michelle Goring and her staff at Forget me not (Thrapston) Ltd., for once again agreeing to be our public point of sale and for having such a well-named shop!

Inkwell Printing for once again producing a quality book.

Finally, my wife Mary for encouragement and support over many years.

Eric Franklin

General Notes

All illustrations are acknowledged individually – any omissions or errors should be notified to the author who will willingly amend these in any future editions.

Where found in newspapers, the paper and dates are included. As you will see, quality is variable. The main newspaper sources of information were: *Kettering Leader* (published weekly on a Friday); *Kettering Guardian* (published weekly, also on a Friday) and; *Northamptonshire Evening Telegraph* (published six days a week). The *Rushden Echo* provided a few items during the early days of the war. One major source which has not survived would have been the *Thrapston Journal*, a weekly newspaper focussing on Thrapston which is mentioned in other papers. Despite extensive enquiries, there does not appear to be any surviving archive of issues before circa 1938, a great loss to local history. Even the British Library Newspaper Archive does not have a single copy from before 1938.

Items from the *EDF Collection* are in the ownership of Eric Franklin, who has an archive of over 360 items of local interest. These are mainly in the form of original postcards, photographs and documents covering the last 150 years. Where a publisher or photographer is named on the original, they are appropriately acknowledged.

Significant events recorded in "In the Springtime of their Lives" are included in the text in ***bold italics*** with the relevant page number. Casualties with an individual entry in the book are shown in **bold**, again with the page number their biography appears on.

During the period covered by this book, British currency was pounds (£), shillings (s) and pennies (d). Twelve pennies made one shilling with twenty shillings to the pound. In modern money, 1d equates to slightly less than ½p whilst 1s is 5p. On occasions in the book, I have given the approximate modern day value to give an indication of the amount.

Where reference is made to the "Guardians", this refers to the Board of Guardians administering the Thrapston Poor Law Union. They were elected annually by people eligible to pay the poor rate and each civil parish in the Union was represented by at least one guardian.

Although thoroughly checked for errors by my team of proofreaders, any remaining are purely my responsibility. Corrections and amendments will appear on Thrapston District Historical Society's website at:

www.thrapstonhistorysoc.co.uk

Eric Franklin
June 2013

1914

January

The year began with the news that the late rector's wife and daughter, Mrs. and Miss Kingsford would shortly be leaving town and moving to Peterborough to live with Mrs. Kingsford's youngest son. A silver hot water kettle to Mrs. Kingsford and a music cabinet and two books of music to Miss Kingsford constituted their parting gifts. They left town on 24th. *(Picture shown left from the Kettering Leader, Friday 2nd January 1914.)*

On 9th, an official announcement was made concerning the new rector. Rev. Basil Wilberforce Stothert. He had been helping out since the death of Rev. Kingsford and was offered the position after a petition in favour of this appointment signed by between 400 and 500 parishioners was forwarded to the Lord Chancellor. From 1901 to 1913, he was an Army Chaplain. He was a strong advocate of temperance and took part in activities promoting this throughout the country; he was also a Scout Chaplain. *(Picture shown right taken from the Kettering Leader, Friday 23rd January 1914.)*

REV. BASIL WILBERFORCE STOTHERT
Rector-designate of Thrapston.

On Saturday 10th, Thrapston drew with Woodford 2 – 2 in the Kettering Combination. On the same day, Thrapston Harriers travelled to Kettering Harriers for an inter-club race, easily beating their rivals, having the first six runners' home.

A week later, the Thrapston Harriers' committee entered the following names to represent the club in the Midland Junior Cross-Country Championship, to be held at Sutton-in-Ashfield, on 24th January, with the final selection to be made later: - W. Bates, F. Benford, A. Allen, T. C. Tebbs, C. B. Church, L. D. Abbott, E. J. Guest, W. Broughton, S. Minney, W. Wilson, A. Wills, Stanley Smith, Septimus Smith, J. Bates, and F. Leete. Mr. W. Dellar (secretary) and Mr. C. A. Smart would accompany the team, together with two trainers. The committee also considered the Midland Senior Cross-Country Championship, which would take place at Thrapston on 14th February, and appointed the following sub-committee to make all arrangements, and also select a course:- Messrs. J. T. Carress (chairman), W. Dellar (secretary), C. A. Smart, A. Day, and C. J. Ruckwood. It was also decided that they would hold the annual dinner of the club at the end of the present month.

Thrapston Police Court sat on Friday 30th. Amongst the cases dealt with were those of two labourers, both of whom were of "no fixed abode", who were seen begging along Halford Street and Midland Road. Each received fourteen days hard labour.

February

On Saturday 13th, Thrapston lost at home to Kettering White Cross 3 -1.

On Friday 20th, the *Kettering Leader* showed a picture of the Thrapston Shop Assistants' Fancy Dress Ball.

Clockwise, from top left hand corner –
Miss Parrish (C16[th] Lady) – secretary of the Fancy Dress Ball.
Miss Cotton (Billiards)
Miss Peachy (Spanish Girl)
Miss Hing (Gipsy Girl)

The Midland Senior Cross-Country Championship was held at Thrapston on Saturday 14th. Competitors preparing for the start of the race are shown in this picture, published on the 20th in the *Kettering Leader*.

Also on 20th, Thrapston Guardians reported that, for the first two weeks of February 1914, the figures were:-
Week 1 104 inmates.
153 vagrants relieved.
198 in receipt of out relief.
Week 2 104 inmates.
133 vagrants relieved.
198 in receipt of out relief.
The cost reported was £23 9s 6d. each week.

On 19th and 20th, the local amateur dramatics group presented "All Through Martha". The report read, "The town of Thrapston possesses amateur actors of more than average merit, and on Thursday and Friday of last week excellent performances of Howard Keeble's comedy, "All Through Martha" were given to crowded houses.

The whole of the characters appear in the above scene, viz.:-
Jane Box (Miss Dorothy Molden), Monica (Miss Marjorie Gainer), Martha (Mrs. P. F. Ruston), the Squire (Mr. P. F. Ruston), the Curate (Mr. S. C. Ainsworth)."

On 28th, Thrapston beat Ringstead 2 – 1, and on the same day, Thrapston Council School reopened after closure due to measles.

March

On 24th, the following incident occurred, reported in the *Kettering Leader* three days later:-
"On Tuesday afternoon, when there were a good many people about, it being market day, an alarming incident occurred in the main street at Thrapston.
Dr. Cogan, of Northampton, was driving a 20-h.p. Ford car up the street, accompanied by Dr. Bird, of Thrapston, and Mr. L. W. Wood, of Aldwincle. Just after taking the turn adjoining the White Hart Hotel the car skidded owing to the slipperiness (due to rain) and sloping side of the thoroughfare (which was tarred a considerable time ago). The brake was not applied, and the car having turned half way round, located itself partly on the pavement, but fortunately, no one was hurt, although a woman who was passing had a narrow escape.
We are informed that quite a number of other motorists and also motor cyclists have experienced similar trouble at this spot, and that "spills" of ordinary cyclists have been frequent."

On 27th, the Kettering Leader had three reports of interest to Thrapston readers:-
"At a special meeting of Thrapston Parish Council the first steps were agreed towards the town having a public supply of water."
In the same issue, the induction of Rev. Basil Stothert as rector of Thrapston was reported.
In addition, there was a report about the Thrapston District Shire Horse Society's Annual Meeting at the White Hart Hotel on Tuesday afternoon. The society had a balance of £269 1s. The date of the annual show was set for Thursday 17th September."

April

Friday 17th April's issue of the *Kettering Leader* carried the picture shown below, captioned "SHIRE HORSE PARADE. An Interesting Street Scene at Thrapston."

A week later, the Shop Assistants' Committee were pictured in the same newspaper.

Standing:
Miss Parrish (secretary), **Mr. E. Mayes (52)**, Miss Firbank, Mr. T. Loaring, Mr. J. Elms, Miss Bugby, Mr. E. Stapleton, Mrs. Gifford, and Mr. E. Loaring.
Sitting:
Miss Hing, **Mr. Emery (22)**, Miss V. Essam, and Mr. Geo. Stapleton.

May

Friday 1st May saw a celebration of Thrapston's mixed hockey team published in the *Kettering Leader*.

"An Unbeaten Side.
THRAPSTON MIXED HOCKEY TEAM.
Who have gone through the season unbeaten. Among the teams which have had to acknowledge defeat at their hands are Peterborough City, Kettering, Buckden, and King's Cliffe.

Back row: Mr. Gilbert (Thrapston), Mr. Barnett (Thrapston), Mr. Holmes (Slipton), Mr. J. Jellicoe (Titchmarsh), Mr. Unwyatte (Clopton), Mr. Selby, captain (Thrapston).
Front row (left to right): Mrs. Raven (Pilton), Miss Bletsoe (Thrapston), Miss Preece (Drayton), Miss Jellicoe (Titchmarsh), Miss Whitney (Pilton)."

The Kettering Combination Executive Committee met on Thursday 14th at the Angel Hotel in Kettering. Walgrave reported Thrapston for failing to fulfil their fixture on 28th March and claimed 18s 6d for brake fare and 6d for a telegram. Mr. Patrick, the referee, also claimed 3s. The claims were allowed, and Thrapston were fined 3s for breaking the fixture.

On 14th, at the Annual General Meeting of the Institute of Bankers, held at their headquarters in Clements Lane, London, Mr. J. M. W. Barker, of the London City and Midland Bank, Thrapston, was awarded the second prize of £10 in the Institute's essay-writing competition.

Despite these being the early days of motoring, Thrapston Parish Council showed an early interest in road safety, the following being reported on 22nd:-
"THRAPSTON COUNCIL
NOTICE TO MOTORISTS
Mr. Hewitt gave notice to call attention at the next meeting of the necessity that notice boards be erected at each entrance of the town to motorists to drive slowly through the place."

On Sunday 31st, at the Men's Adult School during the morning, Mr. A. H. Touch was in the chair, and Mr. A. C. Harris, of Burton Latimer, was the speaker, giving an address illustrated with diagrams on the blackboard on "The Message of the clouds". In the afternoon, Mrs. E. T. Cottingham presided over the Women's School, and read a very good paper on the same subject, written by Miss Hill, of Royden, late of Thrapston. Mrs. F. Mayes nicely rendered a solo, accompanied by Miss Louise Flanders.

June

At Huntingdon Sports
On Whit-Monday (1st June), C. B. Church, of Thrapston Harriers, won the final of the 880 yards handicap with 60 yards start. In the one-mile flat race, E. Guest and T. C. Tebbs, both of Thrapston, finished second and third respectively.

Tuesday 2nd Market prices were reported as:-
Wheat, very short supply, 35s 6d to 36s; beans, 32s 6d to 33s; oats, 21s 6d to 22s per quarter; Beef, 9s per stone; mutton, 5s 6d to 5s 8d per 8 lbs; pork, 8s per stone; butter, 11d per ld; eggs, 1s 6d per score (wholesale prices).

On Friday 19th, the *Kettering Leader* carried this story:
"Queen Mother's Letter.
Troop of Thrapston Boy Scouts and Their Dog.
The 1st Thrapston Troop of Boy Scouts has received a high honour this last week. The scoutmaster, the Rev. B. W. Stothert, sent a letter to her Majesty Queen Alexandra, who on Saturday inspected 10,000 Boy Scouts in London, enclosing photographs of the troop, and mentioning to her Majesty that the troop dog was named "Cæsar" after King Edward's dog. The following reply was received on Saturday morning:-
Marlborough House, 11 June.
Dear Sir. – I am desired by Queen Alexandra to thank you and your Scouts for the letter and most interesting photographs of the 1st Thrapston Troop of Boy Scouts with "Cæsar", which you have been kind enough to send her.
Her Majesty, as you know, takes the greatest interest in the Scout movement. I am, yours faithfully,
(Signed) HENRY STREATFIELD, COL.
Private Secretary to H.M. Queen Alexandra.
Rev. Basil Stothert, Scoutmaster,
1st Thrapston Troop B. P. Scouts.

THE THRAPSTON BOY SCOUTS.
With their scoutmaster, the Rev. B. W. Stothert, rector, and the Troop's dog "Cæsar".

THE DOG "CÆSAR." *(pictured on page 7)*
With instructor and assistant scoutmaster Skelton, who has charge of the Troops pet. The dog, which was presented by an admirer of the Boy Scout movement, is named after the late King

Edward's favourite dog. Her Majesty Queen Alexandra has been pleased to accept copies of the photographs of the Troop, and has sent a most graciously worded acknowledgement."

Continuing the Scouting theme, the next report read "First Northants Lady to receive Scouts'

"Thanks Badge." Miss Viva Ford *(pictured left)*, of Thrapston, who on Thursday last week was presented with the "Thanks Badge" of the Boy Scouts, in the shape of a pendant with a silver chain attached, by the 1st Thrapston Troop, as a mark of their appreciation for her effort in arranging a concert on behalf of the Troop funds. Miss Ford, who is a well known amateur singer – always ready to give her services in any deserving cause – is a niece of Dr. J. W. Gainer, of Thrapston, and is, we understand, the first lady in Northamptonshire to receive the "Thanks Badge", which carries with it certain privileges."

July

Thursday 16th was the annual summer treat of the Thrapston Parish Church Sunday School, and by the invitation of the rector, the Rev. B. W. Stothert, the Thrapston Boy Scouts, of whom he was the scoutmaster, joined in the festivities.

"Having assembled at the Church of England School early in the afternoon, the children, headed by the Scouts, with their drums and bugle band, marched to the Parish Church, where a short service was conducted by the rector, with an appropriate address by the Rev. F. H. Lang, rector of Twywell.

After service the procession was re-formed in High Street, under the leadership of the scoutmaster, many of the children carrying small flags; and in front of the Scouts was led the troop dog. All being in readiness, the procession proceeded down the street en route for the school, where a bountiful tea was awaiting them.

Subsequently a programme of sports was carried out in the adjoining field, kindly lent by Mr. D. W. David, a number of parents and friends being present. The events included races for

members of the Scout Band and for the other Scouts respectively. Mr. Robinson acted as starter, and Lieut. Humphreys (of the Nigerian Field Force) and Miss Viva Ford were the judges. The prizes were distributed to the successful competitors by Mrs. Stothert, who was presented with a bouquet, which was handed to her by the youngest child in the school. The rector took the opportunity of speaking briefly on the importance of the work of the Sunday School.

The children were given cake, etc., before dispersing at dusk. It may be added that the Sunday School (of which Mr. Cyril Bamford was hon. secretary) had greatly increased during the past few months, and now numbered upwards of 180."

C. B. Church, of the Thrapston Harriers, won the twelve miles Marathon race at Kimbolton on Saturday 18th *(picture, left, from the Kettering Leader, Friday 24th July 1914).*

At the end of the month, on 31st the following items were reported:-

"An application was made by Mr. Frederick Houghton, of the Boot Inn, Wellingborough, for an occasional licence for the Thrapston and District Athletic Sports and Horse Show, to be held at Thrapston on Monday August 3rd. – Granted on the same terms and conditions as last year (as to hours of roundabouts on the various evenings etc.)."

"Thomas Day Bird, medical practitioner, Thrapston, was summoned for keeping two more dogs than he was licensed to keep, at Thrapston, on 17th – Defendant pleaded guilty. – Inspector Campion spoke to finding three dogs on the premises Dr. Bird, who was only licensed to keep one dog, told him two were born about last Christmas, and that he had thought of taking out licenses, but had omitted to do so. He also said he would do so at once, and he had done so. – The chairman: Only about a month late. – Fined 11s inclusive."

There was a lengthy report about a dispute between a local angler and the Kettering, Thrapston and District Angling Association.

"Mr. George Nicholls, formerly M.P. for North Northamptonshire was, on Wednesday, duly appointed Liberal candidate for the Thirsk and Malton (Yorkshire) Association."

"Thrapston Town Silver Prize Band repeated the success gained at the Warboys Foal Show, when on Tuesday they again entered for the band contest held in connection with the show. In the selection "Classic Gems" the band who were conducted by Mr. Nat Smith, retained the silver challenge cup, which has only to be won next year to become the property of the band. In addition, in connection with the selection, Mr. Ernest Abbott secured the medal for the euphonium solo, and Mr. Alf Fletcher gained a similar award for the cornet solo. The band also competed in the march "Defenders," and in this they gained the second prize."

"THE EXCHANGE THEATRE
The lessees of the above are to be congratulated on the enterprise and ability displayed by them in endeavouring to establish in so small a town a permanent place of entertainment. A good house assembled on Monday night to welcome Mr. Alf Jerome's company. It is a question as to whom the honours of the evening should fall, the company's abilities being so evenly balanced. The Great Balfe justified his title of mysterious entertainer the Jerome's are remarkably clever vaudeville entertainers; Carl de Alroy is, undoubtedly, an entertaining ventriloquist; and the novel burlesque, "The man from nowhere," concluded a thoroughly excellent programme. The whole show went with a swing from start to finish. Although we have not numerated each and every individual turn of the company, it is not because of their ability but owing to pressure of space. Our readers of Thrapston and district are reminded not to forget the long-night dance on Thursday night. The price of one shilling includes admission to the entertainment and the long-night dance."

On such a note normality ended, for within four days the world would never be the same again.

August

On Sunday 2nd, there was a crowded congregation at the Parish Church in the evening, when the rector, Rev. B. W. Stothert, held a special service in connection with the European crisis. Basing his text on Jeremiah xiii 28, he gave a forceful discourse on the subject.

August 4 1914 – Britain declares war on Germany.

On Thursday 6th, at the first meeting of the committee of the Thrapston Football Club, held at the Mason's Arms, Mr. E. March was elected chairman and Mr. A. A. Staake vice chairman of the committee, while Mr. March and Mr. W. Cheney (the secretary) were appointed delegates to the meetings of the Kettering Combination. The secretary stated that the club would have a new ground this season, nearer the town. The prospects of the season were very bright indeed, despite the heavy adverse bank balance.

Kettering Leader, Friday August 7 1914.
Headline on page 1.

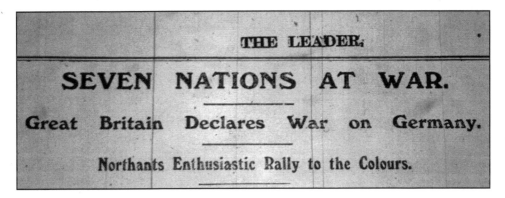

1914 Recruitment Advertisement –
(Rushden Echo)

Sunday 9th was the first Sunday since the outbreak of war. "Special intercessory prayers were read at the places of worship in the town and neighbourhood, and pulpit references to the war were general. At Thrapston Parish Church, the names of all men who had left the parish for active service were individually mentioned in the prayers. At the evening service there was a very full congregation. The hymns were "O God, our help in ages past," "Holy Father, in Thy mercy," and "Peace, perfect peace" (the last-named sung kneeling, after the Benediction). The rector, the Rev. B. W. Stothert, taking as his text Rom. viii., 38-39 (on the love of God), spoke of the war, and urged the need for prayer and unity, and also for calmness in the face of possible reverses. He said the war was the work of the devil. For years the nations of Europe had been drifting into agnosticism; the tendency had been to shelve religion; and now this war had come, and they needed to humiliate themselves and pray for peace. He had been surprised and touched to see how many people during the last few days, in a small town like Thrapston, had, as opportunity offered, gone into church to say their prayers. He hoped they would go on doing so. During the week the tenor bell would be rung every day at five minutes past twelve, and he wanted everyone, when they heard it, to say a prayer for peace. An outdoor service, conducted by the rector, was subsequently held in Chancery-lane, there being a large attendance. Special prayers were used, and the closing hymn was "God be with you till we meet again.""

On the same day, William Rowell, an army pensioner died. "The deceased served in the South African war, and was wounded, being shot through the knee. He had been a sufferer more or less ever since, principally with his heart. About nine months ago he left Thrapston, where he was well known and respected and after living for about six months in Irthlingborough went to reside at Kettering. On August Bank Holiday he came to Thrapston Sports – being determined to see them once more – but on his return home he took to his bed and died on the following Sunday. The deceased married the youngest daughter of the late Mr. Thos. Loveday, postman, of Thrapston, with whom and the two children (boys) much sympathy is felt."

A week later, "the Sunday collections at the Thrapston Parish Church, in aid of the Prince of Wales National Relief Fund, amounted to £10 16s 11d. In the morning the only notice was that given out at the service, but in the afternoon the town crier (who is also sexton), with bell in use, "cried" a further notice round the town. A second collection for the same object will be made later on."

Monday 31st saw the first batch of 35 new recruits leave town on the 8.54 am Northampton train. "Amongst the men leaving were scoutmasters F. Short (Islip), A. Swan (Lowick) and A. G. Swan (Twywell), and assistant scoutmasters W. Skelton (Thrapston), and B. Burdett (Titchmarsh). After the final handshakes and farewells "three cheers for the boys" were given and the train steamed out of the station amid renewed cheers and waving of hats and handkerchiefs. Some other recruits were due to leave during the day, making the total about forty-five."

September

On Tuesday 1st, the Thrapston Christmas Fat Stock Show Committee decided, as a consequence of the war, not to hold a show in 1914.

On the same day, a Thrapston Recruiting Committee was formed, consisting of the Rev. B. W. Stothert, Mr. Geo. Smith (J. P., C. C.), Mr. H. W. Beauford, Mr. J. W. Duthy, and Mr. J. Edmonds. A day later, the clerk to the Thrapston Guardians, Mr. Hunnybun, reported that he had received a telegram from his son, Mr. M. G. W. Hunnybun (deputy clerk and superintendant registrar of births, marriages, and deaths), who was in the Hunts Territorials (Cyclists' Corps), asking whether he could volunteer for the front. – Sanction was given. He later offered himself as a despatch rider and served at the front.

By 3rd September, weekly war prayer meetings had been arranged, held alternately at the Baptist and Wesleyan Churches.

On Friday 4th, the *Kettering Leader* reported that, because of "stirring appeals at a memorable meeting", "...the following members of the Thrapston United Football Club have enlisted in

Lord Kitchener's Army: Messrs. **J. Pollard (25)**, **T. Giddings (13)**, W. Thurlow, and **R. Templeman (14)**. Another valuable United player, C. Booth, has joined the Metropolitan Police." A recruiting office had been opened in the Market Place, manned by Col.- Sergts. Leverton of Oundle and Bethel of Rushden.

By 11th, the Thrapston Boy Scout Troop had commenced patrols in the district. Pictured in the *Kettering Leader* on that date, they were named as :- (Left to right) W. Shelton, R. Knighton, R. Windsor, J. Walton, Rev. B. W. Stothert, L. Shelton, D. Barker, L. Abbott, and H. Wilson, with D. Ingram and the troop dog "Cæsar" in front.

The first batch of recruits *(pictured below hunting for crabs – I found this picture many years ago and failed to note the source - EDF)* was, by now, at Weymouth, undergoing training. One of them wrote from the D Company Battalion, Northamptonshire Regiment, "We joined the 3rd Battalion, who are expecting orders at any time. All of us are in fine spirits, although I

have been in hospital two days with exhaustion. Thrapston fellows have answered the call splendidly, over 50 from our district. We have about 50 scouts from Northamptonshire with us." In another communication, he mentioned that one of the officers spoke of the Thrapston recruits as being "a very smart lot." Two days later, the same writer said "All the boys are fit and well, and enjoy the life very much, especially the bathing parades. Our officers and N.C.O's are the right sort, and keen on their work; and we shall be a smart battalion when we return. With the numbers here from the Thrapston district we ought to get a splendid company of trained men, for we should hold our own numerically and with physique with any other. The weather here has been lovely, and the sun is terrific in the daytime; but at night it is fearfully cold. We have had some rain the last two nights, but the ground is so hard and dry, it has had no effect. An old companion has been put in stores with me, so that we are together once more. I have just had to prepare for a District Court Martial on one of our chaps. Have been told I shall get promotion soon; A. Swan and L. Morris have been appointed acting-corporals for the time being."

"A company of the 6th Battalion Gordon Highlanders marched through Thrapston shortly before one o'clock on Friday 11th, coming from the direction of Huntingdon. During a halt of a few minutes several ladies and gentlemen – including Mrs. Beal, Miss Modlen, and Mr. R. Smith – supplied them with cigarettes; and they left the town, singing a Scotch song."

LETTERS FROM THE FRONT

Letters are now being received in all parts of the country by relatives and friends of our gallant soldiers at the front.

Much of this correspondence will contain matter of public interest, and such communications the "Northamptonshire Evening Telegraph" would be glad to publish, wholly or in part.

All letters of this kind received at this office will be carefully preserved, and will be returned in due course to the senders.

On Monday 14th, the *Evening Telegraph* carried this advertisement on page 1, and for the next four years, many reports were based on letters from combatants.

On the next day, a report about the recruits at Weymouth stated that they had "started on skirmishing drill, and this was a bit of a change from routine company drill. A draft of about 200 Northamptons went away on Friday last on foreign service and included in these were Dick Groom, of Thrapston, and Headland, of Woodford. Corpl. Dick Johnson, of Woodford, who was in the Scout Section of the 1st Battalion has been promoted sergeant."

On September 17th, the White Flag treachery occurred (114) whilst a day later, Thrapston Parish's contribution towards the County National Relief Fund was announced as being £46 1s 5d (collected between 4th and 15th August).

On 24th, news was received from the front – H. Nicholls, a Thrapston postman who previously served in the Boer War, was a corporal at the R.A.M.C. No. 1 Field Ambulance. The report mentioned that the envelope was stamped "Passed by Censor". H. Cooper of Thrapston had left training camp and was now in France. Those still in training were learning trench digging (often to taunts of "think you are digging your father's garden?") and marching, "plenty of it, usually in pouring rain". Uniform was varied – "We do look some pictures here, as at other places where Kitchener's men are, for, of all sizes, we are decked out in various sorts of clothes. Those who are lucky have bought themselves khaki suits, while others, unfortunately, cannot boast a shirt at all, and others have the sleeves right out. Some have been supplied with khaki trousers, or white fatigue suits, owing to their own having given way to the strain; but when on the march, although clothes in raiments varied, all step out briskly with heads erect, shoulders well back, and arms swinging cheerily, marching along to music provided by "the boys", who sing and whistle alternately. We are having plenty of marching. They mean us to keep up the reputation of the regiment and we are all trying to do so ourselves."

On 27th, Pte. Frederick H. Nicholls of the Northamptonshire Regiment was admitted to the Western General Hospital, Manchester, having been wounded in his left arm during action. He arrived in Thrapston four days later to recuperate. He was due to return to depot in Northampton on October 26th.

October

October 3rd saw an appeal in the *Evening Telegraph* for donations of blankets to be sent to the Northamptonshire Regiment at the front. Rev. Basil Stothert, rector of Thrapston, was the co-ordinator. The same day saw a charity fund-raising football match between Thrapston Stadium and Titchmarsh White City in aid of the local Soldiers' Tobacco Fund and Prince of

Wales Relief Fund. The game ended with a win for Thrapston by four goals to three. Afterwards, a smoking concert was held at the King's Arms Hotel. A total of £1 19s 1d was raised, made up to £5. Of this, £4 was given to the local fund and tobacco was later purchased and sent out to the 43 Thrapston and 25 Titchmarsh men on service.

Two days later, Monday 5th, Mrs. J. Rowlett of Chancery Lane was commended for raising 14s by selling asters, grown in her garden, to raise money for the Prince of Wales Relief Fund. The same day worrying news was received in town that Pte. **John Smith (26)**, whose father lived in South Terrace, had been killed. This was later found to be incorrect – he was wounded, and wrote to his father, "It has been hard and rough, but we have to bear it all in good cheer. In the big battle I was up with my regiment. We took up a position on Sunday night, 13th September. I was in the trenches up till the 17th, till I got wounded in the right arm near the shoulder. But I had a fortnights stay in hospital, and am getting on alright now – very nearly well. Then we came to this Convalescent Camp to get well. I am still in good health, only a cold; that is not much."

By the end of the month, Rev. Stothert was able to report that he had over 200 recruits pass through his hands during October. On 28th, he gave the first of six lectures on the European War at the Church of England School. The talk was illustrated with lantern slides, including portraits of prominent persons connected with the war; also English, French, Russian, and German soldiers, views of battleships and great guns. *(Pictured is a typical slide from this era, of transport near Antwerp - EDF).*

November

Philip Makin (3) and Walter Miller (4) were both wounded on 2nd and died on 3rd November, Thrapston's first fatal casualties of the war.

On Saturday 7th, the *Evening Telegraph* reported under the headline "Thrapston recruits in training" – "Sixty out of each company had been transferred to the 3rd Battalion to supply drafts for the 1st and 2nd Battalions as required at the front. In this lot was Assistant Scoutmaster W. Skelton, of the 1st Thrapston Troop of Scouts, and there might be others. The remainder, it was stated, would stay at their present quarters till January, and then be sent to a big training centre, their destination probably being in the Midlands. On Sunday a draft of about sixty went away, the sergeant in charge being Sergt. F. Corbett, the Woodford Scoutmaster. The writer thinks that with the exception of two all the Thrapston boys can report a clean bill of health. He also refers to the interest taken by the recruits in the local papers which reach them."
As well as joining the County Regiment, several youths from the Thrapston district had joined the Hunts Cyclist Corp.

On 9th, Mrs. Webster, of Halford Street, Thrapston, received a postcard from her husband, Sergt. J. Webster of the Royal Scotch Fusiliers, informing her that he had been wounded, and landed on Sunday at Southampton. No particulars were given of the wound. Sergt. Webster, who was a reservist, was a postman at Thrapston prior to the outbreak of the war.

On 10th, reports of the death of **Philip Makin (3)** were received in town.

A recruiting meeting was held at the Corn Market on 14th, resulting in about a dozen young men enlisting.

John Hall, Hortons Lane, received a letter on 18th from his son, **Hugh David Hall (31)**. The *Evening Telegraph* reported "Pte. H. D. Hall enlisted in the first week in August in the 3rd Battalion of the Grenadier Guards (the regiment to which the Prince of Wales belongs). Another son, Robert Hall, enlisted in the Northampton Regiment in September, and is now in training with the 5th Battalion. In his letters he speaks very favourably of the conditions generally, and expresses surprise that more young men do not realise the advantage and duty of joining. In a letter received by his mother on Tuesday night he stated, "We are going firing tomorrow. Real shot. I have passed in one course; if I pass in this course I shall get sixpence a day more, but we have to get 230 points out of 250. We have Rugby, football, running, boxing, and concerts'.""

The *Rushden Echo* reported on 20th that Sergt. Webster had been wounded, whilst the Thrapston Parish total towards the County's National Relief Fund stood at £178 13s 3d. *(Equivalent value, 2012 = £7,693.21)*.

November 25th saw the announcement that, "the Thrapston Baptist Church Sunday School and congregation have subscribed, and forwarded to the "Daily News" Soldiers' Christmas Plum Pudding Fund, the sum of £3, which is equivalent to 120 soldiers' portions of puddings."

Several recruits left town at the end of the month.

December

By the beginning of the month, arrangements for the accommodation of Belgian refugees were nearing completion. Mr. H. H. Bletsoe had given the use of a house in the Market Place and was completing structural repairs himself. The local Relief Committee were only required to provide for decoration and furnishing of the premises. It was expected to be ready for occupation by 18th.

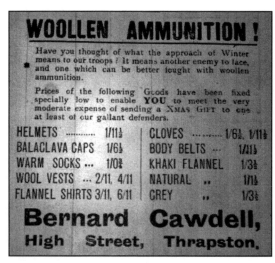

Recruiting was reported to be continuing apace on Thursday 3rd, several leaving for Northampton on Monday 30th November and Tuesday 1st December. On the same day, Thrapston District Council heard that the town's Parish Council had decided to postpone the water supply scheme for three months. Drinking water was being obtained from various wells around town, the engine-house pump and the churchyard spring.

(Advertisement in the Evening Telegraph, Thursday 3rd December 1914)

Recruiting posters appeared everywhere, including the local press. The three shown on page 16 were placed in the *Kettering Leader* on December 4th, 18th and 25th. *(Yes, it was published on Christmas Day! - EDF)*.

Official confirmation of the death of **Philip Makin (3)** was received in town on 7th. In a separate communication, news of the death of **Walter Miller (4)** arrived in town on the same day. The church bell was tolled for both of them. The *Evening Telegraph* reported "Mrs. Miller, of Oundle Road, Thrapston, received a communication from the Infantry Record Office, Warley Station, on Monday morning, conveying her the information that a report had been received from the War Office notifying the death from wounds on November 3rd of her husband, Pte. Walter Miller, No. 7621, of the Northamptonshire Regiment and adding that he had been interred in the Poperinghe Cemetery. On November 7th Mrs. Miller received an Army postcard, dated November 2nd informing her that her husband was in hospital wounded, and going on well, but no further details were given. The last letter Mrs. Miller received from deceased was dated Oct. 25th. Pte. Miller then stated that he was in the best of health, and that they were getting on finely. Two days before receiving news that her husband had been wounded Mrs. Miller had a letter from him in which he mentioned that he had not heard from her for a long time. Then the next day came a postcard informing her that he had just received twenty-one letters from her, although no reason was given why they had accumulated in this way."

On a more mundane level, Thrapston Police Court heard the case of a 27 year old labourer, of no-fixed abode, who was charged with begging in Thrapston. P.C. Short gave evidence of seeing the accused begging from door to door in Halford Street. He was sentenced to 14 days hard labour and told by the bench that instead of begging he should be doing something for his country.

An optimistic letter from Corpl. H. Nicholls was reported on 9th where he said, "Where we are now, everything is so quiet and peaceful that, as far as we are concerned just at present, all points to a speedy end in this dreadful war. Of course we know no more when it will be over than you at home, but according to the victories that the Russians and the other Allies are having, it will not be long before it is over." That evening, a Memorial Service for **Philip Makin (3)** and **Walter Miller (4)** was held in the Parish Church.

On Thursday 10th, a fund-raising day for the Belgian Relief Fund was held in town. The Leader reported "The normally demure town of Thrapston let itself go on Thursday of last week on the occasion of a fete in aid of the Belgian Relief Fund. Everybody turned out to witness the procession, which was headed by a banner inscribed "Help the Belgian Relief

Fund," behind which marched the Town Band, Fire Brigade, Boy Scouts, and the "Ladies" v "Gents" football teams, a hundred silk hats and the "ladies" costumes, provided by Mr. Herbert Abbott, of London, giving the processionists an unwonted appearance, which decidedly tickled the risible faculties of the onlookers. Later the "gentlemen" played the "ladies" at football, where the honours appropriately were even in a 5-5 draw." There was also a gymkhana and in the evening a concert. A total of £30 was raised, £20 being given to the King Albert Fund for Destitute Belgians in London and £10 to the local Relief Committee *(picture shown on page 15 – EDF Collection)*.

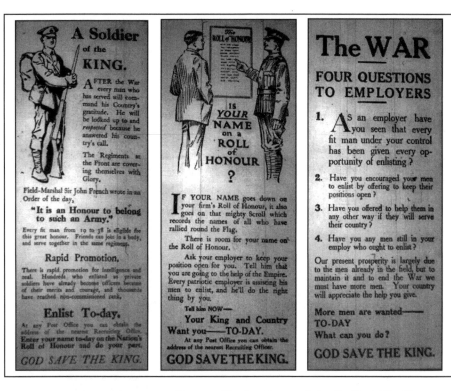

Trooper Charles Bues, of the Bedfordshire Yeomanry, wrote to thank people for the recent gift of cigarettes and tobacco. On 15th, the *Evening Telegraph* reported, "Our duties are as follow: - Reveille at 6 am: stables until 7 o'clock: breakfast until 8 o'clock: saddle up and parade at 8.30, when we have regimental parades and schemes, etc., until one o'clock: dinner and parade for dismounted duties until 4.30: stables again until 5.30, when, if we are lucky, we are done for the day. But as a rule we have a lecture until 7.30, so you see we have plenty to do. I might say I have had one or two exciting moments since we have been mobilised, such as when my horse fell dead under me, and when sleeping in an old barn I woke up to find rats running over my blanket."
(This picture shows Trooper Bues on the horse which died. It appeared in the Kettering Leader on Friday 18th.)

Christmas Day services were held in the Parish and Wesleyan Churches.

The inmates of the Workhouse had a good Christmas Day. The dining room and infirmary were profusely decorated, all work was suspended for the day and a meal comprising roast beef, potatoes (baked and boiled), Yorkshire pudding, leg of mutton, greens, parsnips, plum pudding and custard, and ale and mineral water were served. In the evening, the master arranged the usual concert, which was enjoyed by all. During the interval, oranges and tobacco were distributed. There were very few children in the Workhouse at this time, most being at the children's home in Raunds.

On 29th, the Belgian refugees arrived by train during the evening. Mr. and Mrs. Hollanders and Mr. and Mrs. Vandervalle, and their three sons aged 7, 9 and 10, were given a very warm welcome by both the committee and townspeople. In return, they expressed their gratitude for the arrangements made for their accommodation and comfort.

Thus ended 1914, a year that commenced with the departure of two very popular ladies, and finished with the town's first fatalities and the welcoming of victims of the war from Belgium.

(The above picture shows the corner of High Street and Oundle Road in 1914, Taylor & Downs - EDF Collection).

At the front, all the early optimism about the war being "over by Christmas" had dissipated and the harsh reality of mechanised warfare was starting to enter the public consciousness. Yet patriotism remained high, men were still willingly signing up and Thrapston folk would continue to do all they could to ensure that "our boys at the front" realised that they were remembered and received such gifts as could be obtained for their comfort. "Forget-me-not" days would be held regularly and the flower became the symbol of remembrance, only being superseded by the poppy when the British Legion, which was founded on 15th May 1921, adopted it in 1921.

1915

January

By the end of the first week of the New Year, Dr. Lascelles from Islip (who regularly played cricket for Thrapston) had joined the Scottish Horse as medical officer, accompanied by H. Wilson, B. Cresswell and G. Childs. Two other local men had enlisted with the Hunts Cyclists Battalion, A. Green and **John Guest (42)**.

The *Kettering Leader* reported on Friday 8th that **David Hall (31)** "had a narrow escape the other day. A bullet went through my overcoat and small coat, and smashed four of the cartridges to pieces, but did not hurt me at all. It was very lucky for me".

On the same day, the same newspaper carried the picture *(shown left)* of the Belgian refugees in front of the house in the Market Place.

Mrs. Throssell of Manor House, Chancery Lane, received the worrying news on 12th that her son, Trooper Tebbutt Throssell, of the Northants Yeomanry (B Squadron), who had been one of the first to join up on outbreak of war, had been wounded. One of his comrades wrote, "Our men were digging trenches, and "Tebby" was busy with his spade. Of course this work is done in the dark, as you are in front of the German trenches. Well, "Tebby" was hit in the lower part of the body, about on a line with his hip, and about three inches from the hip, and the bullet went right through him and out the fleshy part. A. E. Smith – you know, our pal – was close to him, and, of course, many more, so he was well looked after at once. Smith came and told me last night about eleven o'clock, when they got back. So first thing this morning I went to hospital to see him, and found him most comfortable and merry and bright. They thought at first it was serious, but now they say the bullet did not touch either the bladder or the stomach, so it is merely a flesh wound. Poor old "Tebby" would have been no more if it had been half an inch either way, but as it is he will soon be home. He always has been one of the best soldiers in our regiment, and now I think he is as good a soldier as there is in France. The Red Cross men told me today he was topping."

He was returned to England on 11th and sent to hospital in Leicester. His commanding officer wrote to Mrs. Throssell, "Your son was in my troop, and I am very sorry to lose him. He is a splendid soldier, and we are all so sorry that he is hors de combat."

A day later, Mrs. Charlton of Oundle Road received a postcard from her son, Pte. Percy Charlton, of the 1st Northants, containing the following: - "Dear Mother, - Landed in England today. Going to hospital. Not serious. – Love, Percy."

On 20th, it was reported that Mr. Donald St. Clair Gainer, older son of Dr. Gainer, of Thrapston, had been appointed, by the Foreign Office, British Vice-Consul at Narvik, Norway, for the period of the war.

Schoolchildren were very involved in "doing their bit" for men on active service. Their gifts were always very gratefully received, as shown by this report from the *Evening Telegraph* on Friday January 22nd:-

"GIFTS FROM THRAPSTON SCHOOL CHILDREN

Fourteen pairs of mittens for the Northamptonshire Regiment were recently knitted by the girls of Thrapston Church of England School, the wool being kindly given by Mrs. Emery (wife of the headmaster Mr. F. W. B. Emery), and each of the girls wrote a little letter to accompany the pair of mittens made by her. The mittens were sent to Oundle and forwarded through Mrs. Capron. On Tuesday one of the scholars, Marjorie Waite, of Oundle Road, Thrapston, (who herself has a brother at the front), received a kind and interesting acknowledgement, as follows: - "British Expeditionary Force, France, January 16th,1915, Trenches. My dear Marjorie – Excuse my writing you, but knowing you knitted the pair of mittens I have received, I thought I would drop you a line to acknowledge them, to let you know what comfort you little ones afford us. No matter how small, you see you are helping in some way, and I can assure you we can do with them, as it's awful what with wet and cold, and the terrible uncomfortable positions we are in. No doubt you read about the terrible war: but it's not war, it's ten times worse than any war: but let's hope it will soon be over. No doubt your teachers tell you lots about it, but they only imagine it; no one can know what it is unless they have been through it. It's awful, you know, to see one's comrades killed each side of you. It's too awful for words. Well, now I will tell you about our living. We get excellent good food – bacon, bread, tea, sugar, tinned meats, cheese, jam, and all sorts of things: and we have fires in the trenches and cook the food as best we can. I can tell you, we get some real good round meals, and we can do justice to them too. Of course, as regards washing days, they are few and far between. If only we could get plenty of clean washing it would be all right. There are lots issued, but some cannot wear flannel. I cannot wear flannel myself, so have to wait for issues of something flannelette or cotton; but there are not many issues of cotton things. Well, now the Germans are shelling us, so must close, wishing you every success in your good work for Tommy Atkins. – Yours sincerely, T. Cheeseman, Corpl. 1st Northamptonshire Regiment." *(Thomas Cheeseman, from Colchester, was killed on May 9th 1915, alongside **George Earle (12)** and **Richard Templeman (14)** and is commemorated with them on the Le Touret Memorial, Bethune, France. He is also named on the Colchester War Memorial - EDF.)*

On 23rd, the local policeman, P.C. Short, was mentioned as having recently lost in action one of his three nephews who had all joined up. On the same day further news was also received from Percy Charlton, who was now in Brighton Hospital, who said "Glad to tell you my side will soon be better, but my feet are so bad; I have no feeling in the toes yet. It is miserable lying in bed all day, but they won't let me get up, so I suppose I must put up with it. We have got some very nice nurses here; it is also a lovely place where we are. It is really a convalescent home for widows, but they have made it into a hospital for us chaps. Did you make any mincemeat this Christmas. If you did mind you save a bit for when I come home. When I saw some of them eating mincemeat in the trenches, it made me think of old times."

The following notice appeared in the *Evening Telegraph* at the end of the month-
"THRAPSTON PRECAUTIONS
The Lighting and Watching Committee of the Thrapston Parish Council have decided to discontinue the public lighting of the streets for the present."

On 31st, **Basil Frederick Emery (7)** was admitted to hospital in Bombay with appendicitis.

February

At the beginning of the month, Corpl. Nicholls wrote home again, "We are resting, but I do not expect it will be for long, as the Germans have just started to send a few shells over, but nothing much, as most of them are duds, and don't explode. The weather is beginning to be more favourable now, so might expect anything to occur." Then, in an addition, headed "10a.m.", he says, "All is quiet now. Our section is remaining here. Have just heard that some of the German guns which sent the shells over here have been put out of action, so hope the news may be true."

A report on Tuesday 2nd said that the County Recruiting Committee were proposing to write to the War Office offering Thrapston as "an excellent ground for training and that the billeting". Two days later came the news that Trooper R. Preece, Northants Yeomanry, had been wounded in the foot. His parents lived at Drayton Home Farm.

Pte. C. A. Westley, for six years a bank clerk in town "and now a resident of Northampton", who was serving with the Gordon Highlanders, had been wounded on or about the 2nd.

The *Evening Telegraph* reported on Thursday 11th, "The Thrapston and Oundle district occupies a very satisfactory position with regard to recruits for H.M. Forces, for since the call came in August, Colour-Sergt. Leverton, of Oundle, has sent 439 men up, of whom only 35 were rejected, making a net total of 404. Of this number, the Rev. B. W. Stothert, Rector of Thrapston, has personally sent 246 from the Thrapston district alone. Moreover, men continue to go in small numbers. Two or three left on Tuesday." On the same day, Pte. Eric St. Clair Gainer, of the Seaforth Highlanders, wrote to the Tobacco Fund and Shop Assistants' Social Club thanking them for their gifts of tobacco, cigarettes and handkerchiefs.

February 17th - Basil Frederick Emery (7) died in Bombay, India, as a result of complications after developing appendicitis.

(His last ship was the Royal Mail steamer, Arankola, shown left).

On 18th, Thrapston Council responded to a County Council request for names of all men who had enlisted or were serving. The report read, "The chairman said that at the last meeting of the County Council the opinion was expressed that some sort of roll of honour should be kept of all who had served during the present war."
It seemed to him that there would be some difficulty in getting a complete list of the Thrapston men, for they might enlist at Northampton, Wellingborough, etc., and the local recruiting officer would not have all the names. He suggested that the only way would be to canvass the town and ask at each house who had served.
Mr. Selby thought that all those fighting for their country are a credit to it, and it was to their honour they wanted to bring their names before the whole of the country. It would be very difficult to get a complete list and it seemed to him it would be best to form a committee from the town generally, for some of the townspeople knew who had joined more than they did themselves. At the suggestion of the chairman Mr. Selby moved that the clerk be asked to take the matter in hand, and that the Councillors should assist in their immediate neighbourhood – Mr. Cheney seconded. – Carried."

March

The March issue of the *Parish Magazine* commented, "To those who are inclined to belittle the Scout movement, it may be of interest to learn that the following members of our troop are serving their country: - Hon. Scoutmaster A. Johnson, Northants Regiment: Assistant Scoutmaster H. Wilson, R.A.M.C.: Assistant Scoutmaster W. Skelton, Northants Regiment: Senior Leader L. Skelton, Hunts Cyclists: Leader H. L. Abbott, Hunts Cyclists: ex-scout W. Guest (1912), Hunts Cyclists."

On Thursday 4th, Trooper Bone, of the Northants Yeomanry, was reported to be in hospital in France suffering from influenza, whilst the next day, a further letter from Corpl. H. Nicholls was quoted in the *Evening Telegraph* – "I am still in good health and wishing for this dreadful war to be over, and to be back home again with you all. We are still at *(place name deleted by censor - EDF)* but we may move about any time before you get this letter: but don't think we are going very far up. Had a jolly good concert here last night: it was in connection with the Reading Room which our minister has been good enough to work up for us, and which passes many a hour away during the day. We try to make ourselves as cheerful and comfortable as possible. So you see, whilst we are away from the firing line we have a few bright hours, but it's nothing like being at home."

Also on 5th, in the same newspaper, an extensive obituary for **Basil Emery (7)** was published.

March 14th - Alfred Edward Waite (8) died in action at Neuve Chapelle, France.

During the same action, **William Reeve (10)** was wounded.

Pte. Percy Charlton returned to Thrapston and was at home for a fortnight's leave in Oundle Road on 15th, having been discharged from hospital in Littlehampton.

Two days later, news reached Thrapston that "Corpl. A. Johnson, of the 1st Northants, had been wounded and was in hospital in Kent, after having been at the front for only a fortnight. Corpl. Johnson was a Reservist, and had served in India with the "Steelbacks." On being called up at the outbreak of the war and proceeding to Weymouth, he for some time acted as musketry instructor with the recruits. In November he went with a draft to Sunderland for coast duty, returning to Weymouth in January. Corpl. Johnson was a postman at Thrapston when the war broke out. The extent and nature of his injuries were not stated." A few days later, his injuries were confirmed as wounds to his left hand, the result of maxim gun fire.

Life in town continued, despite the war. The Parish Council met at the Temperance Hall on Wednesday 17th for only a short time. The meeting was reported two days later in the *Evening Telegraph*. "There were present: Messrs Geo. Smith, J.P., C.C. (chairman), A. Barnett, J. Baines, A. French, W. Hillyard, Alfred Hensman, T. Selby, and Wm. Smith, together with the clerk Mr. Arthur G. Brown.- The District Council wrote agreeing to the proposal of the Water Supply Committee, that the water scheme be adjourned for six months. The chairman remarked that the matter would be placed on the agenda from month to month, so that in case the circumstances altered, the same could be discussed. – The clerk reported that he had arranged the town into districts, and had books prepared for each district in which the names of the men who had enlisted in the Army or Navy would be entered. The books were distributed amongst the several councillors to canvass their respective districts. The chairman mentioned that the books would be kept here and the names added from time to time, a copy being sent to the proper quarter. – Mr. A. Barnett, as chairman of the Lighting and Watching Committee, presented the report of a meeting held on the 9th inst., which recommended:

(a) That any necessary alteration of the route of the lamplighter be left to the chairman to make;

(b) That Mr. Richardson's tender for street watering at 7s. per half day, be accepted;

(c) That the control of the water cart during the ensuing season be left in the hands of the committee.

The report was adopted. - Mr. Selby said there was nothing for the Sewerage Works Committee to report and a little finance business concluded the meeting."

In the same issue, Pte **Hugh Hall (31)** reported "that he had been in hospital for six days with his old complaint, but hoped to be better soon; his joints had always been a little uneasy on account of the wet weather. "But," he proceeds, "I am glad to say the weather is picking up much better the last week, so it will make things better for us when the sun shines a little more." In a further letter, written on March 15th, he says; "Just a few lines to let you know I am all right again, and have been back to the trenches – the same day as I wrote to you last. We have had it very hot, too, but we drove the Germans back a long way and took several trenches from them, and have captured hundreds of them, besides what are killed. I expect you will see it in the papers soon. I have got the cigarettes you sent, and hope you will send some more, and matches with them, and a few cakes – they come in very nice now and then."

Another local man was reported injured on Monday 22nd. Lieut. Spence Sanders, 6th Battalion Gordon Highlanders, who had been home on leave only a few weeks earlier, was wounded in both thighs but was progressing well in hospital. He moved to town in about 1910 and worked as an analytical chemist at the Islip Iron Company. He lived at "The Shrubberies". On the same day, news was received that Pte. C. A. Westley had returned to the front and Pte. **William Reeve (10)** had been wounded.

March 26th - William Edward Cooper (9) killed in action.

March 26th - William Reeve (10) died of wounds.

On 30th, Pte. Percy Charlton returned to depot.

April

On Thursday 1st, Mrs. Earle visited her son Ernest Earle in Manchester Hospital, where he was recovering from two operations. A report on 6th stated, "He had some painful memories to speak of. The Germans, he told his mother, were round them like flies. On the same day that he was wounded, two Thrapston mates with whom he had gone out were struck down. One, **Pte. W. Reeve (10)**, (son of Mrs. Reeve, of Oundle-road, Thrapston), was shot in the head with a bullet and he (Pte. Earle) bandaged the wound and helped to carry him to the dressing station, whence he was sent to Boulogne Hospital. Then he told with clear distress how another friend, **Pte. Alfred Waite (8)**, son of Mr. and Mrs. Waite, of Oundle-road, Thrapston, who was by his side, dropped dead with part of his head blown off by a shell. The narrator begged his mother to break the news to Mrs. Waite as soon as she got home; this she did (on Saturday), and until then Mrs. Waite had heard nothing..."

On 6th, Corpl. H. Nicholls said that he had seen two German aeroplanes, which had been trying to observe their lines. They were repelled by gunfire and the arrival of English and French planes. On the same day, Mr. A. H. Touch had a letter from his brother, Pte. F. Touch of the Cambridge Territorials, who had been at the front for a month, reproduced in the *Evening Telegraph*. He wrote, "Last Saturday night they shifted us to what was a pretty village, but is now a heap of ruins, not one house remaining intact. We slept in these houses on Saturday night and everything was quiet, with the exception of a few bullets from German snipers. On Sunday afternoon, at almost five, they (the Germans) started shelling the place like mad. A few minutes after that the news came that the Germans were making a big attack, and then we had the order that we were to occupy a support of trenches. The shells were flying all around the houses, so you can tell for yourself what it was like when we got into the street. The mud from the shells bursting flew into our faces, so you may depend that those of us who did not get wounded had marvellous escapes. After getting through that and advancing, we had to contend with shrapnel and also bullets from the snipers. We eventually got to the trenches, and kept in them until Monday morning".

Three days later, Mrs. Reeve received official confirmation from the War Office of the death of her son, **William Reeve (10)** whilst Mrs. Cooper had a letter from one of her son's comrades, giving details of the death of **William Cooper (9)**.

On 15th, Mrs. Mault, of the Market Place, Thrapston, received a postcard from her grandson, Sergt. V. H. Gray, of the King's Royal Rifles. It stated that he had been "slightly wounded in the neck, and was in the base hospital. Sergt. Gray was at home at Thrapston not long ago for a fortnight on sick leave, with frost-bite. He has been in the Army for six or seven years, and spent some years in India."

Sunday 18th saw a combined memorial service at St. James' Church for **William Cooper (9)** and **William Reeve (10)**. The Town Band and Fire Brigade attended. The impressive service included the hymns "Days and moments quickly flying" and "Brief life is here our portion" being accompanied by the band and Miss Kingsford. Preaching from the text "And God shall wipe away all tears from their eyes", the rector very feelingly alluded to the sad death of the two soldier heroes who had given their lives for the country. At the conclusion the Dead March was played, the congregation remaining standing.

April 21st - Herbert Frederick Gilbert (11) killed in action.

On 22nd, Pte. W. Skelton, who had recently been an assistant scoutmaster in town, wrote to say the food was good and he was about to go on sentry duty. The same day, Sgt. Webster, drill instructor for the Royal Scotch Fusiliers offered to do his best to help any Thrapston boys to join a Scotch Regiment.

May

At the beginning of May, the Parish Council arranged for a notice to be circulated to all householders:-
"The Council consider it advisable to inform the householders of the town that should there be any sign of AIR RAIDS, or other disturbances, the Supply of Gas will be turned off at the Gas Works. It is consequently most important that All Gas Meters and also Burner Taps should be turned off each night. It is recommended that a small supply of candles be kept in readiness.
BY ORDER".

On Saturday 1st, Corpl. A. Johnson, formerly a town postman was in Bromley Hospital, recovering from septicaemia, and was hoping to have only one finger amputated rather than the whole hand.

On 5th, the Oundle Recruiting Office was transferred to Thrapston, using a room given by the Northampton Brewing Company on Market Place.

On 7th, a letter arrived home from Pte. **J. Waite (15)**, of Thrapston, to say that he and other Thrapston men were in the trenches during the recent heavy fighting.

(Pre-war postcard of Market Place, King & Son – EDF Collection).

May 9th – George Samuel Earle (12), John Thomas Giddings (13) and Richard Edis Templeman (14) all killed in action.

Sunday May 9th was the darkest day Thrapston faced during the course of the war, when three men were killed in action. **George Earle (12)** and **Richard Templeman (14)** were both killed at the infamous Battle of Aubers Ridge in France, whilst **John Giddings (13)** died near Armentieres.

Three days later, the Honorary Recruiting Officer, Rev. Basil Stothert, reported a greatly stimulated surge in recruitment following the sinking of the Lusitania on 9th. A dozen left on 10th, followed by others the next day.

First news of the death of **John Giddings (13)** was received in town on Saturday 15th, whilst four days later, news arrived that **Herbert Gilbert (11)** was missing.

Another casualty was Pte. F. Whitemen of Halford Street who was the very first Thrapston man to enlist. He was wounded at Aubers Ridge, his right hand being blown off. Shortly after, he wrote a postcard to his mother saying, "I am writing this left handed; I have lost my right hand: but cheer up, dear, I have still got my life, thank God."

Thursday 20th brought the news that Trooper Bernard Wright, Northants Yeomanry, had been granted a commission in the Army Service Corps, whilst T. Smith, for several years chauffeur to George Smith, County Councillor, had joined the same Corps in the Mechanical Transport Branch.

There was also a report of the work of the Tobacco Fund, a group raising money to provide comforts to serving soldiers. The *Evening Telegraph* reported, "Meetings have recently been held in aid of the Thrapston and Islip Soldiers' Tobacco Fund. The officials are: president, Mr. W. Beal: chairman, Mr. W. Stobie: treasurer, Mr. F. W. Beal: committee, Messrs. Stobie, Ruckwood, Ireson, Rose, Makin, Newman, Loveday, March, Cooper, Thurlow, and Brudenall. Arrangements are being made to hold a fancy dress and cycle parade, and dance. The Town Band have promised their services, and the Fire Brigade will take part. The patrons include Lord Lilford, Mr. Geo. Smith, J.P., C.C., Lieut-Col. Benyon, J.P., Mr. Czarnikow, and other local gentlemen, and also local ladies."

On Friday May 21st, Mrs. Gilbert received a "returned" letter written to her son Herbert with the word "wounded" on the envelope.

This was also Empire Day. The elementary schools observed their usual celebrations. The report continued, "An interesting feature of the celebration was the distribution to the students (who had cheerfully subscribed) of Empire Day certificates issued by the Overseas Club, of which the King is patron. The certificate *(an example is shown left – EDF Collection)* which is very artistic and fit for framing, records that the recipient "has helped to send some comfort and happiness to the brave sailors and soldiers of the British Empire, fighting to uphold liberty, justice, honour, and freedom in the Great War."

At the end of the month, Miss G. Mansfield from Denford, was appointed an honorary recruiting agent for the Northamptonshire Regiment. The first in the County, she had introduced a number of men to Rev. Stothert. Her uniform comprised a recruiting badge and ribbons.

The last Friday of May (28th) noted that Mr. and Mrs. John Hall of Hortons Lane, had three sons in the Army. **Hugh David Hall (31)** was in hospital in Boulogne with measles, his third hospital admission, the previous two being for treatment for wounds. His older brother John was with the Army Service Corps at Woolwich whilst the third son was about to go to the front with the 1st Battalion, Northamptonshire Regiment.

June

On the first day of the month, Thrapston Police Court sat to decide if the licence for the King's Arms Hotel should remain with Mrs. Beal or be transferred. Mr. Beal had enlisted with the 8th Battalion, Northamptonshire Regiment and was in Colchester. The chairman of the Court decided that it was not necessary to make any change, as long as the house was "properly conducted".

Thursday 3rd reported the anxiety that Mr. and Mrs. Templeman were experiencing concerning their son **Richard Templeman (14)**, after a letter written by his sister was returned stamped "Unable to trace, present location uncertain". The family last received a letter from him on May 6th. The rector was making enquiries. In the same report, the circumstances concerning **Herbert Gilbert (11)** were also being investigated by the War Office. Finally, a list of all eligible men between the ages of nineteen and forty was being compiled for Thrapston and District.

The *Northamptonshire and Hunts Gazette* reported the formation of a Rifle Club and range on Friday 4th. Part of the old foundry off Bridge Street was leased from Mr. W. Hillyard for the range and rifles, targets, etc., had been purchased. Mr. G. V. Charlton was elected chairman of the committee, and it was hoped that the project would be taken up with great enthusiasm.

Saturday 5th saw "gay proceedings" in town when Forget-me-not day took place to raise funds for the Soldiers' Tobacco Fund. As well as a fancy dress and decorated bicycle parade, the Thrapston Town Silver Prize Band and Raunds Ragtime Band played patriotic airs. During the judging, forget-me-not flowers were sold to the crowd in the Market Place. The 1st prizes were awarded to; for lady's fancy get-up – Mrs. Grant (Gypsy Fortune Teller); gent's fancy get-up – Messrs. Newman and Reeves (Italian Organ-grinder and Monkey); girls under 15 – L. Ashley (Milk Float); boys under 15 – W. Chapman (Officer in Khaki); gent's comic get-up – Messrs. Ferry and Hall (Weary Willie and Tired Tim); groups of not less than five – Kettering Ragtime Band. Competitions and refreshments were provided and raffle tickets for the prize of a watch, sold. In the evening, dancing took place at "The Shrubberies", with approximately 300 people paying 4d to attend. A profit of £43 was raised by the event.

Wednesday 9th saw the following notice on the Parish Church notice board:-
"It has come to the notice of the rector that certain persons are stating that he is paid for the recruiting work that he is doing, and receiving so much for each recruit. He wishes people to know that this is a deliberate falsehood, as he neither has received, nor will receive, anything whatsoever. He is only too glad to serve his country in this way, and glad to do it gratuitously."

On Thursday 17th, Mr. Frisby of Midland Road was announced as the winner of the watch in the Tobacco Fund raffle.

A day later, **Richard Templeman (14)** was reported as officially being missing. There was still hope that he had either been cut off from his regiment or been taken prisoner.

On 20th, Sgt. Webster was reported to have been gassed and shot in one eye. He was said to be improving.

Wednesday 23rd brought the news that Corpl. Harold Sutcliffe, formerly employed by the local solicitors, and the son of the late John Sutcliffe of Thrapston, had been wounded in both arms and was in hospital in France. Harold had emigrated to Canada two years before the war started and joined up with the first Canadian Contingent.

On 24th, Corpl. Nicholls said that he was hoping to get some leave in the near future.

Tuesday 29th saw a recruitment event in town, when the recruiting detachment of the 1/4th Battalion, Northamptonshire Regiment visited for the afternoon and evening. 160 men attended, bringing with them twelve new recruits. Five town men enlisted because of this event. The detachment were billeted in town overnight and left next morning, marching to Weldon via Brigstock. *(A Recruitment meeting, at which Lord Lilford addressed the gathering in 1915, is shown above – EDF Collection).*

July

The beginning of the month brought news that, on 7th, **George Earle (12)** had been formally listed as "missing".

On the same day, seven new recruits left town.

On Saturday 10th it was announced that the weekly total of eggs for the National Egg Collection was 250, 70 of which came from Islip. The same day saw the Tobacco Fund committee agree distribution of tobacco and cigarettes to serving soldiers and sailors. Each man would receive 2oz of tobacco and 120 cigarettes, value 2s 6d. These were delivered to family or friends to be passed on. In total, the committee had sent out 165 parcels and still had a bank balance of £16 13s for future gifts.

On Saturday 17th, Mrs. Templeman received a letter from one of her son's comrades, reproduced as below:–
"To Mrs. Templeman. Dear Madam. Having seen your son's photo in the paper, and being one of his chums, I consider it my duty to write and let you know that Dick was killed while running forward at St. Aubers Ridge on May 9th. He was struck by a piece of shell and killed outright. I saw him fall, but had to go on, and never saw any more of him. Your son was a brave lad, and was well liked by all who knew him, and we who have got through wounded are very sorry he is not with us now, but he died a brave soldier's death, as many more of my chums died that fateful morning. – Yours respectfully, Pte. C. E. Webb."
Another soldier, Pte. Freir, wrote from Kent, "Dear Mrs. Templeman. – I expect that by this time you will have heard from Pte. Webb, who was with your son at the time he was killed. I continued making inquiries until I found Webb, and he told me that he had already written to you. I am afraid that what Webb says about your son being killed is perfectly correct. I had heard several rumours of it before, but would not inform you until I was absolutely certain that no hope existed of his being alive. Perhaps after all it is better to know what happened than to remain in a state of horrible uncertainty as to what his fate might be. You have one great comfort, and that is to know that he died bravely and fearlessly, while facing the enemy of our country, and that his death was not long drawn out and painful. From what I can gather, he must have died almost instantaneously, and that is a great mercy. Having had many great friends of mine killed in this terrible war, I can understand to a small degree how you feel about it, and my sympathy for you, his father, and also his sister, is very sincere. The spot where he was killed is about a mile north of Festubert, and his company, together with "D" Company, led the attack. I thank your daughter very much for her letter, and also the very kind gift of cigarettes, which I greatly appreciated. With much sympathy in this time of your great stress, I remain, yours sincerely, C. Glen Freir."

On Thursday 22nd, the recruiting office relocated into premises given by Mr. J. H. Payne in Chancery Lane.

On a more prosaic level, the weekly egg collection resulted in a total of 320.

Sunday 25th saw another memorial service at the Parish Church, this time for **John Giddings (13)**. The rector conducted the service and Miss Kingsford feelingly played "O Rest in the Lord".

The July meeting of Thrapston Rural District Council received a letter from one of their members, Mr. Milligan, who was in Rouen, helping with wounded soldiers and trying to provide some comforts. The Council agreed to raise a subscription to purchase a gramophone and 108 records to be sent out.

Huntingdon Road on a postcard sent in 1915 by "Ethel", in which she says, "I wish this war were over" *(C.W. Vorley, Raunds – EDF Collection)*.

August

Wednesday 4th saw intercessory services held at St. James' Church and the Wesleyan Church (this being a joint service with the Baptist Church). These were held on the anniversary of the declaration of war.

THREATENED PAPER FAMINE.

A WORD WITH OUR READERS.

We urgently request our Readers to place a regular order for the "EVENING TELEGRAPH" with their newsagents, or to buy the paper every night, as far as possible, from one source, thereby assisting newsagents and street sellers in regulating supplies and avoiding waste.

(Left - Advertisement printed in the Evening Telegraph during August 1915.)

Thursday 5th was the day for both the Baptist and Wesleyan Sunday School Treats, held in their respective schoolrooms. Games followed on fields loaned by Messrs. C. and H. Tomlinson of Huntingdon Road for the Baptists, and Mr. Cattell, opposite Thrapston House, for the Wesleyans.

The August meeting of the Rural District Council recorded that the members had raised £7 5s 6d between them, towards the purchase of a gramophone and records. The chairman made up the difference to the required £9 and the machine and records, plus 27 packs of playing cards, were bought and sent off to Rouen.

The same day saw the announcement that the new Wesleyan Church minister was Rev. Harry Shaw. He commenced his duties on September 1st.

At the market on Tuesday 10th, Mr. Bletsoe had an increased supply of eggs which he sold by auction, realising 2s 6d per score.

Two days later, on 12th, the Thrapston Feast garden fete took place in the grounds of the Rectory. The 1914 fete had been abandoned due to the outbreak of war, but a combination of particular financial need and national war claims made it desirable to hold it again. Rain fell from twenty minutes past two until three o'clock, with intermittent thunder, and it remained overcast until four o'clock when the sun broke through. The many sideshows amused a good attendance and the evening entertainment was also well patronised. After deduction of expenses, a total of £45 17s 1½d was raised.

On 19th, the Church Sunday School held its summer treat. After a short service in the church, they had tea in the Church of England schoolrooms, followed by games in the adjoining field. About 150 scholars attended.

On two consecutive Friday's, 20th and 27th, the *Kettering Guardian* reported that two further local men had lost their lives. **Alfred Waite (8)** was officially confirmed as being killed in action between 10th and 14th March, whilst **Herbert Gilbert (11)** was confirmed as being killed at Hill 60, and buried by German troops nearby. A joint memorial service was held on 29th at the Parish Church, and many of the congregation were moved to tears. Miss Kingsford played a selection from Chopin's "Prelude in C Minor" at the close.

On Saturday 28th, the Post Office announced postal restriction, brought about by military calls on men working there and a consequent shortage of staff. These would commence on September 6th. On the same day, the Thrapston branch of the British Women's Temperance Association met to raise funds to enable them to proceed with their patriotic work of making sandbags for the soldiers at the front.

September

Friday 3rd brought news from Corpl. M. Ellson, 10th Battalion Middlesex Regiment, to his father, Mr. Thos. Ellson. He was based at Fort William, Calcutta and had been in India for eight months. In a very long letter, he spoke of being by a river, with paddy fields backed by jungle. The hot season began in March, when they had to stop all work by 10.30am as it became too hot to do so after. He had visited local villages to take photographs but fled quickly when locals began milling around them. Typical of most soldiers, given the chance, they had formed a football team and won the Calcutta League, as well as a charity cup.

On Wednesday 8th, Pte. Fairey Whiteman returned home to Halford Street, on leave from Milbank Military Hospital, London. Houses were decorated with flags and bunting to greet him. He was shortly to be admitted to Roehampton Hospital to be fitted with an artificial hand to replace the one blown off during the Battle of Aubers Ridge. Fairey was one of the first local men to enlist on the commencement of war and received a hero's welcome. Halford Street had, to date, provided five men for Kitchener's Army.

On the same day that Fairey returned home, a local labourer appeared before Thrapston Petty Sessions for the less-than-heroic reason of attempting to poach rabbits. He had been seen by a gamekeeper on two consecutive days, laying wires to trap them. When arrested by Supt. Tebbey he had failed to make a catch. Having previous convictions for similar offences, he was fined 10s.

By 10th, it was reported that all the Belgians had left town, one man having joined the Belgian forces whilst all the others were in London awaiting the documentation to be allowed to return to their home country.

The 15th September saw the 8th Battalion Northamptonshire Regiment in town, based at the White Hart Hotel, recruiting men. On offer were full kit (two suits of uniform, two pairs of boots, overcoat and all necessaries); 3s a day and the promise of staying at home whilst the battalion was in the area. Wives and dependents would receive separation allowance. They remained in the area for ten days.

The local Council reported on Thursday 16th that, "the Roll of Honour had been completed, as far as possible up to date by the several members of the council, who had kindly undertaken to canvass the town, and the books with the names in were ready for the County Council when they required them. He thought the thanks of the council were due to those members for doing their work so well. On the proposition of Mr. Hewitt, and seconded by Mr. Loaring, a vote of thanks was unanimously accorded. On the suggestion of Mr. Selby it was decided to have twenty copies of the list printed and posted in conspicuous places in the town." At the same meeting, Mr. Obadiah Booth, captain of the Fire Brigade, reported that between October 1914 and September 1915, they had four quarterly and four union drills. Two members had enlisted, one with the 2nd Battalion Northamptonshire Regiment who was at the front and one with the Northants Yeomanry who was in training. The Brigade had not been called into action during the year and the fire engine and appliances were in good working order and ready for any emergency. On the same day, managers at the Institute agreed to admit soldiers on furlough free of charge.

The Police Court on Tuesday 21st saw a local carpenter appear charged with being drunk in a public place, namely Horton's Lane. Inspector Campion said that at about 7.30pm on 13th September, he found the defendant lying down in the street. The defendant said he got his foot on something that twisted him round and he fell, striking his head on the wall, which stunned him. He had previous convictions for drunkenness, but, as the last was in 1911, he was given the lenient sentence of a 5s fine.

September 25th - Albert John (Jack) Waite killed in action.

On Wednesday 29th, the *Evening Telegraph* reported four items:
Mr. Milligan had returned from hospital work in France and, whilst he was very grateful to the Rural District Council for the gramophone etc., nothing had yet arrived. He said that everything turns up at the front sometime and just before leaving France, he had received a parcel despatched at Christmas!
Pte. S. Meadows, Oundle Road, had been wounded and was in Norwich Hospital.
Lance-Corpl. H. Cooper, Halford Street, had been invalided home from France with kidney problems. He was in hospital in Birmingham receiving treatment.
Finally, the Annual Parish Meeting at the Temperance Hall had an attendance of just three – Mr. Geo. Smith (chairman of the Parish Council), Mr. Arthur Brown (Parish Clerk) and a member of the public, Mr. Bygrave. No explanation was given for the absence of other councillors.

October

Friday 1st brought reports of injuries to local men:
Pte. William Waite was reported wounded for the second time, no details being currently known.
Pte. Fred Nicholls, of the 1st Northants, of Thrapston, was also amongst those reported to have been wounded (also for the second time), but no particulars were to hand. Private F. Nicholls was the first Thrapston man to return home wounded from the war.
Pte. Jack Parrott, Market Road, Thrapston, of the 7th Northants (Mobb's Corps), and Pte. Harry Clarke, Halford Street, Thrapston, of the Royal Engineers, were also reported wounded, the latter at the Dardanelles, but no details given. Pte. Clarke was formerly captain of the Thrapston football team prior to going to Bedford to work, where he assisted the Bedford Town team.

October 5th - Charles Edward Richardson (16) killed in action.

Have You a Relative
Fighting in the
Great War?

IF so you are
entitled to
wear this Badge.
It is given only
to women who
have relatives
serving.

Send 1/-

and the name of
the relative serving for the Badge
and a Certificate
of Membership
in the Women's
Branch, National
Service.

This advertisement (left) was run during October 1915 in the Evening Telegraph.

Also on Tuesday 5th, a Kettering shoe hand appeared before Thrapston Police Court, summoned by a single Thrapston woman, to show cause *(a paternity case – EDF)*. The case was adjourned for the claimant to bring witnesses. *(No further mention of this case is mentioned in the newspapers – maybe it was settled amicably! EDF.)*

Mrs. Rowlett was again selling asters to raise funds *(see page 13)*. This time, she was pictured in her garden *(right)*, appearing in the *Kettering Leader* on October 8th.

The same day brought the not-unexpected official confirmation of the death in action of **Richard Templeman (14)**.

The 1/1 battalion, Northamptonshire Regiment arrived in town at midday on their recruiting march through the north of the county, where they were met by the rector. After unlimbering in the Sports Field for an hour, they continued on their way to Oundle.

Sunday 10th was another sad day in the life of the town. In the afternoon, an impressive memorial service was held for the late Lance-Corpl. **G. S. Earle (12)** and Ptes. **Jack Waite (15)** and **R.E. Templeman (14)** at the Parish Church, the Rev B. W. Stothert (rector) conducting. The appropriate hymns were "Peace, perfect peace", "O God of wars, O King of Peace", and "Holy Father, in Thy Mercy" and, at the termination of the service, Miss Kingsford feelingly played "O rest in the Lord". The rector delivered an appropriate address, the pulpit being dressed with the Union Jack.

There was a whist drive at the Institute on 11th attended by 80 players.

On 12th, the Thrapston Guardians reported that, during the last quarter, 963 vagrants had passed through the Workhouse at a total cost of £39 19s 6d (i.e. 10d per day per vagrant). The same quarter last year saw 1,277 vagrants pass through at a cost of £15 19s (i.e. 3d each). The increase was due to the order of the Local Government Board, last November, that every vagrant leaving the Workhouse was to be supplied with an amount of food for the day. The Guardians had a profit on the wool account and this was set against the increased costs for vagrants.

October 13th. - George Henry Simpson (17) died of wounds.

Friday 15th brought a report that, on the previous Wednesday, at about six o'clock, Mr. Frank Ferrar, an auxiliary postman, of Huntingdon Road, Thrapston, was cycling from Twywell with a bag of letters. Near Thrapston, his bicycle came in contact with a stone or other obstacle and he was thrown over the handle on to the road, badly grazing his hands and dislocating one wrist. A constable, who happened to be nearby, assisted him and he was able to walk to the Post Office and deliver his postal bag.

On the same day, a 45 year old man of "no fixed abode" received one when he was sentenced to three months hard labour at the Thrapston Police Court. He was accused of obtaining 2s by false pretences from Mrs. Modlen, of the Union Bank House, Thrapston, on the previous Monday. The prisoner told her that he had been wounded in the present war and that he had just come out of Netley Hospital; that the nurse had allowed him to keep the pair of slippers he was wearing; and that he had 17s to come from the Army. He further informed Mrs. Modlen that he had obtained work from Mr. Charles Pettit, a builder in Thrapston, and that he was going to work there the next morning. The prisoner admitted that his statements were false, but alleged that he had intended to repay the money. Mrs. Modlen, Mr. Pettit and Inspector Campion gave evidence. Superintendent Tebbey put in a list of 32 previous convictions against the prisoner. The bench thanked Mrs. Modlen for bringing the matter to the notice of the police.

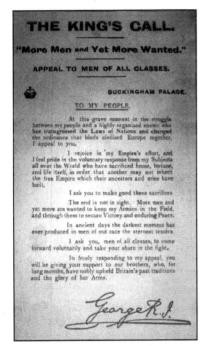

The 18th October brought a letter to Mr. Simpson reporting that his son had been wounded in the leg and been taken to a dressing station for attention.

Further news of the Hall family was reported on 22nd. Corpl. **H. D. Hall (31)** of the 1st Grenadier Guards, son of Mr. and Mrs. J. Hall of Hortons Lane, Thrapston, had been ill in hospital in France for a fortnight. He was now in a London Hospital and going on well. Corpl. Hall's younger brother, Pte. R. H. Hall of the Northants Regiment sent a card dated October 15th, informing his parents that he was quite well. Another son of Mr. and Mrs. Hall's, John who was at the Dardanelles, wrote recently to say that he was all right.

Air raids were happening in London. Whilst on a visit there, the rector, Rev. B. W. Stothert was in one of the affected areas. A house was blown up within a hundred yards of where he was staying; and after his return to his parish, he said that he had never before been so glad to see Thrapston again.

(The "King's Call", shown above, was published in the Evening Telegraph on Monday 25th October 1915).

On 27th, Miss Frances Mary Bletsoe married Mr. Rowland Wood of Titchmarsh at the Parish Church, the rector officiating.

A day later, the *Evening Telegraph* reported, "There has recently been a considerable falling off in the number of telegrams received at the Thrapston Post Office and the delivery is now performed by one girl messenger (with occasional help) instead of the two boy messengers as formerly".

On Saturday 30th, active steps were taken in the North Northants Parliamentary Division in connection with Lord Derby's recruiting scheme. At a meeting held at Thrapston, for the appointment of officers and committee and other business, Col. Stopford Sackville, J.P., C.A., was elected chairman, Mr. Geo. Smith, J.P., C.C., vice-chairman, and Messrs. H. Varah

(Thrapston) and W. F. Corby (Raunds) secretaries. The Central Committee rooms were in the Market Place, Thrapston, with the district recruiting office a few doors below.

November

November 3rd brought the sad news of the death from wounds of **Pte. George Henry Simpson (17)**. One of his comrades expressed his deep sympathy with the relatives and assured them that the regiment had lost a good soldier. The deceased, who was 19 years of age, was not a very strong youth. He had enlisted in September the previous year when the family were living in Thurning. General sympathy was felt with his father and sister (his mother being dead) in their loss. He wrote home regularly and the last letter from him arrived the day before the official notification of his death. His only brother was Staff Sergt. C. E. Simpson of the Northants Yeomanry; he had been serving for several years and was recently made a sergeant.

Mr. and Mrs. J. Clarke, of Halford Street, Thrapston, received a postcard from their son, Pte. H. Clarke, of the Northants Regiment on Monday 8th, stating that he was on the sick list and in hospital in Alexandria, but adding that he was getting on nicely and hoped to be soon out again.

Another report about the Hall family appeared on Friday 12th, under the headline:
"How a Thrapston lad was saved by his ammunition.
Corpl. **H. D. Hall**, son of Mr. and Mrs. J. Hall, of Horton's-lane, Thrapston, of the 1st Grenadier Guards, returned to London on Wednesday after ten days sick furlough at home. He was in hospital at Etaples for ten days with quinsies, and was then transferred to a London military hospital, where he remained for fourteen days. Corpl. Hall went out to the front on the last day in October 1914, and has seen a great deal of fighting in the trenches. While at home he described how he was saved from death on one occasion in the trenches by his ammunition. "We were going", he says, "in support of the Scots Guards and the Gordons. They were going to take a German trench, and the artillery bombarded three quarters of an hour for us. It was daylight when we went to the trenches. We had to go under the main road to Lille to trenches which we were holding at the time, and had to pass over a bridge which the Germans had as a target, and as soon as we commenced to go over the bridge they opened with about five Maxims, and rifle fire from their trenches, which were about seventy yards from the British lines. We had to turn off this road to our trenches, which were only about six yards from the road, and as I was about two yards from the trench a bullet struck me in the pouch and exploded and tattered my ammunition (fifteen cartridges). It went through my overcoat, through my jacket pocket, hit my signalling book, taking a small piece completely out from one side of one cover and making a mark right across that cover, and it must have then passed right on. At so short a range it must have come with terrible force. I stood there as if mesmerised, not thinking of the danger I was in until a comrade in the trench called out "Get in the trench or you'll get killed". I went to jump into the trench, but my feet had got stuck in the mud, and I fell head first into the trench into about three feet of water. We had had orders to go about 150 yards down the trench, and then we waited until about six o'clock at night, when the Scots Guards made their attack. They lost very heavily there, but some men managed to secure part of the trench, which they held until next morning. Then, reinforcements not being available at the time, they came back into the British lines and the Scots Guards went out for five days rest...
Once I was lying in the open, holding my rifle, but not in the usual place – the small of the butt – when a bullet struck the small of the butt, cutting half of it away. I stuck to the rifle as long as I could, but they said it was not safe and would not let me use it anymore, so I had to have another one."

On 19th November, the Roll of Honour for the Parish of Thrapston had just been published, containing 203 names. "It is to be brought up-to-date again immediately after the 30th November. A number of young men have joined since the list was compiled, and satisfactory recruiting is still going on, so that the response must be regarded as highly creditable. The population of Thrapston is given as 1,836. It may be added that on Sunday last a number of Thrapston young men each received a white feather by post. The feathers had been posted in London. A letter on the subject from 'One Who Likes Fair Play' was addressed to the 'Evening Telegraph' on Thursday, pointing out the unfairness of the action."

On the same day, the Parish Council decided, on the motion of Mr. Selby, to enter the town for the Loder Cross, which was to be given to the parish that had the largest percentage of men serving the country. *(Despite extensive searches, I have been unable to find any other information on the Loder Cross – EDF).*

Three days later, on 22nd: "In connection with the Thrapston and Islip Soldiers' Tobacco Fund a final committee meeting was held at the "Red Lion" last week when a report was presented, which showed that the net proceeds of the successful fancy dress and cycle parade, held in June last, amounted to over £40. The money has been spent on tobacco and cigarettes, the last consignment having been just despatched. The goods were supplied by the Co-operative Wholesale Society and Mr. W. Last, Thrapston. It is hoped to shortly call a public meeting to consider the question of raising a fund for something to be sent for Christmas. Many thanks are due to Mr. W. Reeves (the late hon. secretary) and to the committee and others who contributed to the success of the fund. Mr. W. Stobie is now the hon. secretary."

Thursday 25th: "enrolment in the Thrapston district is brisk. It is an interesting fact that since the commencement of the war the Rev. B. W. Stothert (rector of Thrapston and formerly an Army Chaplain), who is hon. recruiting officer for the Thrapston district, has had no fewer than 585 recruits pass through his hands."

November 26th brought news in a short report of **Pte. Charles Edward Richardson (16)** who met a heroic death at the Dardanelles.

In addition, on the same day, three other stories were printed:
"Members of the Thrapston Adult School are interesting themselves in the movement to provide Christmas gifts for Thrapston lads with the forces, and some ingenious and successful methods are being pressed into service in aid of this laudable effort. For instance, one active lady worker bought a sixpenny khaki handkerchief, got a sealed number from an official of the school, and then devoted a good deal of time to obtain guesses at one penny each. In this way the sum of 8s 4d was realised, and the winner of the handkerchief, Miss Hardwick, possesses a trophy which in years to come may be rightly regarded as having played a useful part in British history. The winning number, by the way, was 67."
"Among those who are gazetted second-lieutenants is Mr. G. W. Hunnybun, a leading official of the Thrapston C. and A.C., and an able assistant to the M.C.C.C.A. when it ran its championships at the Northamptonshire town, and also an official of the N.C.C.U.. He is gazetted to the Argyll and Sutherland Highlanders." *(The initials are – Thrapston Cycling & Athletics Club, Midland Counties Cross Country Association, National Cross Country Union - EDF).*
"A local Private soldier appeared before Mr. George Smith, J.P. at Thrapston Police Court charged with being an absentee, since November 22nd midnight, from his battalion, the 3rd Northants, stationed at Bramsholt Camp. Prisoner, who early in the war was very badly wounded, admitted being an absentee, but said he had not been very well. Mr. Smith, in remanding him to await an escort, said his right course would have been to have returned at the proper time and informed the military doctor."

The Thrapston Baptist Church minute book records that, at a church meeting held in the vestry on Tuesday November 30th, "it was proposed by Mr. Simpson and seconded by Mr. C. Crawley that we have an entertainment early in the New Year to raise money for the Tobacco Fund for Soldiers." The motion was carried.

December

On Wednesday 1st, the following was printed in the *Evening Telegraph*. I reproduce it in full as it contains names of many of the town's combatants:

"TOBACCO FUND. Numerous Grateful Acknowledgements at Thrapston

Mr. W. Stobie, hon. secretary of the late Thrapston and Islip Soldiers' Tobacco Fund, has received a large batch of letters of thanks and experiences from the men to whom gifts had been sent. Among the remarks in the various letters, all full of gratitude, are the following:-

"November 23rd. - ... I shared the parcel round the tent, and they all thank you very much. – Shoeing Smith W. H. Brown."

"22/11/16. - ... Perhaps it will interest you to know we are now having a rest, and hope it may be a little longer than usual. – Richard Loveday."

"November 24th. – Thank you and the Thrapston and Islip Fund very much for them. – A. Knight."

"23/11/15. - ...As you know, I have been in the hospital suffering from fever, but I am pleased to tell you I am better. The day I returned to my regiment I met Micky March; he was quite well. Our regiment (1/1 Beds Yeomanry) has moved back into our winter quarters, and we are quite comfortable... It has been market day today. The French lead all their cattle up and down the street on a halter – cows, pigs, and sheep, all just the same; there is no market here, so they parade up and down the street. – C. Bues."

"Sunday , 21/11/15. - ...It is surprising what a weight it takes off our minds when we have an opportunity to get hold of a bit of English baccy and a few fags...My brother has left this part and has been sent out to Egypt...We are having some very cold weather just now. – E. A. Dingley, Staff Farrier Sergeant, Army Service Corps."

"23/11/15. – One fails to adequately express what all this kindness to us means, and such a reminder that we are not forgotten by those at home helps us in no little way to cheer and encourage us. – J. S. Blake, A.O.C."

"21st November - ...My thoughts often wander to the fine times we have had, and I wonder when they will roll round again. We have had a lot of rain here just lately, and it is also very cold. – Sapper J. Nickerson."

"You may believe me that it is pretty rough out here, and so bitter cold and wet; and, as you know, I am getting a bit old, but I still keep pegging along with the young ones. – F. Cooper (6th Northants)."

"21/11/15. - ...I can tell you since I was on leave I have been in a big fight; that was on 25th October, 1915, and I can tell you we were in the trenches five days and nights; but my section was very lucky; we lost only one. E. Munds." (Sergeant, East Anglian Royal Engineers).

"22/11/15. -...We are not having such very bad weather out here yet, but it is very cold nights and mornings. – G. Robinson."

"21/11/15. - ...I can assure you that anything that is sent out here from home goes a long way, and is thought very highly of. – Sapper J. H. Bues."

"November 22nd, 1915. – Please convey to the Thrapston and Islip S.T.F. my sincere thanks. G. March (R.E.)."

"22/11/15. - ...Just now we are getting frost, but not severe. We are about ankle-deep in mud, and it's so delightful trying the "Gaby glide" against one's will – add to that walking into spare shell holes full of water...At time of writing this we are in action, but things are fairly quiet, less a little sniping and occasional gun or two firing just to remind us that the war is still on...I have been right through, and have had a hand in all fights less one – that was the second battle for Ypres: the first was a very hard fight... - Corpl. A. Mayes – 46th Battery R.F.A."

"21/11/15. - ...Today's Sunday, and things go on just as usual. Things are fairly quiet here just now... – Alec F. Slatter."

"Nov. 22nd, 1915. – I am writing on my own behalf, and also on behalf of my fellow comrades of the 5th Northants Reg., Signalling Section. – G. E. Wright."

"25/11/15. – When I am smoking I always think of you all...My hand is well again, but it left me with a stiff finger. I am ready for them again. We shall never forget the 25th at Loos; it was a glorious night, not half, that made one think his number was up. - Pte. J.Parrott (7th Northants)."

In addition to the above, a number of replies have been received from recipients of parcels in this country, including **Pte. J. Stimpson (58)** (Hunts Cyclist Battalion): R. H. Wakefield: Fred Bland (A.S.C.): Lance-Corporal H. Short (Sherwood Foresters): G. E. March and **E. Mayes (52)** (Ammunition Column, 2/4 East Anglian Brigade); and F. W. Beal.

Willie Stobie, the young son of the hon. secretary of the fund, who has joined the Navy, sends some particulars of his life on one of the war vessels. He says: "I have got two good pals from Oundle; the father of one drives the morning mail to Thrapston, and his name is Fox. I like everything but swimming; we go to a different ship to learn, and we have to jump in and can't reach bottom...We go ashore once a week, and that is Wednesday afternoon. We have got a recreation ground on a sort of an island. We have to run three miles before we can play football or have a swing. I have seen some submarines, battleships, troopships, and all sorts. I am in a higher class now."

By Tuesday 7th, Mr. Eric St. Clair Gainer, of the 5th Seaforth Highlanders, second son of Dr. J. W. Gainer, of Thrapston, was in hospital at Rouen, suffering with trench ulcers on the legs and hands. Mr. Gainer had been at the front since March and had seen a lot of fighting, and had some narrow escapes.

An update on the Roll of Honour appeared on 9th when, as soon as it was possible to compile a complete Roll of Honour of Thrapston lads, the rector (the Rev. B. W. Stothert) proposed to have a permanent record placed in the Parish Church.

The egg collectors were commended on the same day; the *Parish Magazine*, in a notice on "The National Egg Collection", in which reference is made to the fact that within a few days twelve million eggs would have been contributed throughout the country, says, "The collection's needs are likely to increase in the near future. Eggs are scarce at present, but our soldier's needs are just as great. Doris Bennett has collected 1,381 eggs since she began her work. The other collectors are Violet Gifford and Jessie Allen."

Saturday 11th, and enrolment at the Thrapston centre had been very brisk during the past week. This was particularly so on Thursday, married men coming up well.

Thursday 16th saw a large gathering at the Corn Exchange for a combined meeting and concert in aid of the Royal Army Temperance Association. The meeting was presided over by Mr. George Smith, (J.P. and County Councillor), and the speaker was Mr. Clare White, secretary of the Association since its formation twenty one years earlier.

Bank closures for the Christmas period were advertised in the *Evening Telegraph* on Saturday 18th *(shown on page 38)*. The war was obviously affecting the banks; staff were being called up for military service and normal opening hours restricted.

THRAPSTON BANKS.

OWING to the War and consequent depletion of the Staffs, the Banks in Thrapston will, on and after 20th December, 1915, CLOSE as follows;

MONDAY, WEDNESDAY, FRIDAY and SATURDAY .... at 3 p.m.
TUESDAY .... at 4 p.m.
THURSDAY .... at 12 o'clock.
The Opening Hours will remain as at present.

BARCLAY & CO., LTD
LONDON CITY & MIDLAND BANK, LTD.
NORTHAMPTONSHIRE UNION BANK, LTD.

T18

Monday 20th and two interesting reports:

An Army aeroplane, en route from Hendon to Peterborough, passed over Thrapston on Sunday afternoon *(a much less common occurrence then - EDF)*.

Lance-Corpl. H. Cooper, of Halford Street, Thrapston (formerly of the Thrapston postal staff), of the 6th Northants Regiment, arrived home on Friday on ten days sick leave. He had been in hospital for twenty weeks altogether (his complaints having been malarial fever, kidney trouble, and trench fever), about four weeks abroad, and the rest of the time in this country. "For six weeks he has been at the Post Office Hospital (20, Kensington Palace Gardens, London), and for five weeks at the hospital's seaside convalescent home. While in hospital, Lance-Corpl. Cooper entered a "Christmas in Wartime" knitting competition, under the auspices of the Professional Classes War Relief Council, the committee of which has, for its president, H.R.H. the Duchess of Albany. The exhibition of the articles sent in took place at the Royal Albert Hall on December 8th, 9th, and 10th. The competition was for soldiers or sailors in British hospitals, and the articles made had to be suitable for members of H.M. Forces serving abroad. Lance-Corpl. Cooper, who was the only representative of the Post Office Hospital, knitted three pairs of socks. Two or three days ago he received an official notification that he had been awarded third prize (10s) in the West of England Section. The proceeds of the competition were for Red Cross funds. It may be added that Lance-Corpl. Cooper is well up in knitting, and that while in hospital he made various other articles, including stockings, body-belt, scarf etc."

By Tuesday 21st, the Thrapston and Raunds Almanac, price 1d, was being advertised as available from Messrs. Taylor and Downs. It included a directory and local information. The front cover had an appropriate picture of a soldier in khaki entitled "Our Daddy's Come Home". This was the forty-first issue of the Journal.

The day after, Thrapston District Tennis Club were reported to have recently sent a donation of five guineas to the British Red Cross Society to assist with their work with sick and wounded soldiers and sailors.

Christmas Day saw four services at the Parish Church, at 6.00am, 7.00am and 8.00am and an after morning service. 161 communicants attended these Holy Communion services, an increase of 25 over the previous year. A total of £9 10s was collected to go to blind soldiers and sailors. There was also a short service at the Wesleyan Church during the morning, conducted by the pastor, Rev. H. Shaw.

At the Workhouse, 75 inmates, of whom 33 were infirmary patients, spent an enjoyable Christmas Day. Amongst their number were five "old boys", who had been placed out in life by the Guardians and had obtained readily-given permission to come home for the festive period. One of them was in khaki - Pte. Coulson of the Northants Regiment, who had travelled from Chatham.

On Sunday 26th, the evening service at the Parish Church included the singing of carols.

The Baptist Church Sunday School held its Christmas Party in the schoolroom during the evening of Tuesday 28th, paid for by old scholars and a few friends.

The Thrapston Shop Assistants Social Club finished off the year with a social and dance at the Corn Exchange on Thursday 30th December in aid of the local Soldiers' and Sailors' Comforts Fund. A large dish of trifle, donated by Mrs. F. W. Beal, realised 30s 6d for the fund. It was first won in a raffle by Mr. Ernest Jellis, who gave it back, after which it was sold by auction four times. (After the second sale, at 4s, Mr. Jellis and a friend gave the lady purchaser 7s for it, and returned it for further competition.) Thrapston was thus enabled to start the year with a new riddle: "When is a trifle not a trifle?" "When it realises 30s 6d for our Soldiers' and Sailors' Comforts Fund." *(No indication was given as to whether the trifle was subsequently eaten or, indeed, if it was in a fit state for consumption! – EDF.)*

1915 marked the beginning of "total war" which involved much effort and sacrifice from those back at home. War would not be won purely by military effort, but would require hard work and a national willingness to keep supplying the forces – the side that could do this for the longest would be victorious. Both sides had to adapt to trench warfare with long periods of inactivity whilst hoping to avoid the effects of continued artillery bombardment. The better the trench, the higher the chances of survival.

The British historian A. J. P. Taylor (1906 – 1990), summed up 1915 as:-
"A year of battles which had no meaning except as names on war memorials."

Not, possibly, the most accurate historical viewpoint, although the sentiment can be understood. Thrapston now had thirteen such names, a number which would more than double over the course of the following year. Yet, such was the belief in the justness of the cause, Thrapston would continue to give of men and resources until victory was attained.

1916

January

The New Year began with a report on 4th that "Mr. and Mrs. Wm. Jeffery, of Market Road, Thrapston, have received official intimation that their son, Pte. Alfred Jeffery, of the 4th Northants, was admitted to the 16th General Hospital, Alexandria, on November 26th, suffering from dysentery, and that on December 10th, he was transferred to the Luxor Convalescent Hospital, Egypt."

That same evening, there was a crowded audience at the Baptist Schoolroom to hear an address by Lieut. V. H. Sykes (who was doing valuable service on behalf of patriotic funds), entitled "Tommy Thinks!!! Incidents from the Battlefield." "The pastor, the Rev. H. Ellis Roberts, presided, and opened with prayer. This was followed by the singing of the National Anthem, and then Mr. William Smith pleasingly sang "We have come up from Somerset," after which the Misses Evelyn and Maggie James gave a vocal duet very nicely indeed. The chairman having introduced the speaker, Lieut. Sykes held the rapt attention of the audience through a deeply interesting and impressive address. The gallant officer, who, it will be remembered, was seriously wounded some months ago, founded his remarks upon his own experiences upon the battlefields of France and Flanders. Numerous instances of bravery and heroism were stated, and 'Tommy's' keen sense of duty and imperturbable hopefulness were vividly portrayed. Life in the trenches, the ruin wrought by bombardments, and various other phases of the war were graphically dealt with, many of the incidents described being of a thrilling character. At the close of the address Mr. Wm. Smith sang "O, Land of Hope." Miss L. Flanders was the accompanist. The collection was for the Thrapston Soldiers' Comforts Fund, and amounted to £1 18s 4d."

At the same time, a specially attractive programme was given at the Thrapston Temperance Hall on Tuesday evening, the proceeds being in aid of the Thrapston Soldiers' and Sailors' Comforts Fund. The members of the local committee interested themselves in the disposal of tickets, and there was a large attendance. At the close of the performance it was announced that the fund would benefit to the extent of £4 10s.

January 7th – George Abery Unger (21) killed in action.

On 7th, Trooper George Watson of the 1st Lovat Scouts (son of the late Mr. Robert Watson, of Thrapston), wrote to his mother from the Military Hospital, Floriana, Malta, on December 19th. He said, "I got wounded on the 3rd in the leg, just above the knee, with shrapnel, and I am sorry to say my thigh is broken, but the doctor says my leg is going along lovely, so I have something to be thankful for. Although it has been very painful, it is easier now: I am afraid it will be a long job. I asked him this morning how long he thought it would be. He said it should not be out of the sling under six weeks. All 'broken legs' get home...I have lost everything. I have only got a belt and a watch left now, and the watch won't go; they cut all my clothes off me."

The Thrapston office for enlistment in the Derby Groups re-opened on Monday 10th, in the charge of the hon. recruiting officer, Rev. B. W. Stothert. Several men came forward.

Friday 14th and another letter from one of the 'Hall boys', Pte. John Hall, A.S.C. (Transit Stores Detachment) *(pictured left, Kettering Leader 14th January 1916)*, recently wrote from Sulva Bay saying he was "stationed on the beach, close to the sea, and that it was cold with rain and snow there now, 'not heat and flies'. He had been laid up for a few days, but was alright again. His work was taking parcels over the water, about five miles. He mentioned that he was getting his letters more regularly."

Saturday 15th saw a successful dance, arranged by the Thrapston Co-operative Society as a further effort on behalf of the local Soldiers' and Sailors' Comforts Fund, held in the Co-operative Hall in the evening, when a company, numbering about seventy, enjoyed dancing to the excellent music supplied by Mr. G. Abbott's Quadrille Band. The arrangements were admirably carried through by a sub-committee comprising Messrs. J. T. Pollard, W. Reynolds, W. Bennett, and S. P. Smart (hon. secretary), with Mr. J. Fletcher proving himself an efficient M.C. Mesdames Pollard, Reynolds, and Bennett served refreshments. It was expected that by the two efforts (concert and dance) a good sum would be handed over to the Central Committee.

Further news of Trooper Watson *(pictured right)* and his brother appeared on Monday 24th. "Trooper George Watson, of the 1st Lovat Scouts (son of the late Mr. Geo. Watson, of Thrapston), was still in hospital at Floriana, Malta. He got wounded on December 3rd in the leg, just above the knee, with shrapnel, his thigh being broken; and after lying in the hospital for about six weeks he had to undergo a further operation for the removal of pieces of bone from the leg.

TROOPER GEORGE WATSON.

Trooper Arthur Watson, of the same regiment (brother to Trooper George Watson), in a letter received by his mother on Saturday, stated that he had got rid of his complaint (dysentery) and was feeling alright again. He mentioned that he was waiting to get some teeth before rejoining his regiment; he was having six false ones. Referring to his brother George he says, "I had a letter from him. I received the parcel alright and sent the box of Woodbines to George and expect to hear from him soon. I suppose that he had a pretty rough time, but that he is getting alright now."

There was a full attendance at a meeting of the committee in connection with the Thrapston Soldiers' and Sailors' Comforts Fund, held at the Co-operative Hall on Monday evening, 24th. The secretary, Mr. W. Stobie, reported the receipt of a donation from the Co-operative Society, the result of the recent concert and dance, of £7 7s, and the best thanks of the committee were accorded. Owing to the watch in the recent competition being unclaimed by the holder of the winning number, it was decided to hold another competition for the watch. It would be wound up by a gentleman in the town, placed in a box, and sealed; the competitors to guess the actual time the watch stopped. It was also arranged, if the present state of affairs continued, to hold a mammoth fancy dress and cycle parade on Whit Monday, June 12th, in aid of the fund. It was stated that the remaining events to be completed were the Wesleyan Church social evening, a whist drive and dance arranged by the Institute Committee, and a dance arranged by the Town Band; all to be held at the Co-operative Hall, free of charge, by the kindness of the society. The secretary also reported that up to the present there was a sum of £50 in hand.

On 25th, pictures of Mrs. Jane Jarvis, in her 98th year, and five generations of her family appeared in the *Kettering Leader (shown on page 43)*.

From left to right:
Standing: Mrs. Wm. Jeffery (daughter), Market Road; Mr. Arthur Jeffery (grandson).
Seated: Mrs. Jarvis; on her lap her great great grandchild (Mrs. Kendel's baby); and Mrs.
          Kendel (great granddaughter), Peterborough.

In the same issue, the death of Mrs. Graveley, Swiss Villas, Huntingdon Road was announced at the ripe old age of 95 years.

January 26th, and the chairman of Thrapston Institute read the roll of honour of members of the institute, as follows:- Messrs. **R. Templeman (14)** (who had given his life for his country), H. Nicholls, W. Barber, J. Barber, W. Guest, **L. Farrer** *(sic – should be Ferrar)* **(51)**, L. Abbott, C. Read, W. Clayson, D. Skelton, K. March, H. Morris, S. George, W. George, J. Nickerson, P. Charlton, M. G. W. Hunnybun, E. March, **E. Mayes (52)**, F. Holley, J. G. Cresswell, H. Guest, and N. Cotton.

On Friday 28th, first news arrived of the bravery and gallantry award to one of the town's bank clerks. "Pte. C. A. Westley, of the 6th Battalion, Gordon Highlanders (of Northampton and formerly of the staff of Barclays Bank Thrapston) who was recently awarded the Distinguished Conduct Medal, has been at home at Northampton on short leave from the front, and on Tuesday visited Thrapston. We are informed by friends of the brave 'Gordon' that the deed which gained the distinction was of a very dashing and timely character. It appears that during the Loos fighting, Pte. Westley crossed a zone of cross-fire, on his own initiative, to warn his officer, who was holding an advanced position with the remainder of the company, of this and the approach of the Germans on each side, thus preventing his comrades from being cut off. He also saved a machine gun from falling into the enemy's hands by himself carrying it back to a protected position."
(His picture, shown above, appeared in the Kettering Leader on Friday January 28th 1916.)

In the same issue, news had been received of Ptes. Arthur and **George Nicholls (28)**, sons of Mr. and Mrs. Thos. Nicholls of Church Lane, Thrapston, both of whom were going on well.

Thrapston Soldiers' and Sailors' Comforts Fund Committee 1916
(Thrapston District Historical Society archives)

Standing:
John Hodson, Horace Abbott, Unknown, Fred Johnson, Sidney Smart, Billy Walker, Walter Bray, Fred Hopkins, Ernest "Cracker" Frisby, Billy Lane, Alf Mayes, Fred Hackney, Arthur Hurrell, Tom Essam, Bill March.
Seated:
William Reynolds, Billy White, Philip Makin, Miss Essam, Miss Firbank, Bill Stobie, William Hillyard, George Raby.
(If you can provide the missing name, please let me know – EDF.)

February

Thursday 3rd was the date for the Thrapston Institute Committee's whist drive and dance in the Co-operative Hall in aid of the Soldiers' and Sailors' Comforts Fund. The whist drive comprised nineteen tables, the prize-winners being: Ladies: 1st, Miss E. Bailey (143); 2nd, Mrs. F. C. Loakes (132). Gentlemen: 1st, Mr. W. Drage (140); 2nd, Mr. W. Dellar (135), after a cut with Mr. J. Headland. Dancing started at ten o'clock to the strains of Mr. G. Abbott's quadrille band, and a good company enjoyed the dancing until the close. Mr. F. Lavender and A. Hurrell were the M.C.'s.

Under the Military Service Act, the Thrapston Local Tribunal was elected at a special meeting of Thrapston Rural District Council at the Workhouse on Friday 11th.
Present were- Mr. Geo. Smith J.P., C.C. (chairman), Mr. T. S. Agutter (vice-chairman), Revs. Canon Lawson and C. F, Bolland, and Messrs. T. Newton, J. T. Knight, F. J. Steward, J. T. Salisbury, W. Whitehead, Jos. Knight, Arthur Abbott, T. Forscutt, J. T. Bonsor C.C., Rowland Wood, and E. Day; together with Mr. Walter Dellar (deputy clerk).
The deputy clerk read the main portions of the circular on the subject received from the Local Government Board, and considerable discussion ensued. It was decided that the tribunal should consist of ten members, namely, the six members who had been appointed the local tribunal in connection with the Derby Group Scheme, and four additional members. A

proposition in favour of having one lady member was rejected. The following were elected to form the tribunal - Mr. Geo. Smith J.P., C.C. (chairman of the District Council), Mr. T. S.

Agutter (vice-chairman), Rev. C. F. Bolland, Mr. Arthur Abbott, Mr. J. T. Bonser C.C., and Mr. F. J. Steward (the members of the Derby Group Tribunal), together with Mr. Thomas Selby (Thrapston), Mr. John Saddington (Islip), Mr. Robert Deans (Brigstock), and Mr. John Brown (Titchmarsh). The tribunal sat on a regular basis for the rest of the war.

(Advertisement, left, Kettering Leader, Friday 11th February 1916.)

Saturday 12th was the occasion of a dance, arranged by the Town Band, at the Co-operative Hall (kindly lent) in aid of the Thrapston Soldiers' and Sailors' Comforts Fund. There was a good attendance.

On 15th, at a meeting of the Board of Guardians, Mr. Milligan referred to the gramophone which the members of the Board kindly subscribed for last June, to be sent out to a military hospital in France, but which miscarried and never reached him. He mentioned that he had found it at Northampton and that as he might not be going to France again for some time he had sent it, together with the packs of cards which had also been given to the Northampton General Hospital, where a number of soldiers were under treatment. This received a round of applause.

The Police Court on Thursday 17th saw the appearance of a local soldier, who was charged with being a deserter from the 3rd Battalion Northamptonshire Regiment, while stationed in the south of England, since 29th January. Inspector Campion stated that he received a description of the prisoner, and at 5.30 on Saturday night he arrested him at his father's home. The prisoner, who was severely wounded in the early stages of the war, admitted being a deserter, and on the Inspector's application he was remanded to await a military escort.

On Sunday 20th, Mr. F. W. B. Emery, headmaster of Thrapston Church Schools, received a letter from Miss Louisa Riches, of Wharton Street, King's Cross Road, London, informing him of the death of an old Thrapston schoolboy, who was killed in action on 7th January; Bombardier **George Unger (21)**, 50406, B Battery, 98th Brigade, R.F.A., Salonika.

The first meeting of the Local Military Tribunal took place on Thursday 24th. The cases before them were of single attested men, all living and working in the area.
Three men from the ironstone industry were first to be considered. The employers had sent all the men they could, some 120. The military authorities were taking the works over and they must be carried on. Two men were granted three months and one total exemption.
Two railway workers were next considered. A shunter was considered indispensible and granted total exemption, whilst a barrow-filler also received the same, being solely responsible for his bedridden father. A delivery driver was refused exemption, whilst two farmers successfully applied for total exemption for their sons. A carpenter and a farmer's workman were both refused.
A further four men received total exemptions, four no exemption and five others periods between one and six months.
The Tribunal sat from 10.30 am to 4.15 pm, with a short break for lunch.

Monday 28th saw the Rifle Club hold a very successful whist drive at the Thrapston Rifle Range, about 60 people being present.

March

On Sunday afternoon (5th) a service for children and young people, in connection with the National Egg Collection for wounded soldiers, was held at the Baptist Church, the pastor (the Rev. H. Ellis Roberts) and the Sunday School superintendent (Mr. G. P. Hepher) presiding. The number of eggs collected was 420.

March 7th – Alexander John Emery (22) killed in action.

Tuesday 7th saw Thrapston Police Court hear a case against a local married woman. She was charged with wilful damage to a window and door, to the amount of 1s, at Thrapston between 12th and 13th February, the complainant being Benjamin Francis Barber, fruiterer, Oundle Road. Mr. Prentice, solicitor for the complainant, stated that the offence was of smearing human excreta on the door and windows. This nuisance had been going on for six to seven weeks. The complainant knew of no known motive. The police had kept watch on the premises on 12th, and did see the defendant out early in the morning. She said that she was trying to find out who was causing the damage and denied it was she. As no evidence of culpability could be brought, the case was dismissed.

The other reported event on 7th occurred at the King's Arms Hotel, Thrapston, in the afternoon, when Mr. Arthur G. Brown, auctioneer, sold, amongst other properties, a small shop and premises on Oundle Road. The price realised was £65.

This advertisement *(left)* was placed in the *Evening Telegraph* on Wednesday 8th.

Also on 8th, the Thrapston Tribunal sat. Amongst the many applications heard were three from Thrapston men.

A cycle agent and repairer, who was also an engineer, received a two month exemption.
A local grocer's vanman said two brothers were in the Army and he was the only son at home with his widowed mother who was not in good health, six months' exemption.
An ironstone worker was refused exemption.

The 9th brought further news of Trooper Watson (of 1st Lovat Scouts). He was still in hospital at Floriana, Malta, and had just undergone his fourth operation. He writes, "I had been up about five days, and was just getting strength so that I could go on crutches. I was expecting to get marked up for England, when the doctor told me I should have to undergo another operation... I was very ill all the week after it, but am all right again now. I have been getting up the last few days, and am looking forward to coming home. They took three pieces of dead bone out of my leg."

Monday 13th saw a man of no fixed abode appear before the Police Court. He was charged with begging at Islip at half-past ten that morning. He was found by P.C. Short making a breakfast of hot tea and bread and butter, which he had begged, and bread and cheese (which had been served to him at the Workhouse) in his pocket. He received the standard sentence of 14 days hard labour.

Thrapston Board of Guardians met on Tuesday 14th. As well as accepting tenders for the supply of foodstuffs and building materials for the Workhouse, they also agreed a tender from Mr. Peacock for haircutting and shaving for £12. Rev. C. F. Bolland reported that an application had been received from Mrs. Knight, assistant matron, for an increase of salary. She had worked at the Workhouse for 26 years and was paid £22 pa. The committee recommended an increase of £2 pa, which was agreed.

NOW is the time to book your requirements for coming Season's Goods to avoid disappointment.

Large Stock of Machinery OF ALL KINDS IN STOCK.

Season's Repairs should be sent in at once.

G. LEWIS & SON, Ltd., KETTERING,

ALSO AT THRAPSTON & WELLINGBORO' MARKETS.

(Advertisement which appeared in the Evening Telegraph during March and April 1916).

Thrapston Tribunal had another very busy day on Monday 20th when they heard 50 cases. Amongst the decisions was one concerning a Thrapston man. He worked as a general assistant in a warehouse. He applied for exemption from combatant service on the grounds of defective eyesight and catarrh in the head. This was granted.

That evening, there was a good muster of the Thrapston and district special constables at a parade held at the Corn Exchange to bid farewell to Mr. J. Edmonds, commandant, who was moving to Wales.

The *Evening Telegraph* reported on Tuesday 28th, "The committee of the Soldiers' and Sailors' Comforts Fund met at the Co-operative Hall last week for the final act in connection with their praiseworthy efforts by which the magnificent sum of £72 had been raised, namely the packing of the boxes to be sent away to our soldier and sailor friends. Besides the committee, (who had Mr. W. Stobie as secretary) willing helpers were found in Miss Essam, Mrs. Gifford, Mr. H. Mundin, and Mr. Page. In all there are 135 soldiers and sailors from the town of Thrapston, and the committee wisely decided to send each man training at home 5s in a registered envelope, with the best wishes of the fund, and to all men abroad 10s worth of goods. Altogether there were 70 boxes despatched by post on Saturday last, and five were delivered to friends of men that had returned to England through illness etc. Each box, which bore the label "With best wishes from the Thrapston Soldiers' and Sailors' Comforts Fund" contained biscuits (half pound), sweets (quarter pound), milk chocolate (half pound), 1 lb. tin of cocoa with milk and sugar mixed, 1 box of Oxo tablets, 1 bar of soap, 1 tin of insect powder, 2 khaki handkerchiefs, one pair of woollen socks, 1 tinder lighter, 1 flash lamp and extra battery, and 25 packets of cigarettes. Non-smokers received an extra pair of socks and a woollen scarf."

Thursday 23rd was the date for a performance of a musical, "The Empire's Honour", at the Corn Exchange, for which a large audience attended. The accompanist was Miss Kingsford.
The picture *(shown on page 48, Kettering Leader, Friday 24th March 1916)* was entitled "Great Britain and her Colonies".
From left to right – Standing - Miss Rowell, Miss Simpson, Mrs. Bland, Miss Margaret Hall, Miss Hall, Miss Musk, Miss Drury, Miss Boosey and Miss Kinch.
Sitting – Mrs. Larkin and Mrs. Newman.

On Tuesday 28th, a snow gale seriously affected the town. Four elm trees were blown down on Oundle Road, smashing telegraph wires and blocking the road. Many other trees were also lost during the storm. About a quarter of a mile on the Thorpe side of Bridge Street Station, a tree fell across the line and a couple of windows on the 3.51 pm train to Peterborough were broken. Nobody was hurt and the line was cleared in time for the next train to pass unimpeded. A train from Cambridge, which should have arrived in town at 4.09 pm was snowed up in Long Stow and had still not arrived by midday the next day. By 10 am on Wednesday 29th, the telegraph wires were still disconnected and all roads out of town impassable, except the one to Titchmarsh. The mail finally arrived by train from Kettering late in the afternoon. The 2.35 pm Kettering train reached Thrapston four hours later and continued to Raunds, where it became trapped. An engine and brake was sent to retrieve it and the passengers returned to town, where they were put up for the night.

On Friday 31st, a coach load of German prisoners (soldiers and sailors) passed through Thrapston London and North Western Station (2.24 pm from Peterborough) in the afternoon. Some of them remarked that they "were tired of it."

April

The *Northampton Independent* carried a report on 1st about Mrs. Gibson, of 88 Dundee Street, St James', Northampton, who had received the sad news that her son Pte. **A. J. Emery (22)** had been killed while serving with the Northamptonshire Regiment.

On Sunday 2nd, Thrapston's special constables were called out twice during the night in connection with Zeppelin warnings.

Further news of **Alexander Emery (22)** arrived in town on 4th.

Also on 4th, the Thrapston District Shire Horse Society held their Annual General Meeting at the White Hart Hotel. There was a good attendance and it was agreed, after much discussion, to bring the show date forward to July 20th, to avoid clashing with harvest.

By Thursday 6th, Midland Railways announced, following the snowfall that, "trains are running nearly to time and are, in fact, very little late."

On the same day, Thrapston Rural District Council reported that during the previous fifteen weeks, only one case of infectious disease, diphtheria, was reported.

Acknowledgements from soldiers to two of the children who collected eggs for the recent egg service at the Baptist Church in aid of the National Egg Collection for Wounded Soldiers (and who wrote on their names, addresses, and suitable messages), were reported in the *Evening Telegraph* on Saturday 8th.

Sergt. A. Palmer (S.F. Regt.) wrote from a Nottingham Military Hospital to E. Clayson: - "Dear Friend – If this card should find you, allow me to thank you for a most enjoyable breakfast. It is such goodness as yours that the British soldier always admires and also appreciates. Thanking you again, I remain, yours sincerely, Arthur Palmer. The egg was splendid."

Pte. Geo. Wadlow, writing from the same hospital to another little contributor says: "Dear Friend. – Just a line to thank you for the egg that I had for my breakfast this morning. I am sure it is a great help to the authorities to have so many eggs forwarded on. As regards your egg, I enjoyed it very much, and noted the words on same. Eggs were scarce over yonder so we enjoy them now. Like other people, I shall be glad when this war is over and peace reigns once more. I was rejected twice before I was passed to fight for my country. It is one's duty. I never thought I should be a soldier. So au revoir. From Geo. Wadlow. Best wishes."

Thrapston Guardians met on Tuesday 8th. Amongst the items on the very long agenda were:
Mrs. Knight's pay rise was increased by £1 pa to £25.
Miss Headland, a 19 year old kitchen maid, who had worked there for two years and three months had her salary increased from £15 to £18.
Miss Cheney, who was very much run down, was given 14 days leave of absence and, for that period, the matron, Mrs. Cook, was to appoint a substitute at as reasonable a cost as possible.

On 18th, news arrived that Capt. R. J.P. Humphrey had been suffering from malarial fever. "For a month he was in hospital in France, and for the past few days he has been at Osborne House Hospital, Isle of Wight. Today (Tuesday) he was expected in Thrapston on sick leave."

The next day, swallows were seen above the town and the *Parish Magazine* reported that "192 splendid cakes had been sent to Berrywood Asylum, Northampton, for the soldiers recovering from injuries".

Friday 21st was Good Friday. Many people attended the 12.00 to 3.00pm service at St. James' Church, whilst Easter Day services, at 6, 7, 8 and 11am were not as well attended as the previous year. This was put down to so many of the young men being away, serving with the armed forces.

Monday 24th was the funeral of Mrs. T. Hodson, widow of a Thrapston butcher, at Lowick Church.

Another dance in aid of the Soldiers' and Sailors' Comforts Fund was held at the Co-operative Hall on Tuesday 25th and was a great success. Between 70 and 80 were present, Messrs. A. H. Hurrell and H. Abbott acted as the M.C's and the refreshments were served by Mrs. Mayes, Mrs. Stobie, and Mrs. Frisby. Miss L. Flanders (piano) and Mr. A. Fletcher (cornet) supplied the music. Dancing was kept up until 2 o'clock.

The Rifle Club arranged a whist drive for the evening of Wednesday 26th, 72 people playing, whilst the next evening, they held a shooting competition for members.

For those of a more spiritual leaning, the Bishop of the Diocese, the Right Rev. the Hon. E. Carr officiated at the confirmation service in the Parish Church on 27th with 23 people coming forward.

May

The *Evening Telegraph* reported that not many children were out with garlands on May Day, no doubt a reflection on the mood of the town.

The Thrapston Petty Sessions had a busy day on Tuesday 2nd when twenty-nine people from the district appeared before the Police Court, each charged with a breach of the Lighting Order (against having lights showing at night) over a period of time. One Thrapston person appeared, a music teacher. P.C. Short said that there was a bright light coming from the kitchen window. She was fined 2s 6d.
Another local man, a coal merchant, was summoned for obstructing a public footpath in Hortons Lane by allowing a horse and coal drag to stand thereon on April 20th. After pleading guilty, he was fined 5s.

On the same day, acting under instructions from the Thrapston churchwardens, Mr. Henry H. Bletsoe let, by auction, "The Church Field", Huntingdon Road, comprising about two acres of accommodation grass land, for a term of three years as from April 6th. The company met the auctioneer on the ground and, after spirited bidding, the land was secured by the Thrapston Co-operative Society at £12 5s per annum.

During Tuesday night (2nd) several Zeppelin warnings were received and a number of Special Constables went on duty.

(One of many advertisements appearing in the Evening Telegraph at this time is shown left – EDF.)

A number of the town's young men left on Monday 8th to join the Army. The best wishes of the townspeople went with them.

On 9th, Mrs. G. Ernest Smith gave the Thrapston Guardians a report on the Children's Home Committee. Five children in the Home had not been vaccinated. One boarded-out boy who had been described as incorrigible, had been received in the Home and was found quite manageable. The eldest girl in the Home had gone into service and had proved to be quite satisfactory. The Committee applied for £1 to purchase an outfit for her, which was granted.

On Wednesday 10th, an aeroplane flew over town at about a quarter to one.

Thrapston Tribunal convened again on Wednesday 10th:
A Thrapston farmer doing his own shepherding asked for total exemption which was granted providing that there was no change in his circumstances.
A managing clerk at the local solicitor's office, who was described as indispensible to both the business and the functioning of the Tribunal, District Council and National Registration Register was granted exemption provided he remained in his present positions.

The *Evening Telegraph* on Tuesday 16th carried two advertisements for bicycles, shown on page 51.

CYCLES ! CYCLES ! CYCLES !—Large quantity of Second-hand Ladies', Gent.'s, Boys' and Girls' Cycles to be sold at bargain prices for cash, from 10/- upwards. Call and see us.—Rupert Smith, Thrapston.

RIDE UNTAXED.—Our present stock of Cycles will be sold without reserve. Over 100 machines to select from. In the matter of New Cycles, Second-hand Cycles, Repairs, Overhauling for the new season, Re-Plating, Re-Enamelling, or, in short, any cycling want, get in touch with the best firm.—Alfred Smith & Son, Midland-rd., Thrapston.   T20

In the same issue, lighting cases and criminal matters were heard at Thrapston Police Court:

A labourer who left his back door open showing a bright light, as well as from a window was fined 5s.

A managing clerk pleaded guilty to going into a room carrying a small benzolene lamp. Fined 5s.

A woman who did not draw the blind and a grocer with a similar offence both received 5s fines.

A widow was fined 4s, whilst a local cycle dealer received a 5s penalty.

A single woman said that she had a double blind and never had any warning that light was showing. P.C. Short told the court that he had warned her. Fined 6s.

A widow received a 4s fine for having a light showing from an upstairs window.

A local auctioneer stated that he had used his best endeavours to comply with the order. They had all the windows duplicated with heavy green blinds or curtains but on this particular night, his wife had been doing some work for prisoners of war or invalids and went into a spare room where the blind was not dawn carrying a candle. It was only for a minute or two. Fined 4s.

The last two cases were against the Wesleyan minister and a widow, both of whom were treated the same, receiving 4s fines.

Five youths, aged between thirteen and seventeen years, were summoned for having in their possession ten eggs from a wild duck, wilfully taken from a nest at a piece of land called "Duck Decoy". All pleaded guilty and were each fined 5s.

A "Wanted" advertisement appeared on Wednesday 17th:
"Lady's second-hand bicycle for cash. Send particulars,
Box No 53, Evening Telegraph, Thrapston."

That evening, the local branch of the British Women's Temperance Association met, with a good attendance. The speaker was Rev. H. E. Roberts, pastor of Thrapston Baptist Church. This was the final meeting of the current season.

Thrapston Appeals Tribunal met again on Thursday 18th. As usual, there were a large number of cases to be heard, those listed below being of local men:

A farmer applied for absolute exemption for his horse keeper and stockman. Exemption to October 31st.

A wholesale and retail grocer applied for a married general assistant. One-month exemption.

A Company applied on behalf of a grocer's manager, married, aged 28. Exemption until July 31st.

A grocer applied for absolute exemption, as did a local fishmonger and poultry dealer. Both were granted this on condition that they remained in their trades.

Two builders, a hairdresser and fruit merchant all received exemptions of between one and seven months.

On Friday 19th, the *Evening Telegraph* reported a promotion. "Sgt. Victor Henry Gray, of the 4th Batt. King's Royal Rifles, grandson of Mrs. Mault, of Market Place, Thrapston, has been promoted to be second-lieutenant. He enlisted in *(unreadable - EDF)* and was for about eight years in India. At the outbreak of the war, he served in France, and is now at Salonika."

Clocks were put forward one hour at 2.00 am on Sunday 21st, under the Daylight Saving Initiative. In Thrapston, most of the public and church clocks were altered at dusk on the Saturday – the Post Office at 9.30 pm and the Parish Church (which has no outside face) between 8.00 and 9.00 pm. A few people "forgot" and arrived at church late. An errand boy, resting at 9.30 am on Monday 22nd, was asked how he liked the new time. "Not much" was the prompt answer. "Oh, but you will leave off an hour earlier." "I don't know", was the doubtful response.

Thursday 25th was Empire Day, which was appropriately celebrated at the Thrapston elementary schools. Patriotic songs were the order of the day.

Also on 25th, the White Hart Hotel was the location for the united annual meetings of the Northants, Leicester and Rutland branch of the Land Agents' Society and the local branch of the Surveyors' Institution. The proceedings were private. Following luncheon, a visit was made to the Islip Iron Company's works, which proved of considerable interest, followed by a tour of Drayton House, including tea.

June

June 1st – Arthur Edward Warren (23) killed in action.

The Thursday 1st June sitting of the Appeals Tribunal included in its cases heard:-
A Thrapston army clicker had his case adjourned to June 30th.
A man working as a hairdresser and photographer was exempted until July 31st.
A master stationer and painter were both exempted until October 31st.

Thrapston Rural District Council also met on 1st. A decision on the water supply was adjourned for a further six months. The Medical Officer reported two cases of scarlatina and one of diphtheria, all of whom had improved.

The *Kettering Guardian* reported on Friday 2nd that Pte. H. S. George appeared in the official casualty list published by the War Office as being wounded.

Saturday 3rd saw the headline shown on page 53 appear in the *Evening Telegraph.*

A day later, news of the Battle of Jutland started arriving in town, including the sinking of the "Tipperary", a destroyer leader. This news, along with confirmation of the death of **Arthur Warren**, was reported on Tuesday 6th in the *Evening Telegraph*.

June 5th – John Isaac Ashton Sutcliffe (24) killed in action.

Some men from the town survived the Battle of Jutland. On 6th, a letter from First-class Stoker Cecil Walter Read, son of Mrs. Read of Midland Road, Thrapston, who was serving on one of the ships (the "Forester") concerned in the recent engagement (the Battle of Jutland), arrived at home to say that he was safe and quite all right. Two days later, confirmation was received that Seaman Bernard Cooper, son of Mr. and Mrs. Edward Cooper, of Halford Street

BIG NAVAL BATTLE.

BRITISH BATTLE CRUISERS AND DESTROYERS SUNK.

SEVERAL GERMAN SHIPS SUNK AND OTHERS DAMAGED.

HEAVIEST SEA FIGHT OF HISTORY.

who joined the Navy about twelve months before the commencement of the war, passed through the recent naval engagement unharmed. He was on the "Warspite", which was in the thick of the fighting and arrived home on Thursday for a week's holiday.

The Guardians met on Tuesday 6th. One of their major concerns was the attestation of Mr. J. L. Mash, the relieving officer. As well as relieving officer, Mr. Mash was also collector, vaccination officer and registrar of births and deaths. It was resolved that the clerk should make representation to the Tribunal for his exemption on the grounds that he was indispensible and engaged in work of national importance. It was commented that, in some districts, ladies could do his job, but not in a widespread rural area. The vice-chairman thought it impossible that a woman could perform his duties in the area of their Union. A couple of voices were raised in dissent to this opinion, although the Guardians agreed that exemption should be sought.

On the same afternoon, a public meeting was held at the Corn Exchange in connection with the women's work on the land movement.

(The advertisement shown right appeared in the Evening Telegraph during June.)

The Thrapston Tribunal sat on Wednesday 7th, when the relieving officer was granted conditional exemption, the condition being that he remained in post.
A local master plumber and decorator received exemption until September 7th.

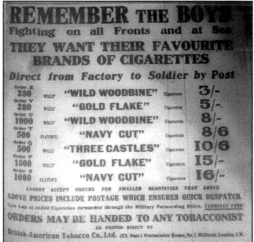

REMEMBER THE BOYS
Fighting on all Fronts and at Sea
THEY WANT THEIR FAVOURITE BRANDS OF CIGARETTES
Direct from Factory to Soldier by Post

Order		Brand		Price
280	WILLS'	"WILD WOODBINE"	Cigarettes	3/-
280	WILLS'	"GOLD FLAKE"	Cigarettes	5/-
1000	WILLS'	"WILD WOODBINE"	Cigarettes	8/-
500	PLAYER'S	"NAVY CUT"	Cigarettes	8/6
500	WILLS'	"THREE CASTLES"	Cigarettes	10/6
1000	WILLS'	"GOLD FLAKE"	Cigarettes	15/-
1000	PLAYER'S	"NAVY CUT"	Cigarettes	16/-

CANNOT ACCEPT ORDERS FOR SMALLER QUANTITIES THAN ABOVE.
Sole Lots of 10,000 Cigarettes forwarded through the Military Forwarding Office, CARRIAGE PAID.
ORDERS MAY BE HANDED TO ANY TOBACCONIST
or POSTED DIRECT TO
British-American Tobacco Co., Ltd. (El. Dept.) Westminster House, No.7, Millbank, London, S.W.

The Police Court heard the case of a labourer of no fixed abode who admitted being drunk in Midland Road on 9th. He was fined 10s and ordered to pay 5s 3d costs.

Monday 12th, and the cost of a 4lb loaf fell by ½d.

Tuesday 13th was the first of two days when the annual meeting of the Northamptonshire Baptist Association occurred in Thrapston. It was their first visit for twenty years. *(A picture of the delegates appeared on 23rd, and is shown on page 55 – EDF.)*

Thrapston Police Court sat on Friday 16th to hear a sad case. A local man was charged with committing wilful damage to a window at his parents' house. His aged mother stated that her son had been away from home for a few days. The previous night they had waited up for him until after ten o'clock, but he did not come, and they went to bed. About eight o'clock next morning he arrived and wanted to enter the house, but they refused. He then broke two windows and used most filthy and threatening language. Inspector Campion applied for a remand in custody, which was granted and he was kept under observation. He was subsequently certified as not being responsible for his actions. The chairman of the Bench made an order for his removal to a Home.

An advertisement appeared in the *Evening Telegraph* on Tuesday 20th, inserted by Alfred Smith and Son, Midland Road, Thrapston.
"Special bargains for June.
Ladies 1916 brand new cycle £5 10s.
Gents BSA light roadster £4 19s 6d.
Gents brand new Rudge-Whitworth at £2 off list price – now £5 19s 6d.
There is nothing in Cycledom we cannot supply.
Phone No. 29"

A memorial service for Lord Kitchener and others who died in the "Hampshire" disaster *(when the ship they were on was sunk by a German mine in the Orkney Islands - EDF)* was held at the Parish Church on Sunday 18th, where the church was "filled in every part". A collection was taken for widows and dependents of sailors, amounting to £4 4s 11d. *(A commemorative Thrapston crested china bust of Kitchener is shown on the back cover – EDF.)*

On Wednesday 21st, the following stories appeared:
At the Tribunal, a market gardener and seed merchant applied for a temporary extension for his son, which was refused. A slaughter man said he would be 41 on July 2nd, and had just been called up. He was exempted until October 31st. A Thrapston outfitter asked for a further two-month exemption for his son. This was granted, but was stated to be the final one.
Thrapston Council decided, after discussion, to keep street watering to just half a day each day *(watering was necessary to settle dust - EDF)*. Trees blown down at the cemetery during the winter had been sold for £5.
A terrier dog owned by Mr. J. W. Stubbs, fishmonger, got onto the line at Bridge Street Station and was killed by a departing train.

A bowls match played at the Institute's green on Thursday 22nd was between the captain's and vice-captain's teams, victory going to the former by 27 points to 12.

On Friday 23rd, the *Kettering Leader* carried the picture shown on page 55 and this article:
"The town of Thrapston was last week the locale of the annual meetings of the Northamptonshire Baptist Association. It is twenty years since the Association last met in the town, and much local interest was taken in the proceedings. Our photograph includes many of the ministers and delegates present at the meetings."

Also on 23rd, the results of the expert and novice Handicap Billiards competition at the Institute were announced, the respective winners being Messrs. J. Meadows and T. Smith.

Tuesday 27th brought a report that the Rev. Cecil Kingsford (youngest son of the late Rev. S. Kingsford, rector of Thrapston), a minor canon of Gloucester Cathedral, who recently offered his services as a Naval Chaplain, had been appointed to the Hibernia, which vessel he joined on Thursday (June 22nd).

On the same day, a drover from Thrapston was summoned to appear at the Police Court for cruelly beating a steer in town on June 4th. After hearing witness and Police statements, he was sentenced to one month's hard labour.

Two days later, on June 29th, a report headed "Thrapston man reported missing" appeared in the *Evening Telegraph*:

"**Ashton Sutcliffe (24)**, son of the late Mr. John Sutcliffe, of Thrapston, is reported 'missing'. He went to Canada seven years ago and joined the Canadian Force shortly after the outbreak of the war. He was in the mounted gun section and had been in France for over a year. His younger brother, Corpl. Harold Sutcliffe, who also went to Canada, and joined the first Canadian Contingent, was wounded, it will be remembered, about twelve months ago, both his elbows being smashed, and other injuries sustained. He is at present at the London headquarters of the Canadian Force, and was engaged in verifying official lists, when he came across the name of his brother amongst the men reported as 'missing'."

During the last week of the month, the Rifle Club organised a week of skittles competitions, resulting in a large entry and keen competition. The overall winners were: Ladies, Miss Cockerill; Gents, Mr. G. H. Gilbert.
After expenses, a total of £2 was raised for club funds.

July

The month began with Freeman and Webb's Summer Sale. Offers included travellers samples, ladies' dress skirts, blouses, robes, neckwear and underwear.

Capt. R.J.P. Humphrey, 1st Northants arrived in town on 1st for a one-week period of leave.

Wednesday 5th was a busy day in town.

The Guardians met and heard that Nurse Attley, who had been at the Workhouse for two years wished to resign her post and asked for a testimonial. This was agreed and the matron asked to place an advertisement for another nurse of some experience at the same salary.
The Guardians also heard that a new pony had been purchased for the Workhouse for £11 4s, the old one being sold for £4.

The Tribunal sat to hear a large number of cases. The Thrapston men were:
A boot maker and repairer, who specialised in repairs. As people preferred to have their old boots repaired rather than buy new ones, he was seen as essential and was exempted until January 1st.

A butcher, working without any help, also received exemption until January 1st.

A local stationer, printer, bookbinder and seller of fancy goods successfully obtained conditional exemption for three employees.

THRAPSTON SOLDIERS' AND SAILORS' COMFORTS FUND.

THE WHIST DRIVE and DANCE postponed from Saturday, July 1st, will be held on THURSDAY NEXT, JULY 6th. If unfavourable weather, will definitely be held in the Co-operative Hall. Don't forget the date, July 6th. Skittle and other competitions.

WM. STOBIE,
T5
Hon. Sec.

This advertisement *(shown left)* appeared in the *Evening Telegraph* on 5th. Although it once again rained, the event went ahead and was moderately successful.

The rector, Rev. B. W. Stothert, had been appointed by the Chancellor of the Diocese of Peterborough for the granting of marriage licences.

July 7th – John Robert Pollard (25) killed in action.

Also on 7th, there was almost a disaster at Bridge Street Station. Between 10.00 and 11.00 am, during goods shunting operations on the Islip siding, the engine backed into a stationary brake van and a dozen other trucks, causing them to run down the slight incline and into the crossing gates, two of which were broken. Mr. Watkins, the manager of Messrs. Wyman's bookstall, jumped onto the permanent way and applied the brakes, bringing the trucks to a standstill. No one was hurt.

On Monday 10th, Mr. W. D. Colley was announced as hon. secretary of the Thrapston Branch of the Church of England Men's Society.

Northamptonshire Council Education Department announced Scholarship awards on 10th. Three Thrapston children were successful:

Kathleen French (Thrapston Council School) received a Class A scholarship for two years to enable her to proceed to secondary school.

William G. Roberts received a one-year extension to continue secondary education, whilst Clifford E. Roberts was awarded a two year extension.

On Wednesday 12th, Mr. Geo. Thurlow, of Halford Street, Thrapston, received two postcards from his fourth son, Pte. William Thurlow, of the 2nd Northants. The first was written in France, dated 6th July, and stated that he was alright. The second came from the General Hospital, Manchester, to which he had been removed, and contained the information that he had been wounded in the left arm. No further particulars were given. Pte. W. Thurlow joined the Northants soon after the war commenced and sailed to France in April 1915.

Also on 12th, the Thrapston School holiday dates were announced – close July 27th and re-open September 4th.

Attendance awards were also made, on that day, to pupils with perfect attendance.

Pupils from the Thrapston Council School:

Alfred Dingley, 5 years, silver medal.

Ivy Dingley, 3 years, bronze medal.

Arthur Perkins, 2 years, white medal.

Sidney Booth, Gladys Frisby and John Wiles, all 1 year.

Pupils from Thrapston Church of England School:

Florence Groom, 5 years.

Ernest Dingley and Florence Loveday, 1 year.

Very few sports matches were either taking place or being reported, but on Thursday 13th, Raunds Conservatives beat Thrapston at bowls by 62 points to 52.

On Saturday 15th, the Thrapston bellringers joined other towers for a meeting at Aldwincle. Ringstead, Raunds, Titchmarsh and Twywell had a pleasant afternoon ringing with the Aldwincle tower, breaking for tea.

Tuesday 18th was when Mrs. Pollard, Halford Street, received a letter from Lance Corpl. Abbott concerning her son, **John Pollard (25)**. The letter was reproduced in the *Evening Telegraph* on the 19th, and read "12/7/16. B.E.F., France. – Dear Madam, - Just a few lines hoping to find you quite well, but I am very sorry to say that No. 13827 Pte. J. Pollard, was killed on Friday. I and 13 Platoon are very sorry to hear about him, and please accept our sympathy. Those that were near him said he was killed outright. He was a good, strong man, and will be missed by all very much. Also, he did not fear anything, and he died or got killed during a very trying time. I am sorry to have to write this, so please accept my sympathy. – Yours faithfully, S. Abbott."

One day later, on 19th, came the news that a former Thrapston man, Pte. William Groom, 2nd Northants, (son of Mrs. J. Groom, of Finedon, and formerly of Denford Ash), had been wounded. He enlisted soon after the outbreak of the war, this being the second time he had been wounded.

Also on 19th, the Tribunal refused a signalman any exemption, whilst the Rural District Council successfully obtained conditional exemption for their steamroller driver.

Thursday 20th saw the Annual Shire Horse Society's show, held in a field off Chancery Lane. It had been cancelled for the two previous years, due to the war, and it was not surprising that entries were down on pre-war days, although there were sill 59 horses on show.

Friday 21st July carried a picture of the **"Thrapston Sporting Chums" (115)**.

The next day, 22nd, formal confirmation was received from the Admiralty of the loss of **Arthur Warren (23)**. Included were these lines "I regret to inform you that his name does not appear on the list of prisoners of war received from the Prussian Ministry of War through the American Ambassador in Berlin, and it is feared that there can now be no doubt that he has lost his life." On the same day, **John Samuel Smith (26)** was injured.

The 22nd was also the day of the Thrapston Industrial Co-operative Society Ltd's annual treat for members' children. They met at the Market Road stores and split into two groups for tea, one going to the Co-operative Hall and the other to the Wesleyan Schoolroom. After tea, they re-formed and marched to a field rented by the Society on Huntingdon Road, where games were freely indulged in. On leaving at 8 pm, each child was given a bag of sweets, biscuits and a bun.

Sunday 23rd marked Thrapston Sunday School's anniversary, whilst on the next day, services were held at the church in the afternoon and evening to celebrate the church's anniversary.

Thrapston Police Court sat on Tuesday 25th. Unusually, there were no miscreants from town to answer for their deeds, although many from other local communities did.

The annual garden fete and sale of work for the Thrapston Habitation of the Young Helpers' League (Dr. Barnardo's Homes) took place in the afternoon and evening of Thursday 27th. Both "The Hollies" and "Nene House" were used, courtesy of Mr. and Mrs. Geo. Smith and the Misses Larter respectively. There were many stalls and competitions. The evening concert was at "Nene House" and many local people contributed to an enjoyable entertainment.

(Pictured above at "The Hollies", Hazel Evans Archive - EDF).

July 29th – John Samuel Smith (26) died of wounds.

The same day, Thrapston Institute put on their flower show and sports competitions (bowls and skittles), at which there was a good attendance.

August

The month began with the funeral, with full military honours, of Pte. **John Samuel Smith (26)** on Tuesday 1st, followed by burial at Oundle Road Cemetery.

Thrapston Guardians met on 1st and agreed that the matron should select the new nurse from the three applications received.

At the Thrapston Tribunal on the same day, two hairdressers aged 28 and 29 years were given three and two months exemption.
A Nottingham company made one more application on behalf of their manager of a grocer's and provisions store. A final one month was allowed.

Friday 4th brought news of Corpl. Gerald March, son of Mr. and Mrs. W. March, of Halford Street, Thrapston, who had been wounded and was in hospital in France. He had been buried by the explosion of a shell, and had staggered out and just got onto his feet again, when he was hit in the fleshy part of the thigh. His brother, Driver Kenneth March of the Royal Field Artillery, was in hospital at Preston Hall, Aylesford, Kent, with skin disease.

On the same day, the *Kettering Guardian* reported "Pte. Sidney Meadows, Northants Regt., son of Mr. and Mrs. Meadows, Oundle Road, Thrapston, is in the 2nd Western General

Hospital Manchester, having been wounded on July 20th in one leg, which had to be amputated halfway up the thigh. This is the second time that he has been wounded. On the first occasion he was wounded by a bullet in the thigh. Mrs. Meadows had a son killed in the early stages of the war **Walter Miller (4)** and she has another son at the front, Pte. **Herbert Miller (33).**"

At the Thursday 5th session of the Police Court, an able-bodied man of no fixed abode appeared charged with begging. P.C. Short said the prisoner had been seen begging all along King Edward Cottages, Islip, the previous day. He said that he only wanted some hot water. Failing to judge his situation correctly, the prisoner was insolent to the magistrate, who promptly awarded him fourteen days hard labour.

On Saturday 5th, Misses C. and V. Mault and Miss M. Rowlett sold carnations, given by Mrs. Buckby of Clopton Manor, in Thrapston streets during the evening, raising £1 1s 11½d for Red Cross Funds.

This advertisement appeared in the *Evening Telegraph* on Monday 7th:
"Wanted at once, two young ladies for the Grocery and Provision Department (for duration of war only); applicants preferred with experience. Apply, stating age, wages required and copies of references, not later than Thurs. Morning, Aug 10th.
Co-operative Society, Thrapston."

August 8th – Horace Dingley (27) died of malaria.

On Wednesday 9th, a letter was received by Mr. and Mrs. B. Barber, of Highfield Road, Thrapston, from their son, Pte. J. Barber, informing them that his brother, Pte. William Barber (Northants Regiment) was wounded on Thursday last week (August 3rd) in his legs and one foot, by the explosion of a bomb, and that he was in hospital. Pte. W. Barber joined the Army in November 1914, and had been in France about fifteen months.

August 10th – George Ernest Nicholls (28) killed in action.

On Thursday 10th, an afternoon garden party was held at the Rectory, lasting until the evening. The chief features were a sale of works, public tea, whist drive and dancing, along with numerous amusements and attractions. Liberal support was received from a good attendance. The proceeds, which amounted to £50, were for Army charities, with a small portion for the "church new hassocks fund".

Also on 10th, an agriculturalist in the district gave the following particulars:
"The cutting of winter oats commenced at the end of last week and the yield is good. Winter beans will follow, the crop being pretty good. The wheat and barley harvest will commence in about ten days. Wheats are not very heavy, but a fair crop; and barleys as a rule are good. The hay harvest is now over; the crops are very good, and have for the most part been got in very good condition. The rains which interfered with the early hay crops (clovers suffered the worst) were beneficial for the corn crops, while rain would now do much good to the grass and roots; the present weather is favourable for the harvest."

On 11th, it was reported that Pte. Herbert George, son of Mr. Alfred George, Chancery Lane, Thrapston, "who was wounded a short time ago in the arm, is going on fairly well. A report that his arm had been amputated is fortunately not correct. It may be necessary to amputate one finger."

On Monday 14th, a man of no fixed abode was fined 5s and police costs for hawking picture postcards in Huntingdon Road without a licence. P.C. Short stated that besides a number of cards, he had 7s on him.

Wednesday 16th's issue of the *Evening Telegraph* carried this "For Sale" advertisement:-
"Ladies second-hand cycle, purchased this year; plated rims, roller brakes, little used; cash £4 10s; approval. Linnell, River View, Thrapston."
It appeared daily for the next two months! *(I suspect this is the cycle advertised as "wanted" on page 51 – EDF.)*

On Wednesday 16th, the County Court sat. The full report follows:
"A holiday atmosphere pervaded the sitting of the Thrapston County Court on Wednesday. In the absence of the Registrar (Mr. Gurney Coombs, solicitor, of Oundle, on vacation), Mr. S. M. French, of Thrapston, a former Registrar, acted as his deputy. There were only twenty original plaints, and but four judgement summonses came before his Honour Judge Wheeler, K.C., and in one of these the rate of payment was reduced from 5s to 2s 6d a month. The only person (a woman from Little Addington) sitting at the back of the Court was told that her case had been withdrawn, although she had heard nothing about it; and when the parties to an action were called outside, there was no response, except, it maybe, a slight laughing echo from the holiday sprites frolicking around. Nor were there any answers to the formal query "Any application to this Court?" and the calm of mid-August, the drowsy holiday month, once more settled upon this many-sided local seat of justice". *(They don't write them like that anymore! – EDF).*

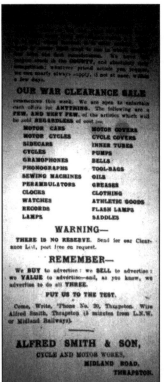

Whilst motorcycling from Thrapston to Bolnhurst, Beds to visit his brother on the evening of 16th, Mr. Herbert Roughton, late of Thrapston and now living in Wolverton, son of Mr. J. W. Roughton met with a serious accident. His machine collided with a trap at Pertenhall, Beds, and he was thrown off, being severely injured about the head and face and rendered unconscious. He was seen by a local doctor, kept in Kimbolton overnight and brought to his parents' home in Thrapston during the afternoon, at the time a heavy thunderstorm hit town.

News of **George Nicholls's (28)** death reached town on Friday 18th.

The County Tribunal sat on Friday 18th in Northampton. Two Thrapston cases were heard:
A single 19 year old horsekeeper, working for his father, was said to cart 2,000 tons of coal a year. His father requested time to dispose of the business so his son could serve. A final two months was allowed.
A married hairdresser and photographer applied for further exemption on business grounds. He offered to teach his wife the photography business and was given until October 18th.

The *Evening Telegraph* carried a new advertisement from Alfred Smith *(shown left)*. He regularly altered his adverts, unlike many advertisers, and often brought humour into them.

Sunday morning (20th) brought Mr. A. H. Dingley, Midland Road, Thrapston, official news from the Machine Gun Corps Record Office, London, that his son, **Horace Dingley (27)** had died, the cause being at that time unknown. On the same day, Mr. and Mrs. Henry Arnold, Victoria Terrace, Market Road, Thrapston, received a field postcard stating that their son, **George Edward Arnold (29)** had been wounded and admitted to hospital at Etaples, France. The sad news of his death reached town on 30th.

Sunday 20th was also the day of a memorial service at St. James' Church for **George Ernest Nicholls (28)**.

A postcard, posted in Birmingham, was received on Monday 21st from Pte. William Barber, Northants Regt., son of Mr. and Mrs. B. Barber, Thrapston. He had been wounded on Aug. 3rd in both legs and one foot by the explosion of a bomb and the message stated that he was on his way to a hospital in this country. In an earlier letter, Pte. Barber, who was a good footballer and very fond of the game, remarked that he thought his football days were over.

On the same day the price of a 4lb loaf of bread was increased by ½d to 8d and the cost of milk was also increased by 1d to 5d a quart.

The bad news continued for a labourer of no fixed abode during the morning, when he appeared in Court charged with begging. P.C. Short said he saw the prisoner begging from door to door in Halford Street between four and five o'clock on Sunday afternoon. He was taken back to one house where the occupant said he had been begging for food. The prisoner was found to have food received from Wellingborough Workhouse, tea and a tramps outfit on him. Unsurprisingly, he received the standard fourteen days hard labour.

The Tribunal sat on Tuesday 22nd and heard a request from a local fruit and potato wholesale merchant for conditional exemption, on the grounds that if he went, he would have to give up his business. He was exempted until January 1st.

August 24th – George Edward Arnold (29) died of wounds.

On the day **George Arnold (29)** died, Mr. Herbert Roughton died in Northampton General Hospital. He never regained consciousness having been admitted four days earlier. An inquest held the next day exonerated the driver of the trap from any blame, the cause of the accident being judged to have been the result of excessive speed on his behalf.

At the Guardians meeting on Tuesday 29th, the shock resignation, due to his wife's continued indisposition, of Mr. and Mrs. Geo. Cook was regretfully accepted. He had served as master of the Workhouse and his wife as matron for 29 years.
Miss Allen, from Maidstone, was appointed matron's assistant, her duties commencing on September 5th.

August 27th – Percy John Holley (30) listed as missing and presumed to have died.

On Wednesday 30th, the "Thanks" section of the *Evening Telegraph* carried these words: "Mr. and Mrs. Roughton and Family, Thrapston, thank all relatives and friends for kind expressions of sympathy and floral tributes in their sad bereavement."

September

On Friday 1st, Mr. Dingley received a letter from his son's officer, Lieut. L. Hume Chidson, paying a warm tribute to Horace and adding, "I would have written to you before, but I was too grieved to write for a little."

Mr. William Smith (of Smith and Grace) was removed to Northampton General Hospital, under the care of Dr. Milligan. He had been unwell for some time.

Several little children sold buttonhole flags around town in aid of the Comforts Fund.

Thrapston Institute held its first flying billiards championship of the season on 1st. Many entered, Mr. C. Stapleton winning first prize.

A day later (2nd) news of two more men arrived in town:
Official information was received by Mrs. Parrott, of South Terrace, Market Road, Thrapston, that her husband, Pte. John Parrott, of the Northants Regt., was in hospital in Bristol with a gunshot wound in his right lung, received on August 18th. A field card was received from him on August 23rd, stating that he had been wounded and was in hospital in France. On Friday, Mrs. Parrott had a letter from him informing her that he was wounded in the chest, and had to go through an operation for the removal of shrapnel, and that if he had good luck to get through he would write again in a few days. He also said that he hoped to be home shortly. Pte. Parrott, who went through part of the South African War, enlisted in September, 1914, and went to France a year later. He was wounded in the hand at the battle of Loos, and was in hospital for some time.
Also, Mr. J. T. Bues, of Thrapston, who had not heard from his son, Pte. C. Bues, Beds. Yeomanry, for nearly five weeks, had a letter from him on Saturday morning, in which he said he was quite well, and had been in the big push for a month.

A united open-air service in connection with the coming National Mission took place in the Market Place during the evening of Sunday 3rd, conducted by the Rector. Several hymns were heartily sung, Miss Kingsford accompanying at the harmonium.

A Thrapston boys' team were reported to have beaten their rivals from Denford in two cricket matches over the weekend on 4th, winning both games, by 14 runs and 15 runs with four wickets to spare.

At the Thrapston Tribunal on Wednesday 6th, a local milkman, working on one farm, was exempted until January 1st.

The Wesleyan Church garden party and sale of work took place on Thursday 7th in the grounds of "The Hollies" in aid of a fund to paint the outside of the chapel. Many entertainments were available, including "Whistle the National Anthem" for ladies. In the evening, a concert was well attended with a variety of local acts on offer.

Saturday 9th was the day of a fund-raising parade for the Soldiers' and Sailors' Comforts Fund. Two pictures of the crowds in the Market Place and one of the "Washing Competition" at "The Shrubberies" are shown on page 63 *(all from the EDF Collection)*.

The *Evening Telegraph* reported on 11th, "The town was made quite gay on Saturday afternoon, when, under delightful weather conditions, the committee of the Soldiers' and Sailors' Comforts Fund held their second fancy dress and cycle parade. The Town Band, who

gave their services, took part in the procession round the town, and also played for dancing in the evening in the grounds of "The Shrubberies", kindly lent for the occasion by Mrs. Sanderson. In the same grounds there were various money-making attractions, in the shape of washing and guessing competitions, bowls, shooting, strafing the Kaiser etc. During the day willing young ladies and children sold forget-me-not flowers, turning "Forget-me-not Day" into "Forget them not." Amongst the results were: Fancy Dress – 1st, Aeroplane, J. Ireson.

Washing competition winners – 1st E. Frisby: 2nd A. Mayes: 3rd W. Reynolds: 4th W. Howe. A bar of soap was given to the unsuccessful competitors."

Also on 9th, Mr. W. Bygrave handed Mrs. Stothert (hon. secretary) £1 4s 6½d for the Thrapston Red Cross Branch, this sum being the proceeds of the sale of cards at the Cinema Hall.

September 10th – Hugh David Hall (31) killed in action.
The Wesleyan Church held their Harvest Festival on Sunday 10th. Gifts of produce were later sold, the proceeds going to Trust Funds.

Mr. Charles Mackness, a builder's labourer aged 55, died on Wednesday 13th. He had been ill for over two years and unable to work. He was diagnosed with an incurable cancer a year earlier but managed to get out and about until two weeks before his death. Under the care of Dr. Gainer, he passed away peacefully during the afternoon. The funeral took place on Saturday 16th.

Thursday 14th brought the news, "respecting Harold Guest, son of Mr. and Mrs. J. T. Guest, of Huntingdon Road, Thrapston, who has received two shrapnel wounds in the thigh. He is now in hospital at Stockport, near Manchester, and it is believed that, happily, he is only slightly wounded, and is going along favourably."

At a meeting of the Soldiers' and Sailors' Comforts Fund Committee, held at the Co-operative Hall on Monday evening, 18th, the secretary's report of the recent parade was presented, and considered highly satisfactory. The receipts reached the grand total of £100, and it was considered probable that after all expenses had been paid there would be a balance of £85. The committee intended to set to work at once upon the task of selecting suitable parcels for all men abroad, and to make every effort that they would reach them before Christmas. The fund had a balance to its credit at the Northants Union Bank of £112.

Tuesday 19th saw a Thrapston labourer appear before the Police Court, where he received a 5s fine for allowing a light to show at his house.

On 20th, Smith and Grace announced that they would close from Friday September 22nd to 29th in accordance with the scheme for holidays for munitions workers.

The bi-monthly meeting of Thrapston Parish Council was held at the Temperance Hall in the evening of Wednesday 20th. The full report in the *Evening Telegraph* read: "There were present: Messrs. Geo. Smith, J.P., C.C. (chairman), F. A. Cheney (vice-chairman), A. Barnett, J. Baines, A. French, A. Hensman, W. Hillyard, W. Hewitt, E. J. Loaring, J. Pashler, and T. Selby; together with the clerk (Mr. Arthur G. Brown).

According to notice given on the agenda, Mr. Baines called the Council's attention to the deposits of heaps of road sweepings, and said that there had been a great many complaints about the heaps lying in the Market Road and elsewhere. He moved that the District Council and the County Council be asked to prohibit the deposit of sweepings on the side of the road in the town as now usually done. – Mr. Hewitt seconded and the motion was carried.

Mr. Barnett (chairman of the Lighting etc. Committee) said the committee recommended that the town not be lighted during the coming winter, while the present conditions prevail – this was agreed.

Letters were received from the surveyors and engineers engaged in connection with the proposed water scheme with reference to their charges and out-of-pocket expenses. On the proposition of the chairman, seconded by Mr. Pashler, it was decided to ask the District Council to pay £20 on account.

Capt. O. Booth sent in his annual report of the Fire Brigade, which stated that eight drills had been held during the year; that the brigade had not been called to any fires; and that the appliances were in good order. Three members had joined His Majesty's Forces, viz., S. Meadows, who had been twice wounded and had lost one leg, **J. Booth (65)**, and L. Wyman. On the proposition of the Chairman and Mr. Cheney, it was resolved that a vote of sympathy be recorded on the minutes and be sent to the unfortunate man Meadows.

A printed statement of accounts for the past three years was issued to the Council, and the chairman pointed out that the total rates for the past year were 1s 7⅜d in the £, while the previous two years they were 1s 10d and 1s 11⅝d."

On the same day, local drinkers found their activities restricted. "The Order of the Licensing Justices, dated 17th November 1914, closing public-houses at 10 pm on week days and 9 pm on Sundays, now ceases to act, being entirely superseded by the new Licensing Restriction Order which comes into application on Monday, the 25th inst." This restricted opening hours and banned Sunday opening. It was enacted to discourage drunkenness amongst munitions workers and was enforced nationwide.

Finally, on 20th, the Tribunal allowed a motor cycle mechanic exemption to January 1st, whilst a motor-car body maker and a wheelwright were both given conditional exemption.

On Sunday 24th afternoon "a meeting of organised labour was held in the Co-operative Hall, presided over by Mr. C. Arnold of the National Union of Railwaymen, to consider the question of labour representation on the Thrapston and District War Pensions Committee. After a lengthy discussion, the following resolution was moved and carried unanimously: 'This meeting of members of organised labour of Thrapston and District protest against being ignored in the setting up of the local War Pensions Committee. Further, we refuse to recognise the nomination already submitted, as it is not representative of organised labour in the meaning of the Act of Parliament for the setting up of War Pensions Committees.' It was also decided that in the event of being unable to get proper recognition of labour by the above resolution to at once call a town's meeting to deal with the question."

Two meetings were held on Tuesday 26th:
The Guardians appointed Mr. Henry Elks, aged 36, and his wife as the new master and matron of the Workhouse. Mr. and Mrs. Cook were presented with a solid silver tea and coffee service and an inscribed mounted oak tray in gratitude for their service to the Union over many years.
At a farmers meeting held at the White Hart Hotel, it was unanimously agreed to hold a jumble sale in aid of the British Farmers Red Cross Fund.

On Friday 29th, a public meeting was held at the Temperance Hall to discuss appointing a district nurse for Thrapston, Islip and Denford. The meeting strongly supported an appointment and a committee was formed with power to act to bring this to fruition.

October

October began with a memorial service for **Hugh David Hall (31)** on Sunday 1st.

On 2nd, an evening meeting of the congregation of the Parish Church was held at the Co-operative Hall to consider the advisability of providing means of complying with the lighting regulations in order that evening services could be held as usual. An estimate was presented from Mr. C. R. Pettit which guaranteed strict compliance at a cost of £8 3s. This was accepted.

There were three reports on 3rd:
A labourer of no fixed abode caught begging in Islip, who had received 14 days in February, received one calendar month's hard labour at the Police Court.
During the day, Mrs. Stothert and Mrs. Pashler sold flags for the Northamptonshire Red Cross Week, raising £10 4s 8d.
In the afternoon, a well-attended meeting of the committee for the second Red Cross Jumble Sale met at the White Hart Hotel. Local butchers agreed to hire a stand and one member undertook to approach the owner of the Warboys cockerel *(which attended many charity events and was a proven aid to successful money-raising – EDF)*. Many donations of items for sale had been received, as were cash gifts. The total expected to be raised, including the proceeds of the first sale, was in excess of £1000 *(in 2012 this equates to about £43,000 – EDF)*.

The Tribunal sat on 4th, with these decisions:
A milkman working with his 70 year old father – given until January 1st.
A saddler and harness maker, who had already had six months deferment, and whose business had increased, received conditional exemption, as did a baker working for the Co-operative Society.

On Thursday 5th, this item was reported in the *Evening Telegraph*, "On the day that Mr. and Mrs. Cook's resignation was tendered to the Board of Guardians, an inmate who had been in the institution for twenty one years went up to the matron and said 'Matron, I wish to give you one month's notice to leave. I am determined I won't stop after you and the master have gone.'"

On the same day, **Charles Richardson (16)** was remembered in the "In Memoriam" section: "RICHARDSON – In ever-loving memory of CHARLES EDWARD RICHARDSON, son of Mr. and Mrs. Edward Richardson, Thrapston, who was killed in action in the Dardanelles on October 5th 1915.
'Gone from those who loved him best'."

On 6th, the Comforts Fund reported receipt of a number of letters from many Thrapston men. Amongst the writers were C. Bell, **H. Dingley (27)**, **J. E. Cobley (44)**, Lce. Corp. W. Tarrant, C. Jacques, H. H. Amos, J. Barber, E. Newman, H. Nicholls, Bernard Cooper, F. Stapleton, Knight, P. Charlton, T. W. Jeffs, J. E. Cresswell, and F. W. Beal. All were in appreciation of the kindness shown and expressed delight at the gift. In many cases, the cigarettes arrived just when the recipients were "cleared out." Pte. F. W. Beal added, "I was very pleased to receive them, as to have a nice smoke and the sound of guns very often and very close to you go together very nicely indeed, especially as now we have got so used to hear shells, whizz-bangs etc., flying about. I can tell you it was something awful when the "Big Push" was on. We had some risky jobs to do, but got through with a few casualties, considering how other regiments went under, but am pleased to say we have shifted to a quieter spot, where we can have a comfortable smoke and enjoy it."

October 9th – George William Turner (32) killed in action.

A day later, news arrived about Pte. J. E. Cresswell. He was "wounded in the right side of the neck on September 25th, and is now in hospital at Leeds. He was formerly a clerk in the service of the Islip Iron Company. He enlisted in the Hunts. Cyclists Corps, and was subsequently, when in France, transferred to the Bedfordshire Regiment."

Also on 10th, the committee of the Christmas Fat Stock Show agreed to hold the show on Tuesday December 12th. Their current bank balance stood at £35 15s 1d. Messrs. Southam & Beck, auctioneers, had offered to donate a cup or piece of plate as a special champion prize for the best beast, which offer was received with grateful thanks.

Scandal hit town on Wednesday 11th, when news about a local dignitary arrived from Lancashire. The *Evening Telegraph* reported, "At the Warrington Police Court today a woman, twenty years of age, whose name was not given, was charged under the Aliens Restriction Order with giving false information as to her name and permanent address while at Warrington.
A Thrapston man was charged with aiding and abetting her.
Defendant was represented by Mr. Herbert Woods, solicitor.
The Chief Constable explained that the offences were committed at two Warrington hotels. In one case the hotel was visited in August and it was unnecessary to supply the addresses. On Sept. 25th the male defendant went to another hotel and engaged rooms for "himself and his wife", and the male defendant assisted the female defendant in preparing the registration forms. He had suggested to her to fill in her name as his wife. The female defendant was engaged at Thrapston in a public position. There had been a certain amount of familiarity between the couple, and she was removed to Lancashire. The male defendant got into communication with her, and followed her there. Without the male defendant's guidance and help it would have been impossible for her to have carried on in the way she had done. This was an exceptionally serious case, as the girl was only twenty.
Mr. Woods denied that the defendants had to answer any charge of immorality, being charged only with a breach of the regulations passed during the war. He pointed out that the male defendant had rendered conspicuous services to the Army, having recruited 1,682 men.

The charges against the female defendant were dismissed on the application of the Chief Constable, as conviction would mean the loss of her situation.
The male defendant was fined £10 in each case, or a month's imprisonment in default.
The Bench said the case had been aggravated by the fact that the male defendant was a man of education, and had knowledge of Army regulations and civil law."

On Thursday 12th October, the concern felt by Mr. and Mrs. J. Holley, Market Road, Thrapston, for their son, **Percy Holley (30)** was reported. They had not heard from him for six weeks.

On the same day, a well-attended evening meeting of the Christian Endeavour Society was held at the Baptist Church.

The next day, Friday 13th, Rev Basil Wilberforce Stothert resigned as rector of Thrapston.

The same day brought news of three Thrapston men:
Pte. **Percy Holley (30)** was officially listed as "missing".
Pte. **Herbert Miller (33)** was reported as wounded on September 17th. He had written to his wife, Oundle Road, Thrapston, from hospital in France. Pte. Miller stated that he had been admitted on September 18th, and that he was very comfortable under the circumstances. In a letter from the matron of the hospital received by Mrs. Miller on Thursday the writer stated, "I suppose he told you that he was very badly wounded in the buttock, and also his chest is troubling him a good bit? Everything possible is being done for him, and he is in a beautiful ward."
Pte. J. E. G. Cresswell, of the Northamptonshire Regiment, youngest son of Mr. and Mrs. T. B. Cresswell of Market Road, Thrapston, had been wounded in the right side of the neck on September 25th.
Also, on 13th, there was a report of the honesty still prevalent amongst most members of the community. A cheque for £2 10s, lost on Tuesday, was soon restored by the finder, a lad, who was given 2d.
At market on the same day, two hens under eighteen months old were sold for 1s 6d each, whilst three chickens, about three months old, went for 3d each.

This advertisement for an auction *(right)*, appeared on Monday 16th in the *Evening Telegraph*.

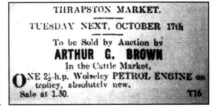

The Courts were not always out to impose the maximum sentence, as shown by a hearing at the Police Court on Tuesday 17th. A local man, lately a farm bailiff, was summoned for non-payment of a poor rate made April 1st 1916, arrears of £2 4s 6d and a special rate of 7s being due. The defendant said that he had been ill, could not pay, was out of work and had four children. The assistant overseer, giving evidence, stated that he did not think the overseers would object to the rates being excused on the grounds of poverty. The Bench agreed, also remitting the costs.

Elsewhere in town, October Fair Day took place on 17th, accompanied by the traditional rain, with the usual stalls. During the afternoon, the secondary schools closed so the children could join in the proceedings.

On Wednesday 18th, Mr. Geo. Johnson, of Huntingdon Road, Thrapston, received official notice from the Canadian Record Office, London, that his youngest son, Pte. Herbert Johnson, of the Canadians, was at No. 14 General Hospital, Wimereux, suffering from a gunshot wound to his legs. On Tuesday Mr. Johnson had a letter from his son, who wrote from a Birmingham Hospital, to which he had recently been removed. Pte. Herbert Johnson had been in Canada for ten years, and came over with a Canadian contingent about twelve months previously. He came home to Thrapston on leave the previous Christmas.

Two days later on 20th, reports that **George William Turner (32)** was missing and that, as all the other members of his relief party were killed when a shell hit them, it was likely that he, too, had not survived.

October 23rd – Herbert Miller (33) died of wounds.

On the same day, the Tribunal decided on these exemptions:
An ostler and bus driver – December 1st – final exemption.
An engine driver, two carpenters and a cycle maker – January 1st.
A bank cashier – February 1st.
A garage proprietor and a carpenter – April 1st.

That evening, a whist drive for the Farmers Red Cross Jumble Sale Fund realised £12.

On Tuesday 24th, the Guardians met. They decided that, owing to the war, no elections would be held next March. The House Committee was delegated the responsibility to consider the three applications for the position of charge nurse and to make an appointment, whilst the laundry woman was awarded a pay increase from 2s to 2s 6d a day. Finally, 871 vagrants had passed through the Workhouse over the previous three months, at a cost of 9d each.

The Rural District Council also met on 24th, where the Thrapston surveyor, Mr. Lloyd, was given a salary increase of £30 to £100 pa.

October 25th – George Alfred Langley (34) killed in action.

The Farmer's Jumble Sale took place on Wednesday 25th. The Warboys cockerel was present with its owner, and the total proceeds from the day exceeded £900. At the sale of final items, a robe and crown worn by Gunner **J. W. Guest (42)**, Machine Gun Corps, at the Thrapston Coronation festivities in June 1911 raised 5s 6d.

On Saturday 28th, a meeting of the Games Committee was held at the Institute. Mr. J. W. Stubbs was unanimously elected games secretary until the end of the year, in place of Mr. J. C. Lavender, who had joined the colours. The number of serving members of the Institute serving was 32. The winner of the flying billiards handicap on Oct. 25th was Mr. F. Dartnell. There were twenty entrants.

The month ended with a local labourer appearing before the Police Court charged with riding his bicycle at 5.25 am without a lighted lamp on a public highway. He initially told the Police that the lamp had just gone out and was believed, until closer inspection showed no lamps at all. Despite this untruth, he received the standard 5s penalty.

November

On Friday 3rd, Mrs. Meadows, of Oundle Road, Thrapston, received a letter from the matron at No. 9 General Hospital, B.E.F., dated Oct. 27th, respecting the death of her second son, Pte. **Herbert Miller (33)**, of the Surrey Regiment, who had been wounded some weeks earlier.

The matron wrote, "I am very sorry I can only give you the worst news. Your son died at 7am, 23rd October... He was very patient, and for a long time I hoped he was getting better. He was very badly wounded in the back. Everything possible was done for him, and he was in a beautiful ward... He was buried in St. Sevora Cemetery, Rouen, on the 25th, with military honours."

Thrapston Post Office announced that it was now closed daily from 12.30 to 1.30.

The County Tribunal met in Northampton to hear military appeals on 3rd November with these local decisions:
A baker, aged 26, employed by his father had his exemption reduced by one day to January 31st.
A 31 year old stereotyper had the military appeal dismissed on technical grounds.
A 32 year old man appealed on the grounds of exceptional hardship on his mother. Five sons had died from consumption; he was the only surviving child and had returned from America to look after her. The appeal was dismissed. The appellant then said "Then they will have to fetch me: I shan't go, I'm willing to work, but I'm not going for my mother's sake. They'll have to fetch me!"

On 4th, this advertisement appeared in the *Evening Telegraph*:
"Required in Thrapston, a sitting-room and a bedroom for District Nurse.
Applications to be sent to Mrs. Waller, Manor House, Islip."

Thrapston Tribunal met on Thursday 9th.
An auctioneer and valuer, a cabinet-maker and undertaker, a chauffeur and a horseman and delivery driver were all exempted until January 1st.
A machinist was given until March 31st.

During the evening of 9th, the Wesleyan Church arranged a "high-class" concert in the Co-operative Hall to raise funds to pay the annual Circuit assessment. The acts included a pianist, violinist, elocutionist and vocalist.

On 10th, Mrs. Holley received this letter, "No. 602, Pte. W. Miles, 1st. Hunts Cyclists' Batt., Red Cross Hospital, Spilsby, Lincolnshire. Dear Mrs. Holley, - I have just picked up a paper saying your son is missing. I hope by the time this reaches you you will have heard of him. I was with him the whole time he was in France. The night before we went into action I slept with him in a small dug-out we cut in a bank about a mile behind the line. There were him and me, and a chap named Lake; we had given each other our home address in case anything happened to us, but I got wounded, and they cut my clothes off me, and I lost your address. Your son went up the line with me, but I lost him when the order came to charge, but I wrote a letter to him and to the chap named Lake yesterday, so perhaps Lake may be able to tell you something about him; that is if he isn't knocked out himself. We were badly cut up; I never thought for a minute that I should ever come out alive, it was awful. I may say your son was a splendid soldier. I was taken ill while we were marching up the line, and he carried my rifle and pack for miles for me, and he looked after me day and night until I was better. He was the best mate I ever had or ever shall have. The night before we charged we were both on gas patrol: we had to patrol up and down looking for and listening for gas alarm. We were both talking and thinking of home, but he always kept cheerful, no matter where he was, and never grumbled. Please excuse this scribble, as I am all of a shake from shock, and I'm not at all well. It was six weeks last Sunday since I was wounded. Well; I think I must close, hoping you will hear from him very soon. – Yours, W. Miles."

For a change, some good news arrived on 11th, being reported in the *Evening Telegraph*.
"PROMOTIONS FOR THRAPSTON MEN
Two sons of Mr. J. Ireland, Halford Street, Thrapston, have recently been promoted. Quartermaster-Sergt. Herbert Ireland, Royal Engineers (sixteen years in the Army, and since August 15th, 1914, in France), has been given the rank of sergeant-major: and Sergt. David Ireland, R.F.A. (seventeen years in the Army, twelve in India, and for some time past at Salonika) has been made quartermaster-sergeant. Another son, Pte. Charles Ireland, is in the City of London Volunteers."

The same newspaper carried a report on a recent meeting of the Thrapston C. of E. School managers, when Miss K. F. Modlen was appointed as a temporary teacher for the infants' school.
Miss W. E. Ward had written to resign her position on December 31st. She had taught there for fifteen years and was wished every happiness in her future married life.

Sunday 12th was the Baptist Church's Choir Sunday. The pastor, Rev. H. Ellis Roberts, conducted the morning and evening services. At the end of the evening service, Mr. C. Freeman jun, who had been the voluntary organist for two years, was presented with £5 as a mark of appreciation as he left to join the colours. His replacement was Miss M. Roberts, the pastor's daughter.

The Institute held a whist drive on 13th in aid of their own funds.

A local man, Thomas Layton, was admitted to Northampton Hospital on Wednesday 15th having sustained a broken arm through a runaway horse.

This advertisement appeared on Thursday 17th:
"To Let. Superior apartments for board-residence; good cooking and attendance.
Apply, "Evening Telegraph" Office, Thrapston."

The Tribunal met on the same day and allowed a carter exemption until April 1st, as his wife had tuberculosis.

On Saturday 18th, the Red Cross Working Party held a very successful sale of work at the Co-operative Hall, raising a total of £7 6$ 8½d for both national and local funds.

The C. of E. School appointed Miss May Hornsby to replace Miss Ward on Monday 20th.

Amongst the names in the Casualty list announced on 21st was:
Missing – Royal Warwickshire Regiment – Parrott T. J. 20810 – Thrapston.

The Guardians met on 21st, when they were informed that Mr. and Mrs. H. Elks had taken up their duties as master and matron on Tuesday 7th.
The same meeting also heard that Miss Clowes, from Ellesmere, Cheshire, had been appointed nurse at the Infirmary and had commenced her duties on 11th.

At the County Tribunal in Northampton on Thursday 23rd, a motor mechanic was given until January 1st and an auctioneer a final exemption until February 1st.

This advertisement appeared in the *Evening Telegraph* on the same day:
"£19 extra profit from the same number of hens in six months was made by one poultry-keeper who added Karswood Poultry Spice, containing ground insects, to the soft mash. 2d, 6d, 1s. Hensman, Bridge Street, Thrapston."

A report of the death of **George Langley (34)** appeared on Friday 24th November in the *Kettering Guardian*.

On the same day, the *Evening Telegraph* reported on the Comforts Fund. "The committee of the Thrapston Soldiers' and Sailors' Comforts Fund, as a result of the parade, etc. held in September (when nearly £100 was cleared), had a busy evening on Monday last, when they met to pack the parcels for the boys at the front. The committee relied on almost the same contents as last season. These included ½lb chocolate, two ½lbs of biscuits, tin of cocoa and milk and sugar mixed, box of Spearmint, tin of Oxo cubes, tablet of toilet soap, tin of nit ointment, one pair of socks, two khaki handkerchiefs, ¼lb peppermint sweets, laces, flash lamp with spare battery, etc. In all ninety parcels were packed."

A further report appeared on 27th, "The committee, in addition to sending parcels to the Thrapston soldiers at the front, wisely decided to send to the sailors, and also to men in hospital, money equivalent to value of the parcels, viz., 11s. It was also decided that cigarettes and tobacco to the value of 2s 9d should be sent from bonded warehouses (free of duty) to all men, so that they should enjoy a smoke in addition to the parcel; also that all men in training at home should receive a substantial cash gift."

Mr. Reuben Cotton died in his 84th year on Wednesday 27th. He had lived in Thrapston for 38 years, where he carried out a successful boot and shoe manufacturing business. He was a regular attendant at the Parish Church, where his funeral took place the next day.

Two married women appeared before the Police Court on Thursday 28th charged with Lighting Offences. One, who forgot to draw the blind was fined 2s 6d. The other, who was looking after her ill husband and failed to draw the blind quickly, received a caution.

Two local criminal cases were also heard:-

A 14 year old boy, employed by a marine stores dealer, left his round with the money and was seen by his employer in Kettering the same day. He was arrested and sent to the Workhouse, from where he escaped. He said that he was trying to get back to his mother in Luton. He was brought to Court by his mother, who told the Bench that her husband, who was in the Army, was a brute. The boy pleaded guilty to the offence. As he had no previous convictions, the Bench dealt with him leniently, binding over him and his mother in the sum of £10 for twelve months.

The final case was of a young married woman charged with stealing two £1 notes and one 10s note from her father-in-law. Her husband was serving in the Army and she had two children to care for. After pleading guilty, she was fined £1.

On Thursday 30th, in the Temperance Hall, Thrapston, a well-attended public meeting was held in furtherance of the scheme for raising a company of the Northamptonshire Volunteer Regiment for Thrapston and district. The representative audience included a number of farmers, tradesmen, etc., some of whom had exemption under the Military Service Act, and much interest was taken in the proceedings. The top table comprised:- Col. Stopford Sackville, J.P., C.A., presiding, supported by Lieut. Col. Willoughby (Daventry), Capt. R. B. Wallis, J.P. (Kettering), Major Nightingale (Oundle), and Mr. F.J. Porter (Thrapston), who, by the desire of the Officer Commanding, had called the meeting. Others present included Mr. G. E. Abbott, J.P. (Islip), the military representative at the Thrapston local tribunal; Mr. T. S. Agutter (Islip), and Mr. F. J. Steward (Brigstock), (members of the Thrapston local tribunal); Mr. E. Waller (Islip), Mr. Gurney Coombs (Oundle), Dr. Gainer, Mrs. R. J. P. Humphrey, Mr. C. Modlen, Mr. H. Varah (Thrapston), and others.

After many speeches exhorting the merits of forming a Volunteer Regiment, it was agreed to form one and volunteers sought. Twenty-five men signed up at the end of the meeting.

I addition, just for a change, a committee was formed to look after the company's formation, comprising Mr. Porter, Dr. Gainer, and Mr. G. E. Abbott who were asked to act as a temporary committee to get gentlemen from the different villages who would form an executive committee.

December

Friday 1st December was the first time "war bread" was delivered to householders in town. Neither in appearance nor in taste did it differ much from ordinary bread.

Mr. Ellson was very anxious about his son, Pte. M. Ellson, Middlesex Regiment. In response to enquiries, he received an official reply on 1st, dated November 29th. This stated "I am directed to inform you that his name has not appeared in any casualty list yet received in this office. I am to add that if your letters to him are not being returned it may be presumed that he is still serving with his unit."

The *Evening Telegraph* reported on Saturday 2nd that, "last month was one of the wettest Novembers on record".

Mr. Edward Tarry, Midland Road, Thrapston, died aged 74 during the evening of Wednesday 6th. In 1879, he was appointed to Thrapston as Police Inspector, retiring in 1894. His wife pre-deceased him by six years. His funeral was on 11th.

On Thursday 7th, Pte. Harry Spencer, 2nd Northants Regiment, youngest son of Mrs. William Spencer, of Wadenhoe, and his bride, Miss Elsie May Jeffs, second daughter of Mr. and Mrs. J. P. Jeffs, Victoria Terrace, Thrapston, were married at Thrapston Parish Church. The bridegroom was home on short leave from the front. (*Picture from the Kettering Leader, Friday 22nd December 1916*)

The Rural District Council met at the Workhouse on 7th, where Mr. W. Beal was appointed veterinary inspector at a salary of £75.

Responses from recipients of the Comforts Fund parcels were reported on Saturday 9th in the *Evening Telegraph*:
"Mr. William Stobie, the indefatigable hon. secretary of the Thrapston Soldiers' and Sailors' Comforts Fund has received a large number of grateful acknowledgements of gifts recently forwarded. We can only find space for a few brief extracts: - W. Jacques: "I hope the aristocracy of little Thrapston will help you in your good work." Pte. W. B. Smith: "Anything like your parcel is a great change out here, as we don't have much chance to buy anything like it." A mother: "Will you please accept my thanks as a mother of a boy that will reap the benefit." Sec.-Lieut. John R. Pettit A.S.C.: "Life is very hard out here, especially in the winter, but it raises one's spirits wonderfully when one finds that our friends at home do not forget us." T. W. Jeffs: "It rained when we got back from leave, and it was raining for about three weeks, but still we get over it; but it was rough." W. H. Brown: "Such acts of kindness brighten up these distressing times quite a lot." Percy Charlton: "Have had a very bad foot, but it is getting on fine now." **W. Guest (42)**: "I am the only Northamptonshire lad in our

company, and I am envied by a good many of the other boys." Hector H. Morris: "For miles and miles around us it is practically up to our knees in mud and slush; but never mind, we are on the winning side." Fred Rowlett: "At present we are resting in a village, but suppose we will be on the move again shortly."
Sec.-Lieut. M. G. W. Hunnybun writes: "I only wish every man in my platoon had the good luck to come from Thrapston, and be entitled to receive such a gift. Thrapston may be a small place, but the inhabitants have jolly big hearts." H. Baker: "I have been six months in France, and have not had a wound, so I think I have been very lucky." G. Waters (writing from a Kent hospital): "I am sorry not to have acknowledged it before. At the time I received it I was just going under another operation. I don't know how they will finish up with me; I'm not getting on so well as I thought." Arthur Morris: "There is nothing a "Tommy" appreciates more than a good substantial, all-round, parcel – one he can tuck into and come again." E. A. Dingley: "Notwithstanding the conditions under which we have to labour, I am pleased to say I am keeping in good health and spirits, and trust that it is likewise with you all." F. W. Beal: "Well, be of good cheer. Wish them all a Merry Christmas and a prosperous New Year." C. Bell: " I was ill in hospital when the parcel came, and the contents were divided among the boys, so it did good." W. Thurlow: "I have been in hospital over twenty weeks now. I may say my arm is getting on very nicely, but it's a slow job."
Equally thankful acknowledgements have also been received from: - C. W. Shadbolt, E. Munds, R. March, C. Frisby, W. Wright, **J. E. Cobley (44)**, J. A. C. King, F. G. Cobley, T. H. Throssell, Fred Holley, H. Nicholls, J. Nickerson, "Sep" *(probably **Septimus Leslie Ferrar (51)**)*, H. H. Amos, C. G. Ferrar, E. H. Longfoot (for her husband), G. Herby, "A Thrapston Bird", S. Gilbert, **J. Booth (65)**, J. Herby, R. Horn, G. Winsor, A. Green, J. Barber, and Sid."

On the same day, Mrs. R. J. P. Humphrey, of Belmont House, Thrapston, received a telegram informing her that her husband, Capt. R. J. P. Humphrey, 1st Northants, was in hospital in France, with malaria and jaundice. Four days later, she heard that he was in the Fishmongers Hall Hospital, London.

Also on 9th, an advertisement was placed by the Thrapston Union inviting tenders from bakers and butchers to supply goods from January 1st.

On Tuesday 12th, a labourer of no fixed abode appeared before the Police Court. He pleaded guilty to a charge of begging. The magistrate asked him why he was not working, to which the prisoner replied that he could not because he was not fit to work. Possibly in a gesture to help his fitness level, he was sentenced to double the usual penalty for begging – one month hard labour.

The 12th was also the date for the twenty-first Christmas Fat Stock Show, held at the Cattle Market. This had been cancelled the previous year, and entries were down on the last show, 45 beasts, 25 sheep and 15 pigs being entered. Many visitors from throughout the county had an enjoyable time. At midday, the sale of live and dead poultry attracted keen bidding. The champion beast was sold for £61 15s.

Finally on 12th, a Special Meeting of the Board of Guardians was called to discuss a replacement relieving officer. In the interregnum, Mr. Cook, the late master, offered temporarily to undertake the role, which offer was accepted.

Rev. Henry Edward Fitzherbert was formally appointed the new rector of Thrapston on 13th and was expected to begin his new duties early in the New Year.

Two local cases came before the Tribunal on 13th. A shepherd received conditional exemption, whilst a builder was given a final exemption until January 31st, to give time for him to complete a contract.

A full house attended a concert at the Temperance Hall, raising funds for the Red Cross.

Friday 15th saw the announcement that Miss Okey, sister of Mrs. G. Cook, the late matron of Thrapston Workhouse, had been awarded the War Medal granted for distinguished services rendered in France. Miss Okey was invalided home with rheumatism contracted in winter 1915, and returned to light duties in Wales during the week the announcement was made.

The *Evening Telegraph* reported on Saturday 16th, "Mrs. W. Fletcher, who as Miss Essam, was for a number of years an ardent and faithful teacher in the Baptist Sunday School was recently, on the occasion of her marriage, presented by her fellow teachers with an electro-plated teapot."

A lengthy meeting of the Board of Guardians occurred on Tuesday 19th:
The clerk reported that official intimation (on a magistrate's order) had been received from Northampton requiring the Guardians to receive into the Workhouse a vagrant about to be released for breaking windows at a doctor's surgery in Thrapston. The clerk said that if the man stayed at the Workhouse, and he did not think he would, inquiries would be made into his place of settlement. However, as he was a vagrant, he was not very hopeful of success.
Mrs. Knight had resigned as assistant matron, Miss F. Headland being appointed as replacement with a salary of £22.
Mrs. Jakins, the laundress, had also resigned and Miss Hewlett, the under-laundress, was promoted into the position.
A Rural District Council meeting followed directly and agreement was giving to increases of pay to roadmen and the engine driver by between 1s and 2s per week.

A day later, the Parish Council met:
They agreed to apply to the proper authorities for permission to light a sufficient number of streetlights to render the town a safer place, there having been a number of minor accidents at night.
Mr. L. Thompson, caretaker at the sewage works, was given a pay rise of 3s, to 28s a week.

The Police Court on 20th heard just one case, as was often usual, for begging, with an unsurprising 14 days hard labour resulting.

On Friday 22nd, Mr. T. D. Morton, High Street, was working at Messrs. Smith and Grace, scraping a pulley, when a piece of metal entered his right eye. He was seen by Dr. Gainer and promptly removed to Northampton Hospital where, after an operation, it was hoped his eye might be saved.

Christmas Day saw the usual activities around town. The Parish Church held a number of services, the 8.00am one having a very large congregation. The Wesleyan Church held a short morning service.

The usual festivities took place at the Workhouse. There were 65 inmates, 30 being in the Infirmary, and six vagrants, four of whom stayed for the day. The meals, treats and entertainments were very much appreciated.

On Thursday 28th, it was announced that, by means of a penny guessing competition, Mrs. Jeffs, of Victoria Terrace, Market Road, had raised 10s in aid of the Thrapston Adult School Fund for parcels for soldiers serving abroad. The prize was awarded to Miss Mabel Rowlett. On the same day, she heard that her son, Pte. W. Q. Jeffs, was in hospital in France suffering from trench fever.

In 1916 Thrapston lost 14 men and the town witnessed its first military funeral of the conflict, that of **John Samuel Smith (26)**. The infamous Battle of the Somme claimed eight men, five of whom are recorded on the Thiepval Memorial in Picardy, France, to those with no known grave *(pictured below, 2010 – EDF Collection)*, whilst the only major naval battle of the war, at Jutland, claimed another casualty. Dark days were still ahead before cessation of hostilities and many were still to suffer the pain of the "official letter".

1917

January

The price of bread was raised from 9d to 9½d a loaf on the first day of the New Year.

On Tuesday 2nd, a special meeting of the Thrapston Guardians was called to appoint a relieving officer, vaccination officer and collector for the Union. Twenty-five applications were received, Mr. Thomas Boyden being the successful candidate.

Three days later, the County Tribunal, sitting in Northampton, heard the Military Representative ask for a review of the exemption granted a Thrapston stereotyper. This was shortened by a month to March 1st and was announced as the final one he would receive.

During the afternoon of Sunday 7th, two aeroplanes descended in fields adjoining Huntingdon Road, Thrapston, and remained for about half an hour. A large number of people went to see them.

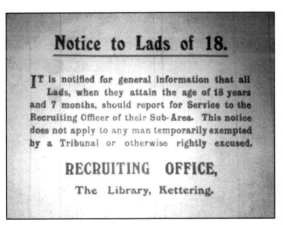

The advertisement *(shown left)* appeared in the *Evening Telegraph* in the second week of the year. The on-going need for recruits was forever expanding the eligible age both upwards and downwards.

Wednesday 10th marked the fourth annual children's fancy dress party of the Thrapston Habitation of the Young Helpers' League (Dr. Barnardo's Homes) held at Nene House Schoolroom. Almost 90 people attended. After judging the fancy dress entrants, there were various musical games and performances. A total of £4 was raised.

The *Evening Telegraph* printed a number of items on Tuesday 16th:
Train alterations had necessitated local postal alterations. First delivery would now commence 20 minutes earlier, whilst second delivery would begin at 2.00 pm rather than 10.40 am as previously.
A former Thrapston signalman, Mr. Wm. Morley, had retired due to ill-health from his position as stationmaster at Grafham. He was signalman in town between 1882 and 1887.
The Thrapston Guardians met and amongst the items discussed were-
The master's book recorded that "On Sunday January 7th, a sacred play entitled "Three Roses" was given by Mrs. E. Waller and party in the dining hall, and was greatly appreciated by the old people." The thanks of the Board were recorded.
There was some discussion about the relative costs of inmates and vagrants. There was general agreement that vagrants were, in fact, a source of some profit, their task of sawing logs for sale before being allowed to leave easily returning the 11d cost of provisions they had to give each vagrant on leaving.
Finally, the deputy clerk, Mr. Dellar, was recommended to the Local Government Board for an honorarium of £15 to thank him for all the extra work he had done to help the Guardians through a very difficult period.

At a hearing of the Thrapston Tribunal on Wednesday 17th, seven local men each received short periods of exemption.

The *Evening Telegraph* carried this notice *(left)* on 18th advertising the sale by auction of the effects of the previous rector, Rev. B. W. Stothert and the recently deceased Mr. Reuben Cotton of Oundle Road.

The forthcoming marriage of Rev. Cecil Kingsford, youngest son of the late Rev. S. Kingsford (for many years the town's rector) to Miss Mary Crick from Peterborough was announced on 18th.

On the same day, the second annual general meeting of the Thrapston and District Rifle Club was held at the Rifle Range in the evening. Mr. G. V. Charlton was re-elected chairman for the year. The accounts showed a deficit of £19 9s 4d, almost £3 less than the previous year. 31 members were serving with the Armed Forces. The meeting ended with the presentation of medals and certificates to the winners of various competitions.

The funeral of Stephen John Kirby, aged 40, who had died on 15th, took place at the Baptist Church followed by burial in their burial ground on Saturday 20th.

At the weekly Thrapston Market auction sales on Tuesday 23rd, Mrs. Walter G. Brown took the sales in the poultry, butter and egg departments *(shown right - Kettering Leader, Friday 9th February 1917)*. Her husband was due to leave for military service and Mr. Arthur G. Brown (auctioneer), in introducing her said "Mrs. Brown has pluckily agreed to help with her husband's work whilst he is away. She will now commence to sell from the rostrum... show her the utmost courtesy and respect in this novel position." Considerable enthusiasm was shown to purchase the first lots in each department. The first couple of fowls made 14s, the first score of eggs 5s and the first pound of butter 4s 8d.

The local Tribunal on 24th granted short periods of exemption to a local milkman, motor mechanic and motor engineer.

On the same day, Mrs. Coates, Bridge Street, widow of William Coates, builder and contractor for over 40 years, died at home. She had come to Thrapston 60 years previously when she was married. The funeral took place at the Wesleyan Church on Saturday 27th followed by burial at Oundle Road Cemetery.

On Friday 26th at the Annual Meeting of the Thrapston Institute, Mr. H. A. Hurrell, the hon. secretary, reported that annual membership fees amounted to only 15s 3d less than last year, although they had lost 10 more members, making 35 since the war commenced. They had done remarkably well with the four public whist drives held, the proceeds of one being given to the local Soldiers' and Sailors' Fund (£3 17s 1d.).

The *Evening Telegraph* carried an interesting report on Saturday 27th about the London explosion on January 19th *(when the Brunner Mond chemical factory in Silvertown, London, was destroyed. It processed TNT for munitions. 73 people were killed and soldiers in France heard the explosion – the Government denied that it happened at Woolwich Arsenal or was the result of German activity - EDF).* It appeared to have been felt in Thrapston as, just before 7 o'clock on 19th, a lady resident noticed the dining room windows shaking violently, there being no wind at the time or any other obvious cause. As it was so unusual, they specifically noted the time. It was concluded, when news of the explosion came through, that a probable cause had been identified.

February

At the beginning of the month, it was very cold. During the previous few days, a considerable number of people took advantage of the opportunity for skating in the meadows.

(An earlier picture of flooded meadows is shown above – dated circa 1908, it shows Midland Road and the side of the Gas Works. No publisher is named, but it is possibly by Frederick Knighton from Kettering – EDF Collection).

The induction of Rev. H. E. Fitzherbert as rector of Thrapston took place on Saturday 3rd at St. James' Church before a large congregation.

At the Thrapston Police Court on Tuesday 6th, Mr. Wm. Loasby was sworn in as a special constable. Supt. Tebbey presented his annual licensing report; the White Hart, Thrapston, had ceased trading during the year, as had three other licensed premises in the district. Renewal of the licence for the King's Head, Thrapston, was adjourned.

Later on the same day, the funeral of Mrs. Rogers, widow of Mr. John Rogers, for many years the Thrapston representative of Messrs. Phipps and Co., brewers, took place at the Parish Church, followed by burial at Oundle Road Cemetery.

During February, the Government had a big push to raise money for the war effort. Advertisements such as this *(Evening Telegraph)* appeared throughout the country.

The Tribunal sat again on Wednesday 7th. Exemptions of between one and three months were granted to two agricultural workers, a stone dresser working as a miller, and a carpenter and joiner.

This advertisement appeared in the *Evening Telegraph* on Thursday 8th:-
"Wanted. Grocery and Provisions – Experienced all-round Assistant and Canvasser: Good wages and permanency.
H. and C. Tomlinson, Thrapston."

Mr. Enoch Cole, Oundle Road, died during the evening of Saturday 10th aged 83 years. For many years, he worked on the Drayton Estate as a carpenter and joiner.

At the meeting of the Thrapston Guardians on Tuesday 13th, Messrs. Pashler and Cheney, coal merchants, asked if, as they had lost so many of their employees to the military, there were any inmates with experience of working with horses and deliveries who they could employ as coal carters. The Guardians regretted they were unable to assist, as most of the inmates were over 70 years old.

February 17th – Joseph George Morley (37) killed in action.

The Police Court heard the case of a local man who was summoned for trespassing on a willow bed adjoining the London and North Western Railway on 27th January. The defendant

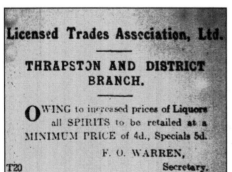

was seen crossing the fence, carrying a gun and entering a willow bed. All access to railway-owned land had been forbidden by the military authorities. The defendant disputed ownership of that piece of land and the case was adjourned for this claim to be investigated.

The Court also granted the King's Head their licence to continue trading. Unfortunately for local drinkers, the notice shown left appeared on the same day in the *Evening Telegraph*, raising the price of liquors.

The Thrapston and District Branch of the Northamptonshire Farmers' Union held their annual general meeting at the White Hart Hotel on Tuesday 27th, about 40 members attending. After electing officers for the forthcoming year, there was much debate about the minimum wage of 25s a week for agricultural labourers. Should this be for a 57 hour week by the worst employee, with enhancements for the more able, and what extras, if any, should be payable for overtime and the harvest? There was also debate about costs associated with tied cottages, and how the new wage structure would affect rents. The only conclusion reached was the necessity to get as many farmers as possible to join the Union to give weight to members who were going to lobby Parliament.

At the County Court on Wednesday 28th, two local business men, E. R. Midgley, grocer, and E. J. Loaring, clothier and outfitter, were given judgement with costs against the former rector, the sums owed being £25 17s 3d and £1 10s 10d respectively. The defendant had tried to raise sufficient to cover these debts by selling his possessions *(see page 78)* with only partial success. He was now engaged in military duties in Essex.

March

On Tuesday 6th, the *Evening Telegraph* carried a report about Mr. and Mrs. Morley and family, Swan Hotel, Thrapston, who had received a letter concerning their son, Joseph. "March 1st, 1917. Dear Madam – having received a parcel containing eatables addressed to Pte. Morley, of this battalion, the contents were divided amongst the remaining men of his platoon, as P. O. regulations do not allow us to return parcels containing food. – I am, yours truly, 12784 J. C. Tite, Sergeant, Northants, B. E. F." The report continued:
"Having regard to the wording of this letter, it is hoped that no very serious news is implied, and that reassuring information may soon be received. The last communication from Pte. Morley was a field card in February 16th. On leaving Kettering Grammar School, a little over three years ago, Pte. Morley entered Barclay's Bank at Grimsby, where he made excellent progress. He joined up in August last, and was in France a fortnight before Christmas. His

numerous friends, both in Thrapston and Grimsby, will sincerely hope to get news that he is safe and well."

Rev. C. E. B. Kingsford, son of the late rector, was married in Peterborough on 10th *(picture from the Kettering Leader, Friday 16th March 1917)*.

Confirmation of Mr. and Mrs. Morley's worst fears was received from the War Office on Thursday 15th with notification of his death in action.

On 19th, a public meeting was held at the Temperance Hall, Thrapston, to promote the formation of a War Savings Association for the town. The *Evening Telegraph* continued:
"Mr. G. E. Abbott, J.P. *(pictured on page 82, Kettering Leader, Friday 27th April 1917)*, of Islip (a member of the County War Savings Association, and acting in conjunction with the National War Savings Association), presided over a moderate attendance, and there was also on the platform Miss Ada Thirsk, of the National War Savings Association. The chairman said they all very much regretted that Mr. Geo. Smith, as chairman of the District Council, was not able to be present to take the chair. The work of war savings associations had been well taken up in neighbouring towns and villages, but for reasons which were known to most

of them there had been a difficulty and delay in regard to Thrapston, and there had been no association there up to the present, although one knew very well that many people in Thrapston had done all in their power to help on the movement. He believed there were still greater sacrifices before them all, but he believed they would rise to the height of those sacrifices. Miss Ada Thirsk, in a very informative address, explained the details of the scheme, which are now generally known. Having spoken of the advantages and safety of investments, the speaker turned to the patriotic side, and said they did not put their patriotism down at 5 per cent.

The Rev. H. E. Fitzherbert moved that they form an association for Thrapston. It was a very desirable thing. Much had been done; still, much remained to be done. – Mr. Pashler seconded, and it was carried unanimously.

Some questions having been replied to, the following officers were elected: Secretary, Mr. F. W. B. Emery; treasurer, Mr. S. C. Ainsworth; chairman, Rev. H. E. Fitzherbert; committee, Rev. H. Ellis Roberts, Mrs. A. Smith, and Mr. O. Griffiths."

On Friday 23rd, this appeared in the Announcements section of the *Kettering Leader*:
"MR. and MRS MORLEY and Family, Thrapston, desire to thank all friends for kindness shown and expressions of sympathy for the loss sustained by them in their bereavement."

Two days later on Sunday 25th, the morning service at Thrapston Parish Church on Sunday was largely of the nature of a memorial service for the late **Pte. J. G. Morley (37)**, youngest son of Mr. and Mrs. J. Morley, of the Swan Hotel, Thrapston. The family, who had attended a celebration of the Holy Communion at eight o'clock, were present, and there was a good congregation. The hymns were "On the resurrection morn", "O God, our help in ages past", and "For all the saints who from their labours rest."

The rector, the Rev. H. E. Fitzherbert, preached a very appropriate sermon from the text "That we, being delivered out of the hands of our enemies, might serve him without fear all the days of our life." At the close of the service, Miss Kingsford played the "Dead March", the congregation standing.

April

A middle-aged labourer of no fixed abode appeared before the Police Court on Tuesday 3rd charged with begging in town on 31st March. He had left the Workhouse that morning after breakfast and was carrying sufficient food for the day. He had eleven previous convictions for begging and two for being an incorrigible rogue. He received one month's hard labour.

A day later, the Diocesan Inspector's report on the C. of E. School was published, stating:
"Very good work appears to have been done throughout the school. I was especially pleased with the interest and intelligence shown in Standards I and II. Both classes of infants are being very suitably taught but a supply of good pictures would be helpful. The general condition of the school is very satisfactory."

The following names were included in the local soldiers Official Casualty list reported in the *Kettering Guardian* on Friday 6th:-
"Killed – Northants Regiment
    Private J. G. Morley (37) - Thrapston
    Private E. Pateman – Thrapston *(Edmund Pateman from Slipton - EDF)*.
    Private E. Waite – Thrapston *(Ernest Waite from Little Addington - EDF)*.

Josiah Boulter, Halford Street, died on 7th aged 57 years. He moved to town 30 years previously and worked as a moulder at Smith and Grace until his health began to fail. He worked for Mr. Selby, butcher, then set up his own pork butcher business. His last few weeks were spent bed-bound and he died of heart trouble and bronchitis. He left a widow and no children. His funeral took place at the Wesleyan Church on 12th followed by burial in Oundle Road Cemetery.

A concert was given in the Co-operative Hall by Miss Leigh and Miss Marks on 10th to raise money for the Church Sunday School.

John Wright, Oundle Road, was reported missing from home after leaving work to go for a walk on Friday 13th. He had been seen near the River Nene and a search was made, to no avail, except for the discovery of his cap on the river bank.

On Saturday 14th, the rector announced that he might have to go away, having been accepted for whole time National Service. He said that he only wanted to go where he would be of most use to the war effort. The vestry thanked him for his patriotic offer, but would be very sorry to see him go.

A recent fund-raising effort was reported on Friday 20th. "Another successful effort to provide cakes, etc., for wounded soldiers at Duston Military Hospital had been organised and carried through by Mrs. Geo. Smith, of "The Hollies." As a result of a house-to-house collection, 23 large cakes, four dozen small cakes, and eight tins of fruit, etc., were sent to the hospital, and the sum of £3 15s 6d was forwarded to Mrs. Wentworth Watson of Rockingham Castle, to be spent for the soldiers."

On 27th news reached Mr. H. H. Bletsoe, auctioneer of Thrapston, that his son Lieut. T. Bletsoe was reported wounded in France. Lieut. Bletsoe, who had obtained his commission a year before, was serving at the time he received his wounds as an observation officer attached to the artillery. News also arrived on the same day that Mr. Eric St. Clair Gainer, of the Seaforth Highlanders, younger son of Dr. J. W. Gainer, of Thrapston, had been gazetted second-lieutenant.

On 29th and 30th, a renewed search of the River Nene was made for Mr. Wright. Water was drawn off as much as possible, although the depth was still 8 or 10 feet in many places. Despite a thorough search, nothing was found.

Mr. Marshall Meadows of Oundle Road died of influenza and pneumonia on 30th, aged 65 years.

At the end of the month, the *Parish Magazine* stated, "The rector has now heard that the Bishop wishes him to stay in the parish for the present."

May

Mr. Wright's body was found on May 1st. Two women spoke to Inspector Campion in the afternoon about spotting something floating downstream near Rarum Bridge. A small group of men accompanied the Inspector and found him near Duck Spinney, close to the railway line. His body was recovered and taken to the Mason's Arms to await an inquest. This took place the next day when Dr. Bird reported that the cause of death was drowning and there were no marks of violence. A verdict of suicide whilst temporarily insane was recorded.

A party of boys from Dr. Barnardo's Homes gave two concerts at the Co-operative Hall on May 3rd, which were well attended. The admission charge and collection monies were donated to the homes.

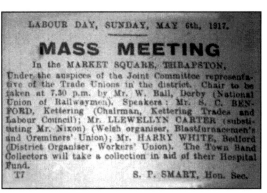

This advertisement appeared in the *Evening Telegraph* on 3rd May 1917.

Friday 4th brought news of two men:
Pte. R. Fetch, Northants Regiment, of Thrapston (lately a postman), who was recently wounded in the thigh and hip, was making good progress in Chichester Hospital, and was able to be wheeled out in a bath chair.
Lieut. T. Bletsoe, recently reported wounded, was badly wounded in the thigh. A telegram was received on Thursday stating that he had been brought to England and was in hospital in Dover. A week later, he was in Shooter's Hill Hospital.

The County Tribunal heard appeals for two men employed by Smith and Grace on 4th. A 28 year old carter was given one month's exemption whilst an 18 year old turner received a final two month exemption.

Band Sunday took place on Sunday 6th. At 9.00am they formed in Oundle Road, marched to the Adult School and then went to the Wesleyan Church for the morning service. In the afternoon, a procession formed in the Market Place, comprising the band, Fire Brigade, Oddfellows' and Foresters' Societies, National Union of Railwaymen, Postmen, St. John Ambulance and Police, amongst others. They marched to the Parish Church where the rector spoke. In the evening, they attended the Baptist Church. The total amount raised was £19 2s 11d which was given to the Northampton and Peterborough Infirmaries.

The Thrapston Tribunal gave the following decisions when they sat on Monday 7th:
A clothier and outfitter received three months exemption.
A 31 year old plumber received two months.
An 18 year old printer was refused any exemption.

The Guardians met on 8th May when Col. Stopford Sackville was unanimously re-elected as chairman. Apart from re-electing various committees, the only other business was to renew their subscription to the Ringstead Nursing Association.

This notice appeared in the "In Memoriam" section of the *Evening Telegraph* on Wednesday 9th:-
"TEMPLEMAN – In ever loving memory of Pte. **Richard Templeman (14)**, Northants Regt., son of Mrs. Templeman, Huntingdon Road, Thrapston, killed in action at Aubers Ridge, May 9th 1915.
Gone but not forgotten."

The Thrapston Education Sub-Committee met on 11th, where attendance figures for all schools in the district were reported. Thrapston Council School reached 86%, a slight fall on the previous year. School holidays for the coming year were approved.

The Thrapston War Saving's Association Committee met on the same day, attended by the Rector (chairman) and Messrs. W. Bygrave, O. Griffith, G. Warner and F.W.B. Emery. It was

decided to ask all local bakers to make 1lb. loaves to facilitate the public obtaining their requirements. It was also resolved to ask teachers at the day schools to get the children to attend school without their lunch. *(It was not reported whether the committee were also prepared to forego their own lunches! – EDF.)*

Also on 11th, the picture *(shown left)*, of an unknown Thrapston lad, undergoing training wearing his gas mask, appeared in the *Kettering Leader*.

The advertisement *(shown below)* appeared in the *Evening Telegraph* on Friday 18th. *(I have been unable to find out whether there was any local take-up – EDF.)*

This letter appeared in the same newspaper on Saturday 19th:-
"SHIRKERS IN THE THRAPSTON DISTRICT.
Sir. – I have read the correspondence in the "Evening Telegraph" re Thrapston shirkers and should like to say a few words. I have lived in the Thrapston district some few years now, and I know the greater part of the people, especially the tradesmen, and I consider it wrong to call Thrapston men shirkers. They are, in my opinion, not shirkers, but it is the Tribunal that I complain of. When some large firms are allowed to get their single men, and also their young married men, a good exemption, whilst smaller tradesmen have to lose their older men, and in some instances have themselves to close down, with only a month or two final exemption, I consider it a great mistake, or otherwise an oversight. Let us have fair play, and put some of these young men in the Army without ruining so many business men. – Yours truly, A TRADESMAN – Thrapston, May 17th."

NATIONAL SERVICE.

250 WOMEN CLERKS

Wanted every week

For Service in France.

To Release Men for the Front.

These women will be employed as clerical workers, general clerks, typists and shorthand writers.

Successful candidates will wear khaki uniforms, live in hostels under comfortable conditions, and receive payment at fixed rate. Age limit 20-40.

Selection Boards are being held at Birmingham to-day, to-morrow, and at frequent intervals, and application forms and conditions of service can be obtained from Miss Bebb, Woman Commissioner, Union Offices, Edmund Street, Birmingham.

WOMEN ENGAGED IN GOVERNMENT DEPARTMENTS OR CONTROLLED FIRMS SHOULD ONLY APPLY WITH THE WRITTEN CONSENT OF THEIR EMPLOYERS.

On Sunday 20th, Mr. J. T. Bues, of Market Road, Thrapston, received a letter informing him that his fourth son, Sapper J. H. Bues, of the Royal Engineers, had been wounded in the head and was in hospital in France. It appears that he was buried by a shell explosion, but was promptly rescued. A little over twelve months before he was wounded in the neck by shrapnel.

On 22nd, with the object of stimulating interest in the Thrapston Volunteers and obtaining more recruits, a Market Day meeting was held at Thrapston. Col. Stopford Sackville, J. P., of Drayton House, presided (first on right), and was supported by Lord Lilford (centre). Col. Eunson, in command of the 2nd Battalion Northamptonshire Volunteer Regiment (left) also addressed the gathering *(picture from the Kettering Leader, Friday 25th May 1917).*

On Wednesday 23rd, a report appeared about the escape of Pte. Bernard Cresswell, R.A.M.C., who was on a transport ship which was torpedoed by a German submarine on April 15th. He wrote, "I was very lucky and never even got a scratch. The bit of swimming came in handy, thanks to the old Low Shot *(pictured right in 1906 – EDF Collection)*... I was in the water for about 4½ hours, hanging on to a piece of wood before we were picked up by a French ship. We had ten days rest, then came to Egypt". His two brothers were also serving in Egypt. *(Censorship did not allow the location of the sinking to be reported although it was probably in the eastern part of the Mediterranean Sea – EDF.)*

Mr. Walter Freeman, of the firm of Messrs. Freeman and Webb, Midland Road, Thrapston, received official news on Wednesday morning, 23rd that his eldest son, Gunner Charles W. Freeman (No 1 Section, No 167 Company, Machine Gun Corps), had been wounded in France behind the right shoulder by a piece of shell, on May 17th, and was in hospital. Before joining up a few months previously, Gunner Freeman was the organist of Thrapston Baptist Church.

A recent house-to-house collection, taken by the Thrapston Red Cross Working Party, was reported on 26th to have raised £11 7s 9d.

A further report appeared on Saturday 26th, concerning acknowledgements received from men for parcels received. As previously, I include the full report:
"A large number of grateful acknowledgements from Thrapston men for parcels sent out by the Thrapston Soldiers' and Sailors' Comforts Fund Committee have been received by the devoted hon. Secretary, Mr. W. Stobie, Midland Road. The recipients write in cheerful and very appropriate terms. Amongst the writers are Corpl. Norman A. Cotton, R. E., motor-cycle despatch rider, Mesopotamia; Pte. A. Green (M. G. Corps) who is ill in bed after an operation for appendicitis, but is going on well; Pte. A. Crofton, who was wounded by shrapnel in the ankle about four hours after receiving his parcel, and has been through an operation and had a piece of shrapnel about an inch long taken out; Bernard Cooper A.B.; Sergt. W. Bishop (Leicestershire Regiment) who has been in the thick of the advance; a Northants Yeoman, B Squadron ("Sid"); Fred J. Holley (R. E.); F. W. Jeffs; Walter Read; **G. Johnson (49)**; C. W. Shadbolt; **Corpl. S. Wright (59)**; Pte. S. Guest; **Corpl. J. E. Cobley (44)**; G. S. Gill; H. H. Morris; Sapper J. Nickerson; H. Ireland; C. S.; M. B. E.; J. W. Bues; Pte. H. Guest; Pte. J. Baker; Pte. E. H. Short and Pte. G. Herby."

At an egg service, held at the Parish Church on Sunday afternoon, 27th, conducted by the rector (Rev. H. E. Fitzherbert), "the children brought 260 eggs and with others collected by the egg collectors and purchased with money subscribed, a total of 480 eggs have this week been sent away for wounded soldiers."

During the afternoon of Tuesday 29th, a very heavy thunderstorm with torrential rain and hail, occurred. A great many shops and houses were flooded whilst some houses in nearby villages were struck by lightning.

June

On Friday 1st, the Northampton Tribunal made the following decisions:
A 35 year old clothier and outfitter had the finality of his exemption removed, as also did a

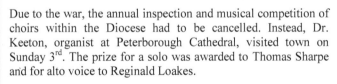

general engineer and plumber, aged 38.

Due to the war, the annual inspection and musical competition of choirs within the Diocese had to be cancelled. Instead, Dr. Keeton, organist at Peterborough Cathedral, visited town on Sunday 3rd. The prize for a solo was awarded to Thomas Sharpe and for alto voice to Reginald Loakes.

A report appeared in the local press on 4th concerning Sapper J. H. Bues. His father had recently received a letter saying that he was progressing satisfactorily at a base hospital in France.

The Board of Guardians met on 5th at the Workhouse. Amongst the many agenda items were:
A 13 year old girl absconded and was found in Kimbolton. She was subsequently discharged when her parents undertook to look after her.

Dr. W. Mackenzie *(shown above, Kettering Leader, Friday 20th July 1917)*, from Raunds, had tendered his resignation as Medical Officer, due to poor health. Instructions were given for the vacancy to be advertised.
A subscription was made to the Thrapston and District Nursing Association.
The matron's salary was increased from £30 to £40 per annum.

Also on 5th, there was an evening meeting of the Thrapston and District Free Church Council, which had been revived. The general feeling was that the town's churches would need to co-operate with each other to ensure that the post-war reconstruction, both physical and spiritual, was effective. There was acceptance of a need to work on their differences and look for common ground.

On 6th, Miss Doris Hillyard, oldest daughter of Mr. And Mrs. W. Hillyard, Laburnum House, married Mr. Harry Childs of Chatteris at the Parish Church *(picture from the Kettering Leader, Friday 15th June 1917)*.

The Thrapston Police Court sat on the same day. Thomas Fuller, of no fixed abode, appeared charged with begging in Halford Street. The prisoner was asked his destination, which was Peterborough, and on promising to leave town immediately, he was discharged without penalty.

These advertisements appeared in the *Evening Telegraph* on 7th and 8th June.

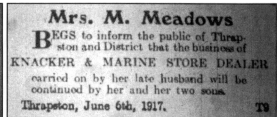

The Rural District Council meeting on 7th included this report:
"HIGHFIELD ROAD THRAPSTON:

Highfield Road, Thrapston

The following letter, with ten signatures, was read – "Gentlemen, - The owners and residents of Highfield Road, who pay rates and taxes, draw the attention of the District Council to the road and footpath, and want to know if something can be done in the matter. The footpath was put down by the owners of the houses at their own expense five years ago and nothing has been done to it by either Parish or District Council; the only thing the Parish Council have done was to place a standard gas lamp on the road, and all we ask is reason and fair play as ratepayers." During the discussion, it was mentioned that the road was a private road, and that there was no

through communication; further, that there was a gateway across the road. – It was resolved to reply that the road was not a highway but a private road, and that therefore the owners must make arrangements."
(The picture shown on page 88, taken later, shows the gas light and general state of the road and footpath. No publisher is named on the original postcard - EDF Collection.)

Rev. Michael Hughes, Northampton, preached the Thrapston Baptist Church Sunday School's annual sermons on Sunday 10th. The services were well attended and collections for Sunday School funds amounted to £7 3s.

This advertisement for Baby Week appeared on Wednesday 13th.

In addition, on 13th, the Thrapston Tribunal sat and amongst many cases, the following Thrapston men were considered:-
A wheelwright, aged 40, was granted conditional exemption, as was a 38 year old motor body builder.
A printing works manager, aged 41, received three months, whilst a deaf market gardener, aged 39, was allowed six months.
Finally, the Workhouse master was granted conditional exemption.

BABY WEEK

(JULY 1—7)

" The race marches forward on the feet of little children"

" Spare that fly "— and risk the well-being of your child !

It is not enough to kill flies : you must strike at the root of the evil. By destroying household refuse daily you destroy the fly's favourite breeding-ground.

Now that the clean and economical Gas Cooker has replaced the coal range, it is necessary to instal a Gas Incinerator in order to dispose of refuse economically and hygienically.

Examination results from Thrapston Evening School (held in connection with the Union of Educational Institutions) were published on Monday 18th:-
Bookkeeping: Elementary, Mabel M. Waite (Class 2, 50 marks), Gladys E. Gifford (Class 1, 77 marks), Phyllis E. Coleby (Class 2, 50 marks).
Shorthand: Elementary, Thomas James (Class 2, 63 marks), Mabel M. Waite (Class 2, 51 marks), Mabel I. Rowlett (Class 2, 69 marks). Intermediate, Gladys E. Gifford (Class 1, 85 marks).
Mr. E. Streather, of Oundle, was the teacher in both subjects.

On Wednesday 20th, the funeral of Mrs. Bone took place at the Parish Church and Oundle Road Cemetery. A full report was printed in the *Evening Telegraph* two days later and is reproduced below:-
"THRAPSTON BEREAVEMENT. Yeoman on Service Loses his Wife.
Sincere regret and sympathy have been evoked by the death of Mrs. Bone, wife of Staff-Sergt.-Major Bone (Northants Yeomanry), and eldest daughter of Mr. W. Winter, of Oundle Road, Thrapston, which took place at Bournemouth on Saturday morning last, at the early age of twenty six.
The deceased, who was well known and respected, was married about four years ago. At that time her husband (who had been through the South African War) was carrying on business as a butcher at Titchmarsh, and at the commencement of the war he went into training with the Northants Yeomanry, to which he belonged, and shortly afterwards left for France, where he has attained the rank of staff-sergeant-major. For some time past the deceased had been residing with her father. Last Christmas she contracted a very bad cold, which developed into

influenza, followed by bronchitis, and she gradually got worse. Her relatives thought a stay at Bournemouth might improve her health, and it was her earnest wish to go, because her youngest sister had derived so much benefit by a visit. Accordingly she was taken to the Royal National Sanatorium at Bournemouth about five weeks before her death, but unfortunately it was found on her arrival that the trouble was too far advanced to hope for a cure. Consumption had developed and she daily got weaker. On Friday evening last her father was with her from four o'clock till nine. She was then quite conscious and able to converse, and was conscious at the last, the end coming at six o'clock next morning. Her husband had been telegraphed to, but the telegram took some days to reach him, being delivered to him in the trenches, where he had just done seventeen days' duty. Consequently he was not able to arrive home until Tuesday morning. It may be mentioned that deceased was passionately fond of music, which gave her pleasure to the last. She leaves one child aged three years.

The funeral was on Wednesday afternoon, the service, both at the Parish Church and in the Cemetery, being conducted by the Rector, the Rev. H. E. Fitzherbert. The mourners were: Mr. W. Winter (father), Staff-Sergt.-Major Bone (husband), Miss Olga Winter (only surviving sister), Mrs. Popple, Peterborough (aunt), Mrs. R. A. Sanderson and Mrs. J. L. Mash, Thrapston (sisters-in-law), Miss Coales (Thrapston), Miss Carr (Kettering), and Mrs. Panter (Kettering)."

A day later, the annual Government inspection of Police took place with a parade in the Corn Market. After the inspection, the Police Station was visited and the books examined. Everything was found to be satisfactory.

On the same day, Leonard Smart, a child, 4 or 5 years old, was running to get into line for assembly at the Church of England School when he slipped and broke his right thigh. This was set by Dr. Bird and the boy was later said to be cheerful.

Notification that Pte. E. F. Parker, A.S.C., M.T., of Church Villa, had received a leg wound on June 8th and was in the 30th General Hospital, B.E.F. was received on 24th June. Before enlisting, he was chauffeur to Colonel Stopford Sackville of Drayton House.

Pte. Rupert Baker was mentioned in a press report *(pictured right, Evening Telegraph, Tuesday 26th June 1917)*. It read:
"A GALLANT "CANADIAN" FROM THRAPSTON
Pte. Rupert Baker (formerly of Thrapston), of the 7th Battalion, Canadians, who has been in hospital at Southport, visited Thrapston prior to proceeding to a convalescent home on the South Coast. His father and mother, Mr. and Mrs. J. T. Baker, and their family, of Huntingdon Road, Thrapston, emigrated to Canada about six years ago, and Mr. and Mrs. Baker have a farm at North Edmonton, Alberta, where they are doing well. Soon after the outbreak of the war Rupert joined the 63rd Canadian Battalion, and was afterwards transferred to the 7th Battalion. He has been in France a little over twelve months, and has been twice wounded: first on the Somme,
with shrapnel in the right arm; and secondly, at Easter, at Vimy Ridge, serious shrapnel wounds in the right shoulder and back. From the latter injuries he has fortunately made a good recovery. In addition to wounds, he has, like so many of our gallant lads, had wonderfully narrow escapes. He has three brothers serving, all in the Canadians."

On Wednesday 27th, several Huntingdon Road residents heard booming, which resembled distant cannonading. This lasted for about an hour. At least two people reported windows rattling slightly. *(It is possible that this was caused by the massive artillery barrage that occurred during the Battle of Passchendaele – the sound was certainly heard in London, and could well have affected town windows – EDF.)*

On 28th, a vagrant appeared before Thrapston Police Court charged with begging. He had previous convictions for the same, having received one month's hard labour in Derby and two weeks in Stony Stratford. Although able-bodied, he had not worked for a long time. He received one month of hard labour.

On Saturday 30th, Lieut. S. E. Buckley of the Northamptonshire Regiment and Royal Flying Corps *(pictured right, Kettering Leader, Friday 6th July 1917)* was received by the King. In December 1915, Lieut. Buckley was reported missing, the War Office report stating, "Aeroplane was seen to land a short distance behind German lines. There is a possibility that the pilot and passenger escaped being killed".

Lieut. Buckley was the son of Dr. T. W. Buckley, Clopton Manor, for many years a resident of Thrapston.

July

The July issue of the Baptist Church Magazine recorded, "We regret to learn that Pte. G. W. Brown has been seriously wounded. – our young friend **Kenneth Smith (64)** is now a cadet of the R.F.C."

The monthly Parish Magazine stated, "We would draw the attention of all our readers to the rough draft of our Roll of Honour now in the church....It is proposed that the Roll of Honour should be in book form, so that other names may be conveniently added from time to time if necessary; while, should a more costly memorial be put up at the end of the war, this book could be put away in the safe with the other parish records – an enduring record for posterity."

Mrs. Parker received a further letter from France, reported on 2nd, informing her that it had been necessary to amputate her husband's left leg on June 27th.

This advertisement appeared in the *Evening Telegraph* on 2nd:
"WANTED. TO BLACKSMITHS.
Wanted – Blacksmith to manage small shop.
C. R. Pettit & Son, Builders & Contractors, Thrapston."

The recent Raunds Wesleyan Methodist Circuit quarterly meeting was reported on Tuesday 3rd. There was a possibility that Rev. Harry Shaw, the Thrapston minister, could be leaving and steps were agreed to secure a possible successor, should the need arise.

The Thrapston Guardians met on the same day. There was lengthy discussion about proposals from the Boundary Commission who were suggesting a reduction in the number of Northamptonshire Parliamentary representatives from seven to five. It was agreed not to submit any proposal to the Commission.
Dr. McInnes was appointed medical officer.
Increases in pay were agreed for the master and matron of the Workhouse. and the laundress.

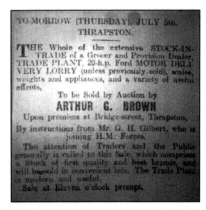

TO-MORROW (THURSDAY) JULY 5th.
THRAPSTON.

THE Whole of the extensive STOCK-IN-TRADE of a Grocer and Provision Dealer, TRADE PLANT, 20-h.p. Ford MOTOR DELIVERY LORRY (unless previously sold), scales, weights and appliances, and a variety of useful effects,

To be Sold by Auction by
ARTHUR G. BROWN
Upon premises at Bridge-street, Thrapston,

By instructions from Mr. G. H. Gilbert, who is joining H.M. Forces.

The attention of Traders and the Public generally is called to this Sale, which comprises a Stock of first quality and best brands, and will be sold in convenient lots. The Trade Plant is modern and useful.

Sale at Eleven o'clock prompt.

The advertisement shown left appeared in the *Evening Telegraph* on 4th July 1917.

On Friday 6th, Mr. and Mrs. Philip Stearne placed a notice in the "Thanks" section of the *Evening Telegraph*. It read:
"Mr. and Mrs. Philip Stearne thank from the bottom of their hearts those kind friends who helped their son Jack in his recent illness, and especially the Committee who organised a collection on his behalf, and for their sympathy in their great loss."

On Tuesday 11th, the Police Court heard an application for the temporary transfer of the licence of the King's Arms from Robert Payne to Harry Sanders, of Titchmarsh. The applicant was of military age with an exemption certificate to July 31st. The Bench retired to consider their decision. On returning, they stated that they were not prepared to transfer a licence to a man who was only exempt from service until the end of the month.

The *Evening Telegraph* reported on 11th, "The committee of the Thrapston Soldiers' and Sailors' Comforts Fund (hon. secretary Mr. W. Stobie) have just despatched another lot of comforts to the Thrapston men now serving. Parcels have been sent to those at the front to the value of £32, and also parcels equivalent in value to men in hospital. There are 81 men in France, 14 in Salonika, seven in Egypt, four in India, one in Mesopotamia, and four sailors; and there are 15 in hospital from wounds or sickness."

The Tribunal convened on 11th, with these decisions affecting local men:
A 39 year old married boot repairer was given until October 31st, conditional on him joining the Volunteer Training Corps.
A 35 year old single postman, blind in one eye and restricted sight in the other had been reclassified B2 after twice being rejected. He was allowed one month's final exemption. *(B2 meant free from serious organic diseases, able to stand service on Lines of Communication in France, or in garrisons in the tropics and able to walk five miles to and from work, see and hear sufficiently for ordinary purposes – EDF.)*
A 26 year old single motor mechanic, general engineer and driver, who was the only skilled agricultural motor mechanic in town was given six months.
A 21 year old builder was exempted until January 1st.
A 37 year old bank cashier and clerk received 3 months final exemption.

On Sunday 15th, the 10th anniversary of the Thrapston Men's and Women's School was celebrated, the speaker being Mrs. Staley from Northampton.

On the same day, Mr. A. Berridge of Oundle Road, employed by Islip Iron Co. Ltd., was thrown off a wagon during the evening, fracturing his collarbone. He was taken home in Mr. Smith's motorcar and attended to by Dr. Bird.

On 16th, the Institute held a billiard handicap of 200 up during the evening. The final was contested between Mr. J. Fletcher and Mr. Theo Smith, the latter winning by 200 – 199. Third place was taken by Mr. S. Jones who defeated Mr. I. French by 21 points. The highest break prize was taken by Mr. E. Abbott (34 points).

On the same night, a crocheted table-cloth, made by Mrs. T. Nichols of "Fair Lawn", Thrapston, in aid of Red Cross funds, was won by Miss Evelyn Smith. Tickets had been on sale for 1s and £5 was raised for the cause.

Northamptonshire County Council met on Thursday 19th, when Mr. Walter Askew, a farmer from Denford, was unanimously elected member for the Thrapston Division, replacing Mr. George Smith who was appointed Alderman.

Thrapston Council School managers met on the same day and amongst the business discussed was:

Mrs. Newman, Huntingdon Road, had been appointed caretaker on a salary of £20 pa.

It was decided not to break up for the summer holiday a week later than planned, on account of the harvest being predicted to be earlier than the previous year.

A list of recipients of attendance medals and certificates was agreed. Council School medals were awarded to Sidney Booth, Ivy Dingley, Gladys Frisby and Arthur Perkins. Certificates went to William Bygrave *(pictured left, with thanks to Mr. Aubrey Bygrave, Cogenhoe)*, Ernest Mayes and Horace March. No medals were awarded at the Church of England School, although certificates were given to Harry Bues, Ernest Dingley and Gerald Wilson.

Finally, an application by a mother to keep her 13 year old daughter at home, her attendance having reached the required level, for housework duties, was refused.

The *Evening Telegraph* carried this item, again on 19th:

"Thrapston in 1737. The following is an extract from "A Tour through Great Britain" by a Gentleman, 5th edition, published in 1753 (four octavo volumes): Thrapston is delightfully situated in a fine valley and surrounded with a rich soil and well watered. It has a fine bridge over the Nyne; but not eminent either for trade or buildings; though it will probably soon change its face by virtue of an Act passed for making the Nyne navigable; which had had so good an effect that, when I was last there, the 17th of November, 1737, on that very day boats were brought up to Thrapston for the first time, which occasioned much joy in the town. Here also is a most beautiful range of meadows and pasture, perhaps not to be equalled in England for length. They stretch uninterrupted, from Peterborough to Northampton, which is near 30 miles in length and in some places near two miles in breadth – the land rich, the grass fine and the cattle which feed on them hardly to be numbered."

On Friday 20th, the Tribunal sat:

Frederick W. Dix, a champion skater and member of Thrapston Harriers, who ran a smallholding and laundry in Raunds, had exemption extended to 30th September. He had previously joined the Army as a motor driver during the early days of the war. After passing his driving test, he was offered 2s 4d a day pay, but refused it and obtained a discharge from service.

A 38 year old plumber and engineer was given three months exemption.

On Saturday 21st, the annual flower and produce show of the Thrapston Institute was held. There was a good attendance and over 100 entries. Various competitions and attractions helped raise between £5 and £6 for the Red Cross.

Whilst this was going on, the quarterly meeting of the Thrapston District Bellringers took place. After electing officers, the 30 members attending then spent two hours ringing in St. James' Church tower.

The *Evening Telegraph* reported, on the same day, that Dartford Grammar School O.T.C. *(Officer Training Corps – EDF)* were forming a camp under the National Service scheme during August to help farmers with the harvest. The camp was to be held at a field opposite Thrapston House and the boys, aged between 16 and 18, would be available to farmers within a 4 mile radius, for between 3d and 4d per hour. Applications were to be made to the rector, hon. secretary of the local Food Production Committee.

Cawdell's announced their Summer Sale with this advertisement *(left)* in the *Evening Telegraph* on Saturday 21st.

Sunday 22nd was a special day for one lady. The *Evening Telegraph* reported, a few days later:

"Thrapston Lady Celebrates 99th Birthday.

Mrs. Jane Jarvis, Thrapston's oldest inhabitant, who lives with her son–in–law and daughter, Mr. and Mrs. Wm. Jeffery of South Terrace, celebrated her ninety-ninth birthday on Sunday. She enjoys very good health, is able to get up and down the garden with assistance, and eats her food with a relish.

On Sunday she got up as usual about eleven, and did not go to bed till nearly nine. There was no family party, but some grandchildren and other relatives came to see her. For dinner – (private details are pardonable on such an auspicious occasion) – she enjoyed her dinner of meat, young potatoes, green peas, and pudding; and at tea a birthday cake made by a granddaughter at Titchmarsh was duly appreciated by the old lady; while before retiring for the night she had a glass of beer and a slice of bread and butter. She loves to listen to the gramophone, and some hymn tunes on Sunday afforded her pleasure.

Her mind seems clear, and although she cannot see to read she still employs herself at times in cutting up pieces of cloth and other material for rug-making etc. A number of grandsons and great-grandsons are in H.M. Forces, and she has lost one grandson. She talks a lot about the war, and hopes she may live to see it over and her grandsons (including Mr. and Mrs.

Jeffery's two sons – one in Egypt, and the other in Salonika) and her great-grandsons safely home again."

The 26th annual show of the Thrapston and District Shire Horse Society took place on 26th July, presided over by Lord Lilford. Entries were described as satisfactory, 41 horses being shown. During the day, the first ever accident to occur during the show happened to

Edward Green, from Islip. He was kicked in the face by a mare, receiving serious injuries. Dr. Gainer attended to him and he was taken home by motorcar. The Champion horse, Orfold Glendoyne, is shown in the picture on page 94.

Also on 26th, Mr. E. J. Loaring, of Huntingdon Road, Thrapston, received a letter from his son, **Pte. W. J. Loaring (39)**, of the 20th Fusiliers (Public School Corps), stating that he had been wounded in the thigh and was in hospital at Paignton, South Devon, and that he was progressing favourably.

July 27th - Gerald Lenton (38) died of wounds.

Thrapston Co-operative Society held their annual treat for children of members on Saturday 28th. About 350 children attended, and were all given tea at the Co-operative Hall and Wesleyan Sunday Schoolrooms. Afterwards they went to the Society's fields on Huntingdon Road for games and races. As they left, all children were given a bun.

The Thrapston Industrial Co-operative Society held a half yearly meeting in their hall on Monday 30th. Sales had increased by £1,220 2s 2d over the last six months, producing the usual dividend of 2s in the £. 34 new members had joined, whilst 13 had left; the total membership was 510. Between January and June, 57,261 2lb loaves had been baked.

On the last day of the month, Mr. Arthur Brown, auctioneer, held a land sale at the White Hart Hotel. Over 10 acres of rich pasture land, situated between Titchmarsh and Clopton was sold for £925.

August

The August issue of the "Wesleyan Magazine" confirmed that Rev. Harry Shaw *(pictured right, Kettering Guardian, Friday 16th November 1917)* would be moving to Rushden and would be replaced by Rev. J. Lewis Gillians.

The "Parish Magazine" included this item:
"ROLL OF HONOUR
 We find that a permanent Roll of Honour in book form would be very expensive at the present time, owing to the high price of vellum. It will be wiser to wait until the end of the war to have this completed, so that there need be no alterations, or unnecessary space left for additions: but a temporary list is being arranged, which will be in the church for August 12th."

On Thursday 2nd, the *Evening Telegraph* carried news of Signaller W. Bishop, Leicestershire Regiment, of Thrapston who wrote from Queen Mary's Military Hospital in Whalley, Lancashire. "I have been invalided over suffering from trench fever, contracted at Bullecourt on June 16th, through lying out, stench and fumes. I am still in bed and have already had three weeks there. I am getting on slowly and the doctor tells me it will be the same time before I am well... I have been in three hospitals in France".

Also on 2nd, the Tribunal sat, with these decisions:
A 36 year old married butcher and a 37 year old married fishmonger and poultry dealer whose wife was ill, both received three months exemptions.

Finally, the Thrapston Habitation of the Young Helpers' League held a sale of works and tea at "Nene House" in aid of Dr. Barnardo's Homes. Poor weather caused the cancellation of outside activities. There were 59 junior members and 8 adults. During the previous three years, they had raised £100 for the cause.

Forget-me-not Day, set for Saturday 4th, had to be postponed to later in the month due to inclement weather.

August 4th - William James Loaring (39) killed in action.

On Monday 6th, it was announced that all 26 boys enrolled in the Thrapston Company of Boy Scouts had passed their "tenderfoot test". 21 of them left town on that day at 9.15 am and marched to Catsworth, arriving at noon. Several fields were made available to them for scouting and drill purposes, courtesy of Mr. John Pashler. Leaving at 5.00 pm, they returned via Hunt's Close and Keyston, reaching home at 8.00 pm.

On Thursday 9th, the *Evening Telegraph* carried two reports of local interest:
Between Sunday night, July 29th and Friday morning, August 3rd, 2.12 inches of rain were recorded in town.

Lord Lilford had arranged for a motorcar to pass through a number of villages on Wednesdays to collect vegetables for the Kettering V.A.D. and District General Hospitals. It would be at the Parish Rooms in town at about 10.00 am to receive donations.

The *Evening Telegraph* on Monday 13th carried this report:
"The services at the Parish Church on Feast Sunday were appropriate to the present war conditions, and due recognition in prayer, hymn, and sermon was paid to those who are fighting for their country, and to those who have already fallen in the conflict. The early celebrations were largely attended, there being 83 communicants at the seven o'clock service, and 41 at the eight o'clock choral service. Preaching to a large congregation at the morning service, the rector (the Rev. H. E. Fitzherbert) took his text from the story of the rich young ruler, "What lack I yet?" (St. Matthew xix., 20). Having referred to the dedication of their church, he spoke of the need of entire dedication of ourselves to God's work if we were to make our country a better one for our soldiers to return to. At a children's flower service in the afternoon there was a good gathering of children, with a few friends. A laurel wreath was placed by the rector on the Roll of Honour, and in an interesting address to the children he dwelt on the words of St. Paul (1st Cor., ix, 25); "Now they do it to obtain a corruptible crown; but we an incorruptible." At the evening service there was a crowded congregation. The choir (with Miss Kingsford at the organ) very nicely rendered an anthem, "What are these that are arrayed in white robes?" The preacher was Rev. J. T. Paddison, vicar of Blidworth, Notts (the rector's late vicar) – who had assisted at the morning celebrations – who based his discourse on the 67th Psalm. The collections during the day were for church expenses, the flowers for the Thrapston Workhouse and eggs brought by some of the children in lieu of flowers for the Red Cross." After the evening services on 12th, a large number of people gathered in the Market Place for an open-air service.

The Wesleyan Sunday School annual treat took place on Monday 13th, starting with tea at Thrapston House. Later, they went to the field opposite *(now the Peace Park – EDF)*, where games took place. As part of this, a cricket match between the teachers and senior boys was played with the teachers being victorious.

August 16th – Leonard Throssell (40) killed in action.

The annual Feast Week garden fete took place in the Rectory grounds on Thursday 16th. Owing to official requests for food economy, the usual public tea was dispensed with. Proceedings began at 4.30 pm, light refreshments being available. Many attractions were on offer and a good attendance raised a total of £83 6s 11d. The money was donated to the Red Cross (75%) and the rest to St. James' Church for church purposes.

On the evening of 16th, the Thrapston Company of Volunteers had a route march under the watchful eye of Sergt.-Instructor Corbett. They went up Kettering Road, through Drayton Park to Lowick and back home via Islip.

The recently formed Thrapston and District Trades and Labour Council met in the Co-operative Hall in the evening of Friday 17th. Mr. Bygrave (Thrapston) and Mr. Wadsley (Denford) proposed, "that the Council approves of the appointment of Mr. S. P. Smart as a Labour representative on the Local Food Control Committee, but are of the opinion that one representative of Labour is inadequate and submits the following names: Mr. F. W. Johnson and Mr. W. T. Hewitt as additional Labour representatives." The motion was carried unanimously.

On Saturday 18th, Mr. E. J. Loaring, outfitter, received the sad news of the death in action of his son **William James Loaring (39)**.

On Monday 20th, an application by Thrapston Parish Council to the Ministry of Food to sell about ½ acre of growing potatoes was granted.

At the Police Court on 21st, a labourer from a nearby village was charged with neglecting to maintain his four children, aged 12, 10, 5 and 2, who were in the care of the Union. He was given two weeks to make arrangements with the Board of Guardians to either agree payment for their continued care by the Board or to make a home and remove them.

The *Evening Telegraph* reported harvest prospects for the Thrapston district on 23rd. "The harvest is now in full progress. Wheat promises to be an average crop and barleys are generally good, but oats are below average. Winter beans are very short and in the majority of cases have to be pulled. Spring beans (very moderate quantity in this district) are up to the average. Potatoes appear very promising. The hay harvest is practically completed; the latter portion was gathered under the very heavy conditions as regards weather; and the crop is not up to the yield of last year."

On 24th, Mrs. Throssell received news of the death of her son **Leonard Throssell (40)**.

On Saturday 25th, these reports were printed in the *Evening Telegraph*:
"Sudden Death. An old man named William Mayes, who had been an inmate of Thrapston Workhouse for a good many years, has died suddenly. He went to bed as usual on the night of 22nd and next morning at six o'clock was found dead in one of the lavatories. He had been suffering from an internal complaint and had been attended by Dr. Gainer, and on the facts being reported to the coroner, it was not considered necessary to hold an inquest. The deceased, who was 73 years of age, had been a very useful man in the gardens and also, latterly, for errands."

The new minister of the Wesleyan Church was confirmed as being Rev. J. Lewis Gillians. He was to commence his duties on September 2nd *(pictured left, Kettering Leader, Friday 31st August 1917).*

The same day was the 3rd Annual Fancy Dress Parade, organised by the Thrapston Soldiers' and Sailor's Comforts Fund. Many people both took part and watched. Takings were estimated to have reached about £100.

Two more reports from Monday 27th:
The coroner had been informed about the death of Mrs. Mary Ann Newman aged 84, wife of Mr. Benjamin Newman, Huntingdon Road. She was admitted to the Infirmary on 18th with an injury to her head. She was seen by Dr. Gainer over the weekend, being unconscious for most of the time. On Sunday, she did not know her relatives when they called and she died shortly after midnight.

Mrs. George Smith had arranged another collection of cakes and other foodstuffs for wounded soldiers at Duston Hospital. Money, totalling £3 11s, was sent to the district organiser, Mrs. Wentworth Watson, Rockingham Castle to purchase further cakes etc.

News arrived in town on 27th concerning Gunner Fred Leete, Royal Field Artillery, of Halford Street. In a letter home, he said: "I was wounded in the right shoulder by shrapnel. I also had some splinters hit me, three in the left thigh, and one in the back of the head, and a bit took a piece off my left ear. Another bit, I don't know where that was off to, but it got stopped half-way through an English and French Dictionary, that Mr. *(name deleted by censor – EDF)* sent me a few days before I got hit...All but the shoulder is about better now, and I have left off the bandages...I expect I shall be here a long time."

The Board of Guardians met on Tuesday 28th. Amongst the items on a lengthy agenda were:
A tender to supply bread to the Children's Home, at 10p per 4lb loaf was accepted.
It was agreed that the minimum age for admission to the Children's Home should be fixed at 3 years.
Acknowledgement was given for a gift of flowers for inmates from the rector.

On 29th, news was received concerning Rifleman H. Cole, 16 Division Intelligence Company, Royal Irish Rifles, whose parents lived in Halford Street. He had been wounded in his left eye on August 8th and admitted to hospital. He arrived in England on 23rd and went to St. Luke's Hospital, Halifax. Aged 18, he had been in France since March and, before enlisting, worked in the offices of the Islip Iron Company.

On Thursday 30th, a Juvenile Tent of the Independent Order of Rechabites was instituted at a meeting held in the Co-operative Hall, where 48 members were initiated.

The Thrapston Rural District Food Control Committee met for the first time on 31st, where the only item discussed was the issue of cards to the public under the sugar scheme.

Finally in August, a 38 year old married compositor was allowed three months exemption by the local Tribunal.

September

The "*Raunds Circuit Wesleyan Methodist Church Record*" for September wished Rev. Harry and Mrs. Shaw success with their move to join the Rushden Circuit and thanked them for their work in Thrapston.

At the County Tribunal on 1st, a 36 year old married clothier and outfitter made a personal appeal. If he went into the Army, his business must close down. He was allowed a three month exemption, at the end of which time, other Thrapston cases affecting outfitters would be considered together.

The Trades and Labour Council sat during the evening of Monday 3rd. The meeting was spent continuing the debate about Labour representation, started on August 17th.

The *Evening Telegraph* reported, on 4th, that the total rainfall in Thrapston during August was 5.32 inches, bringing the year's total to 15.83 inches.

At the Police Court on 4th, two cases involving local people were heard:
A private soldier from Scotland was summoned by a single woman from Chancery Lane to show cause etc. He was ordered to pay maintenance of 3s 6d per week.
A married woman appeared charged with common assault against a local woman. There had been a history of assaults, recently compounded by her sending threatening postcards. The defendant was bound over to keep the peace for twelve months and ordered to pay costs of 4s.

The postponed garden party in aid of Dr. Barnardo's Homes *(see page 96)* took place at "The Hollies" and "Nene House" on Thursday 6th. Bright and sunny weather brought a good crowd in who enjoyed a wide variety of amusements.

Two local men, from Thrapston and Denford, appeared before Huntingdon Petty Sessions on 7th, charged under the Poaching Prevention Act for having a gun in their possession at Keyston on Sunday August 12th. After hearing evidence from P.C. Piggott and statements from the defendants, the Chairman said that the circumstances were very suspicious and the Police were thoroughly justified in bringing the case. However, the evidence was not sufficient to justify conviction and the cases against Campbell Edmund Morris, Market Road and Charles Horace Manning, Denford, were dismissed.

The *Evening Telegraph* reported on 10th concerning Driver Frank Whiteman, whose parents lived in Halford Street. He had been wounded in the mouth on July 28th and was in hospital in France for a month. He had now returned to the front.

At an evening meeting on 10th at the Swan Hotel, *(the entrance to which is shown left – EDF Collection)*, butchers from Thrapston, Oundle, Raunds and neighbouring villages formed themselves into a group, in accordance with a suggestion from the District Commissioner, for the purpose of arranging agreeable prices to lay before the Local Food Control Committee.

An obituary was printed on the same day for Mr. Frederick Fisher, aged 50 years, in Wolverton. He moved to Thrapston in the early part of the 1890s as organist at St. James' Church. He married Miss Fanny Smith, youngest daughter of Mr. George Smith and, as well as being an organist, taught music. He was a regular visitor to "The Hollies" and took much pleasure in keeping up his old friendships in town. He died after suffering creeping paralysis for the final years of his life. He was buried in Wolverton and had no children.

An evening whist drive was arranged by the Town Band on 13th to raise money for Mr. Ernest Abbott, an old bandsman who had been ill for a considerable time. The event was expected to raise a "capital" sum for his benefit.

On 14th, the *Evening Telegraph* carried these two stories:
The Thrapston Red Cross Committee was arranging a door-to-door collection, whist drive, organ recital, flag day and social evening to raise funds.
A jumble sale arranged by the Thrapston Branch of the British Women's Temperance Association was held at Nene House Schoolroom on the previous day. About £9 was raised.

A notice was placed in the *Evening Telegraph* on 14th, which read:
"IN MEMORIAM
In loving memory of **Pte. H. D. Hall (31)**, Grenadier Guards, killed in action on the Somme, 14th September, 1916, aged 21.
What though in lonely grief I sigh
For him beloved no longer nigh;
Submissive would I still reply,
Thy will be done."

The Thrapston Council School Managers Meeting Minute Book recorded on 17th:
"Blackberry Picking.
A circular from the Education Committee was before the meeting with regard to the scheme for gathering blackberries to be made into jam for the Navy and Army, for which two half holidays a week would be allowed, without prejudice to the grant should the number of openings during the school year fall below 400."
It was agreed to give support to the scheme.

A day later, the *Evening Telegraph* reported:
"Northamptonshire Scholars Picking for the Soldiers.
All the head teachers of the elementary schools of the county of Northamptonshire have been requested by the county educational authority to allow the schoolchildren to pick blackberries during this and next month.
One or two half days in the week are to be given to the picking, it being left to the discretion of the head teacher as to the number of sections into which each school may be divided. The different sections will proceed in different directions. When the day's work is over scholars are to bring their fruit to the school and have it weighed, the county paying 1d per lb. The county has for this purpose been divided into a number of sections, each having a depot for the reception of fruit, Victoria School being the depot for Wellingborough. When the fruit has been weighed it is to be dispatched by the head teacher to some jam factory, where it is to be pulped for the Army and Navy. It is estimated by the county authority that this effort will give a yield of five hundred to a thousand tons."

Also on 18th, the local Food Control Committee met and prices submitted by butchers, grocers and bakers were discussed. Perhaps due to a lack of clarity from Central Government as to what they should do with this information, the clerk was requested to file it.

A monthly meeting of Thrapston Parish Council took place on 19th in the Temperance Hall. Mr. E. J. Loaring had written to the Council placing his resignation before them owing to continued ill-health and inability to resume his duties. With regret, this was accepted.

A letter was written to the Midland Railway Company asking for the 9.20 am train to leave earlier, to ensure catching the 9.47 am London train from Kettering.

The annual report of the Fire Brigade was given. Eight drills had been held during the year and the engine and appliances were in good order. Three members of the brigade were serving abroad with the Army. The brigade had attended one fire, at Woodford on February 8th when five cottages were burnt down. £3 3s had been paid to the Council for the use of the fire engine. Four members were called to a small outbreak of fire at a cottage in the Baptist Chapel yard on August 4th. The report was accepted.

September 20th – Edward Percy Raworth (41) killed in action.

This report appeared on 21st:
"ON H. M. SERVICE.
On two afternoons during the past week the scholars of the elementary schools have been out blackberrying with their teachers for the benefit of our gallant soldiers and sailors. A good quantity of the fruit was obtained."

Harvest Festival was celebrated in St. James' Church on Sunday 23rd. There was a good supply of fruit, vegetables and flowers, although not as extensive as usual. Collections were taken for Church funds.

Thrapston Guardians met on 25th:
The master reported that the Harvest Festival service was held in the House Chapel on Sunday where there were many vegetables, including a "profusion" of marrows.

Estimates of costs for the coming year were approved, resulting in a reduction of the rates by 1d to 7d in the £.

Various tenders for the supply of foodstuffs were agreed, as were tenders for drugs, coke and coal, Portland mixed cobbles and animal feed.

The *Evening Telegraph* included these items on 27th:
"See tomorrow's Thrapston and Raunds Journal for exclusive pictures of the Drayton Fete."

The sale of fruit and vegetables given for the Baptist Church Harvest Festival took place last Monday, Mr. H. H. Bletsoe taking the rostrum. £8 3s 7d was raised which, when combined with Sunday's collections, amounted to £11 13s 7d for Church funds.

The name of Sec.-Lieut. T. H. Bletsoe, R.F.A., who was recently awarded the Military Cross, appeared in the "Times" on Thursday, amongst a long list of the recipients of this high distinction.

A train alteration was announced on 28th. For October, the 3.00pm Northampton train would leave at 3.10 pm and thus arrive in town approximately 10 minutes later than timetabled.

October

The two Thrapston schools' total weight of blackberries from three afternoons' picking was 1,199½ lbs.

On Tuesday 2nd, at the Police Court, Mr. Bernard Cawdell, Thrapston and Mr. J. W. Smith, Ringstead, were sworn in as special constables.

A married woman from Halford Street was summoned for failing to subdue the lights of her house at 8.45 pm on September 20th. P.C. Short stated the facts. She drew the blind up before she went to bed, but her husband then lit a candle to have his supper. She was fined 2s 6d.

The Food Control Committee met on the same day. 41 applications from caterers and manufacturers were received for the authority to obtain supplies of sugar. All but three were allowed at least a proportion of their request. Seven applications had been received to deal in potatoes, five being granted. All butchers in the district had submitted their price lists as displayed in their shops.

Finally, on 2nd, this advertisement appeared:-
"To Let. Two houses to let, York Terrace, Thrapston. 2s 6d per week rent.
Perkins and Son, Irthlingborough."

The Thrapston Branch of the Women's Temperance Association met on 3rd at Nene House Schoolroom. They decided to allocate monies raised to: Y.M.C.A. Huts, £6; Central Union funds, £2; and £1 10s 2d to local funds.

Thrapston Rural District Council met on 4th, where they agreed that it was "ridiculous" to submit estimates for water supply works until the war was over.
They had received a letter from the County Surveyor inquiring about advertisements that disfigured the scenery. Col. Sackville spoke strongly in favour of preserving as far as possible the natural beauty of their district. It was resolved that the surveyor take the necessary steps.

On the same day, news arrived in Thrapston of injuries received by Pte. **John Stimpson (58)**, who was recovering in hospital in Cardiff.

Rainfall during September had been recorded as being 2 inches.

This advertisement appeared in the *Evening Telegraph* on Saturday 6th.

NORTHAMPTON TOWN AND COUNTY RED CROSS £15,000 FUND.

THRAPSTON SOCIAL,

Next THURSDAY, Oct. 11th,

In CORN EXCHANGE. DOORS OPEN 3 p.m.

GREAT ATTRACTIONS. For Details see Bills.

October 7th – John William Guest (42) killed in action.

October 8th – Frederick William Newman (43) killed in action.

The Food Control Committee met again on 9th, where five sugar and four potato applications were approved. The maximum price for new milk was fixed at 6d a quart delivered and 5d undelivered.

On the same day, there was a report that, during the Harvest Services on the previous Sunday, a plain oak stand was placed in the font, on which was placed the Thrapston Roll of Honour in book form. This had been made by Messrs. W. and H. Halford of Thrapston and paid for by the Sunday School children. *(The original cover and title page are shown on page 103 – EDF).*
(The title page reads:
"This book containing the list of those from Thrapston who served in the
Great War 1914 – 1918 was first placed in Thrapston Church August 1917
and remained there until July 25th 1920 when it was replaced by a complete and
permanent Roll presented by the Teachers and Scholars of the Sunday School.
Signed Henry R. Fitzherbert, Rector." – EDF)

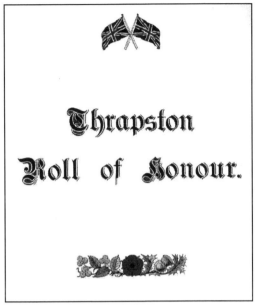

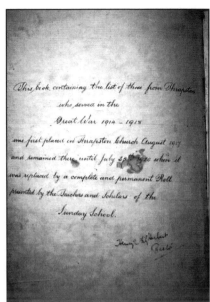

This advertisement was placed in the *Evening Telegraph* on 11th October:-
"One beginner made £2 10s profit from 8 birds in the first four months he used Karswood. 2d, 6d, 1s packets from Thrapston Industrial Co-operative Society Ltd., Market Street, Thrapston.

The local Tribunal announced these decisions on Friday 12th:
A 41 year old married printer and 35 year old married horseman both received three months, conditional on joining the V.T.C.
A single 40 year old vanman received six months exemption.

The School Managers met on 15th. Attendance figures were Thrapston C. of E. School, 91%; Thrapston Council School, 89.9%.

It was announced on 16th that Thrapston would be receiving a visit early in December from his Excellency Count Cheddo Mijatovitch (formerly Serbian Minister to the Court of St. James and other diplomatic posts) who would lecture in aid of the Serbian Red Cross. Mrs. R. J. P. Humphrey had arranged this and it was hoped that Lord Lilford would preside.

Also on 16th, the death of **Frederick Newman (43)** was reported.

Mr. Arthur G. Brown conducted a property auction at the White Hart Hotel during the evening of 16th for a corner building site and dwelling houses, by instructions from the trustees of the will of the late Mr. Reuben Cotton. Lot 1 was a freehold building site at the junction of High Street and Oundle Road including offices, greenhouse and workshops. It was sold to Mrs. Fry for £265. The second lot was two brick and slated dwelling houses in Oundle Road, near lot 1, called Jubilee Cottages (occupied by Messrs. Clarke and Horn), which went for £360, again to Mrs. Fry. The final lot, two more brick and slated houses known as St. James' Terrace (occupied by Messrs. Richardson and Guest) went for £170 to the same purchaser.

Finally, the *Evening Telegraph* wrote, on 16th:
"An aeroplane sustained slight damage in alighting in a field near the Huntingdon Road on Friday. Repairs having been made, it left early on Saturday afternoon. Many people, including a large number of schoolchildren, went to see it."

The 17th brought confirmation of the death of **John William Guest (42)**.

At a meeting of Thrapston Parish Council on 17th, Mr. Thompson, who worked at the sewage works, was granted a pay increase of 2s a week to £1 10s.
The precept for burials was agreed at a total of £50 for the year, whilst an increase in the general precept was considered unnecessary.

These notices were placed in the *Evening Telegraph* on 17th:
"MR. AND MRS. G. RAWORTH and family, of Market Road, Thrapston, desire to thank all friends for their kind expressions of sympathy with them in the loss of their dear son, Percy. "Greater love hath no man than this, that a man lay down his life for his friends.""
"Wanted, a good bricklayer. Wanted, two good men for trial hole boring. Wanted, a good youth, age 15 – 17, to learn motor engineering. Wanted, good motor mechanic for motor and engineering work, must be used to agricultural work. Apply A. W. Bolton, Thrapston."

On 19th, the Institute announced that Mr. R. J. Selby had taken over as games secretary, replacing Mr. J.W. Stubbs, who had resigned for business reasons.

October 21st – James Edward Cobley (44) killed in action.

On Sunday 21st, the Thrapston platoon received a surprise visit from Capt. and Adjutant Willows, when there was a very fair muster under the commanding officer Lieut. Porter. After watching the drill under Sergt.-Inst. Corbett, the Adjutant briefly addressed the platoon, pointing out the enormous importance of their work, in that a very large number of soldiers, who now had to be kept in this country for its defence would be released for foreign service as soon as a certain number of Volunteers had been passed as efficient. In this way, he said, men who were giving up their time to training were doing most effective work for their country and materially helping to bring the war to an end; and also, incidentally, making it possible for the men at the front to get more frequent leave. He also said that he expected shortly to be able to provide them with uniforms of the ordinary Army pattern. Capt. Willows afterwards expressed to the Commanding Officer his pleasure at the smartness of the platoon and their steadiness at drill. In addition to those mentioned above, Corps. Traynar, Johnson, Young and Sanderson were also on parade.

The Guardians met on Tuesday 23rd:
They agreed to the repainting of the corridors.
The quarterly statement was read. The average number of inmates of the Workhouse was 54 a day and the number of vagrants totalled 314, 500 less than the same quarter in 1916.

The Comforts Fund announced their totals from the Parade held in August on 25th:
Receipts amounted to   £139 3s 1d
Payments were   £15 4s 3d
Balance   £123 18s 10d.

The Food Control Committee met on the same day. As well as agreeing prices for butter and meat, they issued sugar cards. Their only other business was to agree their own compensation for lost work hours, at 1s per hour plus travelling expenses.

This notice appeared on Thursday 25th:-
"IN MEMORIAM
In ever-loving memory of Pte. **George Alfred Langley (34)**, Northants Regiment, beloved son of Mr. and Mrs. Langley, of Denford. Killed in action Oct. 25th, 1916, aged 21 years.
Only a private soldier, only a mother's son
Buried on the field of battle, my duty I have done;
I have served my King and Country, God knows I have done my best,
But now I am asleep in Jesus, a son called to rest!
His King and Country called him,
The call was not in vain;
On Britain's roll of honour
You will find this hero's name.
From his loving father, mother, brothers, sisters, uncles, and grandmother."

Friday 26th brought news that, from November 6th, the price of gas would be 6s 6d per 1000 cubic feet.

It was also reported that Mr. John Meadows had dug a carrot root with 19 distinctive carrots growing from it, weighing 4lb 2oz.

This advertisement *(right)* for butter prices was placed in the *Evening Telegraph* on 27th by the Food Control Committee.

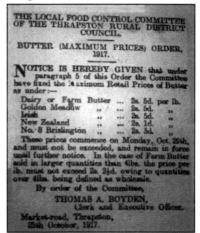

A recent "Bright and Breezy" Social and Parade raised £20, which was shared between St. Dunstan's Hospital for Blind Soldiers and the local Comforts Fund.

A memorial service was held at the Baptist Church on Sunday 28th for Ptes. **Percy Raworth (41)** and **Willie Guest (42)**, where a good congregation paid tribute to them.

On 29th, the County Tribunal allowed a 37 year old married motor engineer a three month exemption.
Also on 29th, the Food Control Committee agreed that Mr. T. A. Boyden, the clerk and executive officer would be paid £150 per annum. From this, he was expected to provide office accommodation and pay his travelling expenses.

The Police Court had a very busy session on Tuesday 30th:
A local motor engineer was summoned for being the owner of a motorcycle and failing to have the registration transferred. Technical difficulties with the case resulted in only an order to pay 4s costs, which were accepted.
An Islip woman was convicted of stealing two pieces of cloth, a sheet, two pairs of scissors and other items, totalling £1 4s in value, from Thomas Arthur Boyden. After pleading guilty and stating that she was only surviving on Parish Relief, she was fined £1, payable in instalments.
The final case was reported in detail, reproduced below:-
"A Thrapston errand boy aged 15 was charged with housebreaking and stealing two £1 Treasury notes, the property of Cyril Barratt, at Thrapston on October 9th and 16th. Cyril Barratt deposed that he lived next door to defendant's parents. On Tuesday, October 9th he had £3 in his bedroom – two Treasury notes and a sovereign in a small cash box which was in

his tin clothes box. On the 15th he went to the box again and found that one Treasury note was missing. He told his mother. The next day, about half-past five he went to the box again and found another Treasury note missing. He made enquiry and in consequence of something he was told went to see the accused the same night. He told defendant's mother. Defendant first said "No," but after a little while he said he did have it and gave him 16s back, saying he had spent the other money. Mary Barratt, mother of the previous witness, said she was in the habit of going for a walk with defendant's mother on Tuesday afternoons. On October 9th, she left home about half-past four. Her door was locked when she went away but when she returned an hour later it was unlocked. On October 16th the same experience occurred. The chairman asked if the door was just unlocked, not broken. It was and she had taken the key with her. Lawrence Bell, a lad, deposed that on October 9th, about a quarter-past seven, he met defendant in the street and asked him where he was going. Defendant said to the Post Office to change a £1 note which his mother and father had given him. He could not get into the Post Office and went into Mr. Touch's who changed it for him. Inspector Campion deposed that this case was not reported to the police but came to his knowledge on October 22nd. He saw defendant at work and told him he was making enquiry about some money stolen from Mrs. Barratt's house. Defendant said "I know nothing about it." Afterwards, he said "A week last Tuesday I went over home for tea about half-past four. My mother went out for a walk with Mrs. Barratt. I took the key from one of our doors, unlocked Mrs. Barratt's door, went upstairs and took a £1 Treasury note. I spent the money in buying flash lights, grapes and sweets. On the 16th I again took our key, unlocked the door, went upstairs to the room and took another £1 Treasury note. I spent some of that and handed 5s back to Barratt." Defendant elected to be tried by this Court, and pleaded guilty. Supt. Tebbey said there was nothing against defendant before. In reply to the Bench, Supt Tebbey said the money stolen had been refunded. The Bench fined defendant £1, to be paid in instalments of 2s per week and bound him over for six months to be of good behaviour. The mother paid the £1."

November

The total rainfall for October was recorded at 3.16 inches.

November 2nd – Arthur William Jeffery (45) killed in action.

The Baptist Church held their second memorial service in a week on Sunday 4th, this time for Gunner **F. W. Newman (43)**.

A day later, the County Tribunal granted a 35 year old married carter and horseman, employed by Mr. Midgley, a final exemption until January 1st.

On 7th, about ten Red Cross cars, several containing wounded soldiers, passed through town. During a short halt, some townspeople brought them tea and gave cigarettes, which were distributed between the soldiers, such kindly attentions being very much appreciated.

The Ekins Charity distributed awards of well-selected books to scholars of Islip C.E. School and Thrapston C.E. and Council Schools on 8th. Charity Trustees and school managers attended the presentations.

On 9th, the *Evening Telegraph* reported that the Boy Scouts had transferred their headquarters to the Old School at the junction of Market Road and Huntingdon Road, which had been refurbished for them by Mr. Bletsoe. *(Pictured on page 107, taken in 1995 before demolition in 1998 – EDF Collection)*. They had recently received a lecture by Capt. R.J.P. Humphrey (who was home on leave from the front), on the mechanism of bombs currently being used in the war.

On Monday 12th, Rev. John Lewis Gillians, the Wesleyan Church minister, married Miss Mary Ann Curtis in Holbeach *(pictured below from the Kettering Leader, Friday 23rd November 1917).*

The Food Control Committee met on Tuesday 13th. The Ministry of Food had approved their list of meat prices and, by request from the Ministry, a reduction of ½d per lb on all joints of beef during November was agreed.

The Tribunal made these decisions on Friday 16th:
A married outfitter and boot dealer, aged 27 and a married fishmonger, aged 37, were both given three months, conditional on their joining the Training Corps.
A married carpenter and plumber, aged 42, received six months exemption whilst a married 36 year old butcher was given three months.

Two advertisements were printed in the *Evening Telegraph* advertisements section on 16th:
"Wanted, for willing girl just leaving school, comfortable situation with a lady. Particulars to Box 99, Evening Telegraph, Thrapston."
"Wanted, strong woman or girl, three or four days a week. Apply, Mrs. S. Nichols, High Street, Thrapston."

Southam & Beck were regular advertisers in the local press, this one appearing in the *Kettering Guardian* on 16th.

On 22nd, the Food Control Committee met to discuss unnecessary overlapping of tradesmen's deliveries by carts and other vehicles, often duplicating routes. Despite lengthy discussion, no conclusions were reached.

Also on 22nd, an afternoon sale of works and evening entertainment took place at the Co-operative Hall in aid of Baptist Church funds. There was a good turnout and expectations were high for a good result.

The Institute held the first round of their billiards handicap for the Conyers Cup on 23rd November. The victor was Mr. W. Stubbs who defeated Mr. C. R. Pettit.

The *Kettering Guardian* ran a story on Friday 23rd, about Mr. F. Brooks, stationmaster at

Mr. E. J. BROOKS (Cranford).   Mr. F. BROOKS, Snr. (Thrapston).   Mr. F. W. BROOKS (Grafham).

Thrapston Midland Road Station and his sons who held the same positions at Cranford (Mr. E. J. Brooks) and Grafham (Mr. F. W. Brooks). Mr Brooks joined the Midland Railway in 1875 at Swadlincote, Derbyshire. He moved to Thrapston in 1902 and, by the time of publication, had been a stationmaster for 35 years. During this time, he had never had a day off ill.

The same day brought the announcement that Mr. J. E. Dixon would be leaving town. He had been postmaster for four years, succeeding Mr. G. Raby. His new appointment was in Kingsbridge, Devon. During the first twelve months of his control at Thrapston, he had carried out several improvements to postal arrangements, giving a more efficient service.

The Thrapston Trades and Labour Council met during the evening of 26th at the Co-operative Hall. Mr. W. H. Bray was nominated for a vacancy on the local Tribunal. There was also lengthy discussion regarding a vacancy on the Parish Council, which had recently co-opted a new member. They were of the opinion that the unsuccessful candidate with the highest number of votes at the election should have been co-opted. They also discussed the lack of good quality housing accommodation available locally for the working classes and requested the District Council took advantage of Government assistance to provide appropriate housing stock.

Lloyd Dennis Knight, the youngest son of Mr. and Mrs. H. Knight, Oundle Road, died of bronchial pneumonia on 26th aged 4 years. He attended the Church Sunday School and was a Junior Rechabite. He was buried on 29th.

The Comforts Fund recent meeting was reported on the same day:
"At a meeting of the Thrapston Soldiers' and Sailors' Comforts Fund Committee it was decided to dispense this year with the usual Christmas parcels, and to send as follows: - to men serving abroad, 7s 6d and 200 high class cigarettes; to men in hospital from wounds or sickness contracted abroad, 10s; and to all men in training at home, 5s. All postal orders were dispatched on Wednesday evening (November 21st), with a copy of the following very appropriate letter from the committee: - "Thrapston, November, 1917. Dear Friend, - We are enclosing herewith a small Christmas present, which we hope may be acceptable to you as a token that we at home have not forgotten you. On behalf of our committee, we wish you as happy a Christmas as possible under the present circumstances, and all good luck in the New Year; and we fervently hope that 1918 will see the end of the war, and that you may safely return home, where a hearty welcome will await you. Hoping you may receive same safely, we are, on behalf of the committee, yours faithfully, Wm. Stobie, hon. sec., P. Makin, chairman." In all there were 200 men serving from Thrapston."

Pears @ Annual
XMAS, 1917   Ready November 30th

Give your   so that

Order now   you may

to your   not be

Newsagent   disappointed

1/-

HOME ONCE MORE

The Annual Contains **5 New Stories** accompanied by

3 MAGNIFICENT PLATES

of All Newsagents and Booksellers **ONE SHILLING** and at All the Bookstalls

COMPLETE

On Friday 30th, two short reports were printed in the *Evening Telegraph*:

The Baptist Bazaar had proved a great success and raised about £80.

The District Bellringers' association had met in town on the previous Saturday, with 18 members attending.

At the end of the month, the Christmas 1917 issue of Pears Annual *(shown left)* went on sale, priced 1s.

December

There was a public dance at the Temperance Hall during the evening of Saturday 1st with a large attendance; the M.C's being Messrs. H. Abbott and H. A. Hurrell. The proceeds were in aid of the Thrapston Soldiers' and Sailors' Comforts Fund.

Two church concerts took place on 2nd. At the Parish Church, Miss L. Kingsford gave an organ recital to an appreciative gathering, whilst the Baptist Church held Choir Sunday, with collection money to be used for choir funds.

The Food Control Committee met on Tuesday 4th. There were concerns about the lack of cheese supplies, lard was unavailable and butter supplies were reduced due to farmers receiving more money for milk than butter. A complaint had been received that margarine was being sold for 1s 2d per lb, which did not accord with the official price.

On Wednesday 5th, the King presented the Military Cross to Second-Lieut. Thomas Bletsoe at Buckingham Palace. The *Evening Telegraph* continued, "Lieut. Bletsoe's conspicuous bravery and devotion to duty in the field was an exhibition of that indomitable pluck which has proved so eminently characteristic of the whole of the British forces. While acting as an observation officer of the artillery a shell dropped on the observation post, blew it out, buried his two men, and knocked him over. He at once set to work and got out one of the men, who was unwounded. He then recovered the other man, and sent him to the dressing station, mended his telephone wire up and continued communicating from the shell hole. And all this time shells were dropping all around him."

This notice appeared in the *Evening Telegraph* on 5th:

"The Thrapston Depot for waste paper is at the Evening Telegraph Office, Corn Exchange. Turn all your accumulations of waste paper into money. Highest prices given."

News was received on 6th that Lance-Corpl. Benjamin Barber, Northamptonshire Regiment, had been wounded in the left wrist and was in hospital in France. In his letter, he expressed anxiety about two of his brothers, Jack and William, who were in the same engagement at Cambrai. His other brother, Ernest, was in hospital with pleurisy. *(The four brothers were featured in the Kettering Guardian on Friday 28th December – see page 112 – EDF.)*

The lectures by Count Cheddo Mijatovitch *(see page 103 for the original announcement – EDF)*, took place in the afternoon and evening of Thursday 6th, with good attendances.

This letter appeared in the *Evening Telegraph* on 6th:
"In the Evening Telegraph on Nov. 22nd appeared the challenging paragraph – in fact the first gossip: "Four Kettering firemen have now served, between them, 90 years". This set historic Thrapston, which never would play second fiddle to Kettering, in a calculating mood, which revealed the conquering record that four of its voluntary Fire Brigade firemen have served amongst them a hundred years "not out" viz: Capt. O. Booth, 46 years; Engineer W. March, 22 years; Secretary and Fireman W. Newman, 16 years; and Fireman H. Loveday, 16 years. Capt. Booth has served under four captains (Messrs. Beadswell, Horn, Siddons and Lord); and as a rounding off fact, it may be added that in the whole of his forty-six years he has only missed two drills and two fires."

Two advertisements were placed in the *Evening Telegraph* on 7th:
"Wanted by young lady (18). Situation in office (in Thrapston if possible). Apply C. Handley, High Street, Thrapston."
"Wanted. Square oak dining table, carved legs. Apply with full particulars to Box 104, Evening Telegraph, Thrapston."

The Annual General Meeting of the Thrapston District of the Northamptonshire Licensed Trades Association Ltd. was reported to have been held at the King's Arms Hotel, Mr. E. Kick, Denford, presiding. The only reported business was the election of officers and representatives.

There was some controversy at the Food Control Committee meeting on Thursday 13th, where Rev. W. St. Geo. Coldwell made a statement. There had been talk in town concerning some tea he had ordered from London. For thirty years, he had bought a year's supply at a time from the City of London Tea Company and recently he made his usual order. The chest was seen arriving at the railway station, and talk started straight away. There were seven in his family and the chest of 50 lbs was for the year. The Chairman of the Committee, Rev. C. F. Bolland, said the only question was whether this was hoarding. Surprise was expressed about the company fulfilling such a large order. Workpeople were only able to buy 2 oz at a time and the Co-operative Society was only allowed 80 lbs a week. Rev. Coldwell stated that he was prepared to resign from the Committee, which was not required at that time. The Clerk was asked to write to the Food Commissioner, giving full details and asking if anything had been done wrong. *(Recently, there had been a widely reported case in Wakefield, where 27 lbs of tea and 17 lbs of sugar had been found in a household of three people. A fine of £1 was levied in respect of the tea – EDF.)*

The Thrapston and District Rifle Club held a jumble sale during the afternoon of Saturday 15th in aid of funds. 47 club members were serving with the Forces and their premises had been offered to the Volunteer Training Corps. About £30 was raised by the effort.

On Monday 17th, the death of George Smith *(pictured on page 111, Thrapston District Historical Society archives)*, managing director of Smith and Grace, occurred after a long illness. He was born on 10th October 1841, in Stamford. Amongst the multitude of his roles in town were chairman of the Board of Guardians, Rural District Council and the Local Tribunal. He had served as a County Councillor since 1904.

The Thrapston Tribunal sat on Tuesday 18th, when a local clothier and outfitter, 36 years old and married, supplying work clothes to ironstone and agricultural workers, was allowed three months exemption.

A market gardener, aged 39, with appreciable hearing loss, had joined the Volunteer Training Corps and was allowed a further three month's exemption.

A single grocer's assistant, aged 18, received a final two month exemption.

The Board of Guardians met on the same day, where the main part of the meeting was devoted to members paying tribute to George Smith.

News was received on Wednesday 19th that Pte. A. H. Roughton, Suffolk Regiment, had been awarded the Military Medal.

On 20th, Rev. F. C. P. Clark from the Society for the Propagation of the Gospel gave an address, illustrated with lantern slides, on life in Burma.

George Smith

The funeral of George Smith took place on Friday 21st at the Baptist Church. The funeral party left "The Hollies" and processed through the streets to Church. A large number of people lined the streets, paying their last respects. After the service, he was buried in the Baptist burial ground. Rev. H. Ellis Roberts conducted the service.

Freeman and Webb, Midland Road, placed this advertisement in the *Evening Telegraph* on 21st.

> CHRISTMAS.—Grand show Useful Presents. Dolls and Toys. Upholstered Wicker Chairs from 13s. 6d.; Toy Perambulators, 18s. 11d. Shop closed Thursday (27th), Friday (28th).—Freeman and Webb, Thrapston.—(Advt.)

With Christmas Day falling on a Tuesday, the market was held a day earlier, on 24th. To quote the *Evening Telegraph*, "It was quite of a holiday character all round."

The only decorations at the Parish Church for Christmas were white flowers on the font and altar. Communion services were held at 7.30am and midday, with a 6.00 pm choral evensong, all conducted by the rector. The collection money was sent to St. Dunstan's Hospital for Blinded Soldiers, and amounted to £5 5s 7d.

The Workhouse held their traditional Christmas Day festivities. There were 29 inmates at the Infirmary, 13 bedbound. The other 16 joined the 48 residents of the Workhouse for a sumptuous dinner, followed by presents and entertainment. Mrs. George Smith assisted with serving the inmates during the day, despite her recent bereavement, which was greatly appreciated.

On Boxing Day, Frederick Kirby, son of Mr. and Mrs. J. Kirby, "Horton House", Thrapston, married Miss Edith Mary Cooke, from Cambridge, at Christ Church, Cambridge.

On 27th December, the Thrapston and District Volunteer Training Corps held a smoking concert at the Co-operative Hall to make a presentation to Sergt. Instructor Corbett, of Woodford, as a token of appreciation for his services. Lieut. J. F. Porter presided and the majority of the platoon was present. The Chairman made the presentation, which consisted of a note case containing six and a half Treasury notes. He also gave the Sergeant-Instructor a personal gift, consisting of a silver-mounted warrant officer's malacca cane. Pte. T. Selby apologised for the absence of Mr. G. E. Abbott, J.P. of Islip, who was very much interested in the movement. Sergt.-Instructor Corbett, who was received with musical honours, made a very suitable reply. A musical programme followed.

On 28th, the *Evening Telegraph* reported the success of Percy Edward Sharp, whose parents lived in Halford Street, who took his B.A. degree at Cambridge on 19th. He trained as a pupil teacher at Thrapston C. of E. School before moving to Wellingborough Technical School for two years. He then worked in Wisbech, Stoke Bruerne and finally Cambridge, where he became an undergraduate at Fitzwilliam Hall.

On the same day, the Barber brothers' pictures appeared in the *Kettering Guardian (pictured below)*. The article read, "The four sons of Mr. Benjamin Barber, engineer of Thrapston, have all been serving at the front in France. Benjamin Barber, a Lance-Corporal in the 5th

FOUR THRAPSTON SOLDIER BROTHERS

JACK BARBER. BENJAMIN BARBER.

WILLIAM BARBER. ERNEST BARBER.

Northants, was wounded in the left wrist in the big push at Cambrai. Jack Barber was also in the big push at Cambrai and has not yet been heard of. He is in the 5th Company Northants. Wm. Barber was in a surprise attack and narrowly escaped being taken prisoner. Ernest Barber, aged 19, Royal Fusiliers, is now in hospital with pleurisy."

On 29th, two items were reported:
The death of Mrs. Jeffs of Market Road, on 18th was noted. She moved to town 44 years previously with her husband, Thomas. Her funeral took place at the Parish Church, followed by burial at Oundle Road Cemetery on 22nd.
The annual Thrapston Church Sunday School prize giving took place at the Co-operative Hall during the evening of Wednesday 26th. After the more traditional musical contributions by scholars, there were dances, sash drill by the Bible Class and selections by a juvenile ragtime band. Prizes were presented by the Rector, each scholar receiving a Bible, Prayer Book or other suitable book.

The year ended with a choral evensong service at St. James' Church, conducted by the rector, whilst the Wesleyan Church held a watch-night service, led by Rev. J. Lewis Gillians. After a brief interval for silent prayer, the New Year was ushered in with the hymn, "Come, let us anew our journey pursue."

The fourth Christmas of the war had now passed and, although there was always hope that it would be the last before hostilities ceased, the town entered 1918 with the certain knowledge that there was still painful news to be received from Europe. 36 men had already died and there were still another 22 telegrams to be received. But, life went on and mixed with the sorrow would be happy times as people endeavoured to make a "home fit for heroes".

1918

Thrapston Market had a very fair show of fat beef, heifers and cows, which were disposed of under the Government scheme on Tuesday 1st. There was also a reasonable show of mutton, in which there was good trade.

The Food Control Committee met on the same day, where the vice-chairman, Rev. H. E. Fitzherbert tendered his resignation, citing a heavy workload. He was secretary of the Local Food Production Committee, which was about to conduct an extensive survey to find additional land for agricultural purposes. As well as a number of other local bodies, he had his normal parish duties. His resignation was accepted with regret.

At the same meeting, the question of the large quantity of tea obtained by Rev. Coldwell *(see page 110 - EDF)* was discussed. At the suggestion of the Divisional Committee, he agreed to retain 10 lb of tea and dispose of the rest.

Finally, there was some debate about whether enforced rationing should be introduced but given there were no queues at shops in the area the suggestion was dismissed.

During the evening of 1st, there was a concert in the Co-operative Hall in aid of Wesleyan Church funds given by a ladies' concert party from Raunds. In excess of £6 was raised.

Finally, a "Wanted" advertisement:-
"Wanted at once, a daily help, apply Mrs. D. C. Taylor, Huntingdon Road, Thrapston."

On 3rd, the whole of the staff at Thrapston Post Office met in the sorting office to make a presentation of an oak revolving bookcase to the postmaster, Mr. J. E. Dixon, who was shortly leaving to take up his new position at Kingsbridge, Devon. He was also given a Swan fountain pen by the sub-postmasters of the district.

This advertisement *(right)* appeared in the *Evening Telegraph* on Friday 4th.

For the National day of Prayer and Thanksgiving, a united afternoon service was held at the Co-operative Hall on 6th. On the platform were Rev. H. E. Fitzherbert (rector), Rev. H. Ellis Roberts (Baptist), Rev. J. Lewis Gillians (Wesleyan) and Mr. H. H. Bletsoe. A crowded hall began the service with the National Anthem and after hymns and prayers, Rev. Roberts gave an address.

THE NORTHAMPTONSHIRE
Licensed Trades' Association, Ltd.
THRAPSTON AND DISTRICT BRANCH

ALL LICENCE HOLDERS are earnestly requested to loyally observe SUNDAY, 6th JANUARY next, by CLOSING THEIR HOUSES for the whole of that day, which is being recognised as one of NATIONAL INTERCESSION.

FRANK O. WARREN,
District Secretary.

The County Tribunal sat on Monday 7th, where a 41 year old married compositor employed by Mr. Taylor, printer, and the last remaining worker was granted three months exemption.

A day later, the *Evening Telegraph* reported on the progress Gunner Edward March was making after being wounded in the shoulder and leg. He had been in hospital in Dorset and was now home on sick leave. Before joining up in early 1917, he was employed by Mr Arthur Brown, auctioneer. He had two brothers who were serving, Sapper T. C. March who was in France and Corpl. R. March, Machine Gun Corps who, after receiving wounds in April 1917, was now engaged at Clipston Training School.

The Police Court sat on Tuesday 8th, where, before beginning the business, the Chairman paid respect to Mr. George Smith.

One case before them involved a leather merchant from Kettering who was summoned under the Motor Spirit Restriction Order, November 2nd 1917, for using a motorcar travelling between Oundle and Kettering when other means of transport were available. In the car were his son and three other boys, whom he had collected from school in Oundle and was taking them home to Kettering. P.C. Short said that he saw the defendant in Bridge Street on 19th December. He pointed out that there were convenient trains – the 11.20 am left Oundle and arrived in Thrapston at 11.39 am. Then the Midland train left Midland Road at 12.29 pm, arriving in Kettering at 12.47 pm. The defendant said that he believed this was one of the occasions where he might have use of the car in connection with reasonable household duties *(as allowed under the Act – EDF)*. The Chairman said that they all knew the present petrol restrictions and that they thought that the trains were convenient. A fine of 10s was imposed.

This advertisement for Chivers' custard powder appeared in local newspapers in January.

On Wednesday 9th, the annual business meeting of the Thrapston Branch of the British Women's Temperance Association was held in the afternoon in the Nene House Schoolroom. Mrs. Cottingham presided over a moderate attendance. During the previous year, membership had remained at about the 50 mark and they held a bank balance of £1 18s 8d.

On Monday 14th, a representative group of butchers met with the Food Control Committee at the Swan Hotel. They agreed that, in Thrapston, to help conserve stocks of meat, all butchers would close on Monday and Thursday.

A day later, the Guardians met at the Workhouse.

The master's book recorded that on 9th, the Rev. A. M. Luckock, rector of Titchmarsh, and his wife entertained the old people with a very interesting lecture in the chapel, illustrated with magic lantern slides. The thanks of the Board were accorded to the entertainers, and to all donors of gifts at Christmas.

During the last quarter, 227 vagrants had passed through the Workhouse.

Thrapston Parish Council met on 16th where, after paying respects to the late Mr. George Smith, the following business was discussed:-

A letter from the General Superintendent of the Midland Railway announced that, from 1st February the 8.00 am train from Cambridge would now run earlier, leaving Thrapston at 8.50 am to enable connection with the 9.45 am express from Kettering to St. Pancras.

Cost of living increases in pay were agreed for their two employees, Messrs. Norman and Thompson.

Finally, Mr. Chattell was elected to fill the vacancy caused by the resignation of Mr. Loaring.

The Thrapston Church of England School managers met on 17th January. The balance sheet showed £157 4s 2d in hand, an increase of over £50 from the previous year. School holidays for 1918, as applied for by the head teacher, were approved for forwarding to the District Sub-Committee.

That evening, Thrapston Institute held the final of the billiards handicap for the Conyers Cup. A large number of members witnessed a good game. Victory went to Mr. J. Meadows who defeated Mr. W. Dellar by 58 points.

SPECIAL SALE
MILLINERY
AND
MODEL HATS
AT
HALF-PRICE
THIS WEEK.

B. CAWDELL,
Commerce House. THRAPSTON.

Cawdell's hat sale was being advertised in the *Evening Telegraph* on 17th *(shown left)*.

The *Evening Telegraph* carried two reports on Friday 18th:
Mrs. Jarvis, Market Road, *(pictured on page 43 – EDF)* who had been ill with sciatica, was confined to bed. She was cared for by her daughter, Mrs. Jeffery. Aged 99 years, with her birthday on July 22nd, she was quoted as saying, "They want me to live to be a hundred, but they don't know what it is." Alluding to food rationing, she exclaimed, with good deal of her old humour and vigour, "They want to starve us out now."
The death in Gainsborough of Mr. David Lambert Pilling, formerly of Thrapston, on 14th was announced. Aged 40, he was clerk at Thrapston County Court for a number of years. During his ten years in town, he was involved with the Liberal Party, secretary of the Boys' Life Brigade and one of the captains of the Thrapston and District Hockey Club. His funeral was held in Gainsborough on 17th.

Thrapston Tribunal met on 18th:
A married stationer and printer, aged 41, who had joined the Volunteer Training Corps and a 27 year old single agricultural engineer and motor mechanic employed under the Food Production Committee, were both exempted until June 30th.

On 21st, the annual meeting of Thrapston and District Trades and Labour Council was held at the Co-operative Hall.

The *Evening Telegraph* reported on 22nd:
C. E. Roberts, of "Cambria", Thrapston, had been awarded a Mathematical Exhibition of £50 a year at Jesus College, Oxford.
The Comforts Fund's annual balance sheet for the year ending December 31st showed a balance in hand of £73 2s 7d.

The Rifle Club held their annual meeting at the Range on Wednesday 23rd, where there was only a moderate attendance. After electing officers for the coming year, the balance sheet was presented, showing £9 13s 6d in hand as opposed to the deficit last year of £19 19s 4d.
Their Roll of Honour contained 41 names. *(The whereabouts of this Roll is unknown – if you have any information about it, please contact me – EDF.)* The club were anxious that the

Volunteers should use their range and the committee were about to consider a proposal which led to the hope that they would be using the range soon.

A whist drive was held in the Co-operative Hall on 24th, attended by 135 people, in aid of funds for the Thrapston Platoon of the 2nd Battalion, Northamptonshire Volunteer Corps.

On 25th, the *Evening Telegraph* announced a price increase to 1d from February 1st, due to paper shortages.

Thrapston Institute *(pictured above, no publisher is named but possibly by Frederick Knighton, Kettering – EDF Collection)* held their annual meeting during the evening of Saturday 26th. A large attendance unanimously re-elected the officers and then heard that there was an end-of-year balance of £29 15s 9d. The evening ended with the presentation of the Conyers Cup to Mr. J. Meadows.

The Thrapston Council School managers meeting, called for Tuesday 29th, could not be held due to being inquorate. Only two members and the clerk attended.

February

Thrapston Police Court sat on Tuesday 5th to hear the case against a 14 year old Islip boy, who was summoned for stealing 10d from the rector. John Hodson, giving evidence, stated that he was a labourer and Sunday School teacher. On Sunday 3rd, a small wooden box was put out for children to put their pennies in, raising money for the Comforts Fund. He left the room briefly and on returning found the lid open and just 4d left in it. Before, there was about 5s. P.C. Short spoke about his enquiries and, after taking the boy to the Police Station, he admitted taking 10d and spending it on sweets. This was the first time he had been in trouble. The boy pleaded guilty, was given a warning as to his future behaviour, bound over in the sum of £10 to be of good behaviour for twelve months and placed under the supervision of a Probation Officer.

The Thrapston Branch of the British Women's Temperance Association had an afternoon meeting at "Nene House" Schoolroom on 6th where Mrs. Graveley of Wellingborough spoke on the recognition of the value of the work they were doing to uproot "the two great evils of intemperance and immorality".

The Guardians met on 7th where the vacancy on the Board was discussed. It was agreed that the Parish Council be asked to nominate, if possible, a lady to join them. Dr. Elliott, Medical Officer, reported seven isolated cases of diphtheria in the district.

On the same morning, the eight o'clock passenger train from Northampton to Peterborough burst a tube at Bridge Street Station. A relief train was supplied, arriving about 30 minutes later and proceeded onwards to Peterborough.

Two advertisements were placed in the *Evening Telegraph* on Saturday 9th, shown left and below.

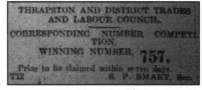

On Tuesday 12th, the *Evening Telegraph* announced:
"Notice: Fresh paper restrictions come into force next month. To make sure of your "Evening Telegraph", a regular order must be placed with your newsagent."

The Board of Guardians met on 12th. Miss Headland, matron's assistant, applied for an increase in salary from her current £22 per annum. It was agreed that this should be raised to £24.

On 13th, reports concerning two sons of Mr. and Mrs. Horace Abbott, Oundle Road were printed. Their elder son, Signaller Leslie Abbott, Machine Gun Corps, had been injured during fighting at Cambrai and was now in a convalescence camp. Their second son, Signaller Arthur Abbott, serving on one of His Majesty's ships, initially went into hospital six weeks previously with German measles, then developed septic sores and finally contracted malaria. He wrote that they were having some lovely weather!

The Food Control Committee placed an advertisement dated 12th, which was printed on 13th:
"Clerk wanted for Local Food Office, as assistant to the Executive Officer (male or female); a knowledge of records and accounts desirable. Applications, stating age, qualifications etc. and salary required to be sent to the undersigned not later than Monday the 18th inst. T. A. Boyden."

The Food Control Committee met on 14th to discuss the proposed adoption of the London and Home Counties Rationing Scheme. This would involve issuing application forms and, on receipt of these, ration and meat cards, to about 4,000 families in the district. The Committee agreed to meet again in one week to work out the fine detail.

Two other items appeared on 14th February:-
Mrs. Jarvis, the town's oldest resident, died at 8.00 am that morning at her daughter's house in Midland Road. Had she lived until July 22nd, she would have attained 100 years.
A petition had been sent to the Postmaster General asking that Mr. J. W. Herring, currently chief clerk, be promoted to the position of postmaster.

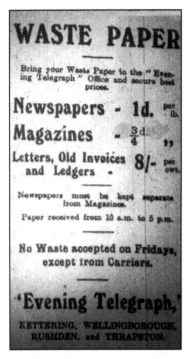

WASTE PAPER
___

Bring your Waste Paper to the " Evening Telegraph " Office and secure best prices.

Newspapers - 1d. per lb.

Magazines - ¾d. "

Letters, Old Invoices and Ledgers - 8/- per cwt.

___

Newspapers must be kept separate from Magazines.

Paper received from 10 a.m. to 5 p.m.

___

No Waste accepted on Fridays, except from Carriers,

___

'Evening Telegraph,'

KETTERING, WELLINGBOROUGH, RUSHDEN, and THRAPSTON.

This advertisement for waste paper appeared in the *Evening Telegraph* on Friday 15th.

A letter from Rifleman Thomas Longfoot, Market Road, was reported on Monday 18th. He had been wounded some time earlier, whilst serving with the Egyptian Expeditionary Force. He wrote, "I have just had a narrow escape. You have read of the advance in Palestine. I was in the Beersheba stunt and the taking of Sherra Wells. That is where I got wounded. A bullet went just over the heart, a very near thing too near for my liking. I am pleased to say I am going on all right now, but still very weak. They did not think there was much hope for me at one time, but I have pulled through, and they have patched me up."

The 18th marked the funeral of Mrs. Jarvis at St. James' Church, followed by burial at Oundle Road Cemetery. Many of her extensive family attended although there were no flowers, at her specific request.

Thrapston Court heard an application for renewal of their licence by the Red Lion, High Street on Tuesday 19th. This was agreed.

Two reports were carried on 21st:
Boys from the Church of England School, as well as tending the school gardens for food production, had also marked out 60 poles of glebe land to the east of the school, offered by the Rector for cultivation. The pupils undertook to take on one plot of 15 poles, initially growing potatoes.
The Volunteers had been inspected on Sunday 17th in the drill meadow near Islip Mill. Of the 53 men enrolled at Thrapston, about 30 had already qualified by their number of drills for inspection, and the whole of them passed.

During the evening of 21st, the Baptist Church Sunday School held their annual prize-giving, where 19 presentations were made for good attendance. The scholars provided entertainment, which was well received by parents and friends. On leaving, each child was given an apple and a bag of biscuits.

Thrapston Rural District Council met on 21st, where, although inquorate (just seven members attending) they were able to talk over what steps, if any, they should take for the forthcoming County Tank Week. Agreement was reached that posters advertising the events would be distributed and Mr. Dellar (deputy-clerk) placed an office at the disposal of the public where he would be willing to receive contributions.

Friday 22nd brought news that Sec-Lieutenant T. H. Bletsoe had been promoted to Lieutenant.

The *Evening Telegraph* reported on 22nd that lectures on "Gardening in wartime" on Wednesdays at the Council School by a county horticultural instructor were being well attended. The most recent attracted 51 people, 14 of whom were boys.

The Food Control Committee agreed at their meeting on 26th to seek help from school teachers in distributing and checking ration applications forms and then handing out cards.

Mr. Arthur Brown held an auction of meadow land at the White Hart Hotel on Tuesday 26th. Three pieces of land were let:
6 acres adjoining Midland Road went to Mr. W. Coales (Aldwincle) at £6 6s per acre.
A meadow by the gasworks went to Mr. Alfred Webb for £5 12s 6d a year.
2 acres off Fair Lane went to Mr. John Barrick at £8 15s per acre.

Rev. Luckock, rector of Titchmarsh, gave another lantern lecture under the auspices of the Thrapston Missionary Association during the evening of 26th. His subject was a tour of the Holy Land he made some years previously.

The annual meeting of the Wesleyan Church took place on Wednesday 27th. The main speaker, from Hertford, presented "With Kitchener's Army in France".

Finally, for February, the Thrapston Council School managers' Meeting Minute Book, dated February 27th 1918 contains this note:-
"It was reported that a quantity of chestnuts had been collected by the children in the autumn, at the request of the Minister of Munitions, but no instructions as to despatch had been received, and they were now almost useless. It was resolved that they be destroyed."

March

Thrapston Tribunal sat on 1st, with these decisions:
A 33 year old married slaughter man received three months.
A 27 year old married working partner at an outfitter and boot dealership had joined the Volunteers and was allowed a further three months exemption.
A 40 year old married boot repairer, also a Volunteer, received three months.
A 37 year old married master butcher who was a Volunteer was exempted for three months.
A 37 year old fishmonger, yet another Volunteer, received three months.
Finally, an 18 year old single grocer's assistant made a personal appeal on health grounds. After much deliberation, he was granted a one month adjournment to enable him to appear before the Medical Board in Northampton.

News of an old Thrapston boy was printed on 1st:
"Thrapston has had the pleasure of welcoming home on leave quite a number of young men recently. Many have been pleased to see Lance-Corporal Henry Baker, of the Canadians, fourth son of Mr. and Mrs. J. Baker, formerly of Huntingdon Road, Thrapston, who emigrated to Canada some eight or nine years ago, and is doing well at Edmonton. He joined the Canadian Force about three years ago, left England for France on 9th June 1916, was wounded in the left knee on August 20th 1917 and has been in hospital in this country ever since, being now on sick leave. He has been through a number of engagements. He has three brothers in the Army; Rupert, Gerald, and Septimus, the last-named at present in hospital in this country."

On Saturday 2nd, the Trades and Labour Council held a dance at the Co-operative Hall, attracting 132 people, to raise funds for the Comforts Fund.

This advertisement appeared in the *Evening Telegraph* on 2nd:
"Two cottages to let, Oundle Road, 2s 3d and 2s 6d per week. Apply A. W. Smart, Thrapston."

Cawdell's placed a number of advertisements in the local press during March, two of which are shown below.

On 5th, the Food Control Committee approved the distribution scheme discussed previously. Meat ration cards were expected to be distributed within two days.

This advertisement was printed on Tuesday 5th in the *Evening Telegraph*:
"Lady clerk wanted; shorthand essential; typist preferred; Taylor and Downs, Thrapston."

Thrapston Parish Council met on Wednesday 6th. Three items were considered:
It was proposed to plant the sewerage works field mainly with potatoes, but with a small amount of sugar beet, to assist with national food production.
They agreed to nominate Mrs. George Smith to fill the vacancy created by her husband's death on the District Council.
A similar vacancy on the Parish Council was filled by Rev. H. E. Fitzherbert who defeated Mr. Edward Loakes by five votes to three.

The *Evening Telegraph* reported on 7th that, in the Thrapston Union area (including parishes in Huntingdon), 4,200 acres had been ploughed under the Government scheme for corn production. Five motor tractors had been used and most of the land had been sown with winter and spring corn.

There were two evening meetings on 7th:
A confirmation service at St. James' Church had six male and 18 female candidates.
The Thrapston Men's Adult School had an evening lecture at the Temperance Hall on phrenology and physiognomy, with explanations and demonstrations of their use.

This appeared in the *Evening Telegraph* on Saturday 9th, and was to continue to feature for many months:
"When spring cleaning, rake together every scrap of waste paper you can and sell it to the "Journal" Office depot, Corn Exchange. By so doing you will help the Government and yourself, for every scrap of paper is now sorely needed."

The Adult School Committee announced, on 12th, that the usual old people's tea and social, which had been a pleasant and much-appreciated annual function for a number of years, had been regretfully abandoned for this year due to war conditions.

After a week with no local news being reported, the *Evening Telegraph* announced, on Monday 18th that:
"A large airship, flying exceedingly low, passed very slowly over Thrapston during the afternoon."

The annual meeting of the Thrapston Branch of the Farmers' Union took place at the White Hart Hotel on 19th. A balance in hand of £15 18s 1d was reported. After some difficulty, members being very reticent to put themselves forward, a committee of 10 people was appointed for the following year.

On 20th, a public meeting resulted in the formation of the Thrapston and District Allotments Association.

March 21st – George Johnson (49) killed in action.

March 21st – Alfred Shrives Loveday (50) killed in action.

The Trades and Labour Council met in the Co-operative Hall on 25th. The recent whist drive and dance raised £11 4s 8d for the Comforts Fund. It was unanimously agreed to hold the usual May Day demonstration.

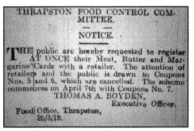

THRAPSTON FOOD CONTROL COMMITTEE.

NOTICE.

THE public are hereby requested to register AT ONCE their Meat, Butter and Margarine Cards with a retailer. The attention of the public is drawn to Coupons Nos. 5 and 6, which are cancelled. The scheme commences on April 7th with Coupons No. 7.

THOMAS A. BOYDEN,
Executive Officer.

Food Office, Thrapston,
26/3/18.

The Food Control Committee placed this advertisement; concerning registering with a retailer so they could use their ration coupons, in the *Evening Telegraph* on Tuesday 26th.

There was no business before the annual assembly of the Parish Meeting on 27th at the Temperance Hall. The only people who were present were Mr. F. A. Cheney (vice-chairman), Mr. Arthur Brown (clerk), Mr. W. Bygrave (hall-keeper) and one other person.

The picture *(shown below)* of men of the Middlesex Regiment, serving in India, appeared in the *Kettering Leader* on Friday 29th. Just one Thrapston man, C. Bamford, appears at the end of the second row and is highlighted with an arrow.

April

The Food Control Committee met on 2nd, when they appointed a sub-committee of five members to consider applications for sugar to make jam.
They also agreed to advertise for an additional assistant to the clerk, Mr. Boyden, due to the overwhelming pressures caused by the continual publication of numerous additional orders and regulations.

The Shire Horse Society held their annual meeting at the White Hart Hotel on the same day when a satisfactory bank balance was reported. It was resolved to hold the annual show on July 25th with no increase to the admission fee.

A "Wanted" advertisement appeared in the *Evening Telegraph* on 3rd:
"Wanted, man (ineligible) to look after horse and trap and assist with other work. John Pashler, Thrapston."

Thrapston District Council met on 4th at the Workhouse.
Mr. T. S. Agutter was elected chairman with Mr. Arthur Abbott as vice-chairman.
A rate of 1s 4d in the £ was set, the same as last year.

An entertainment, by a party of local young ladies called "The Butterflies" *(pictured left, Kettering Leader, 12th April)* provided an evening of musical items at the Corn Exchange on 4th. From left to right, they are:
Back row: Miss Roberts, Miss Cotton, Mrs. Dellar (who trained them), Miss Winter, Miss Hodson, Miss Rowlett.
Front row: Miss Field, Miss Savage, Miss A. Payne, Miss H. Payne, Miss Carress.
The evening was to raise money for the Comforts Fund, which benefitted by £50 0s 6d.

Another concert by the "Bright and Breezy Band" was held at the Corn Exchange on 6th; it raised £38 for the Northamptonshire Regimental Prisoners of War Fund.

April 9th – Septimus Leslie Ferrar (51) killed in action.

On Tuesday 9th, amongst prices paid at the Market, were:
Large hens' eggs 5s 11d and ordinary hens' eggs 5s 8d per score;
Duck eggs between 6s 4d and 6s 7d per score;
A quantity of tame rabbits were sold at "remarkably high prices".

The Guardians met on the same day. They heard from Mrs. Baines (deputy registrar) that her husband, Mr. Joseph Baines, had died on Monday evening. He was the registrar of Births and Deaths, and she requested to be relieved of her duties as soon as possible. As this was an appointment made by the Registrar General, the matter was referred to the Finance Committee. *(Mr. Baines's funeral was held on Thursday 11th at St. James' Church, followed by burial at Oundle Road Cemetery – EDF.)*

Finally on 9th April, results of Scripture examinations were published, with the following Thrapston children recorded as having passed: Connie Hepher, Ivy Grace Winsor, Ellen Hillson, Ivy May Dingley and Audrey Chattell Hepher (all from Thrapston Baptist Church).

Two advertisements were printed in the *Evening Telegraph* on 10th:
"Lost. Left at the "Journal" Office, Thrapston, when lent as cloakroon, an electric torch. Apply at office."
"Respectable intelligent girl or boy required for paper round; able to cycle; reference required. Apply Wyman's Ltd., Thrapston Station."

The same day brought news of Lance-Corpl. F. T. Farrar, Queen's Royal West Surrey Regiment, son of Mr. and Mrs. S. Farrar of Halford Street, who had been wounded in the shoulder and was now in hospital in Exeter, where he was making satisfactory progress. Before joining up, he was an auxiliary postman and boot repairer, living in Huntingdon Road.

A report appeared on Friday 12th that at the Easter Church Vestry, a decision was taken to appoint a committee of the rector, churchwardens, three lay women and four lay men to consider forming a Parochial Church Council.

The Food Control Committee placed this advertisement *(right)* in the local press on 12th.

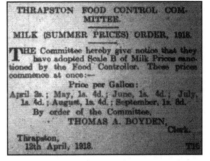

The County Tribunal met in Northampton on Monday 15th, where they allowed a 36 year old married men's outfitter a final two month exemption.

Thrapston Parish Council held their annual meeting on Wednesday 17th. Mr. F. A. Cheney was elected chairman with Mr. T. Selby vice-chairman. Precepts were agreed for the following half year: £5 on the general account and £35 on the burials account. There was some discussion about finding more land for allotments. Messrs. Bletsoe, Pashler and French were appointed to discuss the matter with the Allotment Association.

One day later, the Thrapston Tribunal granted both the assistant clerk to the Board of Guardians and the master of the Workhouse six months exemptions from military service.

Later that day, the Church of England School managers met, the rector and Messrs. A. Hensman and W. Hillyard attending. Two teachers were recommended for a salary increase and the school accounts for the year were audited and signed.

Friday 19th brought news that Mr. Thomas Baxter had been appointed postmaster for Thrapston. He had served the Post Office for 32 years and was moving to town from Castleblayney, Ireland.

Mr. and Mrs. Horner, Huntingdon Road, received news on Monday 22nd that their son, Frederick, Royal Welsh Fusiliers, who was reported missing on March 22nd had been taken prisoner a day later and was now on his way to a Prisoner of War camp in Germany.

Much excitement was felt during the same evening when an aeroplane descended in one of Mr. David's fields adjoining Huntingdon Road after developing a fault. Pending the arrival of air-service men, a guard was provided by the Thrapston Volunteers.

The Parish Council met on 24th to discuss further allotment provision and agreed to offer the local association 2½ acres at the cemetery field. This offer was later rejected and the association sent an appeal to the County Agricultural Committee as they wished to use other areas around town that were in private ownership.

The Comforts Fund met on Friday 26th and agreed to send cash to each man. Additionally, 200 cigarettes would be sent to each man at the front. Recently, every man at the front was sent a 7s 6d postal order, whilst men at home received 5s and those in hospital 10s. The annual parade to raise funds was arranged to coincide with the August Bank Holiday. The secretary reported that he had received a large number of grateful letters from recipients of comforts.

April 29th – Ernest Harry Mayes (52) killed in action.

At the Northampton Tribunal on Tuesday 30th, two married 38 year old Thrapston men, a plumber and a printer's compositor, both received three months exemption.

The final event of April was the Higham Ferrers Second Deanery Conference in the evening of the 30th, held at the Co-operative Hall. Elections were held to appoint members to the Diocesan Conference; Oakham Church Extension Board; the Diocesan Board of Foreign Missions; and the Archidiaconal Board of Finance.

This advertisement for egg substitute appeared regularly during 1918. With many food controls now in place, improvisation became essential.

May

The May issue of the Parish Magazine thanked Mrs. Bletsoe for her donation of altar linen. It also reported that the Thrapston Branch of the Church of England Men's Society had spent a busy winter discussing a report on the connection between Church and State.

May Day was very cold. Many children had taken great pains to make their baskets and maypoles as pretty as possible. They had a day's holiday and a party of girls paraded around town with a banner, singing songs and raising money for the Comforts Fund.

During the evening of 1st, between 30 and 40 special constables attended drill in the Council schoolyard, under the watchful eye of Inspector Campion.

A preliminary meeting was held at the Bank Chambers in the evening of 3rd with a view to forming a One-Man Business Association. A good number attended and it was agreed that the proposed association would cover the Thrapston Tribunal area. A further meeting was agreed.

Sunday 5th marked the Town Band's Annual Church Parade to raise funds for the Northampton and Peterborough Infirmaries. Morning, afternoon and evening parades and services resulted in a total raised of £23 4s 10½d.

A Labour Day meeting took place at the Co-operative Hall in the evening of 5th. A large attendance heard many speeches about the desire to see the Trades Union movement increase in size and effectiveness.

On 7th, the Government announced that postage rates, which were to be doubled, would be held at ½d for letters to men at the front.

At the Guardians meeting on 7th, Mr. Boydon was recommended to the Registrar General for appointment as Registrar for Births and Deaths for the area.

May 7th was the annual May Fair. For the first time in many years, the usual sweet and other

stalls were conspicuous by their absence although the crockery pitch did quite well for customers. It was a disappointing day for the children as it was a fine day; there was, however, some consolation as they were given a half day holiday to allow them to attend.

This advertisement *(left)* appeared in the *Evening Telegraph* on 8th.

An in memoriam notice was placed in the *Evening Telegraph* on Tuesday 9th:
"In ever-loving memory of **John Thomas Giddings (13)**, of Thrapston (Private, Northants Regt.), killed in action at Aubers Ridge, May 9th, 1915, aged 26 years.
"Though death divides, fond memories cling."
From Miss Lyon, Woodford."

The advertisement shown right, appeared on Tuesday 14th.

Two other short reports were printed on the same day:
The Northampton Tribunal allowed a married 37 year old bank clerk at the Northamptonshire Union Bank a three month exemption.
For the second time in succession, there was no business at the Police Court.
(Over the previous year, there had been regular sittings of the Bench – I have included detail of very few cases, as most involved people from other communities – EDF.)

The One-Man Business Association was formed at a meeting in the Temperance Hall on Thursday 16th. Thrapston men elected onto the committee were Messrs. E. T. Cottingham, F. O. Warren, George Savage, B. Cawdell, D. C. Taylor and G. S. Ireson.

Over the next six days, no Thrapston news was reported. The next item appeared in the "Wanteds" on Wednesday 22nd:
"Wanted. Steam tractor driver, good wages. Pettit and Sons, Thrapston."

The Volunteers organised a whist drive on 23rd, 180 attending, raising money for the Northamptonshire Prisoners of War Fund. About £23 was eventually donated.

An army deserter appeared before Thrapston Police Court on Saturday 25th. Inspector Campion recounted how he had seen the man in the High Street the previous evening and was not satisfied with his answers to questions. He was remanded to await an escort.

May 28th – Horace William Reeve (53) killed in action.

The Police Court sat on 28th, where a local motor agent was summoned for driving a motor car at 12.50 am with only one headlight. He had been to Sleaford where he was trapped in floods for three hours. Water entered one of the lamps, extinguishing it. Fined 10s.
Two Thrapston boys admitted riding their bicycles at 10.10 pm without a fitted lamp attached. Fined 5s each.

News of the previous weekend appeared in the *Evening Telegraph* on 28th:
"Four aeroplanes descended in the fields just above Thrapston during the weekend – two on Saturday evening, and two on Sunday morning; and during their short stay a large number of people went to see them."

The month ended with news that Corpl. William Barber, Northamptonshire Regiment, had been wounded in the buttocks by a piece of shrapnel, his third wound of the conflict.

June

The month began with news on 1st that a dance, promoted by the employees of Thorneloe and Clarkson's clothing factory at the Co-operative Hall a few days earlier, had raised £15 7s 3½d for the Comforts Fund.

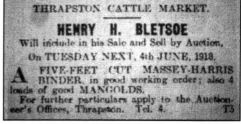

The advertisement shown right appeared in the *Evening Telegraph* on 1st.

During the evening of Sunday 2nd a repair gang were at work strengthening the Midland Railway bridge. Part of the machinery broke, falling into the river whilst George Gunn, from Burton Latimer, was hit by a flailing chain and received lacerations to his leg. After treatment by Dr. Bird and Nurse Mansbridge he was taken home to recover.

Thrapston Tribunal had a lengthy sitting from 10.30 am to 4.30 pm on Monday 3rd. Decisions affecting Thrapston men were:
A 27 year old junior partner in an outfitters with two brothers who had enlisted, one of whom had been killed, received three months exemption.
A 45 year old grocery store manager, a plumber aged 42 years and a fishmonger, 39, all received two months exemption.
Three months were given to a 43 year old draper and a monumental mason aged 45, the latter being required to join the Volunteer Platoon.
Finally, a single farm labourer aged 46 received one month.

The Food Control Committee agreed on 4th that bread could now contain 5% potatoes, rising to 10% on October 1st. Mention was also made of an unproven rumour going around town that butter had been buried in a garden, the consequence of a refusal to allow it to be sold without coupons.

Also on 4th, an aeroplane landed in a field at Islip during the afternoon. It was much damaged owing to the unevenness of the ground, and the airman was considerably shaken. The Thrapston Platoon of Volunteers provided a guard until the arrival, late in the evening, of service men.

June 6th – Thomas Barrick (54) killed in action.

The Rural District Council met on 6th. Amongst the business of Thrapston interest was an announcement from the L.N.W. Railway that they regretted no additional trains could be run, due to services throughout the system being curtailed. A request for a £60 grant from the Food Control Committee was approved.

During the same evening, there was a concert at the Co-operative Hall to raise money for the Wesleyan Church Trust Fund.

At Thrapston Police Court on 11th a young widowed shop assistant employed by the Co-operative store appeared, charged with stealing a tin of Oxo from her employers. After a lengthy hearing with much information about her circumstances, she agreed to be bound over in the sum of £10.

Two advertisements were printed on 11th:
"Wanted. Medium sized table, also plain bookshelves. Box 39, "Evening Telegraph", Thrapston."
"Wanted. Coal carters, apply to Pashler and Cheney, Thrapston."

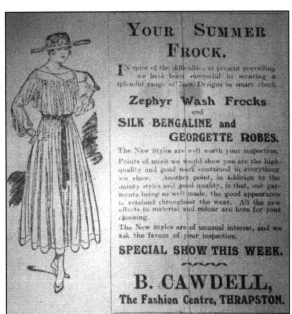

Cawdell's announced their range of new styles for summer, as shown in the advertisement shown left.

Arthur Brown placed the advertisement shown above on 12th announcing an auction of carpets and rugs on 13th.

The following appeared in the *Evening Telegraph* on 13th:
"The "Thrapston and Raunds Journal" will be enlarged with tomorrow's issue by a magnificent Pictorial War Supplement, full of splendid pictures and interesting war items. The very thing for that boy of yours at the Front. No extra postage required for the "Journal.""

Another auction was held at the White Hart Hotel on Tuesday 18th by Mr. Henry H. Bletsoe, where strong bidding saw the sale of many fields and cottages from throughout the district.

Also on 18th, the Food Control Committee agreed extra sugar rations to three applicants for preserving purposes and allowed the purchase of 7lbs. of butter for a function in Islip to raise funds for wounded soldiers.
In the evening, the Supplementary Rations Sub-Committee heard 58 applications for extra quantities, 35 of which were allowed.

The Parish Council met on 19th, where they received notice from the Allotment Association that they were now willing to take up the offer of using the Cemetery field. A three year lease was agreed. The Council agreed that further discussion on the supply of drinking water for the town, held in abeyance for the duration of the war, would not be revisited until hostilities ceased. Finally, Theodore Smith was elected onto the Council to replace the late Joseph Baines.

Restrictions had been announced to preserve paper stocks, this being printed in the *Evening Telegraph* on 19th:
"The "Non-Returns Order" which comes into force on Monday will make no difference to you if you place your order for the "Evening Telegraph" in advance with your newsagent."

The Tribunal made these decisions when they met on Thursday 22nd:
A Co-operative Society manager aged 44, a grocer's assistant aged 45 and a single very deaf carpenter aged 42 each received three months.
A 47 year old watchmaker and his 19 year old son, who worked for the Post Office, were both given three months, conditional on the son joining the Volunteers.
A wheelwright, aged 42, was allowed a final one month exemption.

Friday 21st was the first annual general meeting of the Thrapston Islip and Denford Nursing Association, held at the Temperance Hall. A healthy bank balance was reported. 21 elderly residents and people on outdoor relief were currently receiving a free service.

The *Kettering Guardian* had these words on 21st:
"Wild roses are to be seen growing in great profusion around the Thrapston district and the hedgerows present a most attractive appearance. Wild flowers of all varieties are very plentiful. They make very charming displays for table and drawing room."

Smith and Grace announced their take-over of the entire business of Mr. R. M. Brookes of Twywell on Tuesday 25th, placing this advertisement in the *Evening Telegraph* a day later.

Also on 25th, Thrapston Police Court heard the case of two drovers from Northampton. They were summoned for driving 150 animals on the public highway in Thrapston at 10.45 pm without a light to the front and rear. Pleading guilty *in absentia*, they were both fined 10s with 6s costs.

The Tribunal sat on 27th, giving these decisions:
Three months were allowed for a master tailor (49), a printer (41), a grocer (48), a fishmonger (49) and a jobbing gardener (47) providing he worked on the land for three days a week.
A married 40 year old boot repairer was allowed two months.

That evening, the summer meeting of the Northamptonshire County Union of the British Women's Temperance Association met at the Wesleyan Church, holding afternoon and evening meetings. Various awards were presented to ladies who had gathered "pledges" during the year.

The County Court sat on 28th. Alfred Bolton, motor engineer, claimed £12 9s for goods sold to and work done for Mr. Coulton from Northampton. He sold him a used motorcycle for £16, allowing £5 part-exchange on an old machine. The defendant promised to pay by instalments to clear the debt, but had failed to make any, claiming that it was sub-standard. After hearing the evidence, the judge found for Mr. Bolton and ordered payment of 10s a month.

Finally for June, an advertisement from the *Evening Telegraph*:
"Wanted at once, a good general servant or kitchen help aged 16 to 30. Apply with particulars to Mrs. H. H. Bletsoe, Thrapston."

July

A number of staffing issues were discussed at the Board of Guardians meeting on Tuesday 2nd. Miss Edwards, from Sutton Coldfield, had been appointed matron's assistant, succeeding Miss Oliver who had resigned. Miss Allen, infirmary assistant and Miss Headland, assistant matron, had also resigned. Staffing and salaries were referred to the Finance Committee for their consideration. A discussion about whether the Workhouse had accommodation to spare to take German prisoners and their guards came to no firm conclusion and was referred to the House Committee.

This notice appeared on the same day:
"To gosling buyers. A quantity of goslings will be sold by auction, Thrapston Market, July 2nd."

An evening meeting of the Church Council took place in the Parish Rooms on 4th to consider recommendations to form a Parochial Church Council. It was unanimously decided to form one and to forward the constitution to the Bishop for his approval.

On Sunday 7th, an afternoon organ recital by Miss L. Kingsford raised £2 10s for the Northants Prisoners of War Fund. In the evening, the rector led an open-air service in Chancery Lane, which was well attended.

This advertisement appeared in the *Evening Telegraph* on 8th:
"Domestic help required some mornings. Larter, Nene House, Thrapston."

An auction of glebe land at Bythorn and Brington was held at the White Hart Hotel on 9th, raising many thousands of pounds.

The Food Control Committee met on the same day, where 29 applications for change of retailer were received from customers, the majority wishing to obtain supplies from the Co-operative Society, where they would receive a dividend. Twelve were allowed. The Committee also agreed to make application forms for extra sugar available, to convert surplus fruit into jam.

Also on 9th, E. Loaring & Sons made this business announcement:
"To the Public of Thrapston and District.
May we take this opportunity of thanking all our numerous customers for their valued support in the past.
Mr. E. J. LOARING established this business as far back as 1885, but is unfortunately, through ill-health, now rendered unable to take any active interest in its management.
Mr. E. G. LOARING, the eldest son and partner, has been serving his Country since September 1916, but with the sympathy and assistance of our many clients we have been enabled to carry on.
But now, owing to the exigenses of the War, the Government are making still further demands upon the man power of the nation, and the time has arrived when the only remaining son and partner is being called upon to enlist for military service.
Most of you are no doubt aware that the other brother was killed in France last August.
We therefore ask you to rally round the firm, which is contributing its all in defence of its country.
Soliciting support and co-operation until "the boys come home."
We are, yours faithfully,
E. LOARING & SONS."

Finally on 9th, the Police Court heard the case of a 15 year old Woodford youth who admitted stealing a bicycle "for devilment". He was fined £2 and bound over for 12 months in the sum of £10.

The *Northamptonshire and Hunts Gazette* gave details of the newly published voters' registers on 12th:
"The new register for the Peterborough Division contains the names of 33,638 persons entitled to a Parliamentary vote, 17,772 of whom reside in the Peterborough area and 15,866 in the North Northants old area. The local government electors number 13,333. In the Thrapston Parish there are 515 men and 349 women on the register, total 864; local government 381 men and 349 women."

This appeared in the *Evening Telegraph* on 13th:
"Wanted, a milkman for small dairy (about eight cows) and for small kitchen gardens – good wage to good man. Apply Box 333, "Journal Office", Thrapston."

Miss Marjorie St. Clair Gainer was married to Captain F. Hunt (Queen's Regiment), from Tufnell Park, London at St. James' Church on Wednesday 17th. There was no reception. The couple left town on the 4.32 train for London en route for their honeymoon in Devon *(pictured above, Kettering Leader, Friday 19th July 1918).*

The County Tribunal met on 19th. Amongst the large number of cases was that of a Thrapston boot repairer who had received a two months exemption. The military appealed unsuccessfully against this decision.

Thrapston Rural District Council also met on 19th, where it was reported that Mr. T. S. Agutter had been appointed chairman of the Food Control Committee. Mr. T. Lloyd, surveyor, was appointed to act as the local fuel overseer.

July 23rd – Frederick Bowman Angood (55) killed in action.

News of Lance Corporal Leonard Skelton, Lancashire Fusiliers, *(pictured right, Kettering Leader)* who received wounds to his face and foot in France on 1st July, was received on 24th. He was progressing well in hospital in London.

School attendances were reported on 25th. The Church of England School achieved 88.8% whilst the Council School was at 83.4%. The managers of the latter put this down to an outbreak of whooping cough.

The annual Shire Horse Show *(picture from the Kettering Leader, Friday 26th July 1918)* was held in a field adjoining Chancery Lane on 25th, where there was a small increase to 47 in the number of horses shown. At the close of the show, a public luncheon was held at the White Hart Hotel.

The Young Helpers' fete was held at "The Hollies" and "Nene House" on Thursday 25th. They had raised almost £50 during the previous year for Dr. Barnardo's Homes.

Mrs. Angood received a letter on Saturday 27th from the Commanding Officer of her husband's Regiment, informing her of his death. Just the day before, she had received a field card from him, which he had written on the day he was killed, acknowledging receipt of a parcel.

The *Evening Telegraph* reported on the same day the success of Leslie Smart of "The Laurels" who had gained a scholarship at Kimbolton Grammar School, tenable for six years.

The advertisement shown to the right, requiring all coal merchants and dealers to be registered or licensed, was published on 30th in the *Evening Telegraph*.

The Guardians met on the same day and agreed that 58 beds could be offered for German prisoners and their guards, providing that the master not be taken for military service. *(He had been allowed a three month exemption but was still liable to be called up – EDF.)*

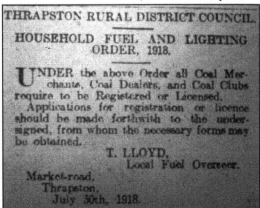

THRAPSTON RURAL DISTRICT COUNCIL.

HOUSEHOLD FUEL AND LIGHTING ORDER, 1918.

UNDER the above Order all Coal Merchants, Coal Dealers, and Coal Clubs require to be Registered or Licensed.

Applications for registration or licence should be made forthwith to the undersigned, from whom the necessary forms may be obtained.

T. LLOYD,
Local Fuel Overseer.

Market-road,
Thrapston.
July 30th, 1918.

Finally on 30th, the Food Control Committee met to discuss a verbal application from the Volunteer Training Corps for additional meat during their August Bank Holiday week training camp at Lilford Hall. The committee, having no authority to accede to the request, regretted they were unable to allow it.

On the last day of the month, this advertisement was printed in the *Evening Telegraph*:
"Wanted, Steam Tractor driver at once, (ineligible). Apply C. R. Pettit and Son, Thrapston."

August

The Tribunal sat on Thursday 1st, making these decisions:
A horsekeeper aged 39, a managing clerk to a firm of builders aged 44 and a 45 year old grocer's assistant each received a three month exemption. A 50 year old fruit and potato merchant was required to join the Volunteers, which he agreed to do.

The advertisement shown right *(Evening Telegraph, Thursday 1st August 1918)* gives details of activities and prize money available at the Forget-me-not Day Parade.

Thrapston Industrial Co-operative Society held a general meeting on 2nd. Profits were good and a dividend of 2s in the pound was agreed. A majority of members present voted for the Society to join the National Labour Party. They also agreed to send a donation of £7 7s to Northampton Hospital.

An open-air service involving the three churches was held in the Market Place on Sunday 4th with a fair congregation.

A very large number of people attended the Grand Parade and Garden Fete at "The Shrubberies" on Monday 5th. The Comforts Fund benefitted by £170.

A slack week for local news followed, not a single item appearing in the newspapers.

DON'T FORGET THE
GRAND FANCY DRESS PARADE
And
FORGET-ME-NOT DAY
AT THRAPSTON,
BANK HOLIDAY MONDAY,
AUGUST 5th.

1—Ladies' Fancy Get-up: prizes, 7s., 3s., 2s.
2—Gent.'s Fancy Get-up: 7s., 3s., 2s.
3—Girls' Fancy Get-up (under 15): 5s. 3s., 2s.
4—Boys' Fancy Get-up: 5s., 3s., 2s.
5—Gent.'s Comic Got-up: 7s., 3s., 2s.
6—Fancy Dress Groups (Ladies—not less than 6): 10s., 5s., 2s. 6d.
7—Fancy Dress Groups (Gent.'s—not less than 6): 10s., 5s., 2s. 6d.
8—Comic Groups (not less than 8): £1, 10s., 5s.

Entrance free to all events. Entries close Saturday, Aug. 3rd. (First Post Monday morning in time.)

SKITTLES, HOUP-LA, SHOOTING, BOWLS, and other Competitions and Amusements.

DANCING in the evening on Splendid Lawn. Particulars and entry forms

W. STOBIE,
Midland-road,
Thrapston.
T2

The Food Control Committee met on Tuesday 13th. The price of milk was fixed at 6d a quart from 19th August. They agreed to buy a new typewriter for £12 12s and also to take part in another blackberry collection. The education department had stated support for this venture and it was announced that 3d per 1 lb would be paid.

The Fuel Organiser announced on 14th that anyone requiring a supply of coal exceeding 1cwt a week should, at once, make application to a registered supplier.

On Friday 16th, Mr. and Mrs. W. Smith, formerly of Thrapston and now living in Yielden, gave a children's tea and treat in celebration of their silver wedding. The swings proved very popular and small prizes were given for the little ones' races.

"LOST. Between Saturday and August Bank Holiday. Gent's silver presentation watch and chain, owner's name engraved inside. Good reward to anyone returning to Mr. P. Makin, Halford Street, Thrapston." *(Evening Telegraph, Friday 16th August 1918).*

August 20th – Arthur Tarrant (56) died of pneumonia.

A Petty Sessional Court was held in town on 21st to consider revisions to the voters' lists under the new Representation of the People Act (1918). Miss S. E. Hillyard had her claim for a Parliamentary vote allowed, although 22 serving soldiers whose claims were received after the 25th July deadline had them refused.

August 22nd – Robert Lewis Hiam (57) killed in action.

The Wesleyan Church witnessed the marriage of Miss Dora Roughton and Lance-Corpl Thomas Smith (Army Service Corps), formerly of Thrapston and now living in Kettering, on Thursday 22nd. The couple left town by train for their honeymoon in Bedford.

The County Tribunal allowed a 37 year old tailor a further three month exemption when they met in Northampton on 23rd.

The picture, shown below, of Thrapston Girls' Band who had recently performed at Ringstead Fete, appeared in the *Kettering Leader* on Friday 23rd.

August 25th – John Thomas Stimpson (58) killed in action.

The Guardians heard, on 27th, that the local Government Board had written accepting the offer of accommodation for prisoners of war. They also heard that the master had been allowed a further three month exemption.

On the same day the Food Control Committee met. A warning to the public was given after they heard of a woman who had two ration books. She stayed with her two daughters, one in Thrapston and the other in Kettering. Unknown to her daughters, she had obtained books from both places and was using them both. One book was confiscated, no other action being deemed necessary.

The Comfort's Fund Committee met at the Co-operative Hall on 30th. Gross takings from the recent Parade and Fete were £190 12s, reduced to £170 after the payment of expenses. It was decided to send all men serving abroad a postal order for 5s and a parcel of tobacco or high-grade cigarettes. Men in training or hospital each received a 5s postal order. It was estimated that there were 225 Thrapston men serving with his Majesty's Forces.

The *Kettering Guardian* reported on Friday 30th that Mr. H. Blackwell, 3 Midland Road, had received news of his son, Pte. L. Blackwell of the Inniskilling Dragoons, who was wounded on 13th in a cavalry charge. His horse was blown from under him and he suffered leg injuries. He was recovering at Cambuslang War Hospital, Glasgow.

September

The *Evening Telegraph* carried this "Wanted" advertisement on Monday 2nd:
"Wanted. Two furnished bedrooms and a sitting room, with attendance, in Thrapston or immediate neighbourhood.
Apply Miss Walters, London & City Bank, Thrapston."

Mr. Alfred Smith, "The Laurels", Huntingdon Road died suddenly on 2nd at 11.00 pm after suffering a brain haemorrhage.

New list prices for coal, to commence on 1st October, were announced on 3rd. In Thrapston, "best hards" would cost 38s 6d per ton whilst "best brights" would sell for 39s 0d per ton. *(Hards were a hard coal, such as anthracite, whilst brights were softer with a higher carbon content, with consequent better burning – EDF.)*

A memorial service for **Arthur Tarrant (56)** was held at the Parish Church during the afternoon of Sunday 8th, the rector officiating. At the close, Miss Kingsford played Chopin's "Funeral March".

THRAPSTON, MIDLAND ROAD

Two advertisements were printed on 9th:

"Milliner wanted (practical) to take and execute orders; good wages, live out. Freeman & Webb, Midland Road, Thrapston." *(Freeman & Webb's Store is shown on page 134 and is now "Thrapston Farm and Garden" – EDF Collection.)*

"Wanted. Cook-general for small house in Kettering; two in family. Write stating age and wages required to Miss Pike, Thrapston House."

Also on 9th, Mrs. Smart placed the following in the *Evening Telegraph*:

"Mrs. A. W. Smart and family of "The Laurels", Thrapston, desire to extend sincere thanks for the numerous expressions of sympathy shown to them in their irreparable loss, and for the beautiful and expressive floral tributes."

The Food Control Committee met on 10th. Complaints about the small tea allowance (2 oz per person per week), the cost of animal feed and a request from a local farmer to discontinue butter making formed the majority of the discussions.

THRAPSTON HOUSEHOLD FUEL AND LIGHTING COMMITTEE.

CLERK WANTED to assist in the Fuel office, 8 working hours per day. In making the appointment preference will be given to Discharged Soldiers, but applicants of either sex will be considered. Apply, stating wages required, to the Secretary, Fuel Committee, Thrapston; on or before the 16th September, 1918.

W. DELLAR, Secretary.

Thrapston, 10th September, 1918.

On the same day, the Fuel and Lighting Committee placed the advertisement shown right.

The Thrapston Branch of the Women's Temperance Association held a Jumble Sale on Wednesday 11th, raising £16 for St. Dunstan's Hostel and the County Band of Hope Union.

On 12th, whilst making deliveries for the Co-operative Society along Halford Street, Benjamin Stapleton, driver, and George Johnson met with an unfortunate accident. The horse was startled and ran onto the footpath. One of the shafts broke and deliveries were scattered over the street. Both men escaped with only minor abrasions.

Mrs. Manning, daughter of Mr. E. J. Loaring, clothier, Thrapston, received official news on 14th that her husband, Corpl. Manning, of the Norfolks, had been severely wounded in both legs. She had received a letter from him stating that he had arrived at Newcastle Hospital, and was progressing favourably.

An evening meeting of the Kettering Branch of the National Federation of Discharged and Demobilised Sailors and Soldiers was held at the Co-operative Hall on Saturday 14th. About 30 local men had joined the Federation and the main thrust of the meeting was the inadequacy of pensions to both soldiers and widows.

The Parish Council met on 18th. A draft agreement to lease the Cemetery Field to the Allotments Association for three years at £10 18s annual rent was approved. Concern was expressed that the Association had sprayed the potatoes growing at the Sewage Works. This had been done on a Sunday, which met with the general disapproval of the Council.
The Fire Brigade reported attendance at two small fires since December.

On the same day, Mr. and Mrs. Hiam received official news of the death in action of their son, **Robert Lewis Hiam (57)**.

This notice was printed in the *Kettering Leader* on 20th:

"IN MEMORIAM

In loving memory of our dear son, **Edward Percy Raworth (41)** (Rifle Brigade), who was killed in action on Sept. 20th, 1917, aged 22 years.

Twelve months have passed, our hearts still sore;
As time goes on we miss him more –
His own sweet smile and loving face;
No one on earth can fill his place.
From his mother, father, sister, and brother."

On 21st, Miss Kingsford took the Parish Church choirboys to Peterborough for an outing. Before the war, they had been to the seaside but it had not been practicable to arrange this over the last four years. They still had a very enjoyable day out.

The Baptist Church Sunday School had a collection for Serbian Relief on 22nd, raising £2 2s.

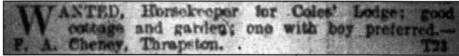

An advertisement in the *Evening Telegraph on Monday 23rd September 1918* is shown above.

The estate left by Mr. Marshall Meadows, late dealer of Thrapston, was published on 23rd. He left £50 to his son, Mr. S. Meadows, £20 a year to his wife and the remainder to his sister Mrs. O. Booth. (*Due to a paper fold in the original, I have been unable to ascertain the total amount left – EDF.*)

September 24th – Samuel Wright (59) killed in action.

The Food Control Committee met on Tuesday 24th. Milk prices, pig feed, meat coupons and provision of sugar for jam making were the topics under consideration. They also agreed that if a farmer sold poultry or rabbits from his own premises, he need not be registered as a meat dealer. The Committee hoped to be able to trust people's honesty to cancel their own coupons if they bought from a farmer.

September 26th – Ralph Buckby (60) killed in action.

October

The last full month of the war brought optimism that "the boys" would soon be home with major gains made at the front. However, this month was to be the town's heaviest ever for losses, five men being killed.

October 1st – Sidney Newman (61) killed in action.

At the Rural District Council on Thursday 3rd, the Medical Officer reported very little infectious disease in the district over the two previous months, although it had been necessary to close Clopton School for a while due to an outbreak of measles.

The Thrapston Tribunal heard a large number of cases on 4th. Five men received three months whilst another six were allowed six months. They were aged between 38 and 49 years.

This tribute to **John Guest (42)** was printed on 7th:
"In loving remembrance of J. W. GUEST, M.G.C. (Thrapston), died in action, 7th Oct., 1917, aged 19 years. Buried in Belgium by the spot where he fell.
"To live in hearts we leave behind,
Is not to die."
- From father and mother, and brothers at home and abroad."

A day later, **Frederick William "Benny" Newman (43)** was also remembered:
"In loving memory of our dear "BENNY" FREDERICK WILLIAM NEWMAN (Thrapston), killed by shrapnel Oct. 8th 1917 at Ypres. Buried at Caesar's Nose.
We never thought when you said goodbye
It was for ever and you were to die;
Too far away your grave to see,
But not too far to think of thee.
From his loving wife, also mother, father, brothers, and sister."

The Food Control Committee met on 8th and fixed the price of milk at 7d per quart collected and 8d per quart delivered. They also instructed butchers to open their shops on Wednesdays, non-compliance being threatened with enforcement action.

The Women's Temperance Association met at "Nene House" School on Wednesday 9th, where they agreed nine points to increase temperance in the community. They called on Government to:
1. Enforce Sunday closing.
2. Restrict public houses opening times.
3. Eventually, to close all public houses.
4. Give licensing authorities more powers.
5. Take more control over private clubs.
6. Abolish the licensing of grocers.
7. Raise the legal drinking age.
8. Allow local people to decide on licensing.
9. Provide alternative meeting places to public houses.

News arrived in town concerning two brothers on 10th:
"Pte. Irvine Geo. Ireson, of the Royal West Surrey Regiment, eldest son of Mr. and Mrs. Geo. Ireson, of Midland Road, Thrapston, was wounded on September 29th in France, by shrapnel, in the forehead, neck, and chest. He is now in an Australian hospital in France, and going on favourably.
Rifleman Joseph A. Ireson, of the Rifle Brigade, Mr. and Mrs. Ireson's second son, during operations in France on 20th September got caught in barbed wire entanglements, which caused a poisoned knee. He was taken to hospital, and the last news stated that he was going on well."

Also on 10th, the Baptist Christian Endeavour Society held their anniversary meeting during the evening.

This Smith & Grace advertisement *(right)* appeared in the *Kettering Guardian* during October.

Thrapston Council School was reported, on 15th, as having collected 1,562 lbs of blackberries.

October 13th – John James Rogers (62) died of wounds.

The Police Court heard three cases on Tuesday 15th. A Ringstead man was fined 5s for failing to subdue lights in his house, whilst the license of the Rose and Crown, Islip, was transferred to Alfred Nutt. A Twywell farmer was fined the great amount of £20 for failing to plough 69 acres of grassland for food production. *(Although not specifically of Thrapston interest, I have included these to indicate the level of crime, which must have allowed locals to sleep easy in their beds at night – EDF.)*

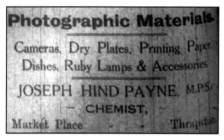

Joseph Hind Payne was advertising his photographic wares in the *Kettering Guardian* during the month. The picture below *(Hazel Evans Archive)* shows him standing in the doorway of his shop some years earlier.

The Parish Council met on 16th. Sales of mangolds, beet and potatoes, grown at the Sewage Works had raised £106 1s. Mr. W. Smith tendered his resignation as a member, due to his relocation to Wolverhampton, which was accepted. There was much discussion about the price of gas, which was felt to be too high. A delegation of members was agreed to discuss the matter with the Gas Company.

October 17th – Arthur Randolphus Abbott (63) died of tuberculosis.

A film show, reported below, arrived in town on 17th.
"A large and keenly interested crowd assembled in the Market Place on Tuesday evening to witness an open-air display of film war pictures from one of the cine-motors now touring the country under the auspices of the National War Alms Committee, the screen being against a portion of the "White Hart" premises. The hundreds of scenes vividly depicted the colossal nature of the sacrifice which has been cheerfully made to achieve the decisive victory for world peace which is now within the grasp of Great Britain and her Allies. During an interval the speaker with the van (Mr. Wilson) gave a short and stirring address."

News of the death of **Samuel Wright (59)** reached town on 18th.

The County Tribunal allowed a grocer, aged 45, six months exemption on 18th.

Dr. Gainer was called to attend Thorpe Station during the 18th when an aeroplane crashed through telegraph poles, narrowly missing the signalbox and track.

Arthur Randolphus Abbott (63) was buried at Oundle Road Cemetery on 19th.

An evening dance at the Co-operative Hall on 19th raised £8 for the Comforts Fund. Mr. E. March acted as master of ceremonies and there was an excellent attendance. Music was

supplied by Miss A. Flanders and Mr. H. Fletcher. The Baptist P.S.A. *(believed to stand for Pleasant Sunday Afternoon – EDF)* raised £2 with their own event.

News that Rev. Ellis Roberts, pastor of the Baptist Church was leaving was announced towards the end of the month.

The Adult Schools held their Harvest Festival at the Temperance Hall on Sunday 20th. Produce was sold the next evening; Mr. W. Bygrave being the auctioneer *(pictured left, with thanks to Mr. Aubrey Bygrave, Cogenhoe).*

October 22nd – George William Kenneth Smith died of wounds.

The following two memorial notices for **George Alfred Langley (34)** were printed in the *Evening Telegraph* on 25th, the first placed by his father, the second by his mother:

"In ever-loving memory of Pte. GEORGE ALFRED LANGLEY, Northants Reg., the beloved son of Mr. and Mrs. Langley, of Denford; killed in action, Oct 25th, 1916, aged 21 years.
Two years have passed since that sad day
When one we loved was called away;
God called him home – it was His will –
But in our hearts he liveth still.
From his loving father, mother, brothers and sisters, uncles, and grandmother."

"In ever-loving memory of Pte. GEORGE ALFRED LANGLEY, the dearly-loved son of Mr. and Mrs. Langley, of Denford, who was killed in action in France, October 25th, 1916, aged 21 years.
Peace be you at rest dear George,
'Tis sweet to breathe your name;
In life we loved you very dear,
In death we do the same.
From his loving Mother, Father, Brothers, Sisters, Uncle, and Grandmother."

The Thrapston Branch of the Northamptonshire Farmers' Union announced a special general meeting on 25th, to be held at the White Hart Hotel on 29th. The President of the National Union, Mr. E. M. Nunneley, was expected to address the meeting.

The Trades and Labour Council met on Monday 28th to hear speeches about to which political party they should affiliate.

A "Thanks" printed on 28th:
"Mr. and Mrs. HORACE ABBOTT and Family of Thrapston, desire to sincerely thank all friends for kind sympathy in their bereavement, and for floral tributes."

The Farmers' Union meeting on 29th was very well attended, with the main sentiment expressed being the hope that the next Government would be a Labour administration.

October 30th – Jonathan Booth (65) killed in action.

News was filtering into town by 30th of the death of **George William Kenneth Smith (64)**. Much sympathy was felt with his parents, Mr. and Mrs. Theodore Smith, "Orchard House".

Another "Thanks" notice was printed on 31st.
"Mr. and Mrs. WILLIAM NEWMAN and Family, of Huntingdon Road, Thrapston, return sincere thanks for the many kind expressions of sympathy with them on the death of Private **Sidney Newman (61)**.

Coal was in short supply *(along with everything else – EDF)*, which helped "Rinso", the cold water washer, to promote the benefits of their product. They claimed that a scuttle of coal could be saved every washday.

November

The month began with good news for three local men when the County Tribunal met in Northampton on 1st. The Workhouse master was exempted until 1st February whilst two 39 year old men, a timber haulier and a compositor, both received six months.

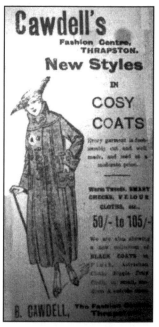

Also on 1st, two advertisements appeared in the *Evening Telegraph*:
"Wanted.
Smart boy or girl for newspaper delivery. Apply Whyman and Sons, L & NW Railway Station, Thrapston."
"For sale.
Smart whippet dog, 14 months old, courses and picks up well. 30s. L. H. Thompson, Oundle Road, Thrapston."

Cawdell's latest advertisement, shown right, was printed from Saturday 2nd.

On the same day, two local men were named in the "Wounded List":
Lance Corporal R. W. Loveday (13792) and H. Wright (16769). Both were serving with the Northamptonshire Regiment.

140

A memorial service was held at the Baptist Church on Sunday 3rd for **Sidney Newman (61), Arthur Randolphus Abbott (63)** and **George William Kenneth Smith (64)**. A large congregation paid respects to their three friends.

The Comforts Fund Committee met on 7th. After sending comforts recently, a bank balance of £180 remained and it was agreed to send 10s to all men abroad and 5s to men in training.

The Wesleyan Church held an evening lecture on "The Church and the Present Crisis" which was given by Rev. Thomas Waugh to a good audience.

On the same day, Canon Burroughs was announced as giving two lectures on 12th, his subject being "Democracy and the Individual". The first would be at 3.15pm in St. James' Church on "The Faith of a Christian Democrat", whilst the second was booked for the Temperance Hall at 8 pm on "Brotherhood or Bolshevism". Further lectures were planned for the coming month.

During the evening of Friday 8th, Mr. and Mrs. Skinner from Woolley, Huntingdonshire left Mr. David's home at Elm Farm where they had been visiting to return home in their motorcar. About half way along the road from Titchmarsh turn and the bridge, they encountered a cow on the road and, in trying to avoid it Mr. Skinner lost control, the car ending up on its right side, blocking the road. Mrs. Skinner was much bruised, whilst her husband escaped with a severe shaking. Dr. Gainer attended with Mr.Carress, from Heighton's Garage. After treatment, Mr. Carress took them home to Woolley.

END OF THE WAR

Germany Surrenders.

Armistice Signed Early This Morning.

Hostilities Cease To-day.

The Prime Minister makes the following announcement:—

(OFFICIAL.)

The Armistice with Germany was signed at 5 a.m. this morning.

Hostilities to Cease on all Fronts at 11 a.m. To-day.

At 5.00 am on Monday 11th November, the Armistice was signed and at 11.00 am, hostilities ceased. The Great War was over and the hope was that, finally, bad news would stop arriving in town. This was not to be the case, a further five men were still to become casualties of war. As the day went on, the display of flags became general and the Town Band paraded around town collecting for blind soldiers. Early in the evening the Church bells were rung, to be joined by other towers in the locality and fireworks were let off with great exuberance. A very well attended public dance took place in the Corn Exchange in the evening, raising much money for patriotic funds.

More prosaically, the Education Committee met during the day, transacting their usual business. Attendance figures were: Council School, 84.2% whilst the Church of England

School attained 87.4%. In both cases, the reason given for the rather low figures was sickness amongst the children.

On Tuesday 12th, morning celebrations of Holy Communion took place in local parish churches, Thrapston having 60 communicants.

At the Petty Sessions on the same day, Superintendant Tebbey advised the Bench that lighting restrictions for houses and cars had been lifted. The Chairman, Col. Stopford Sackville said he should like to congratulate the town and district on the glorious news they had heard the previous day. They had all hung well together like brothers during the war, and he only hoped that good feeling and concord might be established among them for all generations. They had set an example to the world, they had held together for the past four years and he prayed that God's blessing might rest upon them.

A day later, a united thanksgiving service was held in the Co-operative Hall with a full attendance.

During that evening, Mr. Arthur Barnett, of Bridge Street, died after a short illness, aged 56. He had moved to town in 1897 from Eaton Socon, taking over the coach-building business in the White Hart Backway, previously run by the late Charles Papworth. He transferred the business to Bridge Street where he built motor-bodies and, to some extent, aeroplane parts. Mr. Barnett was a member of both the Rural District and Parish Councils.

On 15th, the *Evening Telegraph* reported that influenza was prevalent in town and some of the villages. There were many serious cases and two people had died in Sudborough. Some schools had been closed, including Thrapston Church of England and Islip.

Also on 15th, Henry Halford aged 60, of Market Road, died suddenly at home. He was a sidesman at St. James' Church and his funeral took place on Monday 18th.

The planned lectures, announced on 7th were postponed due to the influenza outbreak on 16th.

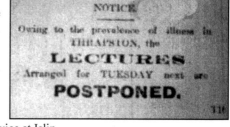

Special thanksgiving services took place at the Parish, Baptist and Wesleyan Churches on Sunday 17th, all were very well attended. Nearly twenty members of the Thrapston Platoon of Volunteers attended the morning service at Islip.

Also on 17th, Arthur Barnett's funeral took place. The cortege left the family home in Bridge Street at 2.00 pm and, after a service at St. James' Church, the interment took place at Oundle Road Cemetery. A very large number of people attended.

Yet another death from the effects of influenza on Tuesday 19th, the victim being Sidney Jones, aged 28, who died at home in Huntingdon Road. An employee of the foundry, he was also a member of the Baptist Church, where his funeral service and burial took place on Saturday 23rd.

This notice was printed in the *Evening Telegraph* on 19th:
"Mrs. A. Barnett of Bridge Street Thrapston and family return all thanks for the many expressions of sympathy with them in their bereavement, and for beautiful floral tributes."

With the cessation of hostilities, the country was in the throes of preparing for a General Election. The old North Northamptonshire Constituency had been altered to form the North (Peterborough) Division and candidates were beginning to put their campaigns together. Polling Day was set for Saturday 14th December with the results to be published two weeks later.

Sunday 24th marked Rev. H. Ellis Roberts's last day as minister at the Baptist Church *(picture from the Kettering Leader, Friday 29th November 1918)*. Services were held in the morning and evening as well as the usual afternoon Bible Classes. At the end of the evening service, he was presented with a wallet containing 21 £1 Treasury notes as a token of their gratitude for his ministry over the previous 24 years.

Also on 24th, another death from influenza occurred. Mr. John Bell, plumber of "The Plantation", Thrapston had begun packing his furniture two days earlier in preparation for his removal to Kettering when his illness started. Aged 46 years, he left a wife and family. His funeral service was held at St. James' Church on 28th with burial at Oundle Road Cemetery.

The Conservative and Unionist candidate for the forthcoming General Election was announced on 26th. Major Henry Brassey, who had held the North Northamptonshire seat since 1910, was announced at a meeting in the Temperance Hall.

The *Evening Telegraph* reported on Friday 29th that there was still a lot of illness in Thrapston and district, chiefly influenza and its complications.

Judge Farrant sat for the first time at Thrapston County Court on 29th, and was warmly welcomed. Twenty original complaints and two judgement summonses were disposed of by the Registrar, and the Judge heard two other cases, not of Thrapston people.

Mr. Lloyd, Fuel Overseer for Thrapston made this announcement on 29th:
"1.   No delivery of coal, coke or any other solid fuel to a private dwelling house shall exceed one ton in the month except with my express consent.
2.   No trolleyman, hawker or other retailer of coal, coke or any other solid fuel shall deliver more than one hundredweight at a time to any private dwelling house and not on any account more than three hundredweights in two consecutive weeks.
Month means a calendar month."

Finally for November, the planned lectures in December were postponed due to both the prevalence of influenza and the nearness of the General Election. It was hoped that Rev. R. Sturdee, Bishop of Peterborough, would be able to deliver his lecture during the afternoon of 29th January 1919.

December

On Tuesday 2nd, Colonel Benyon, Islip House, died aged 74. A local magistrate for many years he was also a regular attendee at St. James Church. His funeral took place on Monday 9th, at St. James' Church.

A notice was placed in the *Evening Telegraph* on 3rd:
"Short Notice Sale.
Denford Cottage, Midland Road, Thrapston.
Useful household furniture and other effects.
To be sold by Auction by Arthur G. Brown
On Wednesday, December 4th 1918.
By instruction from Mr. H. Adams.
Sale at one o'clock."

December 4th – Charles Loakes (66) died of pneumonia.

December 4th- Arthur William Wright (67) died of influenza.

The full candidate list for the North (Peterborough) Division was announced on 4th:
Henry Leonard Campbell Brassey (Coalition) *(pictured right on a 1910 election card, Alfred King & Sons, Oundle and Thrapston – EDF Collection).*
John Mansfield (Labour).
Thomas Ivatt Slater (Liberal).

Two local names appeared in the Casualty List published on 7th:
Prisoner released – Essex Regiment – Upchurch (40002) W. O. (Thrapston). *(This was Walter Oliver Upchurch from Clopton – EDF.)*
Wounded – Queens (Royal West Surrey) Regiment – Cottingham (39791) L. Corpl. C. MM (Thrapston). *(Cyril Cottingham – EDF.)*

Two advertisements were printed on 9th:
"Wanted, man for trial lob-digging and boring.
Also engine driver. Bolton, Thrapston."
"Mr. Jack Mansfield, the Labour candidate, will be holding an open meeting in the Co-operative Hall between 2 and 4 pm on Tuesday 10th."

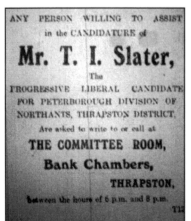

Thrapston Petty Sessions Court sat on Tuesday 10th, where respects were paid to the late Colonel Benyon. A drover, who was staying at the lodging house, Thrapston, was summoned for kicking a dog at Islip on 24th November. After hearing extensive evidence, he was found guilty and ordered to pay a £2 fine.

Mr. Slater placed the advertisement shown left in the *Evening Telegraph* on 10th.

Four days later, after the candidates had held meetings throughout the district, the electorate went to the polls on Saturday 14th. Voting in town took place at the Church of England School, Market Road with Mr. W. Dellar presiding. The first to vote was Mrs. S. P. Smart followed by her husband. By midday 165 votes had been cast and at 4.00 pm there had been 350. When the poll closed, 624 Thrapston voters had attended out of a total number of 740.

At the close of the evening service at the Baptist Church on Sunday 15th, Mr. John Fletcher, choirmaster, was presented with an oak framed address stating:
"Thrapston Baptist Church.
Presented to Mr. John Fletcher by the members of the choir, together with a baton *(silver mounted – EDF)* as a token of their esteem and appreciation of his services as choirmaster for several years.
Annie S. Flanders (secretary)
H. Ellis Roberts (Pastor)
Dec 5th 1918."

News of the death from influenza and pneumonia, of **Charles Loakes (66)** reached town on 16th.

The Guardians met on 17th and agreed to increase outdoor relief by 25% for Christmas week.

At the Food Control Committee meeting on the same day a jam shortage was reported, and the clerk was instructed to communicate with the Commissioner to obtain better supplies.

At Thrapston Police Court on 17th, a recently discharged soldier, who was a hay and corn merchant, appeared charged with obtaining credit for £26 and £25 12s 6d without disclosing he was an un-discharged bankrupt. He was sentenced to two months imprisonment.

On 19th, the Institute held the first round of the billiards competition for the Conyers Cup. 52 people entered.

An advertisement was printed in the *Evening Telegraph* on 19th:
"Wanted, good shepherd, house and garden provided and lambing money. Farm labourer, house and garden provided. Apply F. A. Cheney, Thrapston."

At the Co-operative Hall during the evening, an entertainment was held raising money for Sir Arthur Pearson's fund for the children of blinded servicemen and the Thrapston Juvenile Ragtime Band.

Freeman and Webb announced on 20th, that their Christmas Bazaar was now open.
"New goods just arrived. Grand show of dolls, toys and fancy goods. All the latest novelties at Freeman and Webb, Thrapston."

The Casualty List published on 21st included this name:
"Released Prisoner of War and arrived in England.
Coldstream Guards – Richardson (20068) A. (Thrapston)." *(Extensive research through available records has failed to identify the man who does not appear in the Roll of Honour held in St. James' Church – EDF).*

On Christmas Eve, Mary Sanderson was summoned for a breach of the Lighting Heating and Power Order, 1918, for using gas after 10.30 pm at a dance held in town on 4th December at the Temperance Hall. The event was a fund-raiser for St. Dunstan's Hospital. Superintendent Tebbey advised the Court that the Order was to be revoked and requested to withdraw the case. The Bench acceded.

The Christmas card shown below was specially printed for and sent by Mr. and Mrs. Freegard, of Market Road *(EDF Collection)*.

With Christmas and
New Year Greetings
from
Mr. & Mrs. E. H. Freegard,
Agnes and Margaret.

Market Road
Thrapston   Xmas 1918

Christmas Day services were held at the Parish and Wesleyan Churches with high attendances. The Workhouse had their usual Christmas Day festivities.

The Post Office reported very brisk business before Christmas, which greatly helped them to fulfil expectations. Deliveries on 25th in Thrapston and district were completed before 11.00 am.

An evening dance was held at the Co-operative Hall on Boxing Day in aid of the Comforts Fund. About 150 people attended raising £47.

The general Election results were announced on Saturday 28th and were as follows:

Major Brassey	9516
J. Mansfield	8832
T. Slater	3214
Majority	684

Special memorial services were held at St. James' Church for those who had fallen, on Sunday 29th. 42 names were read out of parishioners who had been killed in action or succumbed to wounds or illness while in H. M. Forces. Two other men were named who were still reported missing. The Roll of Honour in the church contained 227 names of those serving or discharged as well as the 44 named earlier. A total of 271 had "done their bit" and the community afforded them due respect and honour.

A dance was held at the Co-operative Hall on New Year's Eve to raise funds for St. Dunstan's Hostels who benefitted to an amount of £8 10s 2½d.

The Great War had finally ended. Hopes of it being 'over by Christmas' had been delayed by five years but now that it was, there was great rejoicing. The War was won and there was an optimism that a "land fit for heroes" as promised by Lloyd George could now be created.

1919

January

Two advertisements were printed on 1st:
"Wanted, strong girl to work in the kitchen under good cook. Mrs. Fitzherbert, Thrapston House."
"Electrician seeks permanent situation, 15 years experience (5 years in charge of lighting plant). Apply Box 131, "Evening Telegraph" Office, Thrapston."

A Fancy Dress Dance was held between 8.00 pm and 1.00 am by the Thrapston Butterflies on 2nd drawing a large crowd. The proceeds were donated to St. Dunstan's Hostels.

On 3rd, the *Kettering Guardian* carried the following report:
"Now that the war is over it is possible to state that the well-known firm of Messrs. Smith and Grace, Ltd. played an important part in helping those industries which were so much needed for providing our Navy and Army with munitions of war. Their patent screw boss pulleys were in great demand wherever speed of production was essential. Their pulleys were used by the thousands in the great engineering and munition shops all over the country, and the firm were responsible for the refitting of all those munition works which had to be reconstructed following the disastrous explosions which had from time to time destroyed the original work. Throughout the war Messrs. Smith and Grace have been kept at high pressure and their output has been enormous. During the latter part of the period the firm added a department for the making and repairing of agricultural implements, and this proved most useful to farmers and agriculturalists generally in the country who had up to that time experienced very grave difficulties in getting new machinery supplied or existing machinery repaired."

Also on 3rd, the *Kettering Leader* printed the following:
"THANKS.
MRS. CHARLES LOAKES and Family, and MR. and MRS. WILLIAM LOAKES, Thrapston, return sincere thanks for the many expressions of sympathy received by them in the loss of Pte. **Charles Loakes (66).**"

Thanksgiving Services were held in the Parish Church on Sunday 5th. Indifferent weather adversely affected attendances. The rector said, "The real thanksgiving was not only for the triumph in the war, but for the triumph of the cause of righteousness to which the nation had consecrated itself." Collections were taken for the National Tribute to Nurses Fund.

January 7th - John Harry Shadbolt (71) died of pneumonia.

At the market on 7th, only a few samples of wheat and barley were offered, some of which did not reach maximum price owing to poor condition. There was a surplus of fat cattle, a fair show of store lambs and only a few pens of store pigs.

The AGM of the Thrapston District Branch of the Northamptonshire Farmers' Union took place in the White Hart Hotel during the afternoon of 7th under the chairmanship of Mr. T. S. Agutter. 25 members attended. An end of year balance of £31 9s 4d was sent to the County fund and membership during the year had increased from 32 to 66. They agreed to hold monthly meetings. The County Executive were requested to follow up their request for a Sunday train to send milk to London.

On Wednesday 8th, the sixth annual children's fancy dress party was held by the Thrapston Habitation of the Young Helpers' League in "Nene House" School. 41 competitors entered the competition, the three winners being Winifred Cheney (Japanese Girl), Phyllis Askew (Night) and Pat Hawkings (Golly). £5 9s 6d was raised for the cause.

Also on 8th, this advertisement was printed in the *Evening Telegraph*:
"To commemorate the Peace year, Messrs. Taylor and Downs, printers, bookbinders and stationers of Thrapston, Kettering and Peterborough, have reduced the hours of their printing and bookbinding staff from 50 to 48 per week."

The Fitzwilliam Hounds met in Thrapston on 10th with a very small muster.

Also on 10th came news that Pte. H. Knight (10495), Northants Regiment, who had been a prisoner of war in Germany, had now arrived back in England.

An advertisement printed on Monday 13th:
"Wanted, a lady help and give lessons to boy of 11; good needlewoman. State age, salary and reference. Mrs. Frank Cheney, Thrapston."

The Guardians met on 14th. Amongst many agenda items, it was reported that the Workhouse was still without a matron's assistant. The difficulty filling the vacancy was not due to wages, but the lack of room to provide applicants with a sitting room. They agreed that it would be better to employ a cook-general.

The minutes of a Parish Council meeting held at the Temperance Hall on 15th state:
"Peace Memorial -
Proposed Fitzherbert Seconded French –
"That a committee be appointed to consider the question of a town memorial of the Peace and that the Chairman convene a Public Meeting when requested to do so by the Committee".
Carried.
Peace Memorial -
Resolved that Fitzherbert, French and Bletsoe constitute the committee."

A day later, news arrived in town concerning the death of **John Shadbolt (71)**. Much sympathy was felt with his parents. His brother, Pte. C. Shadbolt had spent the previous four years on service in France.

W. T. HEWITT,
BOTANIST AND HERBALIST,
HUNTINGDON ROAD, THRAPSTON,
BEGS to announce that after 16 years' careful study under the direction of some of the most highly skilled Botanists and Herbalists in the country, he has for sale all kinds of non-poisonous ENGLISH and FOREIGN MEDICINAL HERBS, ROOTS and BARKS, etc., also COMPOUND HERBS, in packets.
Orders by post receive prompt attention.
T18

On the same day, news that Major Kenneth Hunnybun (Hunts Cyclists Battalion, attached to the 7th Battalion Somerset Light Infantry) had been awarded the D.S.O.

Mr. Hewitt, Botanist and Herbalist of Huntingdon Road, placed this advertisement *(left)* in the *Evening Telegraph* on Saturday 18th.

The Petty Sessions Court sat on Tuesday 21st, hearing the cases of two local butchers:
Samuel Nichols was fined 40s for supplying a shoulder of mutton without taking the required coupons.
Thomas Selby received a £3 fine for supplying a leg of mutton and three kidneys, this being in excess of the prescribed amount.

Later on the same day, two disabled pieces of artillery, which were on tour around the country, passed through town. Despite rain, a large number of people inspected them with great enthusiasm. The guns were a 4-inch German howitzer captured by the 6th Northants Regiment on 18th September 1918 and a standard field gun, now withdrawn from service. The picture printed in the *Kettering Leader* on 24th *(above)* shows the same guns in Wellingborough.

Recent Royal Academy of Music examination results were announced on 23rd, Miss Violet Bamford being successful in passing the theory examination.

The Guardians placed an advertisement for a cook-general at the Workhouse on the same day.

That evening, a social was held at the Corn Market by the local section of the Labour Party, where Mr. John Mansfield, candidate at the recent General Election, was present. A large gathering gave him an enthusiastic welcome and, after speeches, the Town Band played for dancing.

On Saturday 25th, Mrs. W. Freeman, Midland Road, died suddenly from a cerebral haemorrhage. She was taken ill during the previous evening, Dr. Bird attending. Despite his best efforts, she died at 8.30 am.

On the same day, this Notice appeared:
"Freeman and Webb have postponed their sale from January 28th to Tuesday February 4th."

During the same evening, the Bright and Breezy Band held a benefit dance at the Corn Exchange, raising £20.

On Thursday 30th, Mr. William Beal, Springfield House, Oundle Road, died at home aged 64, having been in failing health for a long time. He was tenant of the King's Arms Hotel between 1901 and 1908 and a veterinary surgeon. He had been very involved with many local organisations and was one of the leading lights in the Thrapston Sports.

The 30th was also the day when the new bank manager at the Northants Union Bank was announced as being Mr. E. A. Law.

The *Kettering Leader* had this picture printed *(right)* of Mr. S. P. Smart with their report on 31st. He had been a signalman in town for some time, working for the Midland Railway and had just been unanimously appointed secretary to the Midland District Council of the National Union of Railwaymen.

February

On Sunday 2nd, Mr. Charles Freeman died at home, Azaelea House, Midland Road, aged 81 *(pictured left, Kettering Leader, 5th February 1919)*. He had the house and shop (Manchester House) in Midland Road built during the mid 1870s and was the founder of Messrs. Freeman and Webb.

The Police Court, sitting on Tuesday 4th, was devoted to the licensed trade. Superintendant Tebbey gave his report covering the previous year. Although there were over 200 licensed premises within the district, there was not a single prosecution for drunkenness.

Also on 4th, this advertisement was printed:
"Waggoner wanted, cottage and garden, at lodge, good wages to suitable man.
David, "Cambria", Thrapston."

On 8th, General Election expenses were published in all the local newspapers:

Major Brassey	expenses £1,053 5s	votes received 9,516	cost per vote 2s 2½d
Mr. Mansfield	expenses £250 15s 5½d	votes received 8,832	cost per vote 0s 6¾d

Details of the forthcoming February lectures at St. James' Church were announced on 8th.
On 11th, Rev. R. J. Sturdee would speak on "The limits of democracy."
On 18th, the Ven. Archdeacon of Nottingham's subjects were "The discipline of democracy" and "Who is my neighbour?"
On 25th, Rev. O. C. Quick would speak on "The church as a spiritual democracy" and "Is the Church of England free?"

Finally on 8th, the quarterly meeting of the Thrapston District of the Central Northants Association of Bellringers was held at Islip, the following towers being represented;
Raunds, Ringstead, Twywell, Woodford, Addington, Lowick, Higham Ferrers, Burton Latimer, Irthlingborough, Titchmarsh, and Islip.
A short service was held at 4.30 pm, conducted by the rector and followed by tea in the Parish Room with about forty sitting down. A short business meeting followed, the Rev. F. H. Lang (Twywell) presided, supported by the rector of Islip (Rev. W. St. George Coldwell) and the rector of Thrapston (Rev. H. E. Fitzherbert).
Several suggestions were discussed regarding a memorial for members of the association who had fallen in the war, and it was decided to place them before the committee for further consideration. The vote of thanks included one to the ladies for waiting at the tea. The tower was again visited, when various methods were rung by mixed bands.

The Guardians held their monthly meeting on 11th. There was much disappointment that no applications had been received for the position of cook-general. War bonuses for staff were agreed; all indoor workers at the Workhouse, as well as the superintendent and matron of the Children's Home (in Raunds) would receive 10% of their pay; whilst the clerk was awarded £20.

Floods were affecting the whole of the Nene Valley. On Tuesday 18th, as a result of these floods and illness, no magistrate attended Thrapston Police Court, where all police business had to be adjourned.

On 19th, John Prentice, solicitor, placed this advertisement in the local press:
"Mr. William Beal, deceased.
All persons having any claims on the estate of William Beal, late of Titchmarsh, veterinary surgeon, are requested to send in writing the particulars thereof to Mrs. Chapman, Springfield, Titchmarsh, one of the executors of the will of the deceased. And all persons indebted to the deceased's estate are required to pay the amount of their respective debts to her."

February 25th – Ernest Wilfred Barratt (72) died of influenza

On 26th, the candidates for County Council elections were announced. Thrapston voters had a choice between:
Walter Askew   farmer
William Thomas Hewitt   moulder, of Huntingdon Road.

During the evening of the same day, a meeting in connection with the Thrapston and District Area of the National Federation of Discharged and Demobilised Sailors and Soldiers was held to arrange for the formation of a branch. This was agreed and the following were elected to form a committee: Messrs. Frank Lavender (hon. treasurer), Horace Glenn, George H. Gilbert, Sidney Gilbert, Samuel Cooper, William Thurlow, Mr. Watts (Islip), F. W. Beal, and F. Whiteman, jun. (hon. secretary pro tem).

Locally reported news was scarce during February, the final item appearing on 28th:
"Influenza and measles are prevalent in Thrapston and district."

March

On Monday 3rd, the *Evening Telegraph* carried two advertisements:
"Lost on hill entering Thrapston, silver plated top of carburettor. Reward on returning same to Wright, "Belle Vue", Kettering." *(There was no indication as whether it was returned – EDF.)*
"For sale. Strong trolley, good condition, seen any time. F. Short, High Street. Thrapston."

On 5th, Mr. Hewitt, the Labour candidate for the County Council election spoke to a good attendance at the Co-operative Hall.

On the same day, a dance for discharged and demobilised sailors and soldiers was announced, to take place at the Corn Market on 8th. Ex-servicemen were requested to let Mr. F. Whiteman, the honorary secretary of the local association know their names by 10th.

The Churchwardens called a meeting in the Temperance Hall on 6th to discuss what steps, if any, should be taken by the Church people of town to erect a memorial in the Parish Church to those who fell in the Great War. A Committee was elected as follows: the rector (the Rev.

H. E. Fitzherbert) and churchwardens (W. Hillyard and J. Pashler), Mrs. Clipsom, Mrs. Humphrey, Miss Kingsford, Mrs. Leigh and Mrs. Partridge, Messrs. Bletsoe, Emery, F. W. Johnson, W. J. Knighton, C. R. Pettit senr. and Pollard. Subsequently Mrs. Humphreys, Mr. Johnson and Mr. Pollard retired. Messrs. J. B. Carter and F. Lord were elected to replace them. Mr. J. F. Porter accepted the position of hon. treasurer.

The County Council election took place on Thursday 6th. There were 730 registered electors in town and a total of 1,251 for the whole district. The local polling station was at the Church of England School with Mr. F. W. B. Emery presiding. The poll clerks were Miss Smart and Miss Rowlett.

The Election result was announced a day later shortly before 10.00 am:

Askew	554
Hewitt	332
Majority	222

Also on 7th, Mr. Thomas Lloyd, Market Road, died aged 69 *(pictured with his "famous" white horse, Kettering Leader 14th March 1919)*. For the latter part of the war, he had been the local fuel commissioner. He moved to Thrapston from Stourbridge, Worcestershire in 1896 when he was appointed surveyor and inspector of nuisances to the Rural District Council. A memorial service for him was held at the Wesleyan Church on Tuesday 11th with a funeral in his native Worcestershire a day later.

The Bishop of Peterborough held a confirmation service for the whole of the Higham Ferrers Deanery at St. James' Church on Saturday 8th. Of the 92 candidates, 32 were from Thrapston, six men and 26 women.

On 10th, Superintendant Tebbey was reported to be very unwell having contracted influenza.

At the Guardians meeting on 11th, it was reported that there had still been no applicants for the posts of matron's assistant or cook-general. They agreed to offer a salary of £30 with the addition of the 10% war bonus, to see if this would encourage interest. There was also a lengthy discussion as to whether the relieving officer should receive a war bonus. There was uncertainty whether they could give one, as he was a Government appointment. No resolution was reached.

The annual old people's tea was held during the evening of Thursday 13th at the Temperance Hall, after an absence of one year. A lengthy programme of entertainment was provided, with Mr. D. C. Taylor acting as Master of Ceremonies. The rector provided motor transport for those unable to walk whilst suitable parcels were sent to people unable to attend.

Just before noon on Saturday 15th, Mr. C. R. Pettit, builder and contractor, Bridge Street, discovered a haystack fire on his premises. With help from willing volunteers, it was extinguished without the need to call the Fire Brigade. About half of the hay was saved. It was supposed that the cause was little children playing with matches.

On Sunday 16, a memorial service was held at St. James' Church for the late Ptes. **John Harry Shadbolt (71)** and **Ernest Wilfred Barratt (72)**. Pictured below is the memorial card

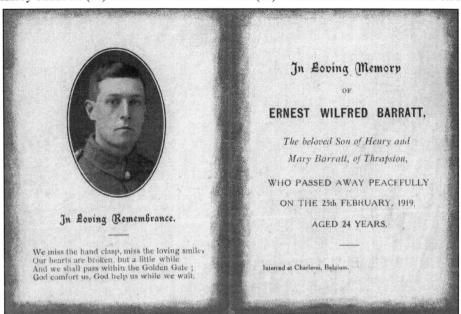

produced for Ernest Barratt *(reproduced with kind permission from Ray Barratt, Thrapston).* A good number of relatives and friends were present. The rector, the Rev. H. E. Fitzherbert, officiated. At the close, Miss Kingsford feelingly played "O rest in the Lord."

The Parish Council held their annual meeting on Monday 17th, where nominations for councillors were received by the large gathering of over 70 people. Voting was by show of hands; with the votes cast shown below and on page 154. The general feeling of the meeting was that this was unsatisfactory and a proper poll should be held on 7th April. This was agreed.

The candidates and the number of votes for each were:

William Thomas Hewitt	55
Frederick William Johnson	48
William Walter Stobie	47
Edward Ernest Frisby	39
Sarah Ann March	38
Mary Ellen Smart	38
Sidney Packwood Smart	38
Thomas William Reynolds	37
Alfred French	24
Rev. H. E. Fitzherbert	21
Thomas Selby	18
Walter Askew C.C.	17
Francis Alfred Cheney	15
Thomas William Johnson	14
John Pashler	14
John Thomas Carress	14
Henry Hopkinson Bletsoe	14
Alfred Hensman	12

George Theodore Smith	12
David William David	10
William Hillyard	9
Edward George Loaring	7

Other matters raised were as follows: a question about the number of new houses due to be built (25 by the District Council); the need to improve facilities for goods and passenger traffic at the railway stations; improving public lighting during winter; the dangerous condition of some footpaths; and the small number of men in the Fire Brigade, and concern about the advanced age of some of them.

At the Police Court on 18th, no magistrate attended, the only business being the swearing-in of a police constable.

The next week passed without any local news being reported.

On 25th, Cawdell's placed an advertisement in the *Evening Telegraph* announcing their new range of fabrics for spring. These included:
Crepe-de-chines at 6s 11d or 8s 11d.
Crepe radiant at 5s 11d a yard.
Coloured silks at 3s 11½d a yard.
Silk georgettes at 5s 11d a yard.
Jap spun silk at 5s 11d a yard (for ten days only).
Shantung silks at only 3s 11½d a yard.
Botany suiting serges in black or navy, costing 9s 11d a yard.
Armure serges, again in black or navy, for 12s 11d a yard.
Tricolene at 4s 11½d.

At an evening meeting in the Temperance Hall on 27th, it was unanimously agreed to form an Infant Welfare Centre for Thrapston and District. Mrs. Walter, Islip, was asked to become branch secretary, to which she agreed.

The *Evening Telegraph* announced on 27th that: "No further consignments of waste paper of any description can be purchased by this office as paper mills now have no further use for this material. Thrapston Office."

The return to normality after four long years was typified by an advertisement in the *Evening Telegraph* on Friday 28th:
"Northamptonshire Football Association.
All clubs, leagues etc. in affiliation in 1914-15, and newly-formed clubs desirous of affiliating, are asked to communicate with the Hon. Secretary at once, giving name and address of secretary.
A General Meeting of the Association will be held as early as possible.
L. E. Swain, 191 Adnitt Road, Northampton."

The advertisement shown right was also published on the same day.

A coal shortage was announced in town on Saturday 29th with restrictions placed on suppliers who were not allowed to deliver more than 2 cwt of coal a week to each dwelling house.

April

The month began badly for Molly Guildford, aged 10, who lived with her parents in Market Road. Whilst returning from Midland Road Station during the evening of Tuesday 1st, having seen her grandparents off by train, she was playing hopscotch on the pavement with her ball when she slipped and broke her left leg above the knee. Dr. Bird was called, took her home by car and set the fracture.

A day later, a lad named Allen, of York Terrace, Huntingdon Road, who was employed at Islip Furnaces, sustained a severely sprained ankle when he was crushed by a small wagon. He was taken home by his foreman, Mr. Butler.

The County Court sat in Thrapston on 4th, Judge Farrant presiding. There was only one judgement summons before the court and, as the parties were unable to attend, it was adjourned to the next session at Oundle Court. A few undefended cases were heard by the Registrar, Mr. Gurney Coombs.

A Thrapston correspondent wrote on 5th that he thought some electors were not aware that they might vote on Monday 7th to elect two District Councillors. Voting for the District Council and Board of Guardians took place at the Church of England School on Monday 7th, Mr. M. G. W. Hunnybun presiding. The result was announced outside the school shortly after the poll closed, a large number of people being present. The District Council and Guardians vote was:

Rev. H. E. Fitzherbert	350	
Mrs. Geo. Smith	255	- both the above were elected.
S. P. Smart (Labour)	161	

The Parish Council election result was :

Fitzherbert, Rev. H. E.	320	
Askew, Walter	260	
Cheney, Francis Alfred	241	
Bletsoe, Henry Hopkinson	232	
Selby, Thomas	213	
Carress, Thomas	205	
David, David William	197	
Stobie, William Walter (Lab)	197	
Hewitt, Thomas William (Lab)	191	
Hillyard, William	181	
Hensman, Alfred	180	
Smith, George Theodore	180	
Pashler, John	178	- all the above were elected.
French, Alfred	177	
Johnson, Thomas William	163	
Johnson, Frederick W. (Lab)	160	
Smart, Sidney P. (Lab)	142	
Reynolds, T. W. (Lab)	112	
Smart, Mary E. (Lab)	110	
Frisby, E. E. (Lab)	106	
Loaring, Edward George	106	
March, Sarah Anne (Lab)	92	

Whilst the poll was occurring, Mr. H. A. Millington, Registration Officer for the County, attended Thrapston Petty Sessional Court to revise the list of voters. A large part of the business was marking off the names of demobilised men from the Absent Voters List and retaining them on the ordinary list. Over 150 men were dealt with.

The *Evening Telegraph* printed these three advertisements on 7th:
"Lost between Denford and Lowick, lady's half-engagement ring set with two diamonds. Anyone returning same to Police Station, Thrapston will be well rewarded."
"Wanted to hire, plot of ground in Thrapston suitable for tennis court. "E.S.B.", c/o Taylor and Downs, Thrapston."
"Typist, really capable, wanted: knowledge of accounts an advantage. Box no. 299, "Journal Office", Thrapston."

The rector paid for the advertisement, shown right, to be printed on 8th.

THANKS.

THRAPSTON RURAL DISTRICT COUNCIL.

THRAPSTON PARISH COUNCIL.

LADIES AND GENTLEMEN,—

I TAKE this earliest opportunity of thanking those ladies and gentlemen who gave me their votes for the above.

I am conscious that the result of the poll was only obtained by very considerable support being accorded to me from every section of the community.

While I cannot hope to represent the views of all, it will be my very earnest endeavour to work for the good of all, and thus try to deserve the confidence you have been good enough to place in me.

T8   HENRY E. FITZHERBERT.

Also on 8th, the Town Band announced that:
"The Town Band, which has for so many years been a successful institution is pulling itself together after the period of stress and hope speedily to regain their standard."

At the Guardians meeting on 8th, a War Bonus of 25% was agreed for the master and matron of the Workhouse, whilst other indoor staff were awarded a 20% bonus. Col. Stopford Sackville, chairman, announced that, having served for many years, he was standing down. A vote of thanks was passed.

An evening Invitation Dance was held at the Co-operative Hall on 10th, organised by a committee of young ladies. Proceeds were donated to the Parish Church committee who were arranging an "Evening of Welcome" for discharged and demobilised soldiers and sailors on 23rd. Invitations to that event had been sent out and a request was made to any eligible men who had not received one to contact the rector as soon as possible.

The Kettering, Thrapston and District Angling Association held their annual meeting in Kettering on Monday 14th. Membership was in excess of 100 and a bank balance of £13 16s 4d was held.

A day later, the Thrapston and District Shire Horse Society held their annual meeting at the White Hart Hotel. A balance of £164 3s 1d was reported and the annual show date was set for Thursday July 24th.

On Saturday 19th, the Thrapston Branch of the National Union of Railwaymen met where they heard of an accident at the new Midland Railway viaduct. One of the workmen, Ernest Arnett from Raunds, a demobilised soldier, was working on a temporary bridge when he fell into the river, which was much swollen due to recent floods. He was unable to swim and Mr. Bert Clipston, Woodford *(pictured right, Kettering Leader, 6th June 1919)* jumped to rescue him, fully clothed. He held his head above water until colleagues managed to throw a rope to drag them both to the bank. Mr. Clipston was congratulated on his bravery and it was unanimously agreed to award him a silver medal and to make his actions known to the Royal Humane Society.

A Thanksgiving Service for the end of the war, and to honour those who served was held in St. James' Church on Sunday 20th. It began with a parade of about 70 ex-servicemen and was headed by the Town Band. The route marched was Market Place, Bridge Street, Market Road and Huntingdon Road. A very large congregation attended and the service closed with an organ rendition of the "Hallelujah Chorus" played by Miss Kingsford.

A Flag Day was held in town on Tuesday 22nd in aid of the National and County Crippled Children's Fund - £12 was raised.

On the same day, on instructions by Messrs. Smith and Grace Ltd., Arthur Brown let by auction a rich feeding meadow of about six acres adjoining Midland Road. After fierce bidding, it was let to Mr. L. Richardson until 31st December at a price of £10 15s per acre. The purchaser was given permission to mow the land once if desired.

On 23rd, a well-attended dance for ex-servicemen took place at the Temperance Hall.

Thrapston Volunteers held their closing dinner at the Corn Exchange on 24th. The hall was decorated with flags and bunting, and the catering was provided by Mr. and Mrs. F. W. Beal. The platoon presented Lieut. Porter with a silver cigarette case and C.S.M. Corbett with a cheque for ten guineas as a mark of gratitude. Thrapston had 79 men enrol with the Volunteers, eleven going on to join the regular Army. A genial evening ended with entertainments contributed by members and invited guests.
Also on 24th, the general meeting of the Thrapston District Voluntary Work Association was held in the Parish Rooms, Islip. They had formed at the outbreak of war in 1914 and continued throughout. The bank balance of £25 was sent to the Director General of Voluntary Organisations.

A Carnival Ball, in connection with Miss Hillyard's dancing classes was held in the Corn Exchange on 25th.

On Saturday 26th, a memorial service was held in St. James' Church for **Jonathan Booth (65)**. A large number of friends and relatives were present, including many old comrades of the fallen trooper, the regiment having now returned to England, and also members of the Town Fire Brigade, of which deceased was a member, and of which his father was captain. The hymns were, "Jesu, Lover of my soul" and "On the Resurrection Morning." The Rector gave a brief, suitable address.

During the evening, a Benefit Dance was held at the Co-operative Hall for Miss E. Brice, who had been ill for a considerable time. Her fellow workers at Messrs. Thorneloe and Clarkson arranged the event and about 250 people attended.

Snow was reported to have fallen in town for several hours during the afternoon and evening of Sunday 27th.

THRAPSTON PARISH COUNCIL.

THE above Council requests Tenders for STREET WATERING, to be received on or before THURSDAY, May 8th. The terms and conditions relating to the work may be inspected at the office of the undersigned.

ARTHUR G. BROWN,
Clerk.

Finally in April, the Parish Council placed an advertisement *(shown on page 157)* inviting tenders for street watering on 30th.

May

May Day was celebrated, with many children wearing garlands and a number of maypoles in evidence.

The District Council met at the Workhouse on 1st. Mr. J. H. Porter, aged 33, was appointed surveyor and inspector with a salary of £250 plus £5 office allowance. He had previously worked for Kettering Rural District Council.
The Council agreed to draw the attention of the County Roads and Bridges Committee to the bad state of roads in town.
The Medical Officer reported that there had been two cases of scarlatina in Thrapston during the previous two months.

The Wesleyan Church held a sale and social evening to raise money for their organ fund on 1st.

Finally on 1st, an advertisement from the *Evening Telegraph*:
"Wanted, plumbers and bricklayers; permanent jobs for suitable men. Pettit and Son, Thrapston."

The *Kettering Leader*, on Friday 2nd, had this "In Memoriam" item for **Ernest Harry Mayes (52)**:
"In loving memory of ERNEST HARRY, the beloved son of Frederick and Eliza Annie MAYES, Halford Street, Thrapston, who was killed in action in France, April 29th,1918, while serving with the 36th Army Brigade, R.F.A.
We could not clasp your hand, dear Ernest,
Your face we could not see;
We were not there to say farewell,
But we'll remember thee.
Far and often our thoughts do wander,
To the grave so far out yonder;
From memory's page we'll never blot
Three little words, "Forget me not."
From his ever-loving mother and father, brother and sister."

An evening open-air Labour Day meeting was held in the Market Place on Sunday 4th; many speeches were made to the large crowd. A collection was taken for the hospitals.

At the Guardians meeting on Tuesday 6th, Rev. C. F. Bolland *(pictured left, Kettering Leader, 9th June 1919)* was elected chairman with Mr. T. H. Beeby becoming vice-chairman.
They decided to adhere to their resolution not to pay the war bonus to the Relieving Officer, Mr. Boydon, as long as he remained in his dual role (as Food Control Officer). The matter had been raised in the House of Commons for a definitive statement as to whether he was actually employed by the Government as Relieving Officer.

This story, reproduced in full, was printed in the *Evening Telegraph* on 9th:
"SEEKING WORK
Discharged Soldier's Experiences at Thrapston.
A correspondent writes: - A discharged soldier who arrived in Thrapston on Tuesday evening, stated next morning that on reaching the town after tramping from Godmanchester with 5½d in his possession, he went into a shop and asked to be served with a pound of bread and that the attendant had no one-pound loaf and refused to divide a two-pound loaf, as this was not allowed by law.
His desire was to purchase a pound of bread and two ounces of margarine for a meal before seeing about his night's lodging. He did not complain of the law being obeyed, but was strongly of opinion that an exception should be made in the case of ex-servicemen in search of employment.
He gave the name of Private Herbert Fisher, late 1st Garrison Battalion, Northamptonshire Regiment and the following particulars: - Served in that Battalion with the Mediterranean Expeditionary Force from 24th October 1915 to 9th February 1916; also served 363 days in the Labour Corps; discharged 22nd June 1918 on medical grounds; by trade a furrier; not had three months' work since June 1918; travelled over the country a great deal in search of work; on Tuesday he had only one pound of bread on the way over from Godmanchester, and on arrival at Thrapston at twenty minutes to eight he was very hungry.
On being refused the bread he inquired for the Discharged and Demobilised Sailors' and Soldiers' Branch officials and was given 1s 6d by (he believed) the treasurer, which enabled him to get a loaf of bread, night's lodging, supper and breakfast. He showed his papers. His character on discharge from the Labour Corps was "Honest and sober man. Disability aggravated by military service." He was wearing the 1914-1915 Star Ribbon and the King's Silver Discharge Badge.
His pension he said was 27s 6d a week for four weeks and 8s 3d a week for 42 weeks: and he would be notified by the Minister of Pensions as to the amount after that. He further stated that he was medically re-examined on April 15th and recommended for surgical treatment and more pension, but that he had not yet heard anything further. He gave his present age as 50 and stated that he proposed making his way to his native place, Bedford, with the view of getting into hospital.
Before he left Thrapston a lady who had heard his story handed him a package as a substantial contribution to his day's provisions."

A public meeting on 13th at the White Hart Hotel of the Thrapston Christmas Fat Stock Show Committee voted narrowly (six votes to five) to hold a show in 1919, although it was accepted that entries would be lower than previously because of the war.

This advertisement was printed on 13th:
"Wanted, coach and motor painter and finisher. Apply Barnett Motor Works, Thrapston."

The picture *(right)* was printed in the *Kettering Leader* on Friday 23rd. It shows Mr. J. W. Roughton whose retirement after 40 years as a postman was announced on 15th. Staff from Thrapston Post Office presented him with a purse of money.

Two "Wanted" advertisements appeared on Monday 19th:
"Wanted. A young lady as manageress for the drapery department.
Applications, stating age, experience and wages required and copies of references by May 30th 1919 to The Manager, Co-operative Society Ltd, Market Road, Thrapston."

"Motor driver (married) seeks situation, private or commercial. 11 years pre-war, one year in Army Service Corps. All repairs. Box 23, "Evening Telegraph", Thrapston."

Thrapston Parish Council met on 21st. The railway had replied that they could not find any difficulties in respect to goods traffic but if specific cases could be quoted, they would be enquired into. The main road through town was very dirty in dry weather and muddy in wet. They requested the District Council remedy this. A street watering contract was awarded to Messrs. C. Pettit and Son. Finally, a new scale of charges was approved for the Fire Brigade's attendance at fires and agreement reached to purchase two lengths of 50 ft hose and have gas laid on at the engine house.

Also on 21st, the total receipts of the Easter Monday effort by the local branch of the National Union of Railwaymen was reported as being £23 18s 5d with expenses of £8 18s 5d. The balance of £15 was sent to the Orphan and Benevolent Funds.

An informal meeting of the Parish Council a day later to consider a Peace Memorial received a report from Rev. H. E. Fitzherbert giving several suggestions. It was decided to lay these before a public meeting on Monday 2nd June.

The same evening a successful meeting and concert for discharged and demobilised servicemen took place at the Corn Exchange.

On 23rd, the announcement that the King of Italy had awarded the Croci di Guerra *(War Cross – EDF)* to Sgt. Major S. Bone appeared in the *Kettering Leader*.

On 24th, the North Northants Musical Competition Society held a meeting at the Temperance Hall. After much discussion, they agreed to hold competitions in 1920 in both junior and senior sections.

At the Police Court on Tuesday 27th, eleven cases were heard, all of people from out of town. Four married women from Brigstock were found guilty of the theft of one piece of glass, some coal, a scrubbing brush, three boxes and 13 chrysanthemum roots. They were all fined.

That evening, Rev. Kirtlan from Hull gave another lecture at the Wesleyan Church describing his experiences over the last three months speaking to troops in occupied territory on the Rhine.

A day later, Mr. H. Varah resigned as agent to the Unionist Association Executive for the North Northants (Peterborough) Division. This was accepted and a warm vote of thanks was accorded for his loyal service since 1906.

On Saturday 31st, these words were printed in the *Evening Telegraph*:
"IN MEMORIAM
In loving memory of Pte. **Arthur Warren (23)**, who lost his life while serving on H.M.S. Tipperary in the Jutland Battle, May 31st 1916.
Those who loved you, sadly miss you
As it dawns another year;
In the lonely hours of thinking
Thoughts of you are ever near.
From his loving aunt and cousins – Thrapston."

June

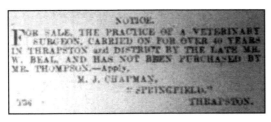

The advertisement *(left)* appeared on Monday 2nd:

Another advertisement from the "small ad's" column of the *Evening Telegraph* on the same day read:
"Wanted. Carter to cart coal, flour etc. Tender form can be had by applying to the Manager, Co-operative Society, Thrapston."

The meeting to discuss Peace memorials was held on 2nd. I include the report in full:-
"A town's meeting was held on Monday evening at the Temperance Hall, Thrapston, to consider the questions of permanent war memorial and peace celebrations. Mr. F. A. Cheney, chairman of the Parish Council, presided, supported on the platform by Mr. Arthur G. Brown (clerk to the Council); and there was a large and thoroughly representative gathering, including a considerable number of ladies.
REPORT OF COMMITTEE.
The chairman, in opening, stated that the questions of war memorial and peace celebrations were brought up at the Parish Council, and a small committee was appointed to go into the matter and make suggestions, the chairman then to call a town meeting. He understood that there was a proposed Parish Church Memorial. There was also a County Memorial, and he believed they would be asked to subscribe to that. He then read the report of the Committee, of which Rev. H. E. Fitzherbert was chairman. With regard to a war memorial, they reported "a recreation ground for the rising generation seems the most appropriate addition that could be made to the town, if a suitable site is forthcoming; or, negotiations might be opened with a view to taking over and renovating the Temperance Hall as a public hall for the town; or, it was suggested that the memorial which it is proposed to erect to the fallen in the Parish Church consisting of reredos and panelling, might be considered by the Parish Meeting as a sufficient memorial for the town. Other suggestions which were brought forward were the erection of an Isolation Hospital; the erection of a Market Cross; and a considerable contribution from the town to the County Memorial: but the Committee does not recommend any of these for reasons which they are prepared to give if required." On the question of Peace celebrations the Committee reported: - "It seems difficult to suggest anything better than sports and a parade, with tea for children and old people. If the celebrations are to extend over two weekdays, the committee suggests that one day should be given up to sports, and tea to children; and one day to parade, garden fete, and tea to old people; and that a committee should be appointed by the Parish Meeting to undertake each department, viz. finance, catering, sports, parade, amusements (in the event of a garden fete)." – (The committee consisted of Rev. H. E. Fitzherbert, and Messrs. H. H. Bletsoe, J. T. Carress, and A. French.)
WAR MEMORIAL
The chairman invited suggestions.
Mr. T. E. Sharp said to his mind the housing question was one of the most burning importance. The houses at present existing in Thrapston certainly had no accommodation for baths. He should like to suggest that a public bath be provided as a war memorial. (Applause.)
Mr. W. Halford suggested that an attempt be made to get a recreation ground. (Applause.) The field known as "The Wilderness" would be central and adaptable.
Mr. T. E. Sharp quite agreed as to the need for a recreation ground. – Mrs. W. March strongly supported a recreation ground. - Mr. W. T. Hewitt thought it was absolutely necessary to provide a place where children could play, not only free from danger but free from the risk of disease. At the same time he quite agreed with what Mr. Sharp had said. (Applause.) – Mr. T.

Selby supported a recreation ground, and suggested the land in front of Thrapston House. A shelter could be provided which might contain the names of those from the town who had served and fallen in the war. (Applause.) – Mr. G. Warner also spoke in favour of a recreation ground.

RECREATION GROUND APPROVED

Mr. Halford then formally proposed, and Mr. Hewitt seconded, that a recreation ground be provided for the town as a permanent war memorial, and that a committee be appointed (with power to add) to carry out the proposal.

The proposal was carried unanimously with acclamation.

CRICKET AND FOOTBALL

The chairman quite agreed that a playground for the children was greatly needed. – It having been remarked that the land in front of Thrapston House would not be suitable for cricket or football, but that a "pitch" could be made in "The Wilderness," Mr. Hewitt thought that cricket or football on the piece of land they were thinking of would hardly be safe for children, who were the chief consideration. – Mr. E. Pickering spoke in favour of having land where football could be played. (Applause.)

Mr. Pashler asked if it would not be better to provide playing fields, say from ten to twenty acres, where cricket or football or any other game could be played. (Much applause.) He suggested it might be possible to obtain a portion, if not the whole, of the Glebe at the back of the Church school. (Hear, hear, and applause.) He believed the money obtained for grazing would be sufficient to pay the interest on the loan. – Mr. Sharp, Mr. Amos, Mr. Porter, and Mr. Halford supported Mr. Pashler's suggestion.

Mr. G. Warner moved that the three sites mentioned be referred to the proposed committee for consideration. – Mr. W. J. Knighton and Mr. J. Hodson both seconded. – This was unanimously agreed to. - On the motion of Mr. Askew C.C., seconded by Mr. Amos, it was unanimously resolved that the committee consider the Glebe land in the first instance.

THE COMMITTEE

The following were appointed to the committee with power to add and with full power to act: Mr. J. F. Porter, Mr. W. Halford, Mr. A. French, Mr. Bletsoe, Mrs. Cottingham, Mr. B. Cawdell, Mr. W. Askew C.C., Mr. Pashler, Mr. J. T. Carress, Miss Kingsford, Mrs. Humphrey, the Rev. H. E. Fitzherbert, Mrs. F. W. Beal, Mrs. Warren, Mr. T. Selby, Mr. Capps, and Mr. F. A. Cheney. – The Rev. H. E. Fitzherbert, alluding to his appointment, said he was entirely in favour of a recreation ground, and would do anything he could to help it. Referring to the proposed Church memorial, he said that he did feel that there should be something done to the glory of God and to keep in remembrance those who had fallen.

PEACE CELEBRATIONS.

The chairman having adverted to the committee's peace celebration proposals, Mrs. March suggested that there should be a tea for the whole of the inhabitants. (Applause.) – Mr. Ainsworth thought all talk of peace celebration was very premature just now. He thought that whatever was done in Thrapston as a matter of peace celebration there should be included a mass meeting – a service of thanksgiving and intercession. – The chairman hoped there would be a day of thanksgiving. – The Rev. H. E. Fitzherbert said the committee thought there would be Sunday, Monday, and Tuesday, three days, and that thanksgiving would come naturally on Sunday. – Mr. Askew suggested that a thanksgiving service be held on the field, and this was unanimously agreed to.

Mrs. March's suggestion was also accepted that a public tea, if possible, should be held for the whole of the inhabitants of Thrapston.

The following were appointed to the committee, with power to add, and full power to act: - Mr. F. W. Lord, Rev. J. L. Gillians, Mr. W. March, Mr. W. Stobie, Mr. Chas. Pettit, Mr. J. T. Carress, Mr. F. C. Lavender, Mr. H. H. Amos, Mr. F. O. Warren, Mr. W. T. Hewitt, Mr. E. Law, Mr. G. C. Ainsworth, Mrs. Humphrey, Mrs. Bletsoe, Mrs. March, Mrs. Carress, Mr. P.

Makin, Mr. John Meadows, Mrs. Warren, Mrs. Beal, Mr. Boyden, Mrs. F. W. Lord, Mrs. F. A. Cheney, and the Rev. H. E. Fitzherbert.
The chairman mentioned that £6 left of the Coronation funds (now £7 1s 10d) would be available."

The Guardians met on 3rd when they agreed that, with the cessation of hostilities, officers whose appointments were sanctioned by the Local Government Board during the war should now have the posts advertised as soon as they became vacant. Salaries offered would remain the same. They also renewed their annual subscriptions to both the Ringstead and the Wadenhoe and District Nursing Associations.

Alfred Smith placed this advertisement, shown right, in the *Evening Telegraph* on 4th.

On 6th an advertisement for Miss Hillyer's plays, in aid of St. Dunstan's, offered tickets for a matinee performance, available from the White Hart Hotel.

The Police Court sat on Tuesday 10th. Several people from the district were summoned for riding their bicycles at night without lights. All were fined 7s 6d, with the exception of one man who received a 10s penalty.

On 12th, the North Northants Conservative and Unionist Association was formally dissolved at a meeting in town. The funds and effects were vested in trustees whilst a new scheme for a central Association was brought to fruition.

On the same day, Rupert Smith, Thrapston offered to buy ladies and boys or girls second-hand bicycles for immediate cash.

Pettit and Son were seeking more employees. On 12th they were looking for a "Plumber and hot water fitter; constant job for suitable man."

Finally, on 12th, the local Labour Council placed the advertisement shown left in the *Evening Telegraph*.

On Wednesday 18th, Thrapston Rectory, opposite Oundle Road *(shown below – EDF Collection)*, was auctioned by Messrs. Henry Bletsoe and Son, the rector having moved into more commodious accommodation at Thrapston House. It was sold as one lot comprising the house and gardens plus an adjoining productive garden with extensive frontages on Market Road and Hortons Lane. It was eventually sold for over £1000 to a buyer acting for the Post Office authorities with a view to adapting it as a Post Office as, for a number of years, the one in Bridge Street was considered cramped and unsatisfactory.

The Parish Council held their monthly meeting on 18th. Following a further letter from the Railway Company, complaints had been received by the Council from Smith and Grace Ltd. and the Co-operative Society, stating that they had no difficulties with rail services and objecting to the implication that they did. The Council agreed to drop the matter. Recent heavy rain had caused flooding along Huntingdon Road which extended to Bridge Street. A small committee was formed to meet with the District Surveyor

to see if anything could be done. Overhanging trees near the Fire Engine House were causing danger to vehicular traffic and it was resolved to request the owner take action. Finally, the clerk reported the cost of the recent election as being £11 12s 5d.

This notice was printed on 18th: "Mrs. C. Bamford, Thrapston, wishes to thank all friends for their kind sympathy on the death of her dear little son."

During the eight months since the Armistice, there had probably been some sporting activity in town, although it was only on Thursday 19th that the first sports report was printed *(shown right)* - a bowls match against Raunds.

RAUNDS v. THRAPSTON.

Played at Raunds on Thursday, resulting in a victory for Raunds by 14 points. Scores:—

W. Cobley, H. Streather, W. Spicer, A. Lawrence (Raunds)	11
S. E. Nichols, W. Dellar, L. Allen, J. T. Carress (Thrapston)	20
H. Bamford, A. Bugby, J. Chambers, P. Harris	21
G. Cooper, W. Bray, G. Gilbert, C. Butler	6
G. Kirk, C. Mason, J. Curtis, W. Patrick	20
E. A. Tinn, W. Halford, A. Pettit, H. Horner	12
	52
	38

Two advertisements appeared on 20th:
"Wanted, ladies cycle or frame, any condition. L. Gunn, Halford Street, Thrapston."
"For sale. Canadian Canoe in good condition, complete. Apply B. B. Wright, "The Hermitage", Thrapston."

After a long and painful suspense of fourteen months, news reached town on 20th that **Septimus Leslie Ferrar (51)**, who had been missing since 9th April 1918, had finally been presumed by the War Office to have died on that date.

The *Kettering Leader* on Friday 20th carried news of the War Office's decision concerning memorial stones for those killed during the war:

"The drawing shows the design of the memorial stone passed by the War Office for the graves of soldiers who have fallen on the Western front, and whose burying places have been recorded.
Each stone will bear the badge of the regiment or unit to which the dead soldier belonged, together with his name, rank, regiment, and date of death. No difference will be made between officers and men, nor will any distinction of rank be attempted in the disposition of the cemetery. The inscription at the base will be chosen by the relatives of the dead.
The number of properly registered graves in France and Belgium is over 350,000, and there will be more than a thousand cemeteries in these countries, the ground on which they are formed, thanks to the chivalrous sense of what is due to the devoted warrior felt by the several Governments, "will be forever England." In each cemetery an imposing stone cross will also be erected."

On 23rd the annual Thrapston wool sales recommenced, taking place in Mr. Selby's field on Chancery Lane. In total, over 10,000 fleeces of varying quality were sold. The best quality ones reached in excess of £4 each.

Another bowls match, against Peterborough, took place in town on 26th with a home victory by 52 points to 31. Thrapston was represented by Messrs. Bamford, Dellar, Savage, Carress, Cooper, Pettit, Horner, Butler, Nichols, Gilbert, Allen and Varah. One of the Peterborough team was Alderman Clifton, still able to take part notwithstanding his 85 years of age.

Saturday 28th marked the official end of the war when the Treaty of Versailles was finally signed in Paris, after six months of detailed negotiation between diplomats representing 32 countries and nationalities.

On 29th Ira Sykes from Westhorpe, Suffolk, who had been staying with her sister, Mrs. McClure in Midland Road, died suddenly aged 23 years.

July

Two advertisements were placed in the *Evening Telegraph* on Tuesday 1st:
"Wanted. Shoeing and general blacksmith; constant job for suitable man. Pettit and Son, Thrapston."

"For sale. Second-hand bicycle, in excellent running order; five guineas *(£5 5s – EDF)*: Harold Guest, Huntingdon Road, Thrapston."

During July, the leaflet pictured below was sent to each house in town, seeking subscriptions towards the cost of the War Memorial, estimated at £420. *(Northampton Records Office)*. This example was completed by the Templeman family, who lost a son during the war.

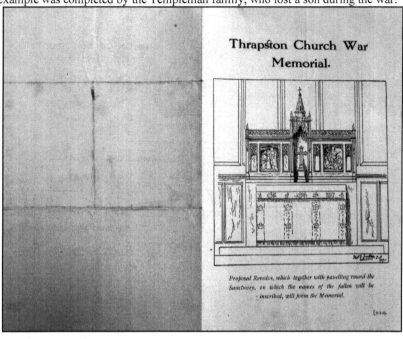

Proposed Reredos, which together with panelling round the Sanctuary, on which the names of the fallen will be inscribed, will form the Memorial.

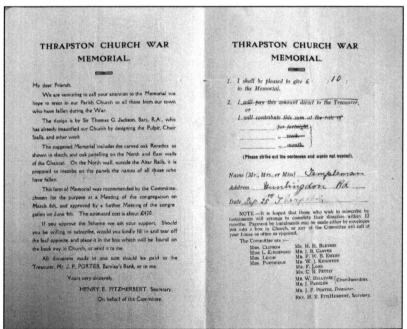

On 5th, the Thrapston branch of the Federation of Demobilised and Discharged Soldiers and Sailors held a successful garden fete and dance in the picturesque grounds of "The Shrubberies" (by the kind permission of Mrs. Sanderson). Music was provided by Thrapston Town Silver Band.

At the Police Court on 8th, six cases were heard, all of people from out of town.

The Institute Flower Show, due to be held on 19th, was postponed for one week on 10th.

Thrapston Bellringers held one of their regular Association meetings at Great Addington on 12th.

The Wesleyan Sunday School celebrated their anniversary on 13th.

The C. of E. School managers met on 15th, where a complaint had been received about youths damaging the school buildings and pilfering from the garden after school hours. It was agreed to take steps to prevent any reoccurrence.

Also on 15th, the rector was instituted as the new Rural Dean by the Bishop of Peterborough in St. James' Church. Tea was served in the Temperance Hall afterwards.

This letter, reproduced in full, was printed on 15th in the *Evening Telegraph*. An intense search failed to find the original letter from "An Inhabitant", the content of which can only be surmised:-
"(To the Editor of the "Evening Telegraph")
Sir, - The letter of "An Inhabitant" is very true to the letter. But the writer, I fear, has failed to grasp what is so palpably obvious to those who have been more fortunate to be born in a place where intelligence in a larger proportion to ignorance is the rule and not the exception, and therefore Thrapstonians are to be pitied rather than blamed. In Thrapston, like in most other similar places, all matters are governed by contaminated narrow minds totally incapable of expansion or conversion.
A person who happens to have been left a house in the year one by his or her great-great-grandmother, and which is still standing upright, and who still has the cheek to call each Monday morning for 1s 6d or 2s rent, is designated one of the "governors" of the village of Thrapston, and so what can "Inhabitant" expect? These places are in many places a disgrace to the universe, and certainly to Britain, and in one part of Thrapston there are places a hundred times worse than the worst slums to be found in Liverpool and other large coast towns. Probably after the next great war a few broad-minded people may have entered the village of Thrapston, although it is very doubtful, and in such cases the middle-class inhabitants may have the opportunity of a bun and a cup of tea to celebrate peace. For any intelligent broad-minded person to be domiciled in Thrapston is equivalent to their being in exile.
Those who may be left out of the marvellous celebrations on Saturday next may have an opportunity of witnessing the celebrations at Kettering or elsewhere, where there are competent and up to date administrators. For corroboration of these allegations analyse the progress of this so-called village of Thrapston during the last 20 years, and it will be observed that facts speak for themselves. – Yours truly,
Sympathiser with Inhabitant.
July 12th."

The Parish Council met on Wednesday 16th, when they received a report from the Storm Water Flooding Sub-Committee. Agreement was reached on extending surface drains by the

C. of E. School. A favourable finance report was received in respect of the Peace celebrations to be held on 19th.

The Comforts Fund Committee were pictured in the *Kettering Guardian* on Friday 18th *(the same picture as on page 44 – EDF)*. A grand finale was planned for 25th, which would finally bring their efforts on behalf of sailors and soldiers to a conclusion. In total, they had raised in excess of £1000.

The Peace celebrations took place in Thrapston over the weekend of 19th, and were reported in great depth by all the local newspapers. *(Full details can be found in our first publication "In the Springtime of their Lives" on pages 106 – 108 – EDF.)*

Alfred Smith placed two advertisements on 22nd that ran for many weeks:
"Sewing machines and prams repaired by experts; no delay. Needles for Prister and Rosemann pattern machines in stock. Any make of needle supplied to pattern. Shuttles, bobbins, needle plates etc.; any make fitted. Pram parts, tyres, spokes, wheels fitted up with the least possible delay. Send your requirements to Alfred Smith and Son, Midland Road, Thrapston."
"Gramophones overhauled and repaired by competent mechanics. Parts always in stock – main springs, governor springs, sound-box parts, tone arm fittings, insulating rubbers, needle screws, elbows. No delay if you bring your repairs to us. His Master's Voice, Zonophone, Winnor, Regal records etc. in stock from 2s 6d. Needles, all kinds, from 9d a box. Alfred Smith and Son, Midland Road, Thrapston."

A well-attended Vestry Meeting was held on 23rd. The only business was to discuss the scheme for the Church War Memorial which was agreed unanimously. 44 names were proposed for inclusion, with their next of kin's approval. The meeting agreed to apply for a Faculty for the necessary work to be done.

The Shire Horse Show was held on Monday 24th, 41 animals being entered. The first picture *(Kettering Leader, 1st August 1919)* shows Lord Lilford in conversation with Mr. Warren.

Below are (left) Lord Lilford's colt which led its class and was sold for a high figure; and (right) Mr. B. Wood's mare, which was voted "Best in the Show".

After four seasons of inactivity, Kettering and District Football Combination held their annual meeting on 28th at the Angel Hotel, Kettering. Amongst the teams who competed in the 1914 - 1915 season, Thrapston United expressed a desire to take part in the coming season. At the meeting, it was announced that nine teams had stated that they would definitely take part with a further three possible.

The Young Helpers held their annual garden fete and sale of work on 31st.

Finally, the total rainfall in town during July was 2.91 inches.

August

On Saturday 2nd, it was announced that Rev. Archibald. W. Smith, late of Rotherham and the Y.M.C.A. had accepted a call to the pastorate at the Baptist Church. His ministry would commence on the first Sunday in September.

This advertisement appeared on 5th:
"Wanted. Lady's cycle, good order, with or without tyres, for cash. Box No. 830, "Evening Telegraph", Thrapston."

The Rural District Council met on Tuesday 7th. They confirmed the continuation of the Fuel Committee and ratified Mr. W. Dellar as Fuel Overseer. They also received a letter from Messrs. Sherard and Coombs, solicitors, Oundle, on behalf of the Oundle Brewery Co. with reference to flooding of their premises at the Swan Hotel. They intimated that the company would hold the Council responsible for any further damage that they, or their tenants, may sustain. A letter from the Parish Council as to remedial steps was also read. The surveyor, Mr. Porter, had prepared a report. After discussion, it was agreed to hold the matter over for one month whilst the clerk investigated the question of liability.

The County Court sat on Friday 8th. Garner Prior Hepher, sweet retailer, claimed £5 12s from Rothon & Co. Ltd., St Helens, Lancashire. In September 1918, Mr. Hepher had ordered 3 cwt. of chocolate, paying £104 4s 9d. On checking the goods, he found there was a shortfall in weight of about 14 lbs. Judge Farrant found in favour of the complainant and awarded the amount claimed with costs.

On 9th, Mr. S. P. Smart *(pictured left, Kettering Leader, 15th August 1919)* was appointed a magistrate by Earl Spencer, Lord Lieutenant of Northamptonshire. He was one of 25 new appointments.

The annual gathering of the Higham Ferrers Second Deanery Sunday School Association met in town on the same day. As many teachers were away on holiday, there was a low attendance of just 25 people.

News during August was a bit slow, as proven by this item, which was printed in the *Evening Telegraph* on Wednesday 13th:
"Mild Sensation.
On Wednesday afternoon, about a quarter-past two, a wild rabbit, believed to have been of an exploring turn of mind, was seen to run down High Street into the Market Place. The curiosity of several boys was excited and one succeeded in catching the wanderer."

The Annual Feast Week Garden Fete was held in the grounds of Thrapston House on 14th. Many stalls were present whilst a number of concerts by local performers were much appreciated. The proceeds were for various church funds and St. Dunstan's Hostel.

The 15th brought official confirmation that **Alfred Shrives Loveday (50)** was presumed to have been killed on 21st March 1918.

The annual treat for Co-operative Society members' children was held on Saturday 16th. This was the first treat since the outbreak of war. Nearly 300 under 14's attended. They assembled at the store on Market Road and, led by the Town Band, paraded to "The Shrubberies", Chancery Lane, where the grounds had been put at their disposal by Mrs. Sanderson. Tea was provided, followed by games and races. The evening finished with the band playing for a few dances. On leaving at 9.00 pm each child was given a bun.

Two advertisements from the 18th issue:
"Football. Thrapston Rovers desire Saturday matches, under 20s. S. Wright, Oundle Road, Thrapston."
"Discharged soldier, competent clerk, desires position of trust; would keep firm's accounts. Kettering district preferred. Box 129, "Evening Telegraph", Thrapston."

This was printed on 19th and continued for a number of weeks:
"Window cleaning.
Ex- Sergt.-Major Webster begs to announce that he has started business in Thrapston as a window cleaner, and respectfully solicits orders."

At the Police Court on the same day, Mr. Michael Williams, Chatteris, applied for a cinema licence for the Temperance Hall, which was granted for a six month period. He was given leave to apply again at this licence's expiry.

This was printed in both the *Evening Telegraph* and *Kettering Leader* on Friday 22nd:
"IN MEMORIAM.
In loving memory of Private **Robert Lewis Hiam (57)**, only son of H.W. and M. Hiam, of Thrapston, 1st 22nd London Regiment ("The Queen's"), killed in action in France, August 22nd 1918, aged 19 years.
Rest well, brave heart, by stream and hill,
Where many a hero's grave grows green;
You live in hearts that love you still,
You live with Christ in realms unseen.
- H.M.B.
- From Mother, Father, and Sisters."

On Friday 22nd, the *Kettering Leader* ran a lengthy article about the maritime adventures of Commander I. A. Sutcliffe *(pictured right, Kettering Leader Friday 22nd August 1919)*, son of Isaac Sutcliffe, a saddler whose business was in the High Street. He first went to sea in 1879 and served many years as first mate, mainly on the South Africa run, with the New Zealand Shipping Company. During the war, he was torpedoed in the Channel and spent much time in the submarine danger zones. In total, throughout his career at sea, he had made eighty voyages around the world.

On 26th, the Singer Sewing Machine Co. Ltd. announced that they had appointed Mr. W. Jacques, High Street, as their agent for Thrapston and district. "Any kind of machine taken in part exchange. Repairs to all machines. Needles, cotton and parts in stock."

The Guardians met on 26th where the following were discussed:
Miss M. Edwards had resigned as matron's assistant on the grounds of ill health after thirteen months in post. She requested a testimonial, which was agreed.
A tender from Messrs. Pettit and Son for £94 10s (the only one received) for repairing the hot water system in the Infirmary was accepted.
There was some discussion about the practicality of keeping a cow in the grounds as an alternative to advertising for milk tenders. This was referred to the House Committee.

Thrapston United played their first match for many years on Saturday 30th. A home friendly game against Brigstock which resulted in a 5 – 2 win for Thrapston.

On 30th, a dance in aid of fundraising for the football club was held at "The Shrubberies."

September

The Parish Newsletter carried the update, *(shown on page 172)*, on the progress being made with both the construction of and raising money for the Parish Church War Memorial.

It was reported on 5th that the Rural District Council had appointed a committee under the Profiteering Act. They also announced that sites had been secured for houses in nearly all the villages in the district that had applied for them.

Thrapston United began their season playing in the Kettering and District Combination League with a home game against Walgrave Amber on Saturday 6th, winning by 2 goals to 1.

On 7th, Rev. Archibald Smith *(pictured below in the Kettering Telegraph on Friday 10th October 1919)* commenced his ministry at Thrapston Baptist Church.

This "Lost" advertisement appeared on Monday 8th:

"Lost, September 3rd in Thrapston or neighbourhood. Gold bracelet; good reward. Apply Mr. A. Wills, Oundle Road, Thrapston."

On 10th, the Selection Committee of the Thrapston and District Shire Horse Society announced that they had hired the five-year-old stallion "Marden Black Prince" for the coming season from Sir Walpole Greenwell.

On Friday 12th Arthur Ferrar, aged 8, was picking up ears of wheat in Huntingdon Road. Hearing a car horn, he went to run off the road, failing to see Mrs. Bright from Halford Street who was cycling past him. She knocked him over whilst falling from her cycle. Arthur received cuts and bruising to his head, Mrs. Bright escaping without injury. Arthur was attended to on the scene and taken home by the car driver.

League football result on 13th: Thrapston United 2 - Broughton United 1.

These two advertisements for future local auctions were printed on Monday 15th.

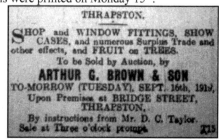

The Parish Council met on 17th, where Captain Booth gave his annual report on the Fire Brigade. Five members had served during the war, L. Wyman and B. Barber, both of whom had now resigned from the Brigade; S. Meadows who had lost a leg; **J. Booth (65)**, who was killed in action and W. Walker who was back with the Brigade. Engineer March had resigned because of his age. The Brigade was described as being on the horns of a dilemma, being unable to obtain a horse to take them to a call of fire. The Council discussed how they might be able to rectify this difficulty, without immediate resolution. It was reported that potatoes grown at the Sewerage Works had realised a total of £23 2s 6d. Finally, this motion was agreed; "That a vote of deep sympathy with Captain Booth and his family in the loss of his son be accorded and that the thanks of the Council be conveyed through him to the other members of the Brigade who have served with H.M. Forces during the war with an appreciation of their patriotism and efforts for our country."

KETTERING AND DISTRICT COMBINATION.

(Week ending 13th September, 1919.)

	P.	W.	D.	L.	F.	A.	Pts
Thrapston United ...	2	2	0	0	4	2	4
Symington's Athletic	2	1	1	0	7	1	3
Desboro' Baptists	2	1	1	0	3	2	3
Rothwell Town	1	1	0	0	10	2	2
Walgrave Amber	2	1	0	1	10	2	2
Desboro' Argyle	2	1	0	1	7	2	2
Finedon United	2	1	0	1	5	12	2
Desboro' Town Res	1	0	1	0	2	2	1
Geddington Stars	1	0	1	0	2	2	1
Broughton United	2	0	1	1	3	4	1
Woodford W.M.	2	0	1	1	1	7	1
Timpson's, Kettering	1	0	0	1	2	5	0
Rushton	2	0	0	2	1	16	0
Corby	0	0	0	0	0	0	0

The Kettering Combination league table was printed on 18th, showing Thrapston United sitting proudly at the top *(two points for a win, one for a draw – EDF)*.

On 18th, Thrapston and District Cycling and Athletic Club met with a view to reforming. It was hoped that all runners and cyclists would attend a general meeting on 2nd October to see if it would be possible to continue the Club's existence. The committee felt that it would be a great pity should Thrapston Harriers become defunct.

Three short reports appeared on 19th:
About 20 members of Thrapston Women's Adult School had been on a motor-brake outing to Bedford on 17th, leaving at 10.00 am and returning a little after 8.00 pm.
A flag day for the Royal National Lifeboat Institution held on 16th raised £7 10s.
The local Branch of the Women's Temperance Association had raised £10 for local charities at their recent jumble sale.

Kettering Leader carried a story on 19th concerning Mr. Donald St. Clair Gainer *(pictured right)*, eldest son of Dr. J. Gainer, who had recently been appointed British Vice-Consul at Tromso, Norway. At the outbreak of war, he was working for the Northern Exploration Company, looking for mineral deposits. He was offered a commission in the Royal Naval Reserve and was almost immediately asked to go to Narvik as Vice-Consul and he served in Norway throughout the war.

Saturday 20th – Thrapston United 5 - Rushton 0.

During the evening, a very successful smoking concert was held at the King's Arms Hotel on behalf of ex-servicemen.

The following was also published on 20th:
"IN MEMORIAM.
In ever-loving memory of our dear son, **Edward Percy Raworth (41)**, who was killed in action, September 20th, 1917, aged 22 years.
When alone in our sorrow our bitter tears flow,
Then stealeth a memory of sweet long ago;
Unknown to the world he stands by our side,
And whispers, "My dear ones, death cannot divide."
From his loving Mother, Father, Sister, and Brother, Thrapston."

At the Guardians meeting on Tuesday 23rd, a further resignation was received, from Miss F. Allen, a nurse in the Infirmary. An increase in the rates by 1d to 11d was agreed. Finally, it was resolved, on the casting vote of the chairman, to buy a cow, as previously discussed on 26th August.

During the same afternoon, the Christmas Fat Stock Show Committee met at the White Hart Hotel where they decided not to hold a 1919 show because of the continuing stock control regulations.

Two local advertisements were printed in the *Evening Telegraph* on 24th:
"Footballs: Footballs: Footballs:
Actually in stock: finest quality, match size. Prices: 17s 9d, 22s 6d. 29s 6d, 35s. Bladders: prices 2s 6d and 2s. Delivery at once. Alfred Smith & Son, Midland Road, Thrapston."
"Lady's cycle, new, unused, £13 13s machine; plated rims, roller brakes. Guaranteed throughout; cash bargain, £9 19s 6d. Approval. Box No. 20, "Evening Telegraph", Thrapston."

Thrapston United had entered the Kettering and District Nursing Charity Cup, the draw for which was announced on 25th. They received a bye in the 1st round and a home game against Wellingborough Athletic in the 2nd.

The same day brought two short items:
"Mr. J. Mansfield (prospective Labour candidate) will preside over the mass meeting in the Market Square on Saturday evening, in connection with the Land Day Demonstration."
"The Temperance Hall will be re-opened as a Picture Palace on Monday next, the lessee and manager being Mr. Michael Williams. There will be performances on four nights weekly (Monday, Tuesday, Friday and Saturday) – two performances on the opening night; and also twice nightly on Saturdays and holidays, as well as a children's matinee each Saturday at 2.30."

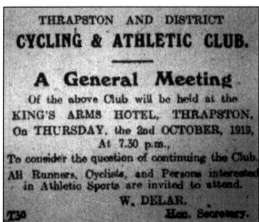

THRAPSTON AND DISTRICT
CYCLING & ATHLETIC CLUB.

A General Meeting

Of the above Club will be held at the
KING'S ARMS HOTEL, THRAPSTON,
On THURSDAY, the 2nd OCTOBER, 1919,
At 7.30 p.m.,
To consider the question of continuing the Club.
All Runners, Cyclists, and Persons interested
in Athletic Sports are invited to attend.
W. DELAR,
Hon. Secretary.
T30

At midnight on 26th, a national rail strike began, curtailing virtually all rail traffic until 5th October.

Thrapston's match against Desborough Argyll on Saturday 27th was postponed.

The Cycling and Athletic Club placed the advertisement, shown left, on 29th.

174

On Monday 29th, railway workers were pictured outside the Co-operative Society's premises in Market Street. The numbers were swelled by staff who had been moved into town to work on the brick viaduct. They then paraded around town, behind the Town Band before returning to their places of work.

(Both pictures shown above were taken from the Kettering Leader, Friday 10th October 1919)

October

The advertisement shown right was printed in the *Evening Telegraph* on Wednesday 1st.

Also on 1st:
"Wanted. Engine driver for timber hauling; must have good experience of traction engine; good wages to permanent and capable man. Bolton, Thrapston."

Sidney Newman (61) was remembered by his family on the 3rd.
"IN MEMORIAM.
In ever-loving memory of our dear son, Pte. SIDNEY NEWMAN, who was killed in action on October 1st 1918, aged 21 years.
Today brings back the memory
Of our loved one gone to rest,
And those who think of him today
Are those that loved him best;
Just when his life was brightest,
Just when his hopes were blest,
His country called – he answered:
In God's hands now he rests.
From his loving Mother, Dad, Sisters, and Brothers, Thrapston."

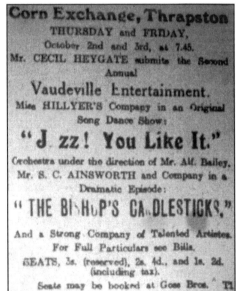

On 4th, only one train ran through Thrapston from Kettering, terminating at Kimbolton. It left Kettering at 1.00 pm.

The Northants Junior Cup first round matches were played on 4th. Thrapston United were defeated at home by Geddington Stars by 1 goal to 0.

The rail strike was called off on Sunday 5th. Businesses were requested to wait a few days before trying to ship goods.

Another "In Memoriam" notice appeared on 7th:
"In loving remembrance of **J. W. Guest (42)**, M.G.C. (Thrapston), died in action, 7th Oct., 1917, aged 19 years. Buried in Belgium by the spot where he so nobly fell.
His battles are o'er,
And God thought best
To take him to a
Beautiful home of rest."

Two reports were printed on 8th:
"Mr. George Thurlow, Halford Street, a signalman at the Midland Road Station, was walking by the side of a hedge on Monday morning last week, when he felt something prick him on a finger. A small red spot was noticed which caused a few twinges, but did not appear to be of any concern. By Thursday there was considerable swelling which Dr. Bird said had been caused by a bite or sting. On Saturday, he consulted Dr. Gainer who diagnosed septic poisoning, directed him to carry his hand in a sling and signed him off work sick."

"Junior football.
In connection with the Parish Church, a boys' (St. James') football club has been formed; and by a dance held recently in the Co-operative Hall in aid of the funds, between £6 and £7 was raised. Mr. T. W. Johnson has kindly lent a field adjoining Market Road, goal posts have been erected and the club is fairly started. George Bailey is captain, Leonard Rickwood vice-captain and the rector has been elected president with Mr. J. B. Carter (Sunday School Superintendent) vice-president. Mr. J. Hodson, one of the teachers, is the honorary secretary."

Three "For Sale" advertisements were printed on 8th:
"Motor-car, Jackson runabout, two-seater, artillery wheels, 6½hp, De Dion; hood, screen. Stepney; three-speeds, reverse, spares; £90 cash or near offer. Rupert Smith, Thrapston."
"Motor-cycle, 1919 James, coach-built, 6hp twin, three-speed, countershaft, as brand new, little used; perfect, any trial: cash £147. Rupert Smith, Thrapston."
"One large and light 20-seater brake, with canopy top, pole and cushions, varnished body and painted wheels, practically as good as new, £25. Also saw-bench with rise and fall spindle, canting fence, suitable for joinery works, 3 saws, complete for power or hand, £25. Bolton, Thrapston."

On Thursday 9th, Rev. A. Smith's recognition service was held at the Baptist Church.

Football results on Saturday 11th:
Kettering Timson's Ltd. 0 Thrapston United 3.
The Reserves played Wellingborough Wesleyans in town on the same day, winning 2 -0.

At the Petty Sessions Court on 14th, Mr. Gerald Hunnybun, clerk for the previous 43 years, tendered his resignation, which was regretfully accepted.

Also on 14th, news of an ex-resident of town was printed. Mrs. Harriett Kelly had died in a mental institution in London aged 77. Her son was very upset about her admission to the home, believing her not to be ill. She died of heart failure. Her first husband was Geoffrey Hawkins, a solicitor in Thrapston who died in 1899. He was clerk to the Magistrates, Board of Guardians, the Highway Authority and County Court, living at Paradise House, Chancery Lane. After his death, his widow remarried and moved to London. She was in Belgium when war broke out and only escaped the country with help from Nurse Cavell.

Another "In Memoriam" notice on 17th:
"In ever-loving memory of our dear boy, **Arthur Randolphus Abbott (63)**, ex-signalman, Royal Navy, who died October 17th, 1918.
"Safe in the homeland."
- From his loving Father, Mother, Sisters, and Brothers, Thrapston.

Saturday 18th:
Geddington Stars 1 - Thrapston United 3.

The annual meeting of the Rushden, Thrapston and District Sunday School Union was held at Woodford Baptist Church on 18th.

The Baptist Christian Endeavour Society celebrated its anniversary on Sunday 19th, the speaker for the day's services being Rev. F. Ward Pollard from Kettering. Collections for the Society amounted to £2 17s 5d. Miss A. Flanders was given special mention for her devoted service as honorary secretary.

The Wesleyan Church had Rev. Joseph Dixon from Brighton speaking to good congregations on 19th and 20th. His Monday evening talk was on Charles Kingsley.

The Guardians met on Tuesday 21st where they agreed a new scale for outdoor relief, an adult receiving an increase from 6s to 7s a week. The two nurses vacancies remained unfilled. There was further discussion about the wisdom of the Union's keeping of cows for their milk supplies and, after much discussion, they agreed to tender for milk as previously.

Two short items were printed in the *Evening Telegraph* on 21st:
"Herbal treatment for piles will quickly relieve the worse case and eventually cure it. W. T. Hewitt, Herbalist, Thrapston."
"Preliminary notice. Mr. S. C. Ainsworth has booked the Corn Exchange for Dec. 4th, 5th and 6th when his Company will present a screamingly funny three-act play."

Bank hours were changing in December, as indicated by the advertisement placed on 21st.

Thrapston United progressed through the second Round of the Kettering Nursing Cup on Saturday 25th with a straightforward 3 – 0 home victory over Wellingborough Athletic.

ON AND AFTER
1st DECEMBER, 1919.
The Hours of Business at the THRAPSTON OFFICES of the undermentioned Banks will be as follow:—
Daily, 10 to 3; except Tuesday, 10 to 4; and Saturdays, 9 to 12 (instead of Thursday, as heretofore).
Barclay's Bank Ltd.
London Joint City & Midland Bank Ltd
Northamptonshire Union Bank Ltd.

PUBLIC ANNOUNCEMENTS.

Thrapston Glee Society.

A MEETING will be held at the WHITE HART HOTEL on WEDNESDAY, 28th October, at 7.45 p.m. All music lovers are invited to attend to discuss the formation of the above. Chairman: Dr. GAINER.

The Glee Society placed the advertisement shown left on 25th

The Baptist and Wesleyan Church choirs united at the Baptist Church on 26th where they held a musical evening service.

On 27th, Thrapston and District Cycling and Athletic Club announced the opening run of the Thrapston Harriers on Saturday 1st November at 3.30pm. They would meet at their Headquarters, King's Arms Hotel and all runners wishing to join were invited to attend.

At the Police Court on Tuesday 28th, Mr. Martin Hunnybun was appointed clerk to the Magistrates, succeeding his father.

The Council School managers met on 28th, when the caretaker was awarded an increase in pay. At the Thrapston District Education Sub-Committee that followed, attendances were announced as being: Church of England School 86.1%, Council School 87%.

In the evening of 30th, the Council School managers met in the Parish Room. Miss Hornsby's resignation was accepted with regret. Three applications had been received for the vacancy and unanimous agreement was reached in offering the post to Miss Gaunt from Great Weldon School, the appointment commencing on 1st December.

Also on 30th, two advertisements appeared:
"Wanted, Young housemaid to work under house-parlourmaid. Mrs. Fitzherbert, Thrapston House, Thrapston."

"Wanted to purchase in Thrapston or district. Detached cottage with about one or two acres of ground. Possession any time up to twelve months. Write Box 726, "Evening Telegraph", Kettering."

November

In the November issue of the Parish Magazine, the rector wrote of his concerns about the possibilities of Nationalisation, especially as to whether the State would fairly compensate those whose industries were to be taken over.

The month began with another victory for Thrapston United, maintaining their unbeaten start to the season with a 1 - 0 home win over Walgrave Amber on 1st.

This notice appeared in the *Evening Telegraph* on 3rd:
"Don't forget the Railwaymen's Victory Dance, Armistice night, Tuesday November 11th, Corn Exchange."

On 5th, Smith and Grace announced that, as a consequence of there being no solution to the moulders strike, they had found it necessary to close the shop at their works in Midland Road.

The Rural District Council met on Thursday 6th. They heard that the full cost of each new house would be about £1,000, most of this having to be met by them. It was formally agreed that the clerk be authorised to advertise for a loan of £40,000 to help with the costs *(this equates to in excess of £1,500,000 in 2012 values – EDF)*.

On 7th, two lorries collided at the junction of Midland Road and Bridge Street. The driver of one vehicle owned by Mr. Freeman, a builder from Oundle, coming from Bridge Street Station took the corner into Midland Road too sharply, not noticing a lorry owned by Messrs. Smith and Grace coming from Midland Road Station. They met in the middle of the road, and both vehicles were damaged. Fortunately, both were travelling slowly and no injuries were sustained. Both lorries were returned to their respective owners for repair.

Thrapston were held to a 1 – 1 draw at home on 8th November to Desborough Town Reserves.

This advertisement appeared on 8th:
"Wanted, a housekeeper in a comfortable cottage home (mother and son, the former an invalid). Apply Mrs. Skelton, Market Road, Thrapston."

On Monday 10th, the first meeting of the Thrapston and District Glee Society was held. Nearly forty enrolled members attended.

On Tuesday 11th, at 7.30 am, Holy Communion was celebrated in St. James' Church. The Church bell was tolled from 10.55 am, ceasing on the stroke of 11.00 am, when the King's injunction for a two-minute silence was loyally observed. Afterwards, the rector conducted a short service.

The Thrapston United team, which defeated Symington Athletic 6 – 0 on Saturday 15th was:
H. Gunn; W. Baxter (captain) and A. Harris; F. Bray, L. Abbott and H. Clark; G. Nicholson, H. Manning, G. Headland, C. Harris and H. Smith.

In the evening of 15th, a highly successful dance was held at the Co-operative Hall, organised by the Peterborough Branch of the Ironfounders' Union, in aid of the Children's Distress Fund, which benefitted by over £10.

A United Thrapston Temperance meeting was held in the Temperance Hall on 16th, with a good gathering.

There was an evening meeting of the Town War Memorial Committee at the Parish Room on 17th, Mr. T. Selby (chairman) presiding. It was reported that the town had been canvassed, and that cash and promises amounting to £600 had been received, leaving £100 still to be raised to complete the sum (£700) for the purchase of the Recreation Field. The hope was expressed that those who had not already subscribed would do so as soon as possible.

Three short items were printed on Tuesday 18th:
"It will be of some interest locally to know that Pte. A. Newman, of Thrapston, and of the Middlesex Regiment, and 1st A.M. G. Cunnington, of Lowick, of the Royal Air Force, who are in hospital at Bagdad with fever, are making rapid progress towards recovery."
"Don't forget. "The Guv'nor" will be at the Corn Exchange on December 4th, 5th and 6th.""
"The famous Apollo Theatre success, "Monty's Flapper" will visit Thrapston Corn Exchange tomorrow (Wednesday) under very distinguished patronage. The entire scenery and effects are travelled by the company. It is many years since a company of this kind has visited the town. Messrs. Goss Bros. have the box plan to hand."

The Guardians met during the morning of 18th. Mr. Gerald Hunnybun resigned as clerk, to the Board's regret. Two assistants to the matron in the Infirmary, appointed only the month before, had resigned. The Board extended thanks to Lord Lilford for the gift of 50 rabbits for the Workhouse inmates.

A block of freehold property in Horton's Lane was sold at the White Hart Hotel on 18th, by instructions from Messrs. H. and C. Tomlinson. The Co-operative Society bought them for £450.

The Fitzwilliam Hounds met in town on 19th with a good many spectators.

The Parish Council met in the evening in the Temperance Hall. Mr. L. Richardson had stated a willingness to continue as town scavenger *(refuse collector – EDF)* provided a pay rise of 1s an hour to 4s was agreed. This was referred to the Sewage Works Committee. Mr. Parker drew the Council's attention to the desirability of all householders and tradesmen clearing the front of their premises after a fall of snow. He asked if an order to force this could be made. The chairman, Mr. Cheney, doubted if this was possible, although agreeing with the sentiment.

Also on 19th:
"Gent's bicycle, good condition, free wheel, 50s. Bird, Bridge Street, Thrapston."

On 20th, it was announced that, due to the successful performances of "Monty's Flappers" the company would remain in town for three more evenings (Thursday, Friday and Saturday). As well as repeating "Monty's Flappers" on Friday, they would feature the Criterion farce "Cynthia Lends her Husband" on the other days. They would be leaving Thrapston on Monday 24th for a season on the Isle of Man.

On Friday 21st, William Dunn, a single man originally from America who came to town in 1915, died of influenza and pneumonia in the Infirmary. He worked as a fitter for Smith and Grace. His funeral was held on 25th in St. James' Church with burial in Oundle Road Cemetery.

Thrapston United had a home victory over Desborough Argyle 2 – 1 on Saturday 22nd.

At an evening meeting at the Baptist Church Schoolroom, Mr. E. T. Cottingham gave an interesting lecture describing his observations and showing photographs as part of the British Eclipse Expedition to Principe Island for the total eclipse on 29th May.

Mrs. Brooks, who had died a few days earlier, aged 42, wife of Frederick Brooks, Stationmaster at Grafham, and daughter-in-law of Mr. and Mrs. Brooks, Midland Road Station House, was buried in Oundle Road Cemetery on 28th, following a service at St. James' Church.

Thrapston United suffered a shock 5 -3 home defeat by Corby on Saturday 29th.

On Sunday 30th the Baptist Church held Choir Sunday with all collections going to Choir funds.

December

A whist drive was organised by the local branch of the Ironfounders' Society on 1st, the 30 tables raising money for the Children's Distress Fund.

Afternoon and evening lectures at the Parish Church on 2nd were given by Rev. R. E. Roberts from Leicester. His subjects were on the theme of "Laity in the Church".

The pictures shown on page 181 were taken at performances of "The Guv'nor" between 4th and 6th in the Corn Exchange *(Kettering Leader, Friday 12th December 1919)*.

Notice of a mass meeting arranged by the National Agricultural Labourers' Union to be held on 7th in the Co-operative Hall was given on 4th.

On the same day, the announcement of the impending retirement of Inspector Campion on 31st December was made. He had served 30 years with the Force and would be sadly missed *(by most of the population! – EDF)*.

The recent death of Mr. Isaac March, shown right, was announced in the *Kettering Leader* on 5th.

Thrapston United were due to play Finedon Argyle in the Charity Cup on Saturday 6th. Finedon, due to a combination of a league match and injuries, were unable to send a team. At a subsequent meeting of the organisers, Thrapston were awarded the tie by default and progressed to one of the semi-finals, being drawn to play Rushden United Trades F.C. at the Kettering Town ground on 29th December.

On Sunday 7th, Mrs. Freeman, widow of Charles Freeman, died at home in Azalea House, Midland Road. Her funeral took place at the Baptist Church on 10th.

Two recent friendly football match scores were given on 7th:
Thrapston Rovers 12 - Denford Rovers 1
Thrapston Sunday School 0 - Titchmarsh Boys 0.

About 50 farmers met on 9th December at the White Hart Hotel, where support was pledged for the Northamptonshire Farmers Ltd., a co-operative organisation designed to assist members with all aspects of their industry. They were particularly interested in setting their own channels for sales of produce, rather than being dependent on Government systems.

An afternoon meeting took place in the Temperance Hall on Thursday 11th and Captain Halton, from Church Army Headquarters, showed a film of their work during the war, both at the front and at home.

In the evening of 11th, a whist drive was held at the Corn Exchange as a benefit for Messrs. J. Webster, J. Rogers and T. Morton, each of whom had been ill for a lengthy period. About £30 was raised.

Arthur Brown placed the announcement *(shown left)* in the *Evening Telegraph* on 13th.

There was an afternoon lecture and demonstration on "Musical Training" in the Co-operative Hall on 13th, given by Dr. Stanley Marchant, St. Pauls' Cathedral.

Thrapston United lost at Rothwell Town by 3 – 0 during the afternoon, and were replaced at the top of the league table by their opponents.

The new Unionist Agent, Mr. Danbury, from Peterborough, spoke to a small audience at the White Hart Hotel on Monday 15th.

The Guardians had a lengthy meeting on 16th. The two nurses, whose resignations were announced at the previous meeting, had now left leaving just one nurse working in the Infirmary. In an attempt to foster some interest, the salary offered was increased to £30 with a £6 bonus and uniform allowance. Whenever an inmate of the Workhouse died, the sexton rang the "passing bell", a service he had performed free for many years. There was now a wish for payment to be made. As it appeared illegal for the Board to use the rates for this purpose, it was agreed to request undertakers add a sum onto their bills to cover the cost. Finally, Mr. M. G. W. Hunnybun was appointed clerk at a salary of £115. He had been assistant clerk since 1908 and, although the only applicant, was considered eminently suitable for promotion.

During December, Cawdell's placed a number of advertisements in the *Evening Telegraph* for Christmas gifts. Part of one of these is shown right.

The Institute held the final of their billiards competition for the Conyers Cup on 22nd. In a close game, Mr. E. Abbott eventually overcame the challenge of Mr. W. Barber; Mr. Dellar took third place.

At Thrapston Police Court on Tuesday 23rd, the Bench paid tribute to Inspector Campion *(pictured on page 183, Kettering Leader, Friday 19th December 1919)* and thanked him for his many years of service.

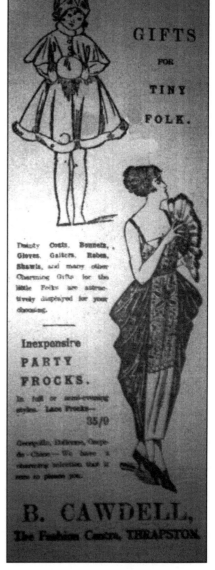

Christmas Day was ushered in by the Parish Church bells ringing, followed by three services in St. James' during the morning. The Baptists and Wesleyans held their traditional joint service at the Baptist Church. At the Workhouse, 52 inmates and 14 Infirmary patients were treated to the usual festivities, which were well received. During the morning, Denford Rovers gained revenge for their heavy defeat *(by 12 – 1, page 181)* against Thrapston Rovers, winning 7 – 2.

The Post Office had a very busy time on 24th and 25th. Staff "put forth all their energy so that the public should receive all their presents by Christmas Day". Breakfast was provided for delivery staff on both mornings before commencing their rounds.

Christmas Day witnessed the wedding between Alec Sawford and Annie Lyford at the Wesleyan Church *(picture below taken from a Family Bible held in the EDF Collection)*.

On Boxing Day, the Town Band paraded around town during the morning. In the afternoon, Thrapston United had a home match against Woodford Working Men, winning by 2 – 1. In the evening, the football club held a very successful long night dance at the Corn Exchange.

The semi-final of the Kettering Nursing Cup was held on Monday 29th. In front of a large crowd at Kettering Town Football Club, Thrapston were represented by: Newman; Barber and Harris; Stapleton, Abbot and Clark; Pettit, Manning, Headland , March and Smith. Smith scored within 15 minutes, the only goal of the first half. Headland netted from a penalty after half-time and sealed the win with a fine goal 18 minutes from the end, leaving Thrapston with a 3 – 0 victory over Rushden United Trades F.C.. Takings at the gate amounted to £20 12s 6d.

On 30th, Alfred Hensman announced the reopening of his shoeing business *(see page 184)*.

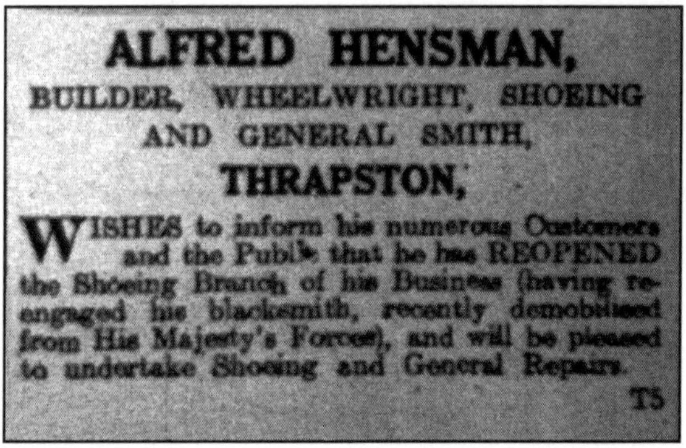

ALFRED HENSMAN,
BUILDER, WHEELWRIGHT, SHOEING
AND GENERAL SMITH,
THRAPSTON,

WISHES to inform his numerous Customers and the Public that he has REOPENED the Shoeing Branch of his Business (having re-engaged his blacksmith, recently demobilised from His Majesty's Forces), and will be pleased to undertake Shoeing and General Repairs.

T5

The first full year of the peace had passed and life was back to normal. Societies and clubs, churches and political parties all sought to bring improvements to the quality of life for their members and the population in general. A new decade would bring a lot of changes, many of them for the better. Robert Laurence Binyon's poem "For the Fallen", written in 1914, contains the words, "We will remember them". And the community continued to cherish the memory of 'lost youth', by erecting Memorials and publishing "In Memoriam" notices to express both their grief and gratitude.

1920

January

The Parish Church Sunday School held their prize distribution in the Temperance Hall during the evening of 1st. Entertainments followed and each child received an orange as they left.

This for sale advertisement appeared on the same day:
"Gloucester incubator, 45 eggs, self-turning and ordinary trays. What offers? Hewitt, Thrapston."

On Saturday 3rd, Thrapston United played a home league match against Corby, running out winners by 6 – 0.

The next week had no news from town until Friday 9th when the County Court sat in town. Charles Cannell, a dentist practising in Thrapston and Kettering, sued A. W. Bolton and Son, Bridge Street for £9, the cost of supplying Mrs. Bolton with a set of teeth. She received them in November 1918 and after a small adjustment, appeared satisfied. When the plaintiff began pressing for payment some six months later, faults started to be reported and the debt was still due in full. After hearing the claims and counter-claims, judgement with costs was awarded to Mr. Cannell.

Also on 9th, the *Kettering Leader* printed this "In Memoriam":
"In loving memory of Gunner **John Harry Shadbolt (71)**, M. G. Corps, who died of pneumonia in the 78th General Hospital, Palestine, January 7th 1919.

> We could not clasp your hand, dear Jack;
> Your face we could not see;
> We were not there to say farewell,
> But we'll remember thee.
> Far and often our thoughts do wander
> To the grave so far out yonder;
> From memory's page we'll never blot
> Three little words, "Forget me not."

From his loving Father, Mother and Brothers. Thrapston."

The local Trades and Labour Council held a whist drive on 10th with sufficient people for 16 tables. The proceeds were sent to Labour's Central Parliamentary Fund.

The Guardians met on Tuesday 13th where they heard that there had still been no applications for the nursing vacancies. A temporary nurse had been obtained from a Northampton Nursing Home at a weekly cost of £3 3s. Figures from the previous quarter showed that the average number of Workhouse inmates was 65, compared to 69 for the year before whilst there had been 400 casuals. Finally, they heard that Lady de Capell Brooke had kindly given a tea for the old people.

Also on 13th, two entertainments were held. The Young Helper's gave one in the Woolpack Club Room, raising £3 3s 6d, whilst another was given to mothers attending the Infant Welfare Centre in the Co-operative Hall.

Smith and Grace commenced their campaign on 13th exhorting local farmers to have their equipment overhauled. *(Their advertisement is shown on page 186).*

On Thursday 15th, a public meeting in the White Hart Hotel agreed to form a Drayton Park and District Cricket Club. Col. Stopford Sackville had offered the use of the estate's ground a month earlier. A temporary committee was formed and an agreement was reached that the annual membership fee would be 5s.

On the same evening, Miss Linda Kingsford organised a concert performed by her pupils in the Corn Exchange. Items were well received and all proceeds were given to the Sunday School Fund.

The Church of England School managers met on 16th. Mrs. Saddington was appointed school cleaner, replacing Mrs. Jeffery who had resigned. Miss Gaunt's memorandum of agreement *(in effect, contract of appointment – EDF)* was signed. Proposed school holidays for 1920 were agreed. The School Savings accounts were audited and found to be correct. The balance was £295 with 157 depositors.

Saturday 17th – Football result – Thrapston United 5 Kettering Timson's 1.

During that evening, the local Branch of the Women's Unionists Associations held their first social in the Co-operative Hall. About 100 people attended and, after tea, heard a speech from the local Unionist agent. Music and dancing ended a very pleasant evening.

An advertisement printed on 19th:
"3 ton steam lorry at liberty for transport work anywhere in the district. Apply Smith and Grace, Thrapston."

Thrapston Union advertised in the *Evening Telegraph* on 21st:
"The Guardians of the Union require the services of a charwoman for their Infirmary, also a woman to assist in the Laundry.
Particulars as to duties and wages can be obtained from the master, Union Workhouse, Thrapston.
Signed: Martin G. W. Hunnybun, clerk to the Guardians."

The Parish Council also met on 21st. Investigations into street and property flooding, after heavy rains were proceeding. Grave-digging fees were received and passed to the Home Office for approval. The state of the roads was again raised and further contact with the County Council agreed.

A hastily arranged Police Court was held on Thursday 22nd, where a man of no fixed abode appeared charged with stealing one dried haddock, value 6d, from John Stubbs on the day before. He was remanded until the following Tuesday whilst enquiries were made.

On Saturday 24th, Thrapston United gained a narrow win at Finedon United by 1 – 0.

The Adult Schools held a Sacred Concert in the Temperance Hall during the evening of 25th, which drew an audience of about 200.

The Kettering Combination Football League held an executive meeting on 26th. One item on the agenda concerned Kettering Timson's who were reported for being late at Thrapston for the match on 17th. The committee excused them on the grounds of the train service being so bad!

The Police Court resumed on 27th to hear the case against the haddock thief. After hearing that the man had been out of trouble for fourteen years and had served with the Army Service Corps during the war, he was found guilty and given the option of a 10s fine or seven days hard labour. He thanked the Bench, but no indication is given as to his choice.

On 28th, Arthur Brown, auctioneer, announced the sale of the effects of Charles Freeman, by instructions of his executors. The sale, to be held at the Corn Exchange, comprised various items of "furniture, ornaments and useful articles" removed from Azalea House. The sale was to occur on 30th with viewing the day before.

On Friday 30th, a Service of Dedication for the Memorial to the Fallen was held in the Parish Church, led by the Archdeacon of Oakham, the Ven. W. G. Whittingham, rector of Glaston, Uppingham. The Memorial contained names in four panels with a central panel inscribed with:
"In grateful memory of the men of Thrapston who died for King and Country in the Great War, 1914 – 1918, the reredos and this panelling were erected, A.D. 1920."
The list of names included was:
"Panel to left of inscription: - Northamptonshire Regiment: Lance-Corpl. J. E. Cobley, Pte. W. E. Cooper, Pte. J. T. Giddings, Pte. W. Jeffery, Pte. P. Makin, Pte. W. Miller, Pte. J. G. Morley, Pte. G. E. Nicholls, Pte. J. R. Pollard, Pte. W. H. Reeve, Pte. C. E. Richardson, Pte. G. H. Simpson, Pte. J. S. Smith, Pte. A. Tarrant, Pte. R. Templeman, Pte. A. E. Waite, Pte. A. J. Waite.
Two smaller panels beneath the inscription: - Left, Rifle Brigade; Rifleman E. P. Raworth, Rifleman H. W. Reeve. Royal Fusiliers; Pte. W. J. Loaring, Pte. J. T. Stimpson. York and Lancaster Regiment: Pte. S. Newman. Royal Army Medical Corps: Pte. G. Johnson. Right, Machine Gun Corps: Gunner H. Dingley, Gunner J. W. Guest, Gunner F. W. Newman, Gunner J. H. Shadbolt, Gunner G. W. Turner. Canadian Contingent: Pte. A. Sutcliffe, Pte. L. Throssell.
Panel to right of inscription: - Royal Navy: Signaller A. R. Abbott. Merchant Service: Wireless Telegraphist B. F. Emery. Royal Field Artillery: Gunner S. L. Ferrar, Gunner E. H. Mayes, Gunner J. Rogers. Royal Engineers: Sapper E. W. Barratt. Royal Air Force: Lieut. G. W. K. Smith. Grenadier Guards: Pte. H. D. Hall. Bedfordshire Regiment: Pte. H. T. Gilbert. Leicestershire Regiment: Sergt. S. Wright. Queen's Royal West Surrey Regiment: Pte. R. L. Hiam, Pte. C. Loakes, Pte. A. S. Loveday, Pte. H. Miller."
The total cost of the memorial was £420.
After the address, a collection for the Memorial fund was taken during the singing of the hymn "For all the saints who from their labours rest," and the service closed with the singing of the "Nunc Dimittis." Miss Kingsford played a fine outgoing voluntary.

A day later, Thrapston United had an easy win over Finedon United by 4 – 0.

February

The Institute held their annual meeting on Monday 2nd with a good attendance. Income for the year amounted to £206 11s 5½d and expenditure £158 2s 5½d. Membership had remained stable at between 80 and 90 paid-up members. A very full year of activities had been appreciated and thanks were extended to the hard working committee who were unanimously re-elected. At the end of the meeting, the Conyers Cup was presented to Mr. E. Abbott.

"Wanted. Man to look after horses and to deliver goods; help given. H. and C. Tomlinson, Thrapston." *(Tomlinson's Store is shown to the right of this picture taken in 1906 – EDF Collection.)*

The Police Court held their annual Licensing Session on 3rd. There were 55 licensed premises in the district, none of which had been prosecuted for any offence – all were very well run. Only one person was prosecuted and convicted of drunkenness during 1919. As well as renewing all current licences, the Bench agreed to extend hours in Thrapston on Tuesdays to include between 11am to 4pm. This was Market Day when up to 300 visitors were in town requiring refreshment.

That evening a whist drive in the Co-operative Hall was arranged to raise funds for the Trades and Labour Council.

Drayton Park and District Cricket Club placed this announcement in the *Evening Telegraph* on 3rd:
"Cricketers in the neighbourhood wishing to join this Club are invited to apply to the Hon. Secretary, Leslie G. Cottingham, The Limes, Thrapston. Annual subscription 5s."

This appeared on 4th:
"Don't forget the Thrapston and District Glee Society's grand concert tomorrow night. Doors open 7.30, commence 8pm."
(The concert was a great success with a large audience and many performers – it was reported in great detail on 6th – EDF.)

At the Rural District Council meeting on 5th, tenders were received for the proposed £40,000 loan to build new houses *(see page 183 – EDF)*. One was accepted, from Mr. Freeman, Highbury, London, which required repayments of £5 17s 6d per cent over 80 years *(a repayment of approximately £80,000 – EDF)*. There was some discussion about how difficult it was to get the Thrapston fire engine to the more remote parts of the district and this was referred to the Parish Council with a suggestion that they consider upgrading it.

The Fire Brigade held their annual dance at the Engine House on 6th.

Thrapston United did not have a league game on 7th, so welcomed Kettering Reserves to their ground for a friendly, losing by 1 – 2.

In the evening, the Institute welcomed Rushden Y.M.I. for a billiards match. Rushden won by 570 – 522.

The Rural District Council placed a Tender notice on 9th:
"The above Council invite tenders for Team Labour from 1st April 1920 to 31st March 1921 in the various parishes in the Northants portion of their District. Forms of tender can be obtained from Mr. J. H. Porter, Surveyor, Thrapston.
Sealed tenders, endorsed "Team Labour", to be sent to the undersigned not later than February 28th.
The lowest or any Tender will not necessarily be accepted.
Gerald Hunnybun, clerk to the Council."

The Sunday School teachers held a social evening in the Temperance Hall on Thursday 12th. Including invited guests, 80 people attended. Entertainments contributed by members were followed by refreshments. The evening finished with dancing to music provided by Miss. L. Fletcher (piano) and Mr. A. Fletcher (cornet).

On 14th Thrapston United played Geddington Stars in town, winning 1 – 0.

An advertisement for a matron's assistant in the Infirmary was placed in the *Evening Telegraph* on 16th with a salary of £30 plus allowances on offer.

At the Police Court on 17th, the cinema licence for the Temperance Hall was renewed for a further twelve months.

The result of a recent football match was printed on 17th: Thrapston St. James 1 - Denford United 0.

On Wednesday 18th, W. Jacques placed this advertisement in the *Evening Telegraph*:
"Motor hire done with motor cycle fitted with comfortable side-car; long or short journeys by day or night; distance no object; 6d per mile up to 25 miles; 30 miles 14s; 40 miles 18s; 50 miles 22s 6d; 60 miles 27s; special quotations for longer journeys. Travellers etc, orders by post or wire will bring machine to your door. W. Jacques, Cycle Agent, Thrapston."

The Police Court held a special hearing on Friday 20th. A Private soldier of the 5th Infantry Battalion, Canadians appeared before Dr. Gainer charged with being an absentee since March 29th 1919. Inspector Baxter stated that the Private's leave expired on that date. He was remanded to await an escort.

The following article, reproduced in full, was printed on Monday 23rd:
"MOTOR ACCIDENT.
Aged Tramp Knocked Down by Kettering Car at Thrapston.
About seven o'clock on Sunday evening Mr. Ernest Blackett of Rockingham Road, Kettering, ale and stout bottler, reported to Inspector Baxter at Thrapston Police Station that a few minutes previously, while driving a motor car from Oundle, he had knocked down on the road, on the Cemetery Hill, Thrapston, an elderly man of the tramping class, and was afraid that the man was badly injured.
He also stated that he did not see the man, who was walking along the centre of the road, until immediately before he was knocked down. He had picked the man up and had him in the car outside the station and wanted to find the nearest doctor.
Dr. Gainer, who lives next door to the Police Station, saw the injured man and at once advised his removal to the Workhouse Infirmary. The inspector went with the car to the Workhouse

where the man was admitted and gave the name of Thomas Brown, of no fixed abode, a labourer, aged 73 years; also that he had spent the night of the 21st at Peterborough, and had walked from that town and was making his way to the Thrapston Workhouse for the night. He had a deep cut above the left eye and near the temple, and abrasions of the hands, and appeared to be rather badly shaken. Dr. Gainer promptly arrived and attended to the injuries.

At the time of the accident it was dark, owing to the fog, and Mr. Blackett stated that for that reason he was driving down the hill slowly, as it was difficult to see.

The Inspector examined the car at the Workhouse but could see no marks upon it, but the right-hand head lamp was smashed and the lamp bracket bent back towards the body of the car. The damage, Mr. Blackett stated, was caused by the collision with the injured man.

On the car were two electric headlights (not powerful ones) and also two oil side lamps. At the time the accident happened Mr. Blackett had with him a young daughter and no one else appeared to have been near.

The injured man informed the Inspector that as far as he knew he had no relatives whatever.

Inquiry on Monday morning elicited that the injured man had passed a comfortable night and was going on as well as could be expected."

On Friday 27th, the Post Office held their first staff social since the end of the war in the Co-operative Hall. Indoor and outdoor staff, with friends, totalled 55 people. After supper, Mr. J. T. Bues *(pictured right and reproduced with kind permission from Mrs. Celia Hope, Thrapston)* was presented with a silver-plated Queen Anne teapot, a pipe, pouch and tobacco to mark his retirement after 32 years service with the Post Office. Dancing began at 11.30 pm and kept going until 1.30 am.

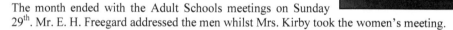

On 28th, Thrapston United defeated Desborough Argyle on their turf by 2 -1.

The month ended with the Adult Schools meetings on Sunday 29th. Mr. E. H. Freegard addressed the men whilst Mrs. Kirby took the women's meeting.

March

At the monthly Police Parade held in Oundle on 1st, ex-Inspector Campion was presented with an easy chair.

Two advertisements were printed in the *Evening Telegraph* on the same day:
"Wanted, immediately, good General, indoors or out; good wages. Mrs. Rupert Smith, Thrapston."
"For sale. A large quantity of gas lime. Apply Thrapston Gas Works, Midland Road."

The Thrapston Rural Food Control Committee placed this advertisement on 2nd:
"Applications are invited for position of Executive Officer and Clerk to the above Committee. Candidates must have had experience in work of Food Office. Salary £200 per annum. Applications should be received by the undersigned not later than the 9th instant.
Thomas A. Boyden, Executive Officer etc.
Food Office, Thrapston."

Saturday 6th saw Thrapston United gain an easy 3 – 0 home win against Desborough Baptists.

At the Guardians meeting on Tuesday 9th it was agreed that all appointments would be made permanent positions from 1st April, and current salaries were confirmed as being appropriate.

The Food Control Committee met on the same day. Fourteen applications had been received for the position of chief executive and clerk and, after discussion, three applicants were selected for interview.

An advertisement was printed in the same issue of the *Evening Telegraph*:

"To let or for sale in Thrapston at the end of September, pleasantly situated house; three bedrooms and bathroom; offers. Apply Box 750, "Evening Telegraph" Office, Thrapston."

The death of Mrs. Arnold, York Terrace, Huntingdon Road occurred on 10th aged 86. She had been widowed for 32 years and lived in town for the last 22 years of her life. A regular attendee of the Wesleyan Church, she was also a member of the Women's Temperance Association. She had been a pillow-lace maker from the age of five and is pictured with some of her work. She was buried in Denford on Saturday 13th *(picture left, - Kettering Guardian, Friday 2nd April 1920).*

The Thrapston Branch of the Farmers' Union held their first annual dinner at the White Hart Hotel on 11th with nearly 100 people attending.

The Town Band held their Annual General Meeting in the Mess Room of Smith and Grace Ltd. on 11th, with all members attending. They had a bank balance of just over £10. Prospects were considered good with several promising junior members.

Motor Cars, Motor Cycles, Cycles & Tractors.

AGENTS for Humber, Overland, Briscoe and other Cars. Triumph, B. S. A., Humber, James, Clyno & Alldays Motor Cycles.
B. S. A., Humber, Centaur, Triumph, Swift, James and Alldays Cycles.
Saunderson, Auston, Fordson & other Motor Tractors.

We Have a Large Number of NEW and SECOND-HAND Machines in Stock, and many more coming in the next few weeks.
Accessories of all Kinds for Cars, Motor Cycles, and Cycles.
All Sizes of Tyres in Stock, Car, Motor Cycle and Cycle.

S. J. HEIGHTON & Co.,
MARKET PLACE, THRAPSTON. 'Phone No. 7.

Heighton's placed this advertisement *(left)* on 12th showing the range of vehicles available.

The Workers' Union held an evening meeting in the Co-operative Hall.

Thrapston United had another match against Desborough Baptists on 13th, winning 1 – 0 from the penalty spot.

On Monday 15th, heavy snowfall caused severe communication cuts, road, rail and telegraphic services were all affected. Horse deliveries from Kettering were expected, although if conditions continued, local deliveries by bicycle would have to be made on foot and only one a day instead of the usual two.

Co-operative Society employees held a staff social in their Hall after work on 15th March. Following a meat tea, they had a whist drive and finished an enjoyable evening with dancing until midnight.

At the Police Court on 15th, five local men were sworn in as Special Constables: Messrs. George Gilbert, J. W. Stubbs, J. H. Chattell, A. H. Touch and F. W. Lord.

Later in the day, the Trades Council met in the Co-operative Hall.

In the evening, the Institute welcomed Rushden Conservative Club for a billiards match. The visitors ran out winners by 582 points to 515.

On Friday 19th, a collision occurred at the Oundle Road corner between a car driven into town by Mr. J. Babb of Titchmarsh and a two-seater driven by a Northampton lady in the direction of Huntingdon. Mr. Babb's car received damage to the front axle and mudguard, whilst the other had a smashed wheel. There were no injuries. After changing wheels, the lady proceeded on her way, Mr. Babb taking his to a local garage for repair. Only the week before, the Parish Council had decided to have warning signs fixed at the junction.

In the evening, the Institute held a whist drive, 22 tables being filled.

On 20th, Thrapston United visited Symington's Athletic (Market Harborough). A 4 – 0 win took them back to the top of the Kettering Combination.

The Annual Parish Meeting was held in the Temperance Hall on Wednesday 24th. As in previous years, it was not well attended, only the chairman, one councillor and the clerk being present. After fulfilling the basic legal requirements, it was closed after five minutes. As they were leaving, a lady arrived who was told that the meeting was over.

The Food Control Committee met for a special meeting on Friday 26th, where Mr. H. T. Stalley was welcomed as the new chief executive. The accounts for the year ending 31st March were submitted to the meeting and handed over to the new officer.

Thrapston United had an easy home win over Rushton on Saturday 27th by 8 - 0.

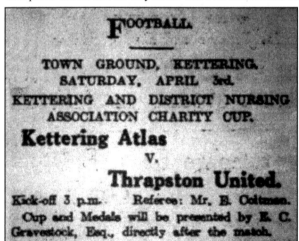

At the Police Court on 30th, Mr. Henry Guest, Huntingdon Road and owner of two old cottages, one in the occupation of Daniel Slater, applied for an order for possession. Every effort had been made to assist Mr. Slater to obtain alternative housing, all of which he declined. Ultimately, an order for possession within 21 days was made.

Publicity *(shown left)* for the forthcoming Cup Final was printed on 31st.

April

At the Rural District Council meeting on Thursday 1st, information was given that the selected site for house-building in town was on Mr. Cheney's field on the east side of Oundle Road. A letter had been received from Edward Loakes, secretary of Thrapston Allotments Ltd. They had many people applying for a plot but no land. They requested that the unused portion of housing land acquired be offered for allotments. The decision was referred to the Housing Committee. The Council had bought a new steam wagon, costing £1,398, payment being due in September.

The Thrapston United team which would face Kettering Atlas on Saturday was announced on 1st: E. Newman; W. Baxter and A. Harris; J. Manning, L. Abbott and H. Clark; G. Headland, H. Manning, F. Stapleton, C. Harris and Smith. Reserves: Williams and Pettit.

Also on 1st:
"Wanted. Motor cycle, solo or combination, for cash. Reginald Cockerill, Halford Street."

Kettering Atlas defeated Thrapston United in the Kettering and District Nursing Association Charity Cup on 3rd (Easter Saturday). Although the presentation of the cup was reported, I have been unable to find the result.

All the Good Friday and Easter services were reported to have been well attended. Miss Linda Kingsford gave an afternoon organ recital in the Parish Church on Easter Sunday.

On Monday 5th, Thrapston United returned to winning ways with victory at Woodford W.M. by 2 – 0.

Thrapston market saw a record price for a pig on 6th, £45 15s being paid by a Kettering resident.

Dr. Kirtlan returned to town to give another lecture on 9th. He spoke in the Co-operative Hall on "The New England".

On 10th, Thrapston played their penultimate match of the season, winning 2 – 0 at Broughton United.

Bad news was announced for all bakers and bread eaters on 10th:
"The Master Bakers and the Thrapston Co-operative Society advance the bread on Monday April 12th.
4lb loaf to 1s and flour 3s 10d per stone.
A. Todd, Secretary."

The championship of the Kettering Combination was decided at Desborough on Monday evening (12th) when Thrapston met Desborough Town Reserves in. The match was reported at some length and is reproduced below in full.
"There was a great crowd of eager supporters, a large number of Thrapston people being present. The ground was in a shocking state, in some parts water lying on the top.
Thrapston set the ball rolling in pouring rain and had the better of the play at the outset. Desborough broke away on the left and forced a corner, but this was easily cleared. Desborough held the Thrapston forwards at bay. With a terrific drive Smith of Desborough hit the crossbar and the visiting goalie had to save twice in quick succession. A fruitless corner then followed for each side. After a corner had been awarded to Desborough the Thrapston

forwards got well away and a minute before the interval, Stapleton gave them the lead with a fine shot.

Interval: Thrapston United   1
                 Desborough Reserves 0

Soon after the re-start the Desborough custodian had to save a high shot from Harris. Desborough then got going, but failed to beat the Thrapston defence. Soon afterwards a penalty awarded to Desborough was splendidly saved. The home team had much the better of the second half and missed many chances, which included two open goals. The game was fought out at a hard pace and when the whistle blew the score was:

                 Thrapston United   1
                 Desborough Reserves 0

Mr. R. Marshall of Kettering was the referee and Messrs. A. Peters (Kettering) and G. H. Patrick (Geddington) linesmen."

Thrapston United's championship winning team, 1920 (EDF Collection).

Four short reports were printed in the *Evening Telegraph* on Tuesday 13th:

The Annual General Meeting of the Shire Horse Society agreed to hold a show in 1920.

A flag day for the County Crippled Children's Society raised £11 12s.

A thunderstorm with hail and torrential rain passed over town in the early afternoon *(picture of the subsequent flooding is shown on page 195 – Kettering Leader Friday 16th April 1920).*

In a local garden, "...a boy felt in a hedge for a thrush's nest, a thrush flew out and landed on his shoulder. There were two eggs in the nest. The boy thought it was the same bird that nested in the hedge in 1919. The nest and eggs were left undisturbed."

On 14th, the Kettering Combination executive meeting was held in Kettering. The chairman congratulated Thrapston on their first ever championship win and Mr. W. Cheney, Thrapston United's secretary, said it was the first time they had won a football trophy. A match between Thrapston and a Rest of the League team was arranged, to be played in Thrapston on 24th.

A children's entertainment in the Baptist Schoolroom took place that evening, raising £6 for the Chapel Restoration Fund.

A view of the flooding on 13ᵗʰ, taken from the Midland Railway Bridge.

P.C. Short's departure from Thrapston and transfer to Brigstock was announced on 16ᵗʰ.

The annual meeting of demobilised soldier's took place during the evening in the Corn Exchange. A time of speeches and entertainment ended with dancing until 1.00am.

On Saturday 17ᵗʰ, Thrapston Rovers beat Lowick 4 – 2 in their last home match of the season.

The final table of the Kettering Combination was printed on 20ᵗʰ, showing Thrapston proudly at the top.

KETTERING AND DISTRICT COMBINATION.
Final table.

	Pld.	Won.	Drn.	Lost.	Goals For	Agst.	Pts.
Thrapston United	26	22	2	2	73	17	46
† Desboro' Town Res.	26	20	4	2	77	16	42
Rothwell Town	26	16	6	4	94	28	38
Walgrave Amber	25	18	1	6	110	27	37
Geddington Stars	26	15	5	6	64	47	35
Symington's Athletic	26	11	3	12	55	65	25
Woodford W.M.	25	10	5	10	41	57	25
Corby	23	9	5	9	47	52	23
Desborough Bapt'st	26	7	6	13	28	50	20
Broughton United	26	7	5	14	51	63	19
† Desborough Argyle	26	9	2	15	51	62	18
Finedon United	26	5	5	16	43	73	15
W. Timpson's, Ltd.	26	3	3	20	35	85	9
Rushton	25	1	0	24	17	142	2

† Two points deducted.

The matches, Corby v. Walgrave Amber, Corby v. Woodford W.M., and Rushton v. Corby, were not played owing to the suspension of the Corby Club by the Northants Football Association.

The Parish Council met on Wednesday 21ˢᵗ. Mr. T. Selby was elected chairman with Mr. Hewitt as his deputy. The Council accepted trusteeship of the Recreation Ground *(to be renamed the Peace Park – EDF)*. The General Account had a healthy balance and required no precept for the coming year whilst the Burial Account needed a £25 precept. Both were agreed. The on-going concerns about the High Street surface were still being discussed with County. The Council School managers met on 22ⁿᵈ and agreed that the summer holiday would start on 30th July. The Council School's attendance figure was 88.1%, compared to the Church of England School at 91%.

Thrapston United welcomed the Rest of the League team on 24th, a 2 – 2 draw providing a fitting end to the season, watched by about 800 people. "Mr. Brightwell, secretary of the Combination, said he was very pleased to be in Thrapston and wished to congratulate them on winning the League. He had been looking up some old records and found that Thrapston had good and bad times, one year being only one point from winning the League. This season they had won, and their record for a junior club was remarkable. They had played 26 League matches, winning 22, drawing two and only being beaten twice. Their success was partly due to their being able to keep to the same team throughout. They had only called on the services of twenty players...

Mr. F. A. Cheney, Club president, was then called to make the presentations. He said it was a great pleasure and honour to present that most beautiful Cup. He thought the Club had done well in getting together so soon after the war. But whatever Thrapston people took on for the town, they always did well.

The Cup was then handed over to W. Barber, captain of the team, who thanked all the supporters of the team, both home and away. He also thanked the players for the way in which they had stuck together to fight their way to victory. Each player was then presented with a medal.

Mr. E. Coltman, Chairman of the League, proposed a vote of thanks to Mr. Cheney and called for three cheers for the Thrapston Club which were given heartily.

Both teams and officials sat down to a splendid tea provided by the Thrapston club."

On 27th, a social and dance arranged by the women's section of the Labour Party took place in the Co-operative Hall.

The Glee Society held another evening concert on the same day in the Corn Exchange. A full audience heard a variety of contributions from the Society's 40 members.

May

Mayday was greeted by many children in the streets with garlands and maypoles.

Mr. William Howe, Huntingdon Road died on 1st aged 66 years after a long illness. He had been the manager of the Thrapston Gas Company for 29 years, only finishing work a month previously. He was married with no children. His funeral took place on 5th in St. James' Church followed by burial in Oundle Road Cemetery.

The *Evening Telegraph* printed this advertisement on 1st:-
"American organ, good playing order, knee swell, stops; £14 or nearest offer. Claude Guest, Huntingdon Road, Thrapston."

The Town Band held their annual parade in aid of the Northampton and Peterborough Infirmaries on Sunday 2nd. Approximately £35 was raised.

During the evening, the annual Labour meeting took place in the Market Place, a good-sized crowd listening to many speeches.

On Monday 3rd, P. C. Frost, recently of Wellingborough, commenced his duties in town.

During that evening, tragedy affected Mr. and Mrs. F. Lord, Midland Road when their 30 month old son, William Trevor, died from meningitis. He had been ill for a fortnight and worsened on Saturday. He had an older sister. His funeral took place on Thursday 6th.

The May Fair took place on 4th. The *Evening Telegraph* reported:
"Pleasure fairs seem to be coming into their own again after the war, in spite of the high prices. On Tuesday at Thrapston there were quite a number of stalls and, with a fine afternoon and a large influx of visitors, business was brisk in the ever-famous "Rock" and other sweets, cheap jewellery, ice cream etc."

The Guardians met on 4th. Rev. Bolland was re-elected chairman for the forthcoming year and Mr. T. H. Beeby, who had not sought re-election to the Board was co-opted and unanimously elected vice-chairman. Mrs. Densem, matron's assistant, who had only been appointed a few weeks earlier, had sent her resignation, citing ill-health as the reason. Mr. Cawdell had tendered a price of £20 for linoleum for the master's sitting room, which was accepted.

The advertisement *(shown right)* was printed on 7th.

The Co-operative Society also advertised on the same day for a first assistant in their grocery and provisions department. Applications were to be received no later than Monday 10th.

Thrapston was mentioned in the House of Commons on Monday 10th, when the President of the Board of Trade was asked if he was aware that the Thrapston Co-operative Society had not received any supplies of coal for their registered customers since 16th March. Enquiries were promised.

THRAPSTON,
Northamptonshire.

VALUABLE GRASS KEEPING.
To be Sold by Auction, by

HENRY H. BLETSOE & SON

On TUESDAY, the 11th day of MAY, 1920,
At 3 o'clock in the Afternoon,
To Michaelmas next, subject to Conditions to be then produced, namely:

12 ACRES, 3 roods, and 22 poles or thereabouts of sound GRASS KEEPING, known as the Home Close, High Farm, Thrapston, and situate in the Back Way, Thrapston.
For further particulars apply to the Auctioneers. Offices: Thrapston.   TB

Demobilised servicemen met in the King's Arms Hotel on 11th. The national organiser, who had hoped to address the meeting, was unable to attend and proceedings took the form of an informal discussion about local and national issues.

On 13th, Rev. Luckock, rector of Titchmarsh, sent 152 fresh eggs to the Workhouse; these were brought to the Ascension Day service by the children.

During the evening, there was a very full house at the Palace Cinema where a variety entertainment was given by the proprietor, Mr. Williams, in aid of the Town Band Hospital Sunday Fund. Takings amounted to £15, which was sent to the honorary secretary, Mr. Stobie, without deductions for expenses.

The Baptist Sunday School took a different format on Sunday 16th. Instead of the usual lessons, scholars gave a program of solos and recitals. 74 eggs were brought along and donated to the Workhouse.

Lord Lilford presided over a dinner at the White Hart Hotel on 17th for Thrapston and District special constables.

Also on 17th, this appeared in the local press:
"Wanted. Several families washing; every convenience. Write Box 1272, "Evening Telegraph", Thrapston."

At the Police Court on Tuesday 25th, a local motor mechanic appeared summoned for riding a motor cycle and sidecar at night without a lamp on the sidecar. He was fined 10s with costs.

A day later, a Stanwick man received a fractured skull whilst bricking a wall in a 53ft deep well on the new building site off Oundle Road. He was initially taken to the Infirmary and transferred to Northampton shortly after. Despite all the efforts of medical staff, he died of his injuries two weeks later.

On 29th, John Stapleton, Huntingdon Road met with one of the more predictable accidents recorded. He was on a short ladder attending to some plants in the window of a house nearby and had placed the end of the ladder in a barrow, to gain extra height. Whilst working, the barrow moved outward causing the ladder and Mr. Stapleton to fall onto the footpath. He was helped onto a chair, and seen by Dr. Gainer and the District Nurse. Messrs. L. and E. Newman took him home. He was badly cut and bruised over his left eye, his left wrist sprained and had general bruising down his left side. Fortunately, no bones were broken.

June

At the Guardians meeting on 1st, they were advised of continuing problems finding nursing staff for the Infirmary. Currently, a cleaner was offering some help. Agency staff were also proving difficult to recruit. Consideration was given to advertising for nursing assistants and the matter left with the Infirmary managers. Estimates totalling £92 2s 6d for external and internal painting submitted by Mr. Prior, Highfield Road, were accepted.

☞ Herbal Remedies are the Best.

IF you wish to be healthy and strong you must avoid the internal use of poisonous drugs, and take the pure and wholesome Herbal Remedies that Nature has supplied for our use in such abundance, to keep the blood pure and the internal organs healthy. Hewitt's Blood Purifying Herbs are a safe and reliable remedy for all skin diseases—Eczema, Scurvy, Pimples, Boils, Blotches, and all impurities of the blood. Price 1s. per packet, post free 1s. 3d.

HEWITT, Herbalist, Thrapston

During the afternoon, Arthur Brown offered by auction two houses just off Midland Road under instruction from Messrs. Loakes. One was sold to Mrs. Densem for £500 whilst the other was withdrawn at £480.

A day later, the Rural District Council were told that house building work in Thrapston had started. They also heard that the steam wagon had been delivered.

Mr. Hewitt placed the advertisement, *(shown above)*, on 4th.

During the evening of 4th, ex-Inspector Campion was the guest of honour at the White Hart Hotel where, under the chairmanship of Lord Lilford, many people came to thank him for his 13 years service in town and to present him with the proceeds of a public subscription, a suitably inscribed gold watch and a cheque for £50. A most enjoyable evening ended with Mr. Campion expressing his thanks and best wishes to the people.

A report was included on 5th concerning the recent coming of age of Miss Jessie Allen, Huntingdon Road, the second daughter of Mr. and Mrs. L. Allen. Between 30 and 40 relatives and friends were entertained at the Co-operative Hall. Following supper, there was entertainment and dancing. Miss Allen received "numerous useful presents including cheques, jewellery etc".

At the Petty Session Court on 8th, application was made for the transfer of the licence of the King's Arms Hotel from Frederick William Beal to his wife Florence Annie Beal, as Mr. Beal was very ill and in hospital. Supt. Tebbey mentioned that all the time that Mr. Beal was away at the war the house was conducted satisfactorily. Transfer was granted for six months.

The Council School managers met on 8th and recommended the appointment of Miss G. Fox as a pupil teacher.

Finally on 8th, Thrapston Cycling and Athletics Clubs met to consider holding a small sports meeting. They had previously agreed not to hold their Bank Holiday Sports in 1920. They decided to have this on 7th August and formed a committee to make the arrangements.

Rushden Bowls Club visited Thrapston on Thursday 10th for a match, the visitors running out winners by 62 – 49.

The Bridge, Thrapston. From the Midland Station.

The new viaduct over the River Nene was opened in June, being reported on 11th. Pictures of the old and new ones are shown left and on the following page *(EDF Collection)*. The first train passed over it on Sunday 6th. The work had taken about thirty months and about 1,500,000 blue bricks had been used. The cost was between £60,000 and £70,000. 150 workmen had been employed and, considering that many had never worked on such an undertaking before, only three minor accidents had occurred. 220 yards in length, it had fourteen arches in total. At 7.00 am on 6th, staff commenced diverting the permanent way from the old to the new road and at 3.10 pm, the first train, driven by Mr. Stevens of Kettering, began the crossing. It stopped in the middle to enable photographs to be taken. Restrictions on traffic were expected to remain in place until the Board of Trade made their inspection. Once the new viaduct was approved, the old one would be taken down.

The Baptist Church Sunday School held their anniversary on Sunday 13th. A total of £9 2s 6d was raised through collections for their funds.

On 14th, Henry H. Bletsoe and Son reminded potential bidders of their auction of mowing grass on the Recreation Ground the next day.

The Christmas Fat Stock Show Committee met at the White Hart Hotel on 15th, when they agreed to hold their first show since 1916, 14th December being the agreed date.

The New Viaduct, Thrapston

In June, it was announced that Mr. D. St Clare Gainer, shown below, son of Dr. Gainer, had been given a permanent appointment as Vice-Consul in the General Consular Service. *(Picture below, Kettering Leader 11th June 1920).*

The Parish Council met on Wednesday 16th. No tenders had been received for storing street lamps, so it was decided that they be left in position during the summer. It was hoped that the Recreation Ground would very soon become available for use. Agreement was reached on calling a public meeting to discuss the high price of gas in town.

A public dance, organised by the Church of England Men's Society, was held on the lawns at Thrapston House on Saturday 19th. Various sports and amusements were provided and, after refreshments, dancing to music provided by the Thrapston Town Silver Prize Band ended an enjoyable time.

On Sunday 20th, the Baptist Church Memorial to members killed during the war was unveiled during an impressive service. *(See page 100 in "In the Springtime of their Lives" for a picture and details of the names included. The memorial is still in the Baptist Church – EDF.)*

The annual wool sales took place off Chancery Lane on Monday 21st. The number of fleeces was very low, being under 3,000 due to the depressed price of wool.

The announcement was made on 21st that the Northamptonshire Union Banks would amalgamate with the National Provincial Bank and the Union Bank of England. This included the Thrapston Branch *(now the site of NatWest Bank – EDF).*

A request for waste paper was printed on 22nd:
"Waste paper for our Thrapston office should be delivered on Tuesday or Friday afternoon, between the hours of two and five, securely tied in 14 lb or 28 lb bundles, or packed in sacks. Every parcel should have a label attached with the name and address of sender, and weight."

Thrapston Women Unionist's held a social afternoon in the Corn Exchange on 24th. A number of stalls selling fancy work and jumble raised £10 for Central Funds.

Arthur Brown held an auction of the effects of Mr. Alfred French at "Ravenswood" on 24th June. Some of the prices realised were:- Chappell pianoforte £88 4s; typewriter £20; typewriter desk £28; oak sideboard £44; oak cupboard bookcase £38; dining table £14; oak bedroom suite £42; brass bedstead £22; satinwood bedroom suite £57. The sale was due to Mr. French's impending removal to the United States.

Thrapston Institute cricket team visited Denford on Saturday 26th, losing by 26 runs. Denford scored 54 and then bowled the Institute out for a paltry 28 runs.

On 30th, a public meeting was held in the Temperance Hall to consider the high price of gas. A good attendance heard many speeches and comments, including representatives from the Gas Company. After much consideration, the following motion was approved:
"This public meeting deplores the high price charged for gas by the Thrapston Gas Company, also the poor quality of gas, and asks the Parish Council to take the matter up with the proper authorities."

July

At the Rural District Council meeting on 1st, Dr. Elliott, Medical Officer of Health, reported that on 10th June, at the request of Mr. Selby, butcher, he inspected 615 lbs of frozen mutton received from Government cold storage in London for local distribution. He condemned the meat and issued a certificate. The meat was dry and had been gnawed by rats and mice. He commended the butcher for reporting his concerns.

An advertisement that appeared on 1st:
"Elderly lady requires middle-aged working housekeeper: good home: small salary. Box 99, "Evening Telegraph", Thrapston."

This report appeared on 2nd:
"The hay having been gathered from the War Memorial Recreation Ground, a number of children took informal possession on Wednesday and appeared to be quite in their element. Having regard to the main thoroughfare, motor danger notices will be more than ever necessary now."

The death of Mr. Horace Walters, Springfield Cottages, Thrapston, occurred on 2nd. He had been engaged for some weeks with the West Yorkshire Anti-Nationalisation Propaganda Committee in Leeds, where he died aged 65 years. He had been a political activist for many years. Sympathy was expressed for his sister with whom he lived. A post-mortem showed that he died after suffering a seizure. His funeral was held at Leeds General Cemetery on 3rd.

The summer gathering of the Kettering Federation of the Church of England Men's Society was held in town on 3rd. Following an afternoon service in St. James' Church, members proceeded to Thrapston House where a sumptuous tea was provided. Although it was a stormy day, the attendance was good.

One of the Kensit Wickliffe Preachers' vans, in the charge of Mr. Adams, arrived in town on 6th and was to stay until Saturday 10th. He planned to address meetings for adults and children each evening in the Market Place.

The advertisement shown on page 202, for a tennis tournament at Lilford Hall was printed on 6th.

A Garden Fete was held at "The Hollies" on 8th, organised by the Thrapston Hospital Week Committee. Overcast weather conditions caused a slow start, very few people being at the opening at 3 o'clock. Many stalls and amusements were available and an hour later, numbers increased. Several little flower girls were very industrious in the good cause. Evening dancing to the Town Band finished off a profitable day.

On 10th, a countywide summer outing for ex-servicemen was held at Althorpe Park. The local organiser was Mr. Cole from Halford Street.

The *Evening Telegraph* printed this article on 12th:
"Eccentric Machines.
Thus a Peterborough contemporary fifty years ago on July 9th 1870: "A novel manufacture appears to have established itself in Thrapston and numerous bicycles and tricycles have been sent out from the Vulcan Iron Works, a refutation of the general belief that these eccentric machines would have their day and cease to be last season.""

This advertisement was printed on Friday 16th, and appeared for the next week:
"ADVERTISER. 16 years in present situation requires change; previous to this holds record beating 80 agents for new business for four years in succession. Unless good money offered, please ignore this advertisement. Traveller or part traveller and book-keeper; thoroughly good appearance and address; first-rate education; gifted conversationalist; could be disengaged month from acceptance of new position, but prefers Oct 1st. Box 1530, "Journal Office", Thrapston."

The Institute held their Flower Show on 17th, raising £11 11s for Northampton Hospital.

On 21st, the Thrapston Sub-Committee of Northamptonshire Education Committee invited tenders for the conveyance of about 20 children, under eight years of age and residing in Denford, to and from the Thrapston schools on a daily basis. A suitable covered conveyance was required for inclement weather.

Cawdell's "Great Half-Price Day" took place on Saturday 24th. Bargains were to be had in all departments, these being:-
Millinery, blouses, costumes, dress materials, figare voiles, bedspreads, ladies' dresses, children's frocks and remnants. Doors opened at 10.00 am and it was promised that every offer was the best ever and would not be repeated.

The 29th Annual Shire Horse Show took place on Monday 26th July. Very bad weather brought fewer entries than usual and the number of spectators was well down on expectations. The horses shown gave the organisers hopes for a bright future, the younger prize winners showing a lot of potential.

Mr. E. R. Midgley, grocer, advertised for a young lady assistant to help with the grocery and provisions part of his business on 26th.

Thrapston visited Oundle on 29th for a bowls match, winning by 86 – 47.

Two events took place on Thursday 29th:

The Young Helpers' League held a garden fete and sale of work at "The Hollies" and "Nene House" during the afternoon, whilst the Town Band were engaged for the evening.

The Thrapston Women's Local Labour Party held a successful meeting in the Co-operative Hall. After an address on "The Food Question", over 50 ladies sat down for tea.

The Co-operative Society held its half-yearly meeting in their Hall on 30th. Trade had amounted to £12,834 8s 0½d with a profit of £1,186 15s 5d. The 623 members received a dividend of 2s in the £.

The two advertisements shown below were printed on 31st:

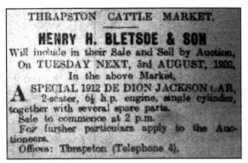

August

At the Police Court on Tuesday 3rd, three local boys appeared for breaking windows at Titchmarsh Mill. The owner said that he did not wish to press the case and, as none of the defendants had been in trouble before, the charges were dismissed upon payment of costs.

The Rural District Council met on 5th and agreed to separate the jobs of surveyor of highways and nuisance inspector, which were at present held by one person. The consensus was that these briefs would be better served by having one full-time person looking after each. The post of nuisance inspector was to be advertised.

At Oundle Court on 6th, Frank Wallace, a saddler who had lived in Thrapston for two years, claimed an injunction against Mr. Williams, proprietor of the cinema in the Temperance Hall, to restrain him from creating a nuisance and for £10 damages. The engine used at the Hall was making a noise to the detriment of the plaintiff and his family, especially his wife and two year old daughter. There was a lot of noise and a perpetual vibration throughout their property. The owner had promised to do something about it, but had not done so. Dr. Bird gave medical evidence as to the effects on the child and wife. The Court decided to adjourn the case to the next Court, to give Judge Farrant time to inspect the premises. *(The case was subsequently decided on 8th November. The injunction was refused and judgement reserved on the claim for damages – EDF.)*

Thrapston Sports was held on Saturday 7th. A composite picture is shown on page 204 *(Kettering Leader, 13th August 1920)*. Over 2,000 people attended. Amongst the Thrapston athletes named were:- Harold Ball, F. K. Webster, Oscar Cooke, J. Webster, W. H. Bygrave, J. E. Blake, L. J. Ruckwood and S. Minney. After the sports, Thrapston Silver Band played for dancing.

The picture shows:
Top left – getting out of the sacks during the obstacle race.
Circled – Sergt. Major G. C. Cairns, starter for all events.
Top right – C. W. Farrow winning the 880yds final.
Bottom left – Mr. W. Askew, Mr. W. Dellar and Mr. H. H. Rose.
Second left, bottom – C. Panter and J. Elmore (both Kettering), first and second in the obstacle race.
Second right, bottom – Master F. K. Webster, winner of the 220yds boys' race.
Bottom right – F. E. Burford (Wollaston), winner of the two-mile race.

Sunday 8th was Feast Sunday, the Town Band giving a concert in the Recreation Ground. £3 12s 6d was raised for band funds.

An item from the "Lost and Found" section, printed on 10th:
"Lost between the Sports Field, Thrapston and Raunds on Saturday last – brown leather wallet containing Treasury notes (numbers known), demobilisation papers, property of working man. Reward on returning same to A. Curtis, 1 Park Road, Raunds or Thrapston Police Station."

Miss Lucy Elizabeth Leigh, Huntingdon Road, married Walter Hitchener, Kettering, at St. James' Church on Wednesday 11th. She had been a teacher at the Council School and Sunday School and was held in the highest esteem. Mr. Hitchener, originally from Staffordshire, had served as a bomber and observer in the Air Force during the war. After a reception in the White Hart Assembly Room,
they left on the four o'clock Midland train for their honeymoon in Derbyshire. *(Pictured left, Kettering Leader, Friday 20th August 1920).*

The annual fete on behalf of the Parish Church took place at Thrapston House on 12th, the usual stalls, amusements and refreshments being available. At 7.00 pm the Town Silver Band struck up for dancing, which continued until 9.30 pm. £148 0s 6d was raised.

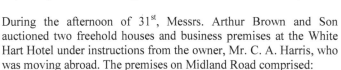

Thomas Neale, Huntingdon Road *(pictured right, Kettering Leader, Friday 20th August 1920)* retired on 13th, after more than 59 years service with the London and North West Railway. He was a driver until 1907, when his foot was crushed and he transferred to Thrapston as a pumper, his final job. Aged over 75 years, he was described as being "of fine physique, tall and upright". He and his wife were looking forward to their golden wedding anniversary in April 1921.

This "In Memoriam" was printed on 21st.
"In loving memory of Private **Robert Lewis Hiam (57)**, only son of H.W. and M. Hiam, of Thrapston, 1st 22nd London Regiment ("The Queen's"), killed in action in France, August 22nd 1918, aged 19 years.
Rest well, brave heart, by stream and hill,
Where many a hero's grave grows green;
You live in hearts that love you still,
You live with Christ in realms unseen.
- H.M.B.
- From Mother, Father, and Sisters."

On 24th, the Guardians met. They commenced the meeting by paying their respects to the late Mr. R. Talbot, Denford, who had been a Board member for many years. There was very little other business and the meeting finished earlier than usual.

On 26th, the Baptist Church held their annual fete at "The Hollies" to raise funds for the Church renovation fund. As well as stalls and amusements, there was an evening concert performed by members. £137 was raised.

On 27th, the picture shown left appeared in the *Kettering Leader* of Mr. W. T. Hewitt, who had just been appointed a J. P., sitting in Thrapston.

At the Police Court on 31st, a temporary transfer of the Swan Hotel licence from Eliza Morley to Mr. E. Miller was granted, as was renewal of the extended licensing hours on market days until the end of the year. A local drover admitted common assault on his employer and was fined 10s. Finally, the Court extended their thanks to Superintendant Tebbey for his valued service *(pictured right, Kettering Leader, Friday 23rd July 1920)* who was leaving the district.

During the afternoon of 31st, Messrs. Arthur Brown and Son auctioned two freehold houses and business premises at the White Hart Hotel under instructions from the owner, Mr. C. A. Harris, who was moving abroad. The premises on Midland Road comprised:
A four bedroomed house with garden, outbuildings, yard and cart entrance with business premises to the rear (three workshops), all in the occupation of the owner.
A three bedroomed cottage in the occupation of Mr. B. Harris.
Bidding started at £100 and at £550, Mr. G. H. Gilbert became the purchaser.

September

The *Evening Telegraph* reported some splendid crops of potatoes in town on 2nd. Mr. H. J. Gurney, Huntingdon Road, had dug a freak-shaped potato, which weighed 1 lb 13 oz.

The Northants Junior Cup first round draw was announced on Friday 3rd. Thrapston United were drawn to play Timson's (Kettering). In the Lower Junior Cup, Thrapston Reserves were drawn to visit Rushden Park Road Baptists.

On 4th, the Trades and Labour Council held a fancy dress parade, fete and baby show at "The Hollies". Pictured are: top, Thrapston Railwaymen, bottom: entries for the fancy dress competition. *(Kettering Leader, Friday 10th September 1920.)*

Thrapston United began the new season in the Kettering Combination on 4th, with a 1 – 2 home defeat by Walgrave Amber.

Afternoon and evening services, with a break for tea, were held at the Baptist Church on Thursday 9th to celebrate the first anniversary of the pastorate of Rev. A. Smith.

Thrapston United visited Mrs. Morris' Boys Club (Kettering) on Saturday 11th, where a 2 – 2 draw was played out.

The Glee Society held their first practice evening in the Baptist Schoolrooms on Monday 13th, where they began rehearsing "Hiawatha's Wedding Feast".

At the Parish Council meeting on Wednesday 15th, congratulations were extended to Mr. Hewitt on his recent appointment as a magistrate.

On Thursday 16th, Miss Marjorie Loveday, Islip, and Mr. Charles William Freeman, Manchester House, Thrapston, were married in Islip. After their honeymoon at Shanklin, Isle of Wight, they were to live at "Fern House", Thrapston.

The *Evening Telegraph* printed this advertisement on 17th:
"Young lady desires clerical position; shorthand typist; knowledge of bookkeeping; 4 years experience. Box 380, "Journal" Office, Thrapston."

A public dance to raise funds for Thrapston St. James' Boys Football Club was held at the Co-operative Hall on the same day.

Thrapston United welcomed Desborough Reserves to their ground on 18th September and gained their first win of the season, by 2 – 0. The team was - Jeffery; Arnold and Harris; J. Manning, Baker and Clark; Headland, H. Manning, March, S. Manning and Knight.

On Sunday 19th, the landlord of the Fox Inn, Mr. Frederick Hodson, died aged 60 years. He had run the establishment for over 20 years and was also involved with Thrapston and Islip Cricket Clubs and the Athletic Sports Committee. His funeral was held at St. James' Church on Thursday 23rd followed by burial at Oundle Road Cemetery.

The first committee meeting of the recently formed Thrapston Branch of the Middle Classes Union was held in the Parish Rooms on 20th, Mr. W. Askew presiding. They agreed to enlarge the committee considerably and to include the surrounding villages.

Another "In Memoriam" advertisement was placed in the *Evening Telegraph* on 20th:
"In loving memory of Rifleman **E. Percy Raworth (41)**, Rifle Brigade, killed in action, September 20th, 1917, aged 23 years.
Fondly we loved him, he is dear to us still,
But in grief we must bend to God's will
Our sorrow is great, our loss hard to bear,
But angels, dear Percy, will guard and care.
From his loving Mother and Father and Brother.

The Guardians met on 21st, where they heard that there had been two applications for the vacant charge nurse post, Miss Davis from Leeds being the successful candidate. The Workhouse master was commended on how well the garden was managed. As well as providing vegetables for the institution, there were also plenty left over for sale, thus providing useful income. This item was also reported as part of the meeting:-
"A circular letter was read from the Guardians of the Northampton Union stating that they had received applications for relief from a number of ex-Service men in consequence of the decisions of Medical Boards that disability was not caused or aggravated by military service, and asking the Thrapston Board to pass a similar resolution to the following and forward copies to the usual quarters: - "Resolved that where men on enlistment into the Naval, Military, or Air Forces were passed fit for service, have been discharged, and are still suffering from disability, they should continue to receive a pension, and not have to apply for Poor Law assistance and become chargeable to local rates." – It was resolved to support the resolution."

An Independent Labour Party open-air meeting in the Market Place on 22nd was abandoned due to exceptionally stormy weather.

The pictures *(shown left)* were printed in the *Kettering Leader* on Friday 24th September 1920. They show an unnamed Thrapston lace maker and Mr. S. Meadows, who lost a leg during the war with his adapted bicycle in Oundle Road.

A whist drive with twenty tables was held at the Institute on 24th September.

Thrapston United travelled to Kettering St. Andrew's on Saturday 25th, winning by 2 – 0 and moving up to 4th place in the table.

An evening open-air meeting took place in the Market Place on the same day, where Major Brassey spoke to the local Conservative and Unionist Association, with a good number attending.

The annual meeting of Thrapston and District Cycling and Athletic Club was held at the King's Arms Hotel on Thursday 30th, where there was a fair attendance. Receipts during the year amounted to £59 9s 11d and the Club had assets, including cash in hand, totalling £161 14s 4d. Mr. Dellar had resigned as secretary, being unable to devote the necessary time and a small sub-committee was appointed to obtain a replacement.

October

Harvest Festival weekend commenced on 1st in St. James' Church and finished with a sale of produce on Monday 4th. £27 1s 10d was raised from collections and the sale, which was shared between the hospitals in Northampton, Kettering and Peterborough.

A "Wanted" advertisement was printed on 1st in the *Evening Telegraph*:
"Wanted, strong man to dig about 20 poles ground. Apply (after 7.30pm) – Gurney, Swiss Cottages, Thrapston." *(These houses on Huntingdon Road are shown above – EDF Collection.)*

In the first round of the Northants Junior Cup, Section 1, Thrapston United had a 1 – 0 home win over Kettering Timson's on Saturday 2nd.

The Council School managers met on 5th. Miss Tarrant, a certificated teacher, had resigned in view of her approaching marriage. They were sorry to see her leave and extended their very best wishes for her married life. Miss Joyce White, Raunds, was appointed into the vacancy.

The District Sub-Committee meeting followed. Attendance figures were - Church of England School 87.8%, Council School 83.2%. Figures were lower than usual, this being attributed to children helping with the harvest. Only one tender had been received for conveying Denford children to school from Mr. Cullum, Titchmarsh. His price of 10s a day was accepted.

On the same evening, an entertainment took place in the Corn Exchange. It was given by a party of twenty children from the London Branch of the National Children's Home and Orphanage and included musical items and a gymnastic display.

Thrapston United beat Broughton in town on 9th by 4 – 0.
The reserve team were due to play Rushden Baptists in the Cup on the same day, but had to scratch leaving their opponents with a bye into the next round.

At the Police Court on Tuesday 12th, an Orlingbury man was summoned for failing to produce a driving licence when asked to by a constable and also for driving through town at 8.45pm on 18th September without lamps. He pleaded guilty to both offences and was fined £2 in each case.

On 16th, a Raunds man was brought before Dr. Gainer in a hastily arranged Police Court. He had been an absentee from his unit of the Royal Air Force since 11th and was remanded to await an escort.

New restrictions on the sale of coal were brought in by the Rural District Council on 20th. A maximum of 1 cwt a week to any premises was imposed.

John Charles Guest, Oundle Road died on 21st. He had been unwell for a long time and spent the last month of his life in the Infirmary. His funeral was held on 26th and two days later, this notice was printed in the *Evening Telegraph*:
"Mrs. Guest, Oundle Road, Thrapston and family wish to thank all kind friends for sympathy and floral tributes sent.
What pain he suffered we did not know,
We never saw him die;
We only know he passed away
And never said goodbye."

A day later, Mrs. A. Barnett, Bridge Street, died from bronchial pneumonia. She was the widow of Arthur Barnett who had died on Armistice Day 1918. Her funeral took place on 25th. Their coach-building business was in the hands of one of their sons.

Thrapston St. James' played against Denford Poppies on Saturday 23rd in a youth game. One of the Thrapston players, Victor Guest, Huntingdon Road, fell on his head and was assisted home in a semi-conscious state. Dr. Gainer and Nurse Mansbridge attended to him. He went to bed, slept for 14 hours and on awaking, was much better.

The Police Court had a 16 year old furnace worker to deal with on Tuesday 26th. He was charged with discharging a firework, to wit a "thunderflash" on the public highway on 16th. There had been a spate of similar activities in town and, after many complaints, this youth was the first to have been identified. He pleaded guilty and, due to him not being the only miscreant, was dismissed with a caution as to his future behaviour.

This report was printed on 26th:

"Several persons in Thrapston have dug remarkably fine potatoes this season. In the garden of the Thrapston Poor Law Institution, in which the master (Mr. H. Elks) takes a keen interest, some of the sizes have been quite noteworthy; one weighed no less than 2 lbs 6 oz and was a good shaped tuber for so large a specimen. It will be recalled that at the September meeting of the Board of Guardians, the master was thanked for the creditable way in which he had managed the garden.

Mr. Gurney, who had advertised for a "strong man" *(see page 208)*, was commended in the *Kettering Leader* on 29th for the huge variety of beautiful flowers in his garden.

Two advertisements appeared in the *Evening Telegraph* on 30th:
"Lost between High Street, Thrapston and Bosworth's Lodge, Islip. Engagement ring (one stone). Reward. Mrs. Percy March, Islip."
"Wanted. Day girl. Apply: Ainsworth, Huntingdon Road, Thrapston."

Thrapston United easily defeated Symington's (Market Harborough) by 3 - 0 in town on Saturday 30th.

The Town Band held a dance in the Corn Exchange during the same evening.

Finally, the Diocesan Board met in the Co-operative Hall on 31st with many clergy, teachers and church workers present.

November

The Bible Society held a meeting in the Co-operative Hall on Monday 1st.

The Rural District Council sat on Thursday 4th when they agreed that the new council houses  on Oundle Road should be called "Addison Villas" *(the completed houses are pictured left – EDF Collection)*. There was much discussion about what rent should be charged. To correlate with the actual cost of building, it would need to be set between 35s and £2 a week, which was much more than the working classes could afford. The Ministry of Health had sanctioned a weekly rent of 8s 6d which was accepted. Mr. Barnes, from Hull, was appointed Inspector of Nuisances. The Medical Officer reported that there had been one case of scarlatina in town since his last report.

The Thrapston Society for the Discussion of Public Questions discussed "The Future of Thrapston" in the evening of 4th. The rector expressed the hope that the town would become a centre, radiating life and activity, rather than becoming an industrial municipality. Well-organised hygiene, recreation and education were needed. They recommended that a proper water supply and electric power should be priorities along with a library. *(Although it appears*

*that this Society had been active for some time, this was the first report of their activity –
EDF.)*

Mrs. Morris' Boys Club (Kettering) visited Thrapston for a league match on Saturday 6th, the
home team winning 3 – 0.

Two short reports were printed on 10th:
The Fitzwilliam Hounds had met recently in town.
Dr. Gainer, who had been very ill with heart trouble and pneumonia, was reported to have
slightly improved to being "gravely ill". *(Daily reports as to his progress appeared for the
next week – EDF.)*

The Temperance Hall hosted a Tennis Club Social on 11th, organised by the Shop Assistants'
Tennis Club. Following whist (21 tables), dancing went on until the small hours.

St. James' Church welcomed a gathering of choirs from local villages who combined to
celebrate "village choirs".

Thrapston United visited Islip for a friendly match on 13th, honours being even at 2 – 2.
Shareholders of the Northamptonshire Union Bank met in Northampton on Tuesday 16th for
an extraordinary general meeting. They confirmed the amalgamation with the National
Provincial and Union Bank of England.

The Parish Council met on 17th in the Temperance Hall. Mrs. Benyon had offered any suitable
spare shrubs she had for the Recreation Ground. She also wished to have two small yew trees
planted at the back of her husband's grave in the Cemetery. Mr. L. Richardson was re-
appointed town scavenger with a daily rate of 3s 6d. There had been a number of complaints
against him of incivility and he was warned to use greater courtesy when speaking to the
public.

The ex-servicemen met for a rally on 18th and agreed the following resolution for forwarding
to the Prime Minister, the Ministry of Labour and Munitions, the Secretary of State for War
and the member for North Northants (Major Brassey, M.P.):
"That we, the Thrapston and District Branch of the National Federation D and D S, and S, do
strongly protest against the discharge of ex- Service men, including a number of disabled,
from various Government departments before the Substitution Committee promised by the
Government have combed the 80,000 odd non-Service men and women still temporarily
employed in Government service; and we call upon the Government to order an immediate
reinstatement of all those affected."

In a second round of the Northants Junior Cup, Thrapston United visited Rothwell Town on
Saturday 20th gaining one of their best ever results, winning 7 – 1.

Pettit and Son advertised for plumbers and hot water fitters on Monday 22nd.

Thrapston Ladies had recently been visited by Kimbolton Ladies for a hockey match. The
Evening Telegraph reported, on 25th:
"The Kimbolton team visited Thrapston with doubting hearts but returned flushed and happy.
Their play was a little faster and not quite so calculating as that of the Thrapston team."
Kimbolton won 5 – 1.

Thrapston United played Kettering Rangers on Saturday 27th in the league. They won 3 – 2.

December

On 2nd, the Co-op Guild met in the Co-operative Hall where Mrs. Swan presided over a meeting of about 50 members and children.

An away game at Desborough Reserves gave Thrapston a 1 – 0 victory on Saturday 4th.

On the same day, Thrapston St. James beat Titchmarsh Juniors by 7 – 0. The scorers were Victor Guest (3), Oscar Cooke (2) and W. Bygrave and Ernest Mayes one each.

At the Women's School on 5th, Mrs. Cottingham gave a musical programme.

The *Evening Telegraph* printed this open letter on 7th:
"Sir. I should like to ask through the medium of your paper if it is not within the range of possibility that a train be run from Thrapston to Kettering earlier in the morning, leaving Thrapston about 7.30.
This would be a great boon to many of the residents of Thrapston and district, and it would be much appreciated, especially by a dozen or so workmen, some tradesmen and schoolchildren who are daily travelling to Kettering.
The first train running at the present time means that tradesmen and schoolchildren are late, and the workman has the option of pushing his cycle (perhaps against a head-wind or through the rain) or probably losing a day's work.
I feel quite sure I am voicing the thoughts of many others when I ask for consideration of the above suggestion.
A Tradesman."

The ex-servicemen held an evening of speeches followed by a concert and dance at the Corn Exchange on Friday 10th. Many people attended to support the Federation.

On Saturday 11th, Thrapston United hosted Kettering Rangers. Letting a two goal lead slip, the match ended in a 2 – 2 draw. As Geddington Stars were not playing, the point gained was sufficient to move Thrapston to the top of the table.

After a lapse of three years, caused by Government restrictions, the Christmas Fat Stock Show was held in the Cattle Market on 14th. 25 cows, 8 sheep and 20 pigs were shown. After the sale, a well-attended dinner was held in the White Hart Hotel.

On 16th, three short reports were printed:
Mr. Lavender, Halford Street, was awarded second and third prizes in the open class for Rhode Island Red pullets at the recent Histon Poultry Show.
The Thrapston Society decided to invite ladies to future meetings.
Freeman and Webb announced their Christmas holidays. They would open all day on Thursday 23rd and close on 27th and 28th. Customers were advised to "buy early and avoid the crush".

Messrs. Cawdell announced big, all-round reductions in prices, in their display advertisements on 18th.

In the Northants Junior Cup on the same day, Thrapston United took on Kettering Atlas, drawing 1 – 1. The replay was arranged for Christmas Day, when Kettering ran out winners by 2 – 1.

Tomlinson's had their Christmas advertisement printed from 20th, shown right.

Thrapston Institute welcomed Ringstead Institute on Wednesday 22nd for billiards and whist matches. The results were; Billiards – Thrapston won by 567 – 443. Whist – Thrapston won by 147 – 135.

On Christmas Eve, a 72-minute peal was rung on the St. James' bells whilst Miss Kingsford took choirboys around town singing carols. A total of £4 5s was raised for the Blind Babies Sunshine House Fund.

On Christmas Day, the postmen completed their deliveries in good time. The usual services were held in town and the Workhouse catered for 45 inmates with 12 in the Infirmary.

A Christmas Day football match was held on the Thrapston ground between Thrapston United Reserves and Thrapston Married Men in aid of the Guild of Help. The Married Men held out well until half-time, when the score was 0 – 0, but crumbled in the second half, eventually losing by 7 – 1. Takings amounted to £4 16s 6d, which the Guild happily accepted.

The Town Band paraded around the town on Boxing Day morning, whilst Thrapston United held a very successful dance at the Corn Exchange in the evening.

The annual invitation dance, arranged by Messrs. I. and J. Ireson was held in the Co-operative Hall in the evening of 26th, about 50 people attending.

The Fitzwilliam Hounds met on 29th with a fair muster. A good number of spectators came to watch.

The Thrapston Shop Assistants Tennis Club held another successful invitation dance in the Temperance Hall on 29th, which ran between 8.00 pm and 2.00 am.

The final event in 1920 was the Guild of Help's long-night dance in the Corn Exchange on New Year's Eve, 160 people attending. Music was provided by George Abbott's String Band.

By the end of the year, the St. James' Church War Memorial had been inaugurated and the Peace Park was now being very well used by grateful children. Just one more name was to appear on the Roll of Honour, the result of illness caused by military service, bringing the total to 58 men; the Roll of Honour in the Parish Church contained 285 names of men who left town to go to war – a fatal casualty rate of 20%. Life was returning to a pre-war state and the mundane was generally considered preferable to the traumas of the previous seven years.

1921

January

The New Year began with a home win for Thrapston United against Finedon by 4 – 0.

Sadly, during the evening of 1st, Miss Emma Johnson, third daughter of Mr. George Johnson, Huntingdon Road, died aged 40 years after suffering a long illness from tuberculosis. She had been bed-bound since the previous October. Before her illness, she had been a keen worker at the Parish Church. Shortly before her death, her father slipped whilst going downstairs, sustaining a cut on his head and some internal injuries.

This advertisement was printed on Monday 3rd: "Christmas Mystery Play, "Eager Heart" at the Corn Exchange, Thrapston. Thursday next, 3 and 8: Friday evening, 8: in aid of the Thrapston and District Nursing Association. Plans and tickets at Messrs. Goss Brothers." *(Goss Brothers premises were in the shop with awning on the*

Market Place, Thrapston.

corner of Chancery Lane shown above – printed by Goss Brothers circa 1919 – EDF Collection.)

The Thrapston branch of the Church of England Missionary Society met in the Parish Rooms during the afternoon of 4th.

Also on 4th, the annual entertainment and prize distribution for St. James' Church Sunday School took place during the evening. Each child received a prize, although it was decided that in future years they would need to have at least 80% attendance to qualify. On leaving, each child was given an orange.

January 5th – Frederick William Johnson (73) died of pulmonary tuberculosis.

The local Women's Temperance Association met in the "Nene House" Schoolroom on 5th, Mrs. George Smith presiding. Membership had remained steady at about 50 and their bank balance was £2 4s. After tea, there was an auction of various gifts brought by members, resulting in a donation of £4 1s 2d being sent to the London Temperance Hospital.

Emma Johnson was buried in Oundle Road Cemetery on 6th, after a service at St. James' Church. Her father was unable to attend, but was represented by family members. Many floral tributes were sent. She was interred in the same grave in which her sister had been buried nearly fifteen years previously.

The annual children's Christmas party took place at the Baptist Church on 6th. Tea was served at 4.00 pm followed by games and competitions. On leaving, each child received a bun and orange.

The Young Helpers' annual children's party was held in the Co-operative Hall on 7th, 50 children attending. They started at 4.30 pm with games and at 6.00 pm, had a short entertainment. Refreshments followed at 7.00 pm and then games and dancing until 9.00 pm. £5 5s was raised during the party for Dr. Barnardo's Homes.

On Saturday 8th, this advertisement appeared:
"Can spare few sittings of eggs from prize winning R.I.R. *(Rhode Island Red – EDF)* (Measure's strain), including 2nd Irthlingborough, 2nd and 3rd Histon; 10s 6d sitting. Lavender, Thrapston."

On the same day, Thrapston United welcomed Kettering St. Andrew's to their ground and gained a 2 – 1 victory. After the match, the club held a whist drive at the Co-operative Hall, with over 50 people attending. The prizes were won by Mr. F. Leete and Miss F. Kirby.

Frederick William Johnson (73) was buried in Oundle Road Cemetery on Monday 10th, the town's final casualty of the Great War.

At the Guardians meeting on 11th, they received the resignation of Miss K. Hill from her post as kitchenmaid. Given the difficulties recruiting staff, they agreed to advertise the vacancy as being for a matron's assistant.

Miss Cottingham gave a children's concert to a well-filled room in the Baptist Schoolroom during the evening of 13th.

This notice was printed in the *Kettering Leader* on Friday 14th:
"Thanks.
Mr. George Johnson and Family, Huntingdon Road, Thrapston, also Mr. and Mrs. W. Johnson and Family, Grove Road, desire to thank all kind friends for the many inquiries and expressions of sympathy with their sad bereavement; also for floral tributes sent."

This report was printed in the *Evening Telegraph* on the same day:
"Master Alfred Turner, aged 15, son of Mrs. Turner, Halford Street, met with an accident on Christmas Eve at Thrapston Foundry which resulted in the loss of an eye. He was working at a machine when a piece of metal flew into his left eye. He did not feel very much pain at the time and continued to work until the foundry closed at noon for the Christmas holiday. He was able to get out on Christmas Day but by the evening his eye had become very bad, he could not see with it and it was bandaged. On the Sunday morning he went to see a doctor who said it was a hospital case. The following Tuesday he was taken to Northampton Hospital and last Friday it was found necessary to remove the eye. It is expected that he will be home on Saturday."

An Inquest was held at Thrapston Police Station on 15th concerning the death of Mr. Ernest Jellis, managing clerk for Messrs. Southam and Sons, auctioneers, who was found dead in the inner room of the firm's Thrapston offices on Friday morning, asphyxiated by gas. There was no jury. The Coroner returned a verdict of "Suicide whilst temporarily insane".

Later in the day, Thrapston United travelled to Broughton where they played out a 2 – 2 draw.

A recent meeting of the Church of England School managers was reported on 18th. Two applications had been received for the headmastership following the resignation of Mr. Emery. Mr. E. W. Newton, Aldwincle, was the unanimous choice, subject to approval from the County Education Authority.

A sparsely attended meeting took place in the Co-operative Hall on 19th January to hear an address on the object and aims of the League of Nations. Those present decided to form a District Branch of the League of Nations Union and elected Mr. H. J. Davies as secretary.

The Parish Council met on 19th, where they resolved not to hold a meeting in February unless necessary. The state of the roads in town was, once again, raised and was subject to on-going discussion with the County Council.

Finally on 19th, the Guild of Help held an evening concert in the Corn Exchange to a large and appreciative audience.

This advertisement was printed on 20th:
"Wanted, wood bundler, in good condition. Apply Jack Rogers, Thrapston."

On Wednesday 26th, a Joint Committee of members from Northamptonshire and Huntingdonshire County Councils sat at the Petty Sessional Court to hear a request from the Rural District Council for increased representation on the Board of Guardians. A number of towns and villages were represented. The Committee agreed that Thrapston should have one extra member.

At the Police Court on Friday 28th, two men of no fixed abode appeared charged with stealing a shirt, value 8s 11d, the property of Edward Barnes. They were remanded to appear on the following Tuesday.

On Saturday 29th, Thrapston United hosted Rothwell Town, winning by 3 – 1.

February

On Tuesday 1st, the two men remanded on the previous Friday appeared for the theft of a shirt. They were also jointly charged with the theft of a painter's dusting brush, the property of Messrs. C. R. Pettit and Son. For the first offence, they received three calendar months hard labour and for the second, one month to run concurrently.

The Farmers' Union met at the White Hart Hotel on 1st. Membership now exceeded 100 and there was lengthy debate about the proposed minimum wage, which did not meet with their approval.

The annual meeting of Drayton Park Cricket Club occured on Friday 4th. The club had 30 vice-presidents and 66 members. During the season, they had played 20 friendly matches, winning eight, losing eleven. The other match was tied.

Thrapston Union placed an advertisement in the *Evening Telegraph* for a domestic servant on Saturday 5th *(shown right)*.

THRAPSTON UNION.

DOMESTIC SERVANT.

THE Guardians of the above Union require the services of a DOMESTIC SERVANT. Candidates must be single women or widows. Salary £27 10s per annum (inclusive of War Bonus), £5 per annum for uniform, and rations, apartments, and washing. Particulars as to the duties can be obtained from the Matron, Poor Law Institution, Thrapston.

Applications, with copies of recent testimonials, to be sent to me, the undersigned, not later than MONDAY, the 7th instant.

By order,

MARTIN G. W. HUNNYBUN,
Clerk to the Guardians.

Union Offices,
Thrapston,
12th January, 1921.   T5

Also on 5th, Thrapston United travelled to Symington's Athletic who inflicted a heavy 8 – 1 defeat on the reigning champions.

A meeting in the interests of junior football took place in St. James' Parish Rooms on 5th to discuss the proposition to form a league. Representatives came from Thrapston, Islip, Cranford, Aldwincle, Woodford, Lowick and Ringstead. A number of other villages had expressed an interest, including Achurch, Titchmarsh, Addington, Twywell and Denford. A league was formed to promote under 15's boys football within a five mile radius of Islip and a committee was agreed. The rector of Islip had already donated a cup for the league winners, which was on display.

This advertisement appeared on 7th:
"Messrs. Thos. E. Gray and Co. beg to inform the public that they have commenced a coal business for Thrapston and District. Coal wharf at Midland Road Station; Order Office, Coate's Yard, Bridge Street, Thrapston."

The Guardians met on Tuesday 8th and appointed Dr. Lascelles as Medical Officer. The average number of inmates during the last quarter was 57 a day, whilst the total number of casuals was 644.

Parker's of Kettering announced regular visits to town on 11th.

In the evening, Thrapston Institute hosted Islip Institute for billiards and whist contests, the home side winning both events.

Thrapston United travelled to Walgrave Amber on 12th, losing 3 – 1.

On Monday 14th, Mr. F. W. Gates, motor engineer of the Wharf Motor Works, Thrapston appeared before the Wandsworth County Court, London to answer a claim for damages of £57 5s 4d from Streatham Engineering Co. Ltd. He had responded to a trade advertisement to have work done on a set of gears. These were sent to London and, after communications, work commenced. The job turned out to be much more complicated than initially thought and required a large number of newly engineered parts. When the gears were returned, Mr. Gates decided that they had done in excess of what was considered necessary. Judgement was sought for the costs incurred and, after hearing evidence from both sides, was awarded to the plaintiff.

At Thrapston Police Court on 15th, Mr. Williams was granted a renewal of his cinematograph licence for the Temperance Hall. In another case, a girl from Twywell was fined 5s for riding her bicycle in town on 26th January without appropriate lighting.

A White Elephant sale took place at the Corn Exchange on Thursday 17th to raise money for improvements at the Recreation Field.

Thrapston people were advised on Friday 18th, "Your grocer is now selling "Aeroplane" self-raising flour, 2 lb bags 11d, 3 lb 1s 4½d. Blended by Henry Barlow and Son Ltd, Confectioners, Kettering."

On Saturday 19th, Thrapston United travelled to Kettering Timson's, winning 2 – 0.

This "For Sale" advertisement was placed in the *Evening Telegraph* on 21st:
"Eggs for sitting from 10 White Wyandottes; records for November 196, December 208, January 223; mated to one of T. Bergon's cockerels', sire Burnley Wonder, dam bred from Lady Barron; 10s down. T. Essam, Market Road, Thrapston."

The Fitzwilliam Hounds met in town on Wednesday 23rd and "...had a fair day's sport. West Fields drew a blank, but a fox from Denford Ash led hounds fast for 15 minutes to Titchmarsh where he beat them. An outlier from near Titchmarsh Warren gave the field a sharp run to Clapton Rough Fields. A brace of foxes was found in Barnwell Wolds, one of which went away, but at Hamerton Grove was given up after a good hunt, the first twenty minutes of which were very fast."

Two evening events took place on 23rd:
The Trades Council held a benefit concert in the Co-operative Hall for families in the District who had no income - state benefits having run out.
The Institute held a whist drive for their own funds.

On Saturday 26th, Thrapston United played a home game against Kettering Timson's, winning 2 – 1.

March

The Police Court sat on Wednesday 2nd. James Sanders, a local labourer and very well known to the Police, appeared charged with disorderly conduct whilst drunk the afternoon before. He pleaded guilty. Inspector Baxter had warned him to go home but he insisted on remaining in the street, so he was taken into custody. He was bound over to be of good behaviour for six months and told to return to Court for sentence during that period if required. A condition was placed upon him that he should abstain from all intoxicating liquor for six months and was also placed under the supervision of Mr. R. A. Claydon, probation officer.

Miss Elizabeth Freeman, Midland Road, died on 1st aged 27 years. Her funeral took place on 4th.

A whist drive organised by the Co-operative Society Committee took place in their Hall on 4th. It was well attended, 30 tables being filled and £7 3s was raised for the Guild of Help.

Thrapston had a difficult away match on Saturday 5th at the league leaders, Geddington Stars. Despite their best efforts, they were defeated in a close game by 3 – 2.

The Guardians met on 8th and heard that there had been no responses to their advertisement for a domestic servant. They agreed that the total rate for Northamptonshire parishes for the next six months would be 5s 5d in the £. Contracts were awarded to cover various periods for services like bread supply and funerals. The previous week had been very busy with vagrants, 68 presenting themselves for assistance.

The ex-servicemen held a whist drive on 11th to raise funds for their group. Over 100 people attended.

The Middle Classes Union met in the Co-operative Hall on Tuesday 15th where the address was entitled "Between the Pincers: the Position of the Middle Classes." The evening finished with a musical entertainment.

On 17th, the Farmers' Union held their annual dinner at the White Hart Hotel. Membership had increased over the year, reaching 104 by the end of 1920.

On the same day, the thirteenth annual tea and social evening for the old folks of Thrapston and Islip was held in the Temperance Hall. 115 guests attended, several being over 80 years old. After tea, an extensive entertainment gave much pleasure. Refreshments, sweets and tobacco were passed around. At the conclusion, Mrs. Cottingham proposed a vote of thanks to all who had assisted with the event. Many of the old people were taken to and from the Hall by motor car and the few who were unable to attend had little packages of refreshments taken to them.

Major Brassey, M.P., addressed a meeting in the Corn Exchange on 18th.

Thrapston United were held to a 1 – 1 draw at Rothwell Town on Saturday 19th.

The letter reproduced below was printed in the *Evening Telegraph* on Thursday 24th:
"I should like to draw public attention to some manly, outspoken remarks of Mr. W. Askew C.C. at the last meeting of the County Council. In order to permit of cinema entertainments being given on Sunday April 3rd for Earl Haig's Warriors' Fund, the Finance Committee recommended that the prohibition of Sunday performances be lifted for that day. Mr. Askew said "he felt he would be cowardly if he did not enter a protest against the recommendation. He had the sincerest sympathy with Earl Haig's object, but if cinemas were opened for this purpose on Sunday, they could not refuse applications for other charitable performances on Sundays. The British character had not been built up on the lines that the end justified the means. They should retain the quiet and sanctity of the English Sabbath and not go in for Continental Sunday". The chairman, I notice, said the Council would respect Mr. Askew's view. The recommendation was carried, but only by 18 votes to 15. Such words as those of Mr. Askew were never more appropriate and necessary than at the present day. I heartily commend them to the notice of all your readers.
A correspondent."

PRELIMINARY NOTICE

THRAPSTON SPORTS,

August Bank Holiday Monday

(UP TO PRE-WAR STANDARD).

FLAT, CYCLE, JUMPING, and TROTTING EVENTS.

Further Details later.

PLEASE NOTE DATE.

W. MILLER and H. ROSE,
Hon. Secretaries

Thrapston Sports placed their preliminary notice *(shown left)* in the *Evening Telegraph* on Saturday 26th.

On the same day, Thrapston United travelled to Rushton winning by 2 – 1.

On Easter Monday, 28th, Thrapston played Woodford. A short report was printed:

"This local "Derby" was witnessed on Monday by the largest crowd at Thrapston this season of almost 1000. Woodford won the toss and kicked with a strong wind in their favour. Woodford had slightly the better of the play, but half time arrived with a blank score, Newman, Thrapston's goalie, only being called upon once. Thrapston overwhelmed the visitors in the second half. K. March opened the scoring and H. Manning added two more goals in quick succession." The final result was Thrapston United 3 - Woodford 0.

The Women's Section of the Labour Party held their annual meeting in the Co-operative Hall on 30th.

Three short items were printed on 31st:
The District Sunday School Union held a meeting at the Baptist Church.
The Easter Church Vestry met with 14 people present. Mr. Hillyard was re-appointed churchwarden for the 25th consecutive year.
Islip Juniors defeated Thrapston St. James' by 2 - 1, Stobie scoring for Thrapston.

April

Thrapston United played a home match against Rushton on Saturday 2nd, winning 3 - 1.

A "Wanted" advertisement, printed on 4th:
"Wanted, experienced man to drive Ford lorry. Pettit and Son, Thrapston."

In the evening of 4th, Thrapston visited Finedon in the Kettering Combination, losing 2 – 0.

The Rural District Council agreed to increase the number of Thrapston Guardians from two to three when they met on 7th.

It was announced that P.C. Frost, who had been stationed in town for eleven months, had been transferred to Rothwell, his replacement being P.C. Baird, who moved in the opposite direction. P.C. Baird had served with H.M. Forces for five years before re-joining the Force at the end of the war.

Finally on 7th, the Glee Club held a concert in the Corn Exchange. The main feature was "Hiawatha's Wedding Feast".

The Institute held an evening whist drive on 8th.

On Sunday 10th, Miss Kingsford gave an afternoon organ recital in the Wesleyan Church. The proceeds were donated to the Organ Upkeep Fund.

On Monday 11th, the Corn Exchange was filled to overflowing for a presentation to Mr. F. W. B. Emery *(pictured right – EDF Collection)* to mark his retirement as headmaster of the Church of England School after 31½ years service. After being given an inscribed gold watch and chain, pupils performed a variety of musical items. The inscription read:
"Presented to F W B Emery by scholars, teachers, managers and friends of Thrapston C E School, for 31 years loyal service.
April 1921."

Tuesday 12th was the annual flower day in aid of the Northampton and County Crippled Children's Fund. £14 2s 6d was raised for the cause.

The Shire Horse Society held their annual parade of stallions in the Market Place on 12th, followed by their annual meeting at the White Hart Hotel.

Thrapston United welcomed Geddington Stars for a midweek match on 13th. Two goals from H. Manning and one from F. Stobie gave them an easy 3 – 0 victory.

A Victor Guest goal for Thrapston St. James' on 14th was the difference in their match against Denford Poppies.

This appeared in the *Evening Telegraph* on Friday 15th:
"Wanted immediately, reliable person for work of small house, help given with cooking. Mrs. Wilkinson, "The Hermitage", Thrapston."

Saturday 16th was the final day of the Kettering Combination season, Thrapston having already completed their fixtures. Walgrave Amber, who finished top of the table, had been deducted 22 points for fielding an ineligible player. Thrapston United therefore finished third, behind Geddington Stars and Symington's Athletic. An appeal was expected from Walgrave.

The Thrapston Gas and Coke Co. Ltd. placed this announcement on 18th, a result of the national miners' strike:
"Owing to the shortage of coal supply the pressure of gas will be reduced daily between the hours of 4.30 and 8pm."

The Parish Council met at the Temperance Hall on Wednesday 20th. The new housing on Oundle Road would need to be connected to the sewer system, which was likely to cost £500. This would greatly increase the rates and it was agreed to approach the Rural District Council for assistance.

That evening, the Labour Party held a social in the Co-operative Hall. Following speeches and entertainment, Miss Ivy Groom played for dancing.

The Young Helpers' League held a concert on 21st, raising £19 16s for their funds.

The Society for the Discussion of Public Questions met at the Council School on 21st, where they were treated to an evening entitled "The Marvel of the Microscope". The speaker, Mr. Rippener from Oundle, gave an illustrated lecture using a magic lantern loaned by Mr. Cottingham.

Thrapston St. James' Boys Football Club finished their season on Saturday 23rd by defeating Islip Juniors by 3 – 1. They had played 23 matches, winning 16, losing 5 and drawing 2. They scored 84 goals and conceded 31. The top scorer, with 54 goals, was Victor Guest.

An accident occurred at the Oundle Road junction on Sunday 24th when a motorcyclist from Twywell collided with a chauffeur-driven car whilst both were taking avoiding action, having realised impact was imminent. The car had two broken windows, dents and a spare petrol can was punctured, depositing its contents on the road. The occupants were unhurt. The front of the motorcycle was badly damaged and the rider seriously cut about the face. He was attended by Dr. Walsh. Inspector Baxter and P.C. Baird attended and rendered assistance.

The 1921 census date of 19th June was announced on 27th.

A number of children paraded through town on Saturday 30th with garlands to celebrate May Day. *(It was not considered acceptable for children to indulge in such frivolity on a Sunday; thus it was held a day early – EDF.)*

May

After evening services on 1st, a Labour May Day meeting took place in the Market Place. There were a number of speeches, which took a little over an hour.

At the Guardians meeting on Tuesday 3rd, they were told of tramps being seen throwing away bread and cheese which they had been given on leaving the Union. The Guardians were appalled by this behaviour and discussed what, if anything, could be done. The Ministry regulated that each should receive ¼lb of cheese and 1½lbs of bread and, being a Government directive, this could not be ignored.

The 3rd was also the annual combined May Fair and market day. There were many visiting stalls, including the ever-popular "Rock Kings".

At the Rural District Council meeting on 5th, the Parish Council's request for help with the cost of sewers in Oundle Road was discussed. This was refused on the grounds that the Parish Council could raise the cost themselves through the rates, rather than the RDC having to do so.

An advertisement which appeared on 5th:
"Grocery and Provisions. Wanted, smart young man as assistant. Apply India and China Tea Co., Bridge Street, Thrapston." *(Pictured below with the company's staff wearing white aprons outside the premises – C W Vorley, Raunds – EDF Collection.)*

Midday on Monday 9th was the closing time for nominations for the extra seats on the Board of Guardians and Rural District Council. Two were received for Thrapston:
Archibald William Smith   (Baptist minister).
Sidney Packwood Smart JP (Railway signalman).
(The election was held on 23rd May, Mr. Smart being victorious – EDF.)

On Tuesday morning, 10th, the sexton of St. James' Church (Mr. Bland) discovered the freewill offering box was missing when he opened up. The church had been open late the previous evening for bellringing practice. He notified the rector and the Police initiated inquiries. It was believed that a number of offerings were in the box.

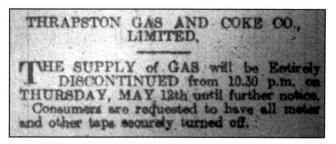

THRAPSTON GAS AND COKE CO., LIMITED.

THE SUPPLY of GAS will be Entirely DISCONTINUED from 10.30 p.m. on THURSDAY, MAY 12th until further notice. Consumers are requested to have all meter and other taps securely turned off.

The continuing miners' strike was beginning to have a dramatic effect on life in genereral. The Gas Company placed this advertisement *(right)* on 11th.

This letter was printed in the *Evening Telegraph* on 12th:
"Sir – By your issue of Tuesday we are informed that there will be an election at Thrapston for an additional Councillor for the Rural District Council, unless one of the nominees withdraw.
Personally, I am a democrat in all its phrases, but in this case I am informed that the tenure of office is only for ten months. If that is so, surely to goodness, if we have any thought for economy it is called for in this case whereby with an agreement between the parties concerned – which should be easy, seeing that one of the nominees was the losing candidate by 30 votes at the last election – the cost of an election, approximately £15, could be saved, which otherwise will have to be bourne by the poor ratepayer. Therefore, let us hope that reason will prevail before Friday noon. Yours etc. Ratepayer."
(There were no withdrawals by Friday noon, the closing date for such an action – EDF.)

The Town Band held their annual parade to raise money for local hospitals on Sunday 15th. Usually held on the first Sunday in May, it had been put back because of the industrial situation with the miners. About £14 10s was raised.

An update on the theft from St. James' Church was printed on 17th:
"The freewill offering box (of oak with a Yale lock), which was missing from the Thrapston Parish Church has been found. During a thorough search of the church on Thursday evening Inspector Baxter discovered it secreted in a dark partitioned corner beneath the seat of a pew, very near to the spot where the box had been fitted. The front had been forced open and the box was empty."

The Parish Council met on Wednesday 18th at the Temperance Hall. Mr. Frederick William Johnson was elected a member of the Council, replacing Mr. D. W. David, who had left the area. Two tenders had been received for taking down, storing, repairing, painting and refixing the street lamps, the one accepted being for £6 10s from Mr. E. Jervis. A preliminary discussion about introducing electric lighting and heating in town was raised by Mr. Hillyard. The estimated cost was £3,500 and it was agreed that he get the ball rolling with a committee, then call a public meeting.

Walgrave Amber's appeal against a 22 points deduction in the Kettering Combination Football League was heard on Monday 23rd. The appeal was allowed and they were reinstated as League Champions for the 1920 – 1921 season. Thrapston United thus finished in fourth place.

Thrapston United held their annual general meeting on Monday 23rd in the Co-operative Hall with a good company being present. The secretary, Mr. A. Harris, presented his report and the balance-sheet which was unanimously adopted. The balance stood at £59 6s 4d. The chairman, Mr. W. H. Bray, paid tribute to the club's loyal supporters. The pitch had been taken on a three year lease and they hoped to put a wire fence around it before the new season started. After electing the committee, agreement was reached that they remain in the Kettering Combination and to apply to the Rushden League for the Reserves.. They would also enter the Northants Junior, Northants Lower Junior and Kettering Charity Cup competitions. The chairman said he hoped they would have as successful a season as the last had been, and appealed to all young players to sign on for the club. He thanked the company for their attendance, which closed a successful meeting.

Thrapston beat Oundle at bowls on Wednesday 25th by 121 – 61.

Two short items appeared on 27th:
"At the Thrapston Elementary Schools, Empire Day was marked by hoisting and saluting the Flag, appropriate lessons and singing of "God save the King" and other patriotic songs. At the Church of England School, the Rector gave a suitable address."
"The Thrapston Horticultural and Poultry Establishment, 4 Swiss Villas, Thrapston (Proprietors Horace J. Gurney and A. F. Gurney). Inspect our stock of summer bedding plants. For quality and price we lead the way. Call and inspect our stock. Also, shortly ready, the finest selection of garden plants in the neighbourhood, grown from all the leading seed producing firms of the country. Also best quality poultry foods of every description, at competitive prices."

On 27th, the *Kettering Leader* reported the retirement of Mr. F. Brooks *(pictured right, published as part of the article – EDF)* as stationmaster of Midland Road Station. He had been there for nearly 23 years and decided that, aged 65 years, he was ready for retirement.
He was succeeded by his youngest son, Ernest, who had been stationmaster at Cranford for eight years.

The same newspaper had an article on a pair of handcuffs, known as "darbies", pictured above, which had been found in town by Inspector Butlin thirty years earlier. It was suspected that a local felon had, somehow, managed to free himself from them after escaping custody.

Mr. Hillyard held an inaugural meeting in the Parish Room to consider providing electric lighting and heating in town on Monday 30th. Fifty people had been invited to attend and 21 did so. It was accepted that Thrapston Mill could not provide sufficient power for their needs and that another source would be needed. It was anticipated that, once installed, electricity could be supplied at half the cost of gas. A committee was appointed from those present to further investigations.

Also on 30th, in the *Evening Telegraph*:
"Two carpenters and joiners wanted at once. Apply W. Loakes, Thrapston."

On 31st, a major fire destroyed the Ringstead Unity Co-operative Society boot factory. The Thrapston Brigade were among three called to attend, but were unable to, as there were no horses available to pull the engine.

The Guardians heard, on 31st, that an inmate had fractured his thigh after falling from a garden seat on Thursday 5th May. This was not reported to the acting master until 8th, when the Medical Officer was called. The patient *(who was described as being mentally defective – EDF)* had walked about on the Friday and Saturday. The injury was discovered on the Sunday when he was unable to move. The Medical Officer stated that the fact that the fracture was not discovered before did not suggest negligence, the patient having not complained of any pain during the intervening period.

June

The Rural District Council discussed diverting surface water from Huntingdon Road to prevent town centre flooding after heavy rain, when they met on Tuesday 2nd. The surveyor was instructed to commence the work, with the Distruct Council bearing the cost.

The Baptist Church held a wedding on 6th between Miss Margaret Fanny Kirby, Horton House, Thrapston, and Mr. Oliver James Steward of Bury St. Edmunds, an assistant at Mr. Touch's outfitters. They honeymooned in Hunstanton.

Also on 6th, Mrs. Ernest Abbott, Oundle Road, died aged 39. She had been ill with consumption for a long time. Her funeral was held on 9th.

The Farmers' Union met for an ordinary meeting on 7th at the White Hart Hotel.

A notice cancelling Thrapston Sports, due to the continuing miners' strike, was published on 14th.

The Parish Council met on Wednesday 15th. Captain Booth spoke about Fire Brigade matters. Mr. Barrick had offered to take the fire engine to the scene of fires at any time using his motor lorry. It was agreed that an iron attachment should be fixed to the fire engine for towing purposes. Captain Booth also brought forward the desirability of the prompt payment of men who attended fires as they often had to wait for months whilst insurance claims were settled. The Council agreed to accept responsibility for payments.
Mr. Hewitt raised his concerns about the water supply and state of the pump near the Fire Engine House in Huntingdon Road. A great number of residents relied on the pump for their water and were concerned about the large quantity of water used for other purposes than human consumption. Water from the pump on Market Hill was not fit for human consumption and he thought that manufacturers should use this supply. After discussion, it was resolved to ask the sanitary inspector, Mr. Barnes to meet with two Councillors.

The Trades and Labour Council held their monthly meeting in the Co-operative Hall on Friday 17th where the main business was to discuss the threatened reduction in State Unemployment Insurance Benefit. A letter of objection was sent to the Prime Minister and local M.Ps.

Miss Kingsford gave another organ recital at the Parish Church in the afternoon on Sunday 19th. A collection was taken for the Church War Memorial Fund.

Messrs. Gurney placed the advertisement shown left in the *Evening Telegraph* on Monday 20th.

The Young Helpers' League held their annual sale of work and fete at Thrapston House on Thursday 23rd, opening at 3.30pm with an admission charge of 6d. In the evening, they held a children's concert and "Fairy Play".

The Guardian's meeting on 28th heard that there were two impending nursing vacancies in the Infirmary at the end of September. They agreed that, when advertised, a salary of £45 should be offered.

Also on 28th, the formal announcement was printed of the end of the miners' strike, with workers due to return to the pits on Monday 4th July.

July

This was printed on 1st:
"Wanted. Warehouse suitable for corn, in Thrapston. Apply T. H. and P. E., Reg, 4 Swiss Villas, Thrapston."

The second meeting of the group considering the provision of electricity in town met in the Parish Room on Monday 4th. Some members had visited Stratford-upon-Avon Electricity Works and reported their findings. There was some discussion as to over-estimations of cost. A letter from the Ashton Electricity Works was read, which gave similar details as the Stratford report. After discussion, they adjourned for four weeks to enable further enquiries to be carried out.

On Tuesday 5th, Mr. E. J. Loaring, Hill House, Thrapston, met with a serious accident during the morning. He trod on a piece of banana skin near the market entrance and fell, breaking his left kneecap. He was taken home and attended to by Dr. Walsh.

On 6th, this advertisement was printed in the *Evening Telegraph*:
"Wanted. Situation for young lady; good knowledge of bookkeeping, typing and general office routine; any position of trust. Box 303, "Evening Telegraph" Office, Thrapston."

The Baptist Church Sunday School were taken by motors to Wicksteed Park for their annual treat on 7th.

The Oddfellows received good news on 8th:
"The Nelson Lodge of Oddfellows, Thrapston, State Section Branch has received sanction from the Ministry of Health for ten payments of the following additional benefits: sickness, 4s per week; disablement, 2s per week; maternity benefit, 8s."
(The Oddfellows were an organization set up to protect and care for their members and communities at a time when there was no welfare state, trade unions or National Health Service. The aim was (and still is) to provide help to members and communities when they need it – EDF.)

Two advertisements were printed on 11th:
"Wanted, temporary daily help for shop and home. Box 22, "Evening Telegraph", Thrapston."
"For sale. Three-burner Perfection stove, with oven, good condition. Viccars, Mill Road, Thrapston."

On Thursday 14th, this item appeared:
"Mr. Richard Shadbolt of Bridge Street, Thrapston, is progressing favourably from the effects of an accident which he met with a few evenings ago while motor-cycling home from Aldwincle. At the turn where the Aldwincle road comes into the Islip – Lowick road a collision occurred between his machine and a car (three wheeler) being driven by Mr. C. Pettit junr., of Thrapston, in the direction of Brigstock. Seeing that a collision was inevitable, Mr. Shadbolt leaped from his machine and fell onto the grass. His left foot was caught by the engine of the car and badly cut and bruised. The front part of both cycle and car were greatly damaged. Mr. Pettit, who was unhurt, went to Islip to fetch another car, but meanwhile the driver of a car which passed from Thrapston conveyed Mr. Shadbolt home."

During the evening, Thrapston Bowls Club welcomed Northampton Borough Police for a match. The home side won by 89 – 59.

The Guild of Help held a public dance on the lawns of Thrapston House on Saturday 16th, the Town Band playing. The attendance was low due to there being many other attractions in the area. *(Thrapston House is shown right – C. W. Vorley, Raunds – EDF Collection.)*

Mrs. Elizabeth Sanderson died on 18th aged 85, widow of the late Mr. Richard Sanderson, for many years a grocer in town. Her funeral was held in the Baptist Burial Ground on Thursday 21st, which was, by coincidence, the 21st anniversary of her husband's death.

With the miners' strike now over and coal supplies returning to normal, the London and North-Western Railway announced excursions for the August holiday on 23rd:
"August 1st from Thrapston at 8.45 am, Irthlingborough at 9.00 am and Wellingborough at 9.10 am to Castle Ashby and Northampton for one day."

The Guardians met on 26th. There had been no responses to the advertisement for Infirmary assistants and the clerk was instructed to advertise again in two local papers and a nursing paper. Two other members of staff had resigned, Miss Davis, charge nurse and Miss Jeffery, kitchenmaid. Approval for these posts to be advertised was given.

On Saturday 28th, Thrapston travelled to Kettering Conservatives Bowls Club and were beaten by 101 – 59.

August

Two items were printed in the *Evening Telegraph* on Wednesday 3rd:
"Obituary.
Our readers will regret to hear of the death of Mr. George Siddons, who was for many years a coal merchant, road surveyor and auctioneer at Thrapston. After residing in London, he went to live with his son in South Africa about 15 months ago, at whose residence he died on June 7th. The deceased, who was 70 years of age, was taken ill with pleurisy a week previous to his death and heart failure supervened. His widow has returned from South Africa and is now residing with her daughter in London."
"Electric lighting. An adjourned meeting held at the beginning of last week heard a full explanation as to the cost of providing electric light, heating and power from Mr. E. Loakes. Lighting was estimated to be about half the cost of gas. Seven people were elected to assist with canvassing the town to ascertain what lighting, heating and power would be required. These were: Messrs. F. Cheney, R. Cawdell, E. Loakes, C. Pettit, F. Stubbs, W. Knighton and W. Hillyard."

At the Police Court on Tuesday 4th, there were no law breakers, the only business being a licence transfer.

The District Council met on the same day, where they agreed to pass on to the Parish Council the issue of public water for urgent resolution. Six of the new houses in Oundle Road were occupied, with six others due for occupation during the month.

St. James' Church annual garden fete was held at Thrapston House on 4th, over 500 people attending. £70 0s 6½d was raised.

Finally on 4th, Melba Berridge, a pupil of Mrs. Marks, Thrapston, was announced as being successful in the preparatory grade in the Trinity College of Music Examination held a week earlier in Wellingborough.

On Sunday 7th, Miss Elizabeth Larter, "Nene House", Midland Road, died at home. She had been suffering from heart weakness for a number of weeks. She had lived in town for many years with her sister, Miss A. Larter. She had been very involved in the temperance movement and was also a great supporter of the Young Helpers' League. Her funeral took place at St. James' Church on 10th.

From 7th, Rev. H. Ellis Roberts, ex-minister of the Baptist Church, visited town for a week.

On Thursday 18th, the Hospital Week Committee held their annual fete in the grounds of "The Shrubberies".

Two advertisements were printed on 19th:
"Wanted. Strong girl or widow as help, day or otherwise. Box No. 118, "Evening Telegraph Office", Thrapston."
"Wanted. Two carpenters and joiners. W. Loakes, builder, Thrapston."

Robert Lewis Hiam (57) was again remembered in the *Evening Telegraph* on 22nd:
"In loving memory of Private ROBERT LEWIS HIAM, only son of H.W. and M. Hiam, of Thrapston, 1st 22nd London Regiment ("The Queen's"), killed in action in France, August 22nd 1918, aged 19 years.
- From Mother, Father, and Sisters."

The 1921 census figures were announced on Wednesday 24th. The Northamptonshire part of Thrapston Rural District showed a decrease in population of 360, the 1921 figure being 10,289.

A news item from fifty years earlier was reproduced on Monday 29th:
"Ragged and dirty children hang about the streets of Thrapston all day and are a nuisance to the town generally and some action has to be taken to put an end to it."

On the same day, the Society for the Discussion of Public Questions held their annual meeting, when they agreed an annual subscription of 2s 6d.

At the Police Court on 30th, two agricultural workers from Keyston were fined 5s each for riding their bicycles at 11.15 pm on August 7th without lights.

The Northamptonshire Football Association held the draw for various cup competitions on 30th. Thrapston United were given a bye in the first round of the Junior Cup, the Reserves were drawn away to Higham Ferrers Wesleyan Institute in the Lower Junior Cup, the Reserves also receiving a bye in the first round of the East Northants Medals competition.

Finally on 30th, the Trades and Labour Council held a poorly attended public meeting to discuss the provisions of the recently enacted Provision of Meals Act and hear responses from the Education Department about feeding schoolchildren.

September

Thrapston United played their first game of the new season at Broughton on Saturday 1st, winning 1 – 0. The team was: F. Bray; E. Turner and A. Harris; A. Jeffery, H. Dodson and H. Morris; H. Barrick, F. Stobie, H. March, T. Essam and H. Smith.

On Thursday 8th, the Raunds Wesleyan Circuit held their quarterly meeting in town. They had 476 full members and 130 juniors.

The Guardians held a special meeting on 9th to hear about 200 applications for outdoor relief from unemployed men from Raunds and Ringstead.

Railway excursions from Bridge Street Station were announced on Saturday 10th:
"Thursday 15th September, leaving at 7.25 am to Yarmouth for one day."
Friday 16th September, leaving at 11.10 am to North Wales, Blackpool and the Lake District for 8 and 15 days."

The Guild of Help held a garden fete, whist drive and evening dance in the grounds of Thrapston House on 10th. About 100 people attended the dance.

Finally on 10th, Thrapston United suffered a 1 – 2 home defeat by Broughton.

The annual show of the Shire Horse Society *(letterhead shown on page 231 – EDF Collection)* took place on 13th in the usual field off Chancery Lane. Approximately 150 spectators saw the collection of 40 entries. The traditional after-show dinner was held in the White Hart Hotel.

The Hospital Week Committee met that evening, and agreed donations to local hospitals as follows: Northampton, £76, Kettering and Peterborough £26 each.

THRAPSTON & DISTRICT
SHIRE HORSE SOCIETY.

Joint Secretaries—
B. WOOD, Clapton, Kettering.
Walter G. BROWN, Market Place, Thrapston, Kettering.
('Phone, Thrapston 18)

19......

In the first round of the Kettering Football Charity Cup on 13th, Thrapston United were given an away draw at Denford.

On Thursday 15th, the funeral of Miss Kathie Harris, youngest daughter of Mrs. Harris of Kettering and the late Mr. John Harris, Midland Road, Thrapston, took place at the Parish Church and Cemetery. The coffin plate read "Kathleen Harris, born May 20th 1892, died September 12th 1921." There were many beautiful wreaths.

Football results from Saturday 17th:
Timson's (Kettering) 2 Thrapston United 0.
In the Islip Schools League –
Lowick 2 Thrapston 1.
Thrapston 12 Aldwincle 0.

The Harvest was celebrated at the Baptist Church on 18th. Collections amounted to £6 6s 3d whilst the sale of produce a day later raised a further £8 11s 11d.

This advertisement was printed on Tuesday 20th:
"Gramophone Records Exchanged.
Bring those you are tired of, and get a fresh supply. All makes in stock from 1s upwards.
Machines repaired without delay; all parts in stock.
Rupert Smith, Gramophone Depot, Midland Road, Thrapston."

Edward Percy Raworth (41) was again remembered on 20th:
"In ever-loving memory of our dear son, EDWARD PERCY RAWORTH, Rifle Brigade, killed in action, September 20th, 1917, aged 23 years.
Only those who have loved and lost
Can understand War's bitter cost.
From Mother, Father, Sister, and Brother, Market Road, Thrapston."

The Parish Council met on Wednesday 21st. They agreed to buy a direction post for the corner of Midland Road, pointing towards Kettering. They also agreed to commence street lighting on 3rd October. Water from the town pump had been analysed and found to be fit for drinking. The Sewage Works reported that the sale of vegetables had raised £99 15s 6d. They also considered the District Council's request to sort out a public water system. The original estimate of £6,100 was now thought to have doubled and they decided that it was not an opportune time to be trying to raise this level of funding *(this equates to about £130,000 today – EDF)*. The Fire Brigade made their annual report to the Council. Mr. Barrick's lorry would convey the engine to future fires. One member required a new uniform to replace his moth-eaten one, whilst eight pairs of new boots were needed, replacing the 30 year old ones currently in use. Captain Booth *(pictured right Kettering Leader 17th February 1922)* had completed 50 years service, serving under four captains before his appointment to that position in 1907. Between 1881 and 1921, they had attended 63 fires. Captain Booth was congratulated on completing 50 years and general thanks were passed on to the men.

The Institute held a whist drive on Friday 23rd.

On 24th, Thrapston United defeated Timson's (Kettering) in town 3 – 1.
In the Schools' League, Thrapston St. James beat Aldwincle Rectory 3 – 0.

Arthur Brown conducted an auction in the White Hart Hotel on Wednesday 28th. On offer was "a commodious freehold dwelling house with garden and premises at Bridge Street, Thrapston with possession on completion". Bidding reached £550, which was below the reserve price, and it was withdrawn.

Colonel Stopford Sackville announced on 27th that he was:
"...affording the public another opportunity to visit the gardens and grounds of Drayton House. They will be open on Thursday, Friday and Saturday September 29th and 30th and October 1st between the hours of 3 and 8pm." *(Drayton House and gardens are pictured below –published by Photochrom Ltd, London – EDF Collection.)*

October

Thrapston United played Mrs. Morris' B. C. (Kettering) on Saturday 1ˢᵗ, winning 4 – 2. Islip Schools' League – Cranford St. John's 2 Thrapston St. James' 6.

Sidney Newman (61) and his brother **Frederick (43)** were both remembered in the *Evening Telegraph* on 1ˢᵗ:
"In loving memory of Pte, SIDNEY NEWMAN, killed in action, October 1ˢᵗ, 1918. Also of Pte. FREDERICK NEWMAN (BENNY), killed in action, October 8ᵗʰ, 1917.
"Death divides, but memory ever clings."
From Mother, Father, Brothers, and Sister, Thrapston."

At the Guardians meeting on 4ᵗʰ, three couples were interviewed for the positions of porter and barber and charge nurse. Mr. Rodwell and Miss Edith Knowles, who were intending to get married, were appointed. Mr. Rodwell, aged 39, had served with the Army for over four years and was previously labour master at Wellingborough Workhouse, whilst Miss Knowles was a charge nurse at the same institution. Their appointments were dependant on their marrying. The salaries offered were, porter/ barber, £45, charge nurse £50 with a £5 uniform allowance.

Another "In Memoriam" notice, this time for **John William Guest (42)** was printed on 7ᵗʰ:
"In loving remembrance of J. W. GUEST, M.G.C., Thrapston, died in action, 7ᵗʰ Oct., 1917, aged 19 years. Buried in Belgium.
One who never turned his back, but marched breast forward,
Never doubted clouds would break;
Never dreamed, though right were worsted, wrong would triumph;
Held, we fall to rise, are baffled to fight better;
Sleep to wake.
From Father, Mother, and Brothers."

Thrapston United were on the receiving end of a crushing defeat on 8ᵗʰ, losing 7 – 2 at Walgrave Amber. In the Schools' League, Thrapston beat Twywell 7 – 0.

At the Police Court on Tuesday 11ᵗʰ, the licence of the Red Lion was transferred from George Cooper to John Whitney.

The Court sat again on Friday 14ᵗʰ. Helen Wright, who gave her age as 66, of no fixed abode, was charged with, "That she on October 15ᵗʰ, at the parish of Thrapston, then being a casual pauper chargeable to the common fund of the Thrapston Poor Law Union did unlawfully abscond from the casual wards of the said Union before she was entitled to discharge herself therefrom, contrary to the Pauper's Inmates Discharge and Regulation Act of 1871". She said that she had been on the road for a good many years and had her round, which included Thrapston, about every three months. She admitted leaving but did not know it was an offence. She was admitted to the casual ward on 12ᵗʰ and supplied with the usual meals. On 13ᵗʰ, she was requested to do certain household work but refused, packed up her things and left. She was reported to the police and taken into custody. She was sentenced to seven days hard labour.

The Society for Discussion of Public Questions heard a lecture on "Corsica" by Rev. Fitzherbert during the evening of the same day.

Football results on Saturday 15th:
Thrapston United 0 - Walgrave Amber 3.
Thrapston St. James' 8 - Islip Reserves 0.

The Guardians heard that out-relief costs had increased greatly at their meeting on Tuesday 18th. This was attributed to local unemployment, caused by the miners' strike. Costs had doubled compared to the same period in 1920 and were now £522 6s 11d.

This advertisement *(right)* for the Corner Cafe appeared on 18th.

The Parish Council received tenders for eight pairs of firemens boots on 19th. Prices were not quoted in the press.

Corner Cafe, Thrapston.

C. LOVEDAY.

CUSTOMERS are kindly requested to note that, although we are not trading with Mr. B. F. LAWSON of Wellingborough, we still have CAKES and PASTRIES of the Highest Quality, which are made under the most careful of hygienic conditions.

Try our HOME-MADE PORK PIES, 1/10 per lb., and SAUSAGES, 1/9 per lb.

Satisfaction Guaranteed.

ALL COOKED MEATS GREATLY REDUCED. TRIAL SOLICITED.

On 20th, this piece was published, on the Fair held in the Market Place on 18th:
"With glorious weather, market day, closed schools and motor omnibuses depositing heavy loads of visitors, the Market Place on Tuesday afternoon was thronged with people, most of them presumably with a little holiday cash to spend. The stalls were of a varied character and the rapid and persuasive eloquence of some of the vendors was quite reminiscent of "the good old times.""

At the Northamptonshire Assizes, held in Northampton on Saturday 22nd, a local 45 year old musical director was charged with bigamously marrying a local lady. He had left his wife and five children and job in a bank to go into revue. His omission to mention to his "second" wife that he was already married resulted in a period of three months hard labour during which he could reflect on his misdeeds.

In the afternoon, Thrapston United were heavily defeated at Mrs. Morris' B. C. by 5 – 1.
Thrapston St. James' won 4 – 0 at Twywell, Victor Guest scoring a hat-trick and E. Mayes the other goal.

Freeman Brothers reminded the population on 26th that Christmas was coming:
"Christmas Club. For particulars apply Freeman Bros, Fancy Bazaar. Grand show of toys, dolls, games etc. The cheapest house for presents."

The Kettering Prize Choir gave a very popular evening concert in the Corn Exchange on 28th in aid of Wesleyan Church funds.

On 29th, Kettering Rangers visited Thrapston United and won 2 – 0.
Thrapston St. James' had an easy 3 – 0 win over Woodford.

On the same day, Mr. Frederick William Lord, Azaelea House, Midland Road, died of a heart attack aged 30 after suffering with consumption for most of the year. He left a wife and child.

The Baptist Christian Endeavour Society celebrated their anniversary on Sunday 30th, the speaker being Rev. Black from Kingsthorpe. Collections were taken for the Society.

The British Legion held their monthly meeting on 31st at the King's Arms with a good attendance. Those present agreed to attend the Remembrance Day service at St. James' Church on 6th and that a wreath should be placed on the Memorial by Messrs. Whiteman and Cole in the name of the Branch. A Poppy Day had been arranged for town and Islip on 11th, the proceeds to go to the Earl Haig Fund.

Finally, the Society for the Propagation of the Gospel held their annual meeting in the Corn Exchange on 31st. This was combined with a missionary pageant. The attendance was described as average.

November

The Farmers' Union met on Tuesday 1st where the main topic of discussion was, once again, the possibility of increasing wages for agricultural workers.

W. Loakes, builder, advertised for two carpenters on the same day.

Frederick Lord's funeral was held on 2nd at St. James' Church and Cemetery. In the evening, a muffled peal was rung on the church bells as a mark of respect.

This notice was printed in the *Evening Telegraph* on 3rd:
"Mrs. F. W. Lord, Thrapston and Mr. Percy Lord desire to return sincere thanks for the many kind letters of sympathy with them in their bereavement; also for the floral tributes sent."

The Rural District Council met on 3rd. There was a proposal that a new road, suitable for all traffic, be constructed from Huntingdon Road, near Elm Farm and the Out-Mear Road, near Page's Lodge to Denford. This was passed to committee. Rev. Bolland moved "that in view of the necessity of finding work for the unemployed and in view of the fact that hundreds of people came into Thrapston every market day, it is desirable to proceed with the provision of public conveniences forthwith." This was referred to the Thrapston Parochial Committee.

Finally on 3rd, Thrapston United were given permission by the Northants Football Association to hold a benefit match for H. Morris.

On Saturday 5th, Thrapston United travelled to Rushton where they drew 1 – 1.
In the East Northants Medals Competition, Thrapston Reserves welcomed Rushden Red Shield to town. A 2 – 2 draw was played out. *(Rushden won the replay – EDF.)*

On 6th, being the nearest Sunday to 5th, the Memorial Service to the fallen was held to mark the third anniversary of Armistice Day. 30 ex-servicemen attended, as did a good number of townspeople. The service ended with the Last Post and Reveille, played by Mr. A. Fletcher, and the National Anthem. Collections taken during the day were sent to the Services Candidates Ordination Fund, which helped to train over 100 officers and men for the ministry.

On 7th, the *Evening Telegraph* printed a lengthy appreciation entitled "The Incomparable Dolph". He had completed over 50 years of public service in town as sexton, verger, town crier, emergency street lamplighter and skilled workman, amongst other tasks. In great demand for all outdoor festivities, he cut a fine figure dressed in his traditional uniform. *(Randolphus Bland (1863 – 1935) is pictured on page 235 – EDF Collection.)*

The Choral Society's recent whist drive was mentioned on 7th as raising between £7 and £8 for their funds.

An advertisement of local interest was printed on 8th:
"Wanted; small knee-hole writing desk. Box 131, "Evening Telegraph", Thrapston."

Also on 8th, the newspaper announced, "We understand that Mr. T. H. Freeman and Company intend to present a Chinese Fantasy in an elaborate eastern setting in the Corn Exchange on December 15th, 16th and 17th."

A meeting of the British Legion Unity Relief Committee was held on 9th, dealing with distress amongst unemployed ex-servicemen. Relief was granted in over fifty cases.

On Thursday 10th, a Social meeting, arranged by the Women's Committee of the National Unionists Association, took place at the Corn Exchange. Over 100 people sat down for tea, after which a number of speeches were made.

On Saturday 12th, notice of two forthcoming auctions was given:
"Without reserve.
Thrapston L. and N. W. Railway Station.
Important sale of about 65,000 feet run of well-seasoned sawn timber, comprising:
8,000 feet; 2in x 2in, 2in x 2½in, 2in x 3in, 2in x 4in, 3in x 5½in.
20,000 feet; ¾in x 1in.
10,000 feet; ⅝in x 3in.
10,000 feet; 1in x 10in, 1in x 11in, P.S.J., P.T. and G.
5,000 feet; ¾in x 5in and ¾in x 7in.
5,000 feet; ½in x 3½in, ½in x 4¾in, ⅝in x 4in, 1in x 4in, 1in x 4½in.
1,000 feet; 1½in x 10in.
To be sold by auction by
Berry Bros and Bagshaw.
Absolutely without reserve, in the Goods Yard at the above station on Tuesday November 15th 1921.
Sale to commence at 11 o'clock punctually.
No catalogues.
Further particulars may be obtained of the Auctioneers, Market Place, Kettering (Tel 158)."

"Thrapston Market.
Arthur G. Brown & Son
Will include in their next sale on Tuesday next, Nov. 15th
Pair horse van, with pole, shafts and tilt; single horse van, with fixed top, set of plated double harness, set of single brass harness, sundry harness, lamps, rugs, van sheet, etc by instructions from Messrs. Tomlinson, who have purchased a motor.
Sale at one o'clock."

In the afternoon, Thrapston United travelled to Desborough Reserves and were on the end of a 5 – 0 thrashing. The heady days of winning the Championship seemed a long time ago!

That evening, a whist drive was held in the Corn Exchange, raising money for St. Dunstan's.

On Monday 14th, this advertisement was printed:
"Dix's Thrapston and Raunds bus route.
The 10 o'clock from Raunds and the 11.30 from Kettering on Saturdays will be discontinued. All other times as usual."

On 15th, the Guardians agreed the same Christmas fare as previous years for the Workhouse and Children's Home. Mr. Steward, who had visited the Workhouse before the meeting, reported that the extreme ends of the hospital were very cold (under 50 degrees) owing to defective hot water pipes. The master had arranged an inspection by tradesmen the following day. Delegates had visited the County Mental Hospital and found that patients from Thrapston were more to their satisfaction than they had expected. As regards ex-servicemen, none were in the asylum as a result of hardships during the war *(i.e shellshock – EDF)*.

The result of poppy sales was announced on 15th. £12 11s 3d was handed to the secretary of the local branch for forwarding to London. 50% was promised to be returned to the local British Legion Unity Relief Fund.

On Saturday 19th, Thrapston United were held at home to a 2 – 2 draw by Brigstock in the 2nd round of the Junior Cup.

During the evening of Monday 21st, a touch of Stedman Triples (1008 changes) was rung in 35 minutes by the St. James' Church bellringers.

The Police Court on 22nd heard the case of a coal miner, now living and working in Nuneaton, who was summoned for a breach of the Poaching Prevention Act in town on 6th. This was his first offence, being of previous good character. He pleaded guilty by letter and was fined 10s.

A day later, a good number of spectators assembled to witness the Fitzwilliam Hounds meet in the Market Place. There were, however, only a few riders.

The Chamber of Trade met on 24th. Sufficient local traders had indicated their willingness to participate in the proposed Shopping Week between 10th and 17th December for it to be a viable event. Prize competitions and a free gift scheme were agreed.

Football results on Saturday 26th:
Brigstock 4 - Thrapston United 1 (Cup replay).
Thrapston 15 - Denford 0 (Schools' League).

The Society for the Discussion of Public Questions heard a presentation on "Factors which determine retail prices in Thrapston" at their meeting on 28th. The hope was expressed that the coming Shopping Week would help town prices to be as competitive as those in other towns in the district.

Details about the Chinese Fantasy (mentioned on page 234) appeared on 29th. "Ah Chee, the Ferry Girl", a musical comedy in two acts, was to be produced by Mr. T. H. Freeman with a large cast of local people. *(The programme cover, signed by the playwright, Ernest Goodwin, is shown on page 238 – Gainer Collection. Money raised was donated to the Peace Park Fund and amounted to £7 10s 0d.)*

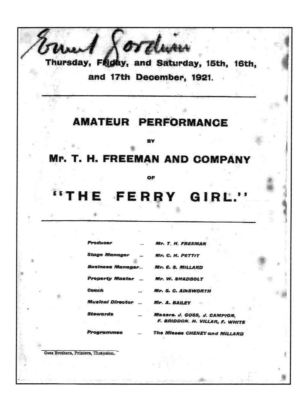

December

The Rural District Council considered the suggested link road from Huntingdon when they met on Thursday 1st. The proposed route was already metalled except for 1000 yards. It could provide work for local unemployed men but, as the estimated cost was £2,460, a decision was deferred. As a number of tenants of the new houses in town had left due to high rents, they agreed to reduce these from 12s to 9s 6d a week.

Edward Marks, Horton's Lane, died on Monday 5th after a short illness. For a number of years, he was market toll collector in town. He left a wife but no family.

The Discussion Society met on 5th and heard a very interesting lecture by Mr. H. E. Salt, Trinity College, Cambridge on "Life in a 12th Century Manor in the Midlands".

The Farmers' Union met on Tuesday 6th for their Annual General Meeting in the White Hart Hotel. They had 112 members and the bank balance stood at £144 13s 11d.

After the meeting, Messrs. H. H. Bletsoe and Son sold by auction two building sites, owned by Mrs. Hewitt, in Oundle Road. They were bought by Mr. A. Pettit of the Mason's Arms, Thrapston for £75.

Shopping Week was publicised in the area with the advertisement shown on page 243 appearing in the *Evening Telegraph* on Thursday 8th. It began on 10th with large numbers travelling into town. Shop windows had been decorated and there were high hopes that the various competitions and novelties would encourage good trade.

On 9th, the *Kettering Leader* reported that Mr. D. St. Clair Gainer *(shown left)* had been appointed British Vice-Consul in Havana, Cuba.

The Annual Fat Stock Show was held on Tuesday 13th. In total there were 31 entries in the cattle section, 15 in the sheep section and 19 pigs. There were also 8 entries in the roots section – mangolds and kohl rabi.

On the same day, the Guardians heard that a new steam boiler and associated pipework had been fitted in the Workhouse kitchen at a cost of £110.

On 17th, Mr. Hepher announced:
"G. P. Hepher's home-made sausages, 1s 8d per lb; every Friday and Tuesday."

The *Evening Telegraph* reported on Wednesday 21st that Shopping Week had more than fulfilled expectations and that more people visited town on the last day than did on the first. It was reported later that one of the balloons released during the week had landed in a field at Gussola, near Cremona, Italy. Balloons were filled with gas until they reached a diameter of 40inches *(one metre - EDF)*.

At the Parish Council meeting on 21st, they heard that the Sewage Works Committee had accepted a tender of 3s per hour from Mr. Morris for the position of scavenger. The question of providing public conveniences was deferred, costs being a major concern.

Christmas Day at the Workhouse followed the usual routine, with a concert in the evening.

On Boxing Day, Thrapston United played out a 1 – 1 draw before a very large crowd in their home match against Woodford.

On Thursday 29th, Mr. Philip Stearne, York Terrace, Huntingdon Road had a stroke whilst on an errand in town. He was returned home by motorcar in a serious condition. *(He did not recover and died a few weeks into 1922 – EDF.)*

Another concert took place at the Workhouse on Friday 30th, arranged by Miss Kingsford. During the interval, inmates were presented with sweets and oranges, with tobacco for the men. The master thanked the performers at the end who were given a resounding three cheers by the inmates.

On 31st, Thrapston United played a 1 – 1 draw at Brigstock.

Finally, the Rural District Council advertised in the *Evening Telegraph* on 31st:
"To let.
Houses known as Addison Villas, Oundle Road, Thrapston. Rent 9s 6d per week, tenant paying rates. For particulars and conditions of tenancy apply to –
W. Dellar, Thrapston."

This marks the end of research into life in Thrapston during the period covered by the World War One section of "In the Springtime of their Lives", 1914 to 1921. The most difficult years ever experienced had, somehow, been survived and hope sprung eternal. I trust it has given some insight into how important it was for the men at war to hear of news from home and the sort of news they would have heard. At times of stress, the minutia of daily-living took them from a place of acute misery to being back at home and a place of safety and comfort.

The British Legion had formed a local branch which would go on to preserve the concept of "Remembrance" for the fallen of all conflicts for all time. I am grateful for their devotion.

Eric Franklin

June 2013

Index

Names Index

Berridge, Mr.A., 92; Melba, 229;
Bethel, Colour Sergeant, 11;
Binyon, Robert Laurence,184;
Bird, Dr. Thomas Day, 3,8,84,90,92,126, 149,155,176,180,203;
Bishop, W., 87,95;
Black, Rev., 234;
Blackett, Ernest, 189,190;
Blackwell, Mr. H., 134; L., 134;
Blake, J.E., 203; J.S., 36;
Bland, Fred, 37; Mrs., 47; Randolphus, 224,235,236;
Bletsoe, Miss Frances Mary, 5,33; Henry H., 14,29,50, 83,101,106,113,123,128,148,152,153, 155,161,162,164,197,199,238; Mrs., 124,129,162; Lt. T.H., 83,84,101,109,118;
Bolland, Rev. C.F., 44,45,47,110,158,197,235;
Bolton, Alfred W., 129,144,175,176,185; Mrs., 185;
Bone, Mrs, 89; Sidney, iv,89,90,160; Trooper, 22;
Bonsor, J.T., 44;
Boosey, Miss, 47;
Booth, C., 11; Jonathan, 64,73,140,157,173; Mrs. O., 136, Obadiah Jnr, iv; Obadiah, 31,64, 110,173,226,232; Sidney, 56,93;
Boulter, Josiah, 83;
Boyden, Thomas A., 77,105,117,122,163,190;
Brassey, Major Henry, 143,144,146,150,208, 211,220;
Bray, F., 179,230; Walter, 44; W.H., 108,225;
Brice, Miss E., 157;
Bright, Mrs., 172;
Brightwell, Mr., 196;
Brooke,Lady de Capell, 185;
Brookes, R.M., 128;
Brooks, E.J., 108,225; F., 108,225; F.W., 108,180; Mrs., 180;
Broughton, W., 1;
Brown, Arthur G., 22,31,46,64,78,95,103,114,119,121,127,144,157,161,182,187,198,201, 205,232,236; G.W., 91; John, 45; Mrs. Walter G., 78; Thomas, 190, W.H., 36,72;
Brudenall, Mr., 25;
Buckby, Mrs., 59; Ralph, 136;
Buckley, Lt. S.E., 91; Dr. T.W., 91;
Bues, Charles, 16,36,62; Harry, 93; J.H., 36,86,87; J.T., 62,86,190; J.W., 87;
Bugby, Miss, 4;
Burdett, B., 10;
Burford, F.E., 204;
Burroughs, Canon, 141;
Butler, Mr., 155,165;
Butlin, Inspector, 225;
Bygrave, Aubrey, v,93,139; William, 31,63,85,97,121,139; William H., 93,203,212;

Cairns, Sgt. Major G.C., 204;
Campion, Inspector, 8,31,33,45,54,84,106,124,126,181,182,183,190,198;
Cannell, Charles, 185;
Capps, Mr., 162;
Capron, Mrs., 20;
Carress, J.T., 1,153, 155,161,162,165; Miss, 122; Mrs., 162;
Carr, Bishop Hon E., 49; Miss, 90;

Carter, J.B., 152;
Cattell, Mr., 29;
Cavell, Nurse Edith, 176;
Cawdell, Bernard, 14,94,101,115,120,125,127,140,154,162,182,197,202,212; R., 229;
Chapman, M.J., 161; Mrs.,151; W., 27; William, iv;
Charlton, G.V., 26,78; Mrs., 19; Percy, 19,20,22,23,43,66,72;
Chattell, J.H., 114,192;
Cheeseman, Thomas, 20;
Cheney, F.A., 64,121,123,145,153,155,161,162,196,229; Miss, 49; Mr., 80,127,180,193;
Mrs.,148,163; W., 9,21,194; Winifred, 148;
Chidson, Lt. L. Hume, 62;
Childs, G., 19; Harry, 88;
Church, C.B., 1,6,7;
Clark, H., 179,183,193,207; Rev. F.C.P., 111;
Clarke, Herbert William, iv; Mr., 31,34,103;
Claydon, R.A., 219;
Clayson, E., 49; W., 43;
Clifton, Alderman,165;
Clipsom, Mrs. 152;
Clipston, Bert, 156,157;
Clowes, Miss, 70;
Coales, Miss, 90; W., 119;
Coates, Mrs., 78; William, 78;
Cobley, F.G., 73; J.E., 66,73,87,104,187;
Cockerill, Miss, 55; Reginald, 193;
Cogan, Dr., 3;
Coldwell, Rev. W. St. George, 110,113,150;
Cole, Enoch, 80; H., 98; Mr., 202,235;
Coleby, Phyllis E., 89;
Colley, W.D., 56;
Coltman, E., 194;
Cook, George, 61,65,73; Mrs. G., 49,61,65,74;
Cooke, Edith Mary, 111; Oscar, 203,212;
Coombs, Mr. Gurney, 60,71,155; Mr. (Solicitor), 169;
Cooper, Bernard, 52,66,87; Edward, 52; F. 36; George, 233; H., 12,31,38; Mr., 25,165;
Mrs., 24,52; Samuel, 151; William Edward, 23,24,187;
Corbett, F., 13,97,104,112,157;
Corby, W.F., 34;
Cottingham, Cyril, 144; E.T., 125,180,222; Leslie G., 188; Miss, 216; Mrs., 5,114,162,212,
220;
Cotton, Miss, 2,122; Norman A., 43,87; Reuben, 71,78,103;
Coulson, Pte., 38;
Coulton, Mr., 129;
Crawley, Mr. C., 36;
Cresswell, Bernard, 19,86; J.E.G., 43,66,67; T.B., 67;
Crick, Mary, 78;
Crofton, A., 87;
Cullum, Mr., 209;
Cunnington, G., 179;
Curtis, A., 204; Mary Ann, 107;
Czarnikow, Mr., 25;

Danbury, Mr., 182;
Dartnell, F., 68;
David, David William, 7,123,141,150,154,155,224;
Davidson, H., iv;
Davies, H.J., 217;
Davis, Miss, 207,228;
Day, A., 1; E., 44;
Deans, Robert, 45;
Dellar, Mrs., 122; Walter, 1,44,77,115,118,144,165,169,182,204,208,240;
Densem, Mrs., 197,198;
Dingley, Alfred, 56,61,62; Ernest A., 36,56,73,93; Horace, 59,61,62,66,187;
Ivy Mary, 56,93,123;
Dix, Frederick W., 93,237;
Dixon, J.E., 108,113; Rev. Joseph, 177;
Dodd, Thomas R., iv;
Dodson, H., 230;
Drage, W., 44;
Drury, Miss, 47,48;
Dunn, William, 180;
Duthy, J.W., 10;

Earle, Ernest, 23; George Samuel, 20,25,28,32; Mrs., 23;
Edmonds, J., 10,47;
Edward, H.M. King, 6,7;
Edwards, Miss M., 129,171;
Elks, Henry, 65,70,210; Mrs., 65,70;
Elliott, Dr., 117,201;
Ellson, M., 30,72; Thomas, 30,72;
Elmore, J., 204;
Elms, J., 4;
Emery, Alexander J., 4,46,48; Basil Frederick, 20,21,22,187; Mr. F.W.B., 20,45,82,85,152,
216,221; Mrs., 20;
Essam, Miss V., 4,44,47,74; Mr. T., 44,219,230;
Evans, Hazel, v,58,138;
Eunson, Colonel, 86;

Farrant, Judge, 143,155,169,203;
Farrow, C.W., 204;
Ferrar, Arthur, 172; C.G., 73; Frank, 32,123; Mr. & Mrs. S., 123; Septimus Leslie, 43,73,
122,165,187;
Ferry, Mr., 27;
Fetch, R., 84;
Field, Miss, 122;
Firbank, Miss, 4,44;
Fisher, Frederick, 100; Herbert, 159;
Fitzherbert, Rev, Henry Edward, 73,79,82,87,90,96,102,113,120,148,152,155,160,161,162,
163,233; Mrs., 147,178;
Flanders, Miss Annie, 139,145,177; Miss Louise, 5,41,49;
Fletcher, Alf, 8,49,189,235; H., 139; J., 42,92,145; Miss L., 189; Mrs. W., 74;
Ford, Viva, 7;
Forscutt, T., 44;
Fox, Miss G., 199; Mr. 37;

Headland, Miss F., 49,74,117,129; G., 179,183,193,207; J., 44; Mr. (Woodford), 12;

Heighton, Garage, 45,141,191;

Hensman, Alfred, 22,64,70,123,153,155,183;

Hepher, Audrey Chattell, 123; Connie, 123; Garner Prior, 46,169,239;

Herby, G., 73,87; J., 73;

Herring, J.W., 117;

Hewitt, Mrs., 238; William Thomas, 5,31,64,97,148,151,152,153, 155,161,162,177,185,195, 198,205, 206,226;

Hewlett, Miss, 74;

Heygate, Cecil, 175;

Hiam, Mr. H.W., 135,171,205,229; Mrs. M., 135,171,205,229; Robert Lewis, 133,135,171, 187,205,229;

Hill, Miss, 5; Miss K., 216;

Hillson, Ellen, 123;

Hillyard, Doris, 88; Miss S.E., 133,157; Mrs., 88; William, 22,26,44,64,88,123,152,154,155, 221,224,225,229;

Hillyer, Miss, 163;

Hing, Miss, 2,4;

Hitchener, Walter, 204;

Hodson, Frederick, 207; John, 44,116,162,176; Miss, 122; Mrs. T., 49;

Hollanders, Mr. and Mrs., 17;

Holley, Fred J., 43,73,87; Mrs. J., 67,69; Percy John, 61,67;

Holmes, Mr., 5;

Hope, Celia, v,190;

Hopkins, Fred, 44;

Horn, Mr., 103,110; R., 73;

Horner, Frederick, 123,165; Mr. and Mrs., 123;

Hornsby, Miss May, 70,178;

Houghton, Frederick, 8;

Howe, W., 63,196;

Hughes, Rev. Michael, 89;

Humphrey, Mrs., 71,73,103,152,162; Captain R.J.P., 49,55,73,106;

Humphreys, Lieutenant, 7;

Hunnybun, Gerald, 10,176,179,188; Kenneth, 148; Martin G.W., 10,35,43,73,178,182;

Hunt, Captain F., 130;

Hurrell, A.H., 44,49; H.A., 79, 109;

Ingram, D., 11;

Ireland, Charles, 70; David, 70; Herbert, 70,87; J., 70;

Ireson, G.S., 125; Irving George, 137,213; Joseph A., 63,137,213; Mr. George, 25,137; Mrs., 137;

Jacques, C., 66; W., 72,171, 189;

Jakins, Mrs., 74;

James, Evelyn, 41; Maggie, 41; Thomas, 89;

Jarvis, Jane, 42,43,94,115,117,118;

Jeffery, A., 207,230; Alfred, 41; Arthur William, 43,106,187; Miss, 228; Mr., 41,94; Mrs. W., 41,43,94,115,186;

Jeffs, Elsie May, 72; F.W., 87; J.P., 72; Mrs., 72,75,112; T.W., 66,72,112; W.Q., 75;

Jellicoe, Miss, 5; Mr. J., 5;

Jellis, Ernest, 39,216;

Lord, F., 110; F.W., 152,162,192,197,234,235; Mrs., 163,197,235; Percy, 235; William Trevor, 197;

Loveday, Alfred Shrives, 121,170,187; Florence, 56; H., 25,110; Marjorie, 206; Richard W., 36,140; Thomas, 10;

Luckock, Rev. A.M., 114,119,197;

Lyford, Annie, 183;

Lyon, Miss, 125;

McClure, Mrs, 165;

McInnes, Dr., 91;

Mackenzie, Dr. W., 87;

Mackness, Charles, 63;

Makin, Mr.Philip Senior, 25,44,46,108,133,163;; Philip, 13,15,187;

Manning, Charles Horace, 99; Corporal, 135; H., 179,183,193,207,221,222; J., 193,207; Mrs., 135; S., 207;

Mansbridge, Nurse, 126,209;

Mansfield, John (Jack), 144,146,149,150,174; Miss G., 26;

March, E., 9,43,113,139,173; G.E., 36,37; Gerald, 58; H., 183,207,230; Isaac, 181; Kenneth, 43,58,221; Micky, 36; Mr., 25; Mrs., 58,161,162; Mrs. Percy, 210; R., 73,114; Sarah Ann, 153,155,; T.C., 114; William, 25,44,58,110;

Marchant, Dr. Stanley, 182;

Marks, Edward, 238; Miss, 83; Mrs., 229;

Marshall, R., 194;

Mash, J.L., 53; Mrs., 90;

Mault, Miss C., 59; Miss V., 59; Mrs., 24,52;

Mayes, A., 37,63; Alf, 44; E., 4,37,43; Ernest, 212,234; Ernest Harry, 93,124,158,187; Mr. Frederick, 158; Mrs. F., 5,49,158; William, 97;

Meadows, John, 54,105,115,116,163; Marshall, 58,83,136; Mrs. M., 58,59,68,88; Sidney, 31,58,64,136,173, 207;

Midgley, E.R., 81,106,202;

Mijatovitch, Count Cheddo, 103,110;

Miles, B.H., 117; W., 69;

Millard, E.S., 238; Miss, 238;

Miller, Herbert, 59,67,68,187; Mr. E., 205; Mr. W. 220, Mrs., 15,67; 220; Walter, 13,15,59, 187; **Milligan**, Dr., 62; Mr., 28,31,45;

Millington, H.A., 156;

Minney, S., 1,203;

Modlen, C., 71; Miss K.F., 11,70; Mrs., 33;

Molden, Dorothy, 3;

Morley, Eliza, 205; Joseph George, 80,81,82,83,187; Mr. Joseph, 81,82; Mrs. J., 81,82; William, 77;

Morris, Arthur, 73; Campbell Edmund, 99; H., 230,235; Hector H., 43,73,87; L., 11; Mr., 239;

Morton, T.D., 74,181;

Mundin, H., 47;

Munds, E., 36,73;

Musk, Miss, 47,48;

Neale, Thomas, 205;

Newman, A., 179; Benjamin, 98; E., 66,183,193,198,221; Frederick William "Benny", 102,103,106,137,187,233; L., 198; Mary Ann, 98; Mrs., 47,48,93,140; Sidney, 136,140,141, 175,187,233; William, 25,27,110,140;

Newton, E.W., 216; T., 44;

Nicholls, Arthur, 43; David, iv; Frederick H., 12,31; George (M.P.), 8; George Ernest, 43,59, 60,61,187; H., 12,15,21,22,23,27,43,66,73; Mr. Thomas, 43; Mrs. T., 43;

Nichols, Mrs. S., 107; Mrs. T., 93; Samuel, 148,165;

Nicholson, G., 179;

Nickerson, J., 36,43,73,87;

Nightingale, Major, 71;

Norman, Mr., 114;

Nunneley, E.M., 139;

Nutt, Alfred, 138;

Okey, Miss, 74;

Oliver, Miss, 129;

Paddison, Rev. J.T., 96;

Page, Mr., 47;

Palmer, Arthur, 49;

Panter, C., 204; Mrs, 90;

Papworth, Charles, 142;

Parker, E.F., 90,180; Mrs., 91; "Shop on wheels", 218;

Parrish, Miss, 2,4; Timothy, iv;

Parrott, Jack, 31,37,62; Mrs., 62; T.J., 70;

Partridge, Mrs., 152;

Pashler, John, 64,80,82,96,122,123,127,152,153,155,162; Mrs., 65;

Pateman, Edmund, 83;

Patrick, G.H., 194; Mr. 5;

Payne, Joseph Hind, 28,138; Miss A., 122; Miss H., 122; Robert, 92;

Peachy, Miss, 2;

Peacock, Mr., 47;

Perkins, and Son, 102; Arthur, 56,93;

Perrin, J., iv;

Peters, A., 194;

Pettit, A., 238; C., 238; Charles R., 33,65,91,108,126,132,152,158,160,162, 163,165,171,211, 217,221,229; Footballer, 183,193; John R., 72;

Pickering, E., 162;

Piggott, Police Constable, 99;

Pike, Miss, 135;

Pilling, David Lambert, 115;

Pollard, J.T., 42; John Robert, 11,56,57,187; Mr., 152; Mrs., 42,57; Rev. F. Ward, 177;

Popple, Mrs., 90;

Porter, F.J., 71,72; J.F., 104,112,152,157,162; J.H., 158,169,189;

Preece, Miss, 5; R., 21;

Prentice, John, 46,151;

Prior, Mr., 198;

Quick, Rev. O.C., 150;

Raby, George, 44,108;

Raven, Mrs., 5;

Raworth, Edward Percy, 101,104,105,136,174,187, 207,231; Mr. G., 104; Mrs. G., 104;

Read, Cecil Walter, 43,52; Walter, 87;

Reeve, Horace William, 126,187; Mrs., 52; William, 22,23,24,187;

Reeves, Mr. W., 27,35;

Reynolds, Mrs., 42; Thomas William, 153,155; William, 42,44,63;

Richardson, A., 145; Charles Edward, 31,35,66,187; Edward, 66; L., 23,157,180,211; Mr., 103;

Riches, Louisa, 45;

Rickwood, Leonard, 176;

Rippener, Mr., 222;

Roberts, Clifford E., 56,115; Miss M., 70,122; Rev. H. Ellis, 41,46,51,70,82,111,113,139, 143,145,229; Rev. R.E., 180; William G., 56;

Robinson, G., 36; Mr., 7;

Rodwell, Mr., 233;

Rogers, Jack, 181,217; John James, 137,187; Mr. John, 80; Mrs. John, 80;

Rose, H.H., 25,204,220;

Roughton, A.H., 111; Dora, 133; Herbert, 60,61; J.W., 60,61,159; Mrs., 61;

Rowell, Miss, 47,48; William, iv,10;

Rowlett, Fred, 73; Mabel, 59,75,89,122,152; Mrs. J., 13,32;

Ruckwood, C.J., 1,25; L.J., 203;

Ruston, Mr. P.F., 3; Mrs. P.F., 3;

Sackville, Colonel Stopford, 33,71,84,86,90,102,142,156,186,232;

Saddington, John, 45; Mrs. 186;

Salisbury, J.T., 44;

Salt, H.E., 238;

Sanders, Harry, 92; James, 219; Spence, 23;

Sanderson, Corporal, 104; Elizabeth, 63,90,228; Mary, 145, 167, 170; Richard, 228;

Savage, George, 125,165; Miss, 122;

Sawford, Alec, 183;

Selby, R.J., 104; Thomas, 5,21,22,23,31,35,45,64,83,112,123,148,153,155,162,165,179,195, 201;

Shadbolt, C.W., 73,87,148; James, iv; John Harry, 147,148,153,185,187; Richard, 228; W., 238;

Sharp, C.G., 127; Percy Edward, 112;

Sharpe, Thomas E., 87,161,162;

Shaw, Mrs., 99; Rev. Harry, 29,38,91,95,99;

Shelton, L., 11; W., 11;

Short, E.H., 87; F., 10,151; H., 37; Police Constable, 15,20,46,50,51,59,60,61,102,114,116, 195;

Siddon, Archibald Charles, iv;

Siddons, George, 229; Mr., 110;

Simpson, C.E., 34; George Henry, 32,34,187; Miss, 47,48; Mr., 33,36;

Skelton, D., 43; Leonard, 22,131; Mrs., 179; W., 6,10,13,22,24;

Skinner, Mr. 141; Mrs., 141;

Slater, Daniel, 192; Thomas Ivatt, 144,146;

Slatter, Alec F., 37;

Smart, A.W., 119; C.A., 1; Leonard, 90; Leslie, 131; Mary Ellen, 153,155; Miss, 152; Mrs. A.W., 135; Mrs. S.P., 144; Sidney Packwood, 42,44,97,117,150,153,155,164,170,223;

Smith, A.E., 19; Alfred, 51,54,60,134,163,168,174; Evelyn, 93; Fanny, 100; George (JP,CC), 10,22,25,31,33,35,37,44,58,64,81,93,100,110,111,114; George Theodore, 154,155; George William Kenneth, 91,139,140,141,187; H., 178,183,193, 230; John Samuel, 13,57,58,75,187; J.W., 101; Miss, 22; Mrs. A., 82; Mrs. George, 58,83,98, 111,120,155,215; Mrs. G. Ernest, 50; Mrs. Rupert, 190; Mrs. Theodore, 140; Mrs. W.,132, 138; Nat, 8; R., 11; Rev. Archibald W., 169,172,176,206,223; Rupert, 51,163,176,231;

Septimus, 1; Stanley, 1; Theodore, 25,54,92,128,140; Thomas, 133; William, 22,41,62,72, 132,138;

Spencer, Earl, 170; Harry, 72; Mrs. William, 72;

Staake, A.A., 9;

Staley, Mrs. 92;

Stalley, H.T., 192;

Stapleton, Benjamin, 135; C. 62; E., 4; F., 66,183,193,194; George, 4; John, 198;

Stearne, Jack, 92; Mrs. Philip, 92; Philip, 92;

Stevens, Mr., 199;

Steward, F.J., 44,45,71,237; Oliver James, 226;

Stimpson, John Thomas, 37, 102,133,187;

Stobie, F., 221,222,230; Mrs., 49; William Walter, 25,35,36,42,44,46,47,56,72,87,92,96,108, 132,153,155,162,197; Willie, 37;

Stothert, Rev. Basil Wilberforce, 1,3,6,7,8,9,10, 11,12,13,21,25,26,32,33,35,37,41,56,67,78; Mrs., 7,63,65;

Streatfield, Colonel Henry, 6;

Streather, E., 89;

Stubbs, F., 229; John. W., 54,68,104,108,186,192;

Sturdee, Rev. R., 143,150;

Sullivan, M., iv;

Sutcliffe, Harold, 27,55; I.A., Commander, 171; Isaac, 171; John (Senior), 27,55; John Isaac Ashton, 52,55,187;

Swain, L.E., 154;

Swan, A., 10,11; A.G., 10; Mrs., 212;

Sykes, Ira, 165; V.H., 41;

Talbot, R., 205;

Tarrant, Arthur, 133,134,187; Miss, 208; W., 66;

Tarry, Edward, 72;

Taylor, A.J.P., 39; and Downs (Printer), 17,38,113,120,148,156;,D.C., 125,152,172; Mrs. D.C., 113;

Tebbey, Superintendent, 30,33,79,106,142,145,150,152,199,205;

Tebbs, T.C., 1,6;

Templeman, Richard Edis, 11,20,25,26,27,28,32,43,85,166,187; Mr., 26,166; Mrs., 26,28,85, 166;

Thirsk, Ada, 81,82;

Thompson, L., 74,104,114,140;

Throssell, Leonard, 97,187; Mrs., 19,97; Tebbutt H., 19,73;

Thurlow, George, 25,56,176; William, 11,56,73,151;

Tite, J.C., 81;

Todd, A., 193;

Tomlinson, C., 29,80,179,188,213,236; H., 29,80,179.188,213,236;

Touch, A.H., 5,23,106,192,226; F., 23;

Traynar, Corporal, 104;

Turner, Alfred, 216; E., 230; George William, 66,68,187; Mrs., 216;

Tusting, Thomas Rawson, iv;

Unwyatte, Mr., 5;

Unger, George Abery, 41,45;

Upchurch, Walter Oliver, 144;

Vandervalle, Mr. and Mrs., 17,19;
Varah, H., 33,71,165;
Villar, H., 238;
Vorley, C.W., 29,223,228;

Wadlow, George, 49;
Wadsley, Mr., 97;
Waite, Albert John (Jack), 25,31,32,187; Alfred Edward, 22,23,30,187; Ernest, 83; Mabel M., 89; Marjorie, 20; Mr., 23; Mrs., 23; William, 31;
Wakefield, R.H., 37; W., iv;
Walker, Billy, 44,173;
Wallace, Frank, 203;
Waller, E., 71; Mrs. E., 69,77;
Wallis, Captain R.B., 71;
Walsh, Dr., 222,227;
Walter, Mrs., 154;
Walters, Horace, 201; Miss, 134;
Walton, J., 11;
Ward, Miss W.E., 70;
Warner, G., 85,162;
Warren, Arthur Edward, 52,57,160; Mr., F.O., 80,113,125,162,168; Mrs., 162,163;
Waters, G., 73;
Watkins, Mr., 56;
Watson, Arthur, 42; George, 41,42,46; Mrs. Wentworth, 83,98; Robert, 41;
Watts, Mr., 151;
Waugh, Rev. Thomas, 141;
Webb, Alfred, 119; C.E., 28;
Webster, F.K., 203,204; J., 13,14,24,27,170,181,203; Mrs., 13;
Westley, C.A., 21,23,43;
Wheeler, Judge, 60;
White, Billy, 44; Clare, 37; F., 238; Joyce, 208;
Whitehead, W., 44;
Whiteman, Frank, 99; Fairey, 25,30,151, 235;
Whitney, John, 233; Miss, 5;
Whittingham, Venerable W.G., 187;
Wiles, John, 56;
Wilkinson, Mrs., 222;
Williams, Footballer, 193; Michael, 170,174; Mr. (Cinema), 197,203,218;
Willoughby, Lt Colonel, 71;
Willows, Captain, 104;
Wills, A., 1,172;
Wilson, Gerald, 93; H., 11,19,22; Mr., 138; W., 1;
Windsor, R., 11;
Winsor, G., 73; Ivy Grace, 123;
Winter, Miss Olga, 90,122; W., 89,90;
Wood, B., 169,231; L.W., 3; Rowland, 33,44;
Woods, Herbert, 66;
Wright, Arthur William, 144; Bernard B., 25,165; Cuthbert, iv; G.E., 37; H., 140; Helen, 233; John, 83,84; Mr., 151; Samuel, 87,136,139,187; S., 170; W., 73;
Wyman, L., 64,173;

Young, Corporal, 104;

General Index

Addington, 150,218; Great, 167; Little, 60,83;
Adult School, 5,35,75,84,92,120,121,139,173,187,190;
Aeroplanes, 50,63,77,104,123,126,127,139;
Airship, 121;
Aldwincle, 3,57,119,216,218,228; Football Team, 231; Rectory Football Team, 232;
Althorpe Park; 202;
Amateur Dramatics, 3;
Armentieres, France, 25;
Armistice, 141,164,178,209,235;
Aubers Ridge, 25,28,30,85,125;

Baptist Christian Endeavour Society, 137,177,234;
Baptist Church, 10,14,29,36,39,41,46,48,67,70,74,78,84,86,89,91,101,105,106,107,109,111, 113, 118,123,136,139,141, 142,143,145,169, 172,176,177, 180,181,183,197,199,200,205,206, 215,216,221,226,227,228,229;
Barclays (Bank) & Co. Ltd., 38,43;
Bedford, 31,133,159,173;
Belgian Refugees, 14,17,19,30; Relief Fund, 15,16;
Bellringers, 57,93,109,150,167,237;
Bethune, France, Le Touret Memorial, 20;
Blind Babies Sunshine House Fund, 213;
Boer War, iv,10,12,62,87;
Bolnhurst, Bedfordshire, 60;
Bombay, India, 20,21;
Boulogne, France, 23,26;
Bournemouth, 89,90;
Bowls Club, 57,164,165,199,202,225,228;
Boy Scouts, 6,7,11,13,16,22,96,106;
Boys Life Brigade, 115;
Bramsholt Camp, 35;
Bridge Street Station, 48,54,56,117,178,230;
Brighton, 177; Hospital,20;
Brigstock, 27,45,71,160,195,228;
Brigstock Football Club, 171,237,240;
British Eclipse Expedition to Principe Island, 180;
British Legion, 17,235,236,237,240;
British Red Cross Society, 38;
British Womens Temperance Association, 30,51,100,102,114,116,129,135,137,173,191, 215;
Broughton United Football Club, 172,193,209,216,230;
Brunner Mond Chemical Factory, London, 79;
Buckingham Palace, 109;
Burton Latimer, 5,126,150;
Bythorn, 129;

Caesar's Nose Cemetery, Belgium, 137;
Calcutta, India, 30;
Cambrai, France, 109,112,117;
Cambridge, 48,111,112,114,238;
Canada, 27,55,68,90,119;

Canadian Record Office, 67;

Cattle Market, 73,126,212;

Catsworth, 96;

Cemetery, Oundle Road, 54,58,78,80,83,89,90,112,118,122,139,142,143,180,196,207,211, 215,216,231, 235;

Chatham, Kent, 38;

Children's Distress Fund, 179,180;

Children's Home Committee, 50;

Chivers Custard Powder, 114;

Christian Endeavour Society, 67;

Christmas Fat Stock Society, 10,66,73,159,174,200,212,239;

Church of England Men's Society, 56,124,200,201;

Church of England Missionary Society, 215;

Church of England School, 7,13,20,45,56,70,82,90,93,100,101,112,115,118,123,131, 144,155,168,178,186,196,209,216,221,225;

Church War Memorial, 166,168,171,187,213,227;

City of London Tea Co., 110;

Clopton, 5,95,136,144; Clopton Manor, 59,91;

Colchester, 20,26;

Conservative & Unionists, 143,163,208;

Co-operative Hall, 42,44,45,47,49,57,63,64,65,69,70,83,84,95,97,98,107,108,112,113,115, 116,119,121,124,125,126,127,134,135,139,142,144,145,146,151,156,157,176,179,180,182, 185,186,188,190,191,192,193,196,199,203,206,210,212,213,216,217,219,220,221,222,225, 226;

Co-operative Society, 35,42,50,57,59,65,95,103,110,128,130,132,135,159,161, 164,170,175, 179,192,193,197,203,219,226;

Corby Football Club, 180,185;

Corner Cafe, 234;

Corn Exchange, 14,37,39,47,53,90,109,120,122,141,149,157,160,175,177,178,179,180, 181,183,186,187,195,196,200,209,210,212,213,215,217,218,220,221,234,235,236;

Council School, 3,56,85,93,100,103,106,116,118,119,131,137,141,178,195,196,199,204,208, 209,222;

County Court, 60,81,115,129,143,155,169,176,185;

Cranford,108,218,225; Cranford St. John Football Club, 233;

Cricket, 19,62,97,162,186,188,201,207,217;

Cycling & Athletic Club,35,173,174,178,199,208;

"Daily News" Soldier's Christmas Pudding Fund, 14;

Daylight Saving Initiative, 52;

Dardanelles, 31,33,35,66;

Dartford Grammar School OTC, 94;

Denford, 26,62,65,93,97,99,105,110,139,156,191,201,202,205,209,218,235,237; Denford Ash, 57,219; Poppies Football Club, 209,222; Rovers Football Club, 181,183; United Football Club, 189;

Derby, 91;

Desborough, Argyll Football Club, 174,180,190; Baptists Football Club, 190,191; Town Football Club, 179,193,207,212,236;

District Allotment Association, 121,123,124,128,135,193;

District Athletic Sports & Horse Show, 8;

District Nurse, 65,69,198;

District Shire Horse Society, 3,48,57,94,122,131,156,168,169,172,194,202,222,230,231;

District Tennis Club, 38;

District Trades & Labour Council, 97,99,108,115,117,119,121,140,164,185,188,203,206, 219,226,230;
District War Pensions Committee, 64,65;
Drayton, 5,52,80,86,90,97,186,188,217,232; Fete, 101; Home Farm, 21;

Earl Haig's Warriors Fund, 220,235;
Eaton Socon, 142;
Egypt, 36,41,86,92,94;
Ekins Charity, 106;
Electric Light & Heating, 224,225,229;
Ellesmere, Cheshire, 70;
Empire Day, 26,52,225;
Etaples, France, 34,61;
Evening School, 89;
Exchange Theatre, 8;
Ex-Servicemen's Federation, 151,211,212,220;

Feast Sunday, 29,96,170,204;
Festubert, France, 28;
Finedon, 57; Argyll Football Club, 181; United Football Club, 186,187,215,221;
Fire Brigade, 16,24,25,31,64,84,101,110,135,152,154,157,160,173,188,226,231;
Fitzwilliam Hounds, 148,179,211,213,219,237;
Floods, 79,87,126,151,156,164,169,186,194,195,226;
Food Control Committee, 97,98,99,100,102,104,105,107,109,110,113,114,117,119,120,121, 122,123,125,127,128,130,131,132,133,135,136,137,145,190,191,192;
Forester's Society, 84
Forget me not, 17,27,63,96,132,158,185;
Fort William, India, 30;
Fox Inn, 207;
Free Church Council, 88;
Freeman's Egg Substitute, 124;
Fuel Overseer, 131,143,169;

Gas Works, 24,79,190,201,222,224;
Geddington Stars Football Club, 175,177,189,212,219,222;
General Election, 143,144,146,149,150;
Glee Society, 177,179,188,196,206,221;
Gloucester Cathedral, 54;
Godmanchester, 159;
Grafham, 77,108,180;
Grimsby, 81;
Guardians, vi,2,10,32,38,45,47,49,50,53,55,58,61,65,68,70,73,74,77,80,84,87,91,97,98,101, 104, 110,111,114,117,122,123,125,129,131,133,145, 148,149,151,152,155,156, 158,163, 171, 174,176,177,179,182,185, 186,191,197,198,205,207, 210,216,217,218,219,221, 223,226, 227, 228,230,233,234,237,239;

Harriers, 1,6,7,93,173,178;
Havana, Cuba, 239;
Hendon, Middlesex, 38;
Higham Ferrers, 124,150,152,170,230;
Hill 60, France, 30;
Histon Poultry Show, Cambridgeshire, 212,216;

Hockey, 5,115,211;
Hospital Week, 202,229,230;

Independent Order of Rechabites, 98,108;
India, 21,22,24,30,52,70,92,121;
Infantry Record Office, 15;
Infant Welfare Centre, 152,183;
Influenza, 22,83,90,142,143,144,151,152,180;
Institute, 31,32,42,43,44,54,58,62,68,70,79,92,93,104,108,115,116,145,167,182,188,189, 192,201,202,208,213,218,219,221,232; of Bankers, 5;
Ironfounders, Society, 180; Union, 178;
Irthlingborough, 10,102,150,216,228;
Islip, 10,19,28,45,46,56,65,71,81,95,97,105,112,116,127,128,142,144,150,151,154,157,206, 210,218,220,228,231,233,235; C.of E. School, 106,142; Cricket Club, 207;
Football Club, 211,234; House, 143; Institute, 218; Iron Company, 23,52,66,92,98,155;
Juniors Football Club, 221,222; King Edward Cottages, 59; Manor House, 69;
Rose & Crown, 138;
Italy, 160,239;

Jutland, Battle of, 52,75,160;
Juvenile Ragtime Band, 112,145;

Kensit Wickliffe Preacher Vans, 201;
Kettering, 10,32,48,71,90,101,110,114,133,135,143,148,151,158,167,170,175,177,178,181, 183,185,188,189,191,193,194,199,201,204,208,212,218,219,230,231,236,237;
Angel Hotel, 5,169; Angling Association, 8,88,156; Atlas Football Club, 193,212;
Conservative Bowls Club, 228; District Charity Cup, 174,177,183,193,225,231;
Football Combination, 1,5,9,169,171,173,187,192,193,194,195,206,221;222,224,225
Grammar School, 81; Harriers, 1; Mrs. Morris' Boys Club Football Club, 206,211,233,234;
Prize Choir, 234; Ragtime Band, 27; Rangers Football Club, 211,212,234;
Rockingham Road, 189; St. Andrews' Football Club, 208,216; Timson's Football Club, 176, 186,187,206,208,219,231,232; V.A.D., 96; White Cross Football Club, 2;
Keyston, 96,99,230;
Kimbolton, 7,60,87,175; Hockey Club, 211; School, 131;
King Albert Fund, 16;
King's Arms Hotel, 13,26,46,92,110,149,173,178,197,199,208,235;
Kingsbridge, Devon, 108,113;
King's Call, 33;
King's Head, 79,80;

Land Agents Society,52;
League of Nations, 217;
Licensed Trades Association, 80,110,113;
Lilford Hall,132,201,202;
Littlehampton, 22;
Loder Cross, 35;
London City & Midland Bank, 5,38;
London & North Western Railway, 80,205,228;
Loos, Belgium, 37,43,62;
Lowick, 10,97,150,156,179,218,228; Church, 49; Football Club, 195,231;
Low Shot, 86;
Lusitania,25;

Thrapston House Names:

    Addison Villas, 210,240;
    Azaelea House, 150,234;
    Belmont House, 73;
    Cambria, 115,150;
    Church Villa, 90;
    Denford Cottage, 144;
    Fair Lawn, 93;
    Fern House, 206;
    Hill House, 227;
    Horton House,111,226;
    Jubilee Cottage, 103;
    Laburnum House, 88;
    Manchester House, 150,206;
    Manor House, 19;
    Nene House, 58,77,96,99,100,102,114,116,129,131,137,147,203,215,229;
    Orchard House, 140;
    Paradise House, 176;
    Ravenswood, 201;
    River View, 60;
    Springfield Cottages, 201;
    Springfield House, 149;
    The Hermitage, 165,222;
    The Hollies, 58,62,83,99,100,111,131,202,203,205,206;
    The Laurels, 131,134,135;
    The Limes, 188;
    The Plantation, 143;
    The Rectory, 29,59,97,164;
    The Shrubberies, 23,27,62,63,132,167,170,171,229;
    Thrapston House, 29,94,96,135,147,162,164,170,178,200,201,204,227,228,229,230;

Thrapston, Islip & Denford Nursing Association, 128,215;
Thrapston & Islip Soldier's Tobacco Fund, 12,21,25,27,28,35,36;
Thrapston Mill, 225;
Thrapston & Raunds Almanac, 38;
Thrapston Rovers Football Club, 170,181,183,195;
Thrapston United Football Club, 10,169,171,172,173,174,175,176,177,178,179,180,181, 182,183,185, 186,187,188,189, 190,191,192,193, 194,195,196, 206,207,208,209,210,211,212, 213,215,216,217,218,219,220,221,222,224,225,230,231,232,233,234,235,236,237,240;
Titchmarsh, 5,10,33,45,48,57,89,92,94,95,114,119,141,150,151,192,197,209,218,219;
Juniors Football Club, 181,212; Mill, 203; White City, 12;
Town Crier, 10,236;
Town War Memorial Committee, 179;
Town Silver Prize Band, 8,16,24,25,27,42,45,63,84,100,125,141,149,156,157,167,170,175, 183,191,196,197,200,202,203,204,210,213,224,228;
Treaty of Versailles, 165;
Tromso, Norway, 173;
Twywell, 7,10,32,57,128,138,150,218,222; Football Club, 233,234;

Vimy Ridge, 90;
Volunteer Training Corps, 71,86,92,97,104,110,111,112,115,116,118,119,123,126,127,128, 132,142,157;
Voters Register, 130,133;

The Author

Eric Franklin was born in Mitcham, Surrey in 1949.

After leaving school, he lived in Birkenhead, Merseyside, then Alresford, Hampshire before marrying Mary in 1973. They moved to Northampton in the same year. After seven years in Earls Barton, they moved to Thrapston in 1982.

After a career with Social Services, Eric took early retirement in 1996. He subsequently started a Welfare Rights Group in town; then managed Thrapston Swimming Pool on Market Road for three years. When the Nene Centre opened, he worked maintaining the pool plant and air conditioning units for nine months.

He was a Thrapston Town Councillor for nine years between 2003 and 2012, serving as Mayor in 2006 – 2007. For five years, between 2007 and 2012, he was a director of the Northamptonshire County Association of Local Councils and Championed the Quality Parish Council scheme throughout this time.

Local history has been a developing interest over the last ten years. As well as joining the committee of the Historical Society, he is also one of a small group of people working on developing a Heritage Centre for the town. Updates on progress can be found on our website at www.thrapstonheritage.co.uk.

Eric was co-author of "In the Springtime of their Lives", the Thrapston Roll of Honour, published in 2009.

He has written two local history booklets for Thrapston Heritage:

> The Thrapston I Remember, an illustrated re-write of George Essex's memories of Thrapston during the early years of the 20th Century.

> Thrapston Harriers, the Early Years 1907 – 1914.

> Others are in the planning stage: The History of Public Houses and Beer Retailers in Thrapston; and Thrapston Men in the 2nd Boer War and Earlier.

> A long-term project, which he hopes to start in 2013, is to record and photograph all gravestones etc. in the Oundle Road Cemetery. With over 1,800 plots, this is a big undertaking and Eric would be grateful if anyone reading this would like to offer any help. Contact details are on page ii.

For four years he was editor of Strapetona, the annual magazine of Thrapston District Historical Society.

In tandem with preparing this book for publication, he was commissioned by the Northamptonshire County Association of Local Councils (NCALC) to research and write a brief history of the Association and its predecessors, covering the years 1947 – 2012).